THE ASPECT OF ETERNITY

1993

OTHER BOOKS BY

BRUCE BAWER

––––––––––––

The Middle Generation (1986)

The Contemporary Stylist (1986)

Diminishing Fictions (1988)

The Screenplay's the Thing (1992)

THE
ASPECT
OF
ETERNITY

ESSAYS BY

Bruce Bawer

GRAYWOLF PRESS

SAINT PAUL

These essays were first published in *The New Criterion,* to whose editors
the author expresses his thanks.

Publication of this volume is made possible
in part by a grant provided by the Minnesota State Arts
Board through an appropriation by the Minnesota State Legislature,
and by a grant from the National Endowment for the Arts.
Additional support has been provided by the Andrew W. Mellon
Foundation, the Lila Wallace-Reader's Digest Fund,
and other generous contributions from foundations, corporations,
and individuals. Graywolf Press is a member agency of
United Arts, Saint Paul. To these organizations
and individuals who make our work possible,
we offer heartfelt thanks.

Published by G R A Y W O L F   P R E S S
2402 University Avenue, Suite 203, Saint Paul, Minnesota 55114
All rights reserved. Printed in the United States of America.

9 8 7 6 5 4 3 2
First Printing, 1993

Library of Congress Cataloging-in-Publication Data
Bawer, Bruce, 1956–
The aspect of eternity / Bruce Bawer.
p.   cm.
"These essays were first published in The New criterion" – T.p.
verso.
I S B N 1-55597-187-3 (cloth)
1. American fiction–20th century–History and criticism.
2. English fiction–20th century–History and criticism.   I. Title.
P S 379.B357   1993
813'.509 – dc20   92-38919

CONTENTS

FOR CHARLOTTE LILIAH

DAVENPORT WITH LOVE

Preface

ONE DAY ten years ago, while poking through the literary magazines in New York's Gotham Book Mart, I discovered the *New Criterion,* a monthly that was then only a few issues old. It was the most beautifully designed magazine I'd ever seen, and after paging through it, I realized that I'd made a discovery.

This discovery took place at a crucial moment in my life. I was twenty-six and about to receive my Ph.D. in English. I'd just finished my dissertation, written at breakneck speed over a period of four months. If I was in a hurry, it was because I'd been feeling increasingly alienated in academia and disillusioned by academic criticism, and I knew that if I lingered over the thing I'd wake up one day and realize I didn't want to be bothered finishing it. I'd won the race against my own disillusionment; but now, though I'd donned a suit and dragged myself to a couple of job interviews at the previous year's MLA convention – and would dutifully but halfheartedly drag myself to two or three more over the next few years – I knew I really didn't want to be a cog in the academic machine.

To be sure, I'd had several top-notch teachers in graduate school, and after four years as an instructor of introductory composition and literature I knew that I loved teaching and was good at it; but I found the English-department atmosphere profoundly exasperating. I'd never seen so many middle-class types in my life – and they all kept themselves busy putting down the middle class. Between class sessions the less inspiring members of the department sat around in the faculty lounge sipping coffee and bonding with each other by quoting Shakespeare and Terry Eagleton and by snidely mentioning names of popular writers like Leon Uris and James Michener. They bonded by telling jokes in which the punch lines alluded to familiar quotations from Swift or Joyce or Dante, and they laughed at the jokes not because they were funny (they weren't) but because if they didn't laugh everyone would think they didn't recognize the allusions. They bonded by having conversations about politics in which it was understood that everyone shared exactly the same opinions about every issue, and in which the only differences were on tactical matters.

After all this bonding, the professors would go off to committee meetings and commit petty treacheries against one another. Or else each would shuffle to his office, pick up a book or two and a handful of yellowing index cards, and proceed to a room down the hall to teach a class. These were the very same classes they had taught for years, with the same reading lists, and in those classes they said the very same things they had always said. All that was different was the student roster. Few of these professors seemed interested in trying anything new; few seemed to have original opinions about anything; few seemed even to *think* about anything. The handful of brave souls who did think about things and who refused to march in academic lockstep were the subject of ubiquitous scorn. The place was, in short, awash in cowardice, mendacity, mediocrity, and careerism, and every year, when yet another aging New Critic or Chicago critic slid with relief into retirement and was replaced by yet another energetic young slave of this or that critical trend, things seemed only to get worse. It was a grim spectacle, and eventually I grew tired of pretending to myself that I could ever fit into such a place, or would want to.

What I did want to do – what I had always wanted to do – was write; the main reasons I had applied to graduate school were that I loved to read and wanted an excuse to write. I had never intended to become a critic; indeed, it came as a surprise to me when, in my first Ph.D. seminar, a professor suggested that I submit a paper I'd written about F. Scott Fitzgerald to a scholarly journal. It came as an even greater surprise when the journal took it – my first professional acceptance. During my four years in graduate school I'd had a few more papers accepted by journals. But this experience only made me realize that I had no interest in making a career of academic writing. For that's what academic writing was: not a vocation but a career, a means by which young scholars built up their résumés in order to secure jobs, promotion, tenure. The vast majority of academic essays were artificial, gratuitous, deadly dull, written not out of a strong emotional response to a work of literature and a compulsion to understand it more fully, but out of sheer, naked professional necessity. These essays sounded alike, and they had nothing to say. I couldn't imagine anybody wanting to read them.

That wasn't true of the *New Criterion*. Nor had it been true of the old *Partisan Review*, whose issues of the 1940s and 50s I had pored through excitedly, a few months earlier, while researching my dissertation. The *Partisan Review*'s critics had been keen, ardent, engaged; they hadn't been academic careerists working their respective specialties like tired farmers plowing a field, but human beings responding freshly and frankly and with all their hearts and minds and souls to a wide variety of cultural phenomena that had moved them to joy or outrage or wonder. Unfortunately, there wasn't anything like the *Partisan* around anymore; to be sure, there were journals I admired greatly, such as the *Hudson Review* and the *American Scholar*, and there were a few non-academic critics – ranging from John Simon to Gore Vidal – who tackled a diversity of subjects with style, intelligence, a real sense of engagement, and a manifest desire to reach the educated common reader and make him think. But no magazine of my own day seemed quite to fill the space that the *Partisan* had once occupied – at least not until I ran across the *New Criterion*. From every angle – style, tone, point of view, range of interests – this magazine seemed almost to have been created precisely for me. If anyone had told me that it was "neoconservative" in orientation, I would have frowned in puzzlement. I wasn't a neoconservative, whatever that was: I was an old-fashioned liberal humanist who was sick and tired of English-department political correctness.

Not long after that day at the Gotham, I sent off queries to the editors of *Commentary*, the *American Scholar*, and the *New Criterion*, politely asking them for review assignments and enclosing clips of a couple of opinion pieces I'd published in *Newsweek* and the *Los Angeles Times*. From *Commentary* I received a form rejection; from the *American Scholar*, a note explaining that I would be hearing shortly from their "reviewing committee." (Though I've written for the *American Scholar* many times since, I'm still waiting to hear from that committee.) From Hilton Kramer, editor of the *New Criterion*, I received a letter asking for "some sort of personal/critical statement from you that would give us a more concrete sense of what contemporary writers most interest you and why." Personal/critical statement? I sweated over this one for a while, then tapped out a rambling, opinionated letter that I regretted sending the moment after I'd dropped it in the mailbox. To my astonishment, I heard back from Mr. Kramer almost immediately. He'd found my letter "very interesting"; I'd be hearing shortly from him or his managing editor, Erich Eichman, about a review assignment. Ten years and a hundred assignments later, I can still remember how liberating it felt to compose that first *New Criterion* book review: for the first time in a work of criticism, I was speaking in my own voice and from my own heart.

In a sense, the *New Criterion* has been my real graduate school. Over the years, Messrs. Kramer and Eichman suggested topics that I would otherwise never have had the nerve to tackle and that I took on only because I didn't have the nerve to say no. I ended up learning a great deal from these assignments; indeed, I came to realize that in a sense I didn't really know what I thought of a given writer until I took on his or her oeuvre in an essay. I should add that I also learned a lot from Erich Eichman, who has an extraordinary sense of argumentative structure and the editorial equivalent of perfect pitch. It is to Erich, too, that I am indebted for the insight that inspired the compilation of this book of essays about twentieth-century novelists with a strong religious, mystical, or visionary element. One day several years ago, when most of these essays had already been written, Erich mentioned casually that my critical work betrayed a conspicuous interest in spiritual questions and in writers who explored such questions. This observation surprised me, because I considered myself a thoroughgoing atheist and Aristotelian. When I looked back at my pieces, though, I realized that he was right. Now, on the other side of a baptism, it impresses me to look back and realize that Erich was aware of my interest in these matters some time before I was. There are no words to express my gratitude to him and to Hilton Kramer, as well as to the other *New Criterion* staffers, past and present, with whom I worked on these pieces and whose friendship and support have been of inestimable importance to me over the years: Christopher Carduff, Marge Danser, Roger Kimball, Donna Rifkind, and the late Eva Szent-Miklosy. I wish also to thank my father, Ted

Bawer, *il miglior fabbro,* for his helpful comments on several of these essays, and to thank Scott Walker, Anne Czarniecki, Ellen Foos, and Tree Swenson of Graywolf for their various contributions. Finally, I am deeply indebted to my companion, Christopher Davenport, who is my constant inspiration and whose idea it was to gather these essays under this title.

Willa Cather's Uncommon Art

If o n e doesn't come across Willa Cather's name as frequently as those of the other major American novelists of her time, a large part of the reason, one suspects, is that she suffers from an image problem. People who have never even read her – or who retain only the vaguest memories of having read her in school – tend to think of her as earnest, proficient, dully respectable; almost universally, it seems, her name conjures up drab images of midwestern prairies and amber waves of grain, images that are likely to strike the typical reader as far less scintillating than, say, Hemingway's soldiers and *toreros*, Fitzgerald's flappers and romantic egoists, or Dreiser's magnificently wretched Jennies, Carries, and Clydes. Perhaps the most celebrated remark about Cather by one of her literary contemporaries is Hemingway's derisive comment, in a 1923 letter to Edmund Wilson, about a battlefront episode in her uncharacteristically flimsy novel *One of Ours.* "Do you know where it came from?" Hemingway asked. "The battle scene in *Birth of a Nation.* I identified episode after episode, Catherized. Poor woman she had to get her war experience somewhere." Later generations may not share Hemingway's overtly patronizing attitude toward Cather; but there does remain, in the minds of many, a perhaps unwitting inclination to dismiss her as a genteel and innocuous (if highly gifted) celebrant of frontier life.

This is unfortunate, for there are few American novelists whose collected works form as substantial, and as consistently masterly, a body of work as Willa Cather's. To read through her fiction – most of which has now been gathered in two Library of America volumes edited by Sharon O'Brien – is to recognize how slender, uneven, and replete with self-imitative works, by comparison, are the oeuvres of most of her contemporaries.[1] The contrast with Dreiser is particularly worth noting. The two novelists were almost exact contemporaries: Cather was born in 1873, two years after Dreiser's birth, and died in 1947, two years after his death. Like him, she was a midwesterner (though born in Virginia, she moved to Nebraska as a child); like him, she grew up during the so-called Gilded Age, and was distressed by what she saw as a rise in crassness and vulgarity and a decrease in refinement, moral probity, and respect for grace and beauty. Yet she by no means shares what Lionel Trilling described as Dreiser's "showy nihilism"; on the contrary, her novels repeatedly underscore the significance of human life and purposeful effort. While Dreiser's prose, moreover, remained clumsy and bombastic throughout his career, as if to mirror his protagonists' raw energies, Cather's prose was from the first more classical than naturalistic, and over the years became increasingly spare, meticulous, and unembellished; clearly, she sought not to capture in her prose the roughness of frontier life, but rather to assert, by means of diction, tone, and syntax, traditional notions of civilization and culture.

The contrasts between the Old and New Worlds, and between civilization and wilderness, have been a favorite subject of American novelists since James Fenimore Cooper; but Cather had her own distinctive perspective on these themes. Growing up in close proximity to Swedes, Germans, and other immigrants, she observed the encounter between America and Europe at first hand, and perceived the high drama and heroism of these newcomers' struggle to adapt to the folkways of their new land while attempting to preserve the most valuable elements of life in the old country. Cather found heroes all over the American landscape: not only in those farmers whose persistence and perspicacity enabled them to subdue nature and prosper, but also in those who, tormented by the cultural limitations of frontier life, strove either to escape the frontier or to bring European-style enlightenment to it. As Alfred Kazin has observed, Cather's protagonists are all pioneers of a sort, living "by a purity of aspiration, an integrity or passion or skill" that can

1. *Willa Cather: Early Novels and Stories* collects *The Troll Garden, The Song of the Lark, My Antonia,* and *One of Ours. Willa Cather: Later Novels* collects *A Lost Lady, The Professor's House, Death Comes for the Archbishop, Shadows on the Rock, Lucy Gayheart,* and *Sapphira and the Slave Girl.*

survive only through vision, willpower, and an unwavering indifference to the petty prejudices of others; they are, as a fellow character says of the heroine of *The Song of the Lark,* "uncommon" individuals "in a common, common world."

It was, indeed, the pioneer spirit, in whatever form, that her Nebraska upbringing taught Cather to recognize and admire; and it was in the extraordinary challenge posed by less than fully congenial environments to these unconventional spirits that she found her most enduring theme. Yet Cather distinguished true pioneers from equally assertive persons with meaner temperaments and less estimable goals. And she appreciated commoner souls as well: some of the most appealing characters in her books are unambitious, down-to-earth folks who are almost childishly simple and notable for their selfless devotion. Cather pays tribute, too – most conspicuously, in the stories about art and artists collected in her first book, *The Troll Garden* (1905) – to those who, through timidity, lack of vision, or untimely death, fail as pioneers. In "A Wagner Matinée," for instance, a young man's beloved aunt, a longtime Nebraska housewife, visits him in Boston, where she was once a music teacher. He thinks she has put her past behind her, but when she is emotionally overwhelmed by a Wagner concert he realizes that, somewhere deep within her soul, an artist has lived in torment. The aunt says she doesn't want to leave the concert hall, and he understands: "For her, just outside the door . . . lay the black pond with the cattle-tracked bluffs; the tall, unpainted house, with weather-curled boards; naked as a tower, the crook-backed ash seedlings where the dish-cloths hung to dry; the gaunt, moulting turkeys picking up refuse about the kitchen door." It is an affecting, well-written story, but the conclusion is pat and predictable, and hinges too strongly on the presumption that the reader shares the narrator's distaste for prairie life.

An even grimmer picture of prairie life is painted in "The Sculptor's Funeral," wherein the remains of a recently deceased young sculptor are returned to his Kansas hometown to be buried by his family and neighbors, virtually none of whom understood him and who even now patronizingly dismiss his accomplishments. The only characters who do not share this attitude are the local attorney and an art student who has escorted the body from Boston. The student, observing the towns-people's scorn, says that the sculptor "was wonderful . . . wonderful; but until to-night I have never known how wonderful." And the lawyer agrees: "That is the true and eternal wonder of it, anyway; that it can come even from such a dung heap as this." Though it may load the dice against the locals, the story's nightmarish vision of small-town igno-rance, intolerance, and ignobility is horrifyingly plausible. The mes-sage – an important one in Cather – could hardly be clearer: an artist's family and hometown folks are not necessarily his "people" at all. (Cather makes much the same point in "Death in the Desert" and "The Marriage of Phaedra.")

The book's opening and closing stories focus on the relation between temperament and the attraction to art. "Flavia and Her Artists" is about a frivolous patroness who reveres artists yet insufficiently appreciates her husband, whom she finds deficient in aesthetic understanding; ulti-mately, however, he proves to have more integrity than any of her art-ists, and the ultimate illustration of this integrity is his quiet refusal to wear it on his sleeve. "Paul's Case," meanwhile, concerns a high-school boy whose enchantment with the world of art is unaccompanied by the qualities of temperament (the story is subtitled "A Study in Tempera-ment") that might make possible for him a fulfilling life as an artist. Paul, a Carnegie Hall usher who hates the "ugliness and commonness" of his life, frequents the backstage area of a downtown theater where he "breathed like a prisoner set free, and felt within him the possibility of doing or saying splendid, brilliant, poetic things." He doesn't aspire to be an actor or a musician, but wants simply "to see, to be in the atmo-sphere, float on the wave of it, to be carried out, blue league after blue league, away from everything." The actors think Paul has a vocation; but this vocation, which might motivate a differently constituted indi-vidual to pursue a brilliant career, can only lead Paul, such as he is, to a tragic end.

"Paul's Case" is the best story in *The Troll Garden,* and it is largely be-cause the protagonist, his tragedy, and the implied view of art are all rather more complex and ambiguous than in the other stories. Indeed, most of these stories share a handful of flaws: they are a bit too self-conscious and simplistic in their devotion to art; they sometimes draw overly neat contrasts between artists and philistines; their view of prairie life is unrelievedly negative; and their prose is less taut and subtle than in Cather's later work. Yet such faults are hardly surprising; these stories, after all, reflect a young author's joy and wonder at discovering her vocation, her outrage at ordinary people's lack of understanding, and her dread of falling back into the world of her childhood. At their best, the stories effectively communicate an almost Jamesian sensitivity to the nuances, ironies, and tragedies of the artist's life, and burn with a passionate awareness that, as Cather wrote elsewhere, "the splendid things of life are few, after all, and so very easy to miss."

SHE FURTHER EXPLORES the life of art in *The Song of the Lark* (1915). This long, discursive novel, as Cather declares in its closing pages, is the story of "how a Moonstone girl found her way out of a vague, easy-going world into a life of disciplined endeavor." The girl is Thea Kronborg, daughter of an immigrant; the "vague, easy-going world" is that of her hometown, Moonstone, Colorado; and the "life of disciplined endeavor" is that of the great, internationally famous singer that Thea eventually becomes, thanks largely to the support of her family doctor, Howard Archie, and a magnanimous freight-train conductor named Ray Kennedy. Many people might think of life in a place like Moonstone as hard and disciplined, and of an artist's life as vague and easy-going; Cather disagrees. Though the lyrical title may suggest otherwise, this is a confident, even an arrogant book, without a trace of misty-eyed nostalgia; Thea is no sweet songbird, but an unsentimental, determined young woman who prefers the company of Mexicans and "rowdies" to that of "nice" girls, and who realizes that her siblings are "her natural enemies."

Cather paints a fine portrait of an artist in embryo. During her childhood Thea moves into an uncomfortable attic room whose acquisition, we are told, "was the beginning of a new era in Thea's life"; the room is an affectingly rendered symbol of Thea's artistic alienation, of her elevation beyond the world of her upbringing into the realm of art, and of the special hazards of her calling. When Thea leaves home to begin her career in Chicago, Cather, far from glossing over the girl's egoism, points out its utility:

> If youth did not matter so much to itself, it would never have the heart to go on. Thea was surprised that she did not feel a deeper sense of loss at leaving her old life behind her. It seemed, on the contrary, as she looked out at the yellow desert speeding by, that she had left very little. Everything that was essential seemed to be right there in the car with her. She lacked nothing. She felt even more compact and confident than usual.

The honesty of this passage gives it a surprising power. Less effective, perhaps, is a later section detailing a journey to the Southwest, where an encounter with old Indian art gives Thea a sense of connection and obligation to the artists of the past that serves to replace her lost sense of family attachment.

In *The Song of the Lark,* Cather demonstrates far more regard than in *The Troll Garden* for the frontier, whose newness and beauty mirror Thea's youth and talent. "There was a new song in that blue air," Cather writes, "which had never been sung in the world before." A similar appreciation for frontier life informs *O Pioneers!* (1914). Like *The Song of the Lark,* this novel is set on the Nebraska prairie and has as its heroine the smart, strong-willed child of an immigrant. John Bergson, in eleven years of farming, "had made but little impression upon the wild land he had come to tame"; but his daughter Alexandra, in the decades that follow, prospers by her intelligent and imaginative dedication to the goal of taming the soil. Like *The Song of the Lark,* the novel has a certain prairielike expansiveness; Cather takes her time about making points, and allows herself ample room for touches of atmosphere, generalizations about man and nature, and descriptions of subsidiary characters. Consequently the book does not focus as steadily as it might on its heroine, who remains a bit too distant and impassive to be a thoroughly engaging character. But it is sensitive and authentic, and contains some captivating lyrical passages.

A more fully successful novel – with an even more sympathetic view of prairie life – is *My Antonia* (1918), whose narrator, a New York businessman named Jim Burden, recalls his relatively prosperous upbringing by grandparents in and near Black Hawk, Nebraska. In particular he remembers his childhood friend Antonia Shimerda, a less well-to-do Bohemian immigrant who is now a hardworking farm wife and mother and who, more than anyone else, represents to Jim "the country, the conditions, the whole adventure of our childhood." Like Thea and Alexandra, Antonia is no delicate flower of the frontier; indeed, Cather implicitly contrasts this sturdy, spirited, and often obnoxious girl with Jim's affected, "unimpressionable" wife, who (like Flavia in *The Troll Garden*) is an art patroness. The contrast between the apparent loathing for Nebraska that is embodied in a story like "A Wagner Matinée" and the affection and regional pride manifest throughout *My Antonia* is striking:

> July came on with that breathless, brilliant heat which makes the plains of Kansas and Nebraska the best corn country in the world. It seemed as if we could hear the corn growing in the night; under the stars one caught a faint crackling in the dewy, heavy-odored cornfields where the feathered stalks stood so juicy and green.... The cornfields were far apart in those times, with miles of wild grazing land between. It took a clear, meditative eye like my grandfather's to foresee that they would enlarge and multiply until they would be, not the Shimerdas' cornfields, or Mr. Bushy's, but the world's cornfields; that their yield would be one of the great economic facts, like the wheat crop of Russia, which underlie all the activities of men, in peace or war.

Despite the poetry of such passages, Cather's depiction of frontier life is never idyllic. In several of her novels, the Edenic imagery comes complete with a snake; in *My Antonia* it is a menacing rattler that Jim destroys with a spade. In *The Song of the Lark,* a tramp pollutes Moonstone's water supply and causes the death of several children by typhoid; in *My Antonia* there is an even more chilling episode concerning a pack of wolves that devour a wedding party. The story, though told in flashback by an immigrant and set in Russia, reinforces Jim and Antonia's sense of the ever-present threat in their own hostile environment.

My Antonia is superior in many ways to Cather's previous novels. In the simplicity of its story, the naturalness of its narrative voice, and the evocative rendering and emotionally disciplined handling of characters and regional settings that plainly derive from the author's childhood, *My Antonia* recalls *Huckleberry Finn*. The novel's plot feels less contrived than those of its predecessors, and Jim, for the most part, is an improvement over the digressive third-person narrators of Cather's earlier books. Finally, *My Antonia* offers a more sharply honed portrait of life on the frontier than either *The Song of the Lark* or *O Pioneers!*; it is as if Cather – who had, since 1906, been based mostly in New York – had finally lived away from Nebraska long enough to bring the meaning of her childhood into perfect focus and to celebrate, at this distance, the commendable aspects of prairie life.

Cather won the Pulitzer Prize for *One of Ours* (1922), but this long, windy novel represents a distinct falling-off from *My Antonia*. Claude Wheeler, a smart, restless boy with high principles and a "sharp disgust for sensuality," leaves his stolid, pious clan's Nebraska farm to attend college and finds himself drawn to the world of culture. Yet Claude, who despite this attraction obediently returns home after college, isn't as decisive or interesting as Thea Kronborg or Alexandra Bergson; his much-reiterated feeling that there must be "something splendid about life, if he could but find it!" comes off as vague and tiresome, and his abrupt marriage to an unsuitable local girl seems motivated mainly by plot necessities. Too often, he seems little more than a bundle of romantic clichés about youth. Though the book does contain some memorable characters and forceful scenes, one's principal impression is that Cather, for once, decided to indulge the expectations of the mass audience. Toward the end, rather than resolve Claude's struggle, she sets it aside altogether and ships him off to fight World War I. This section of the book is extremely synthetic, full of implausibly wholesome battlefield discourses and portentous bits of narration that (whether or not Hemingway was right about specific borrowings from *Birth of a Nation*) do bring to mind the corny solemnity and flag-waving of old war movies. One is especially pained by Cather's glib acceptance of the war's carnage on the grounds that it proves "men could still die for an idea"; the only imaginable defense of her vision of trench warfare is that the book's final chapters were written not to capture the truth of war but to comfort the mothers of dead soldiers.

AN IMPORTANT ELEMENT in *One of Ours* is Claude's dismay over the changes that his native region and its people have undergone since his boyhood: trees have been cut down, the land impoverished, and the residents grown more litigious, small-minded, lazy, and extravagant. "With prosperity," Cather writes, "came a kind of callousness; everybody wanted to destroy the old things they used to take pride in." This view is central to Cather's novels *A Lost Lady* (1923) and *The Professor's House* (1925). The eponymous lady of the first book, which opens in the late nineteenth century, is Marian Forrester, the wife of Captain Daniel Forrester, a retired railroad builder and the leading citizen of Sweet Water, Colorado. The novel's protagonist is Niel Herbert, the local judge's nephew, who admires Mrs. Forrester for her loveliness and charm but mostly for her loyalty to Captain Forrester, whom he comes to recognize, in later years, as one of the dreamers, "impractical to the point of magnificence," who had first settled the West, "a courteous brotherhood . . . who could conquer but could not hold." Contrasted with Forrester is Ivy Peters, a bully who grows up to be a lawyer, one of a breed of vulgar, covetous young operators who ravage the elegant and honorable world created by men like Forrester. After the Captain's death, Mrs. Forrester betrays him to Peters in more ways than one, and Niel comes to loathe her; yet he eventually pities her as a victim of the "sunset of the pioneer."

This short, beautifully shaped novel is one of Cather's finest, depicting the struggle between common and uncommon spirits with unprecedented power and plangency. Its characters, rendered with impressive economy, take on a grander, more symbolic dimension than those in her earlier books. Having in her earliest novels contrasted the wildness of the frontier with the cultural life of Europe and the East, Cather here identifies both with the Forresters, whose house is an emblem of civilized life and whose marsh symbolizes the frontier's natural beauty; Cather makes it clear that men like Peters – who ultimately buys and drains the marsh – are the enemies of both civilization and nature.

The Professor's House is a somewhat longer – and odder – book. It has two central figures. Godfrey St. Peter is a fifty-two-year-old midwestern professor, author of a pioneering multi-volume history of the Spanish in North America, whose isolation from his family is symbolized by his attachment to the attic study that he refuses to abandon after moving to a new house with his wife. He feels less close to her, in fact, than to his memories of Tom Outland, a brilliant student with whom he had a "romance . . . of the mind." Outland, who grew up in New Mexico and died in the Great War, was the inventor of a vacuum device used in aviation, the income from which has enriched his sole heir and sometime fiancée, St. Peter's daughter Rosamond. The first and third parts of the novel depict St. Peter's strained relations with his wife and married daughters and with the repellent modern spirit that has prompted a fellow professor to sue for a cut of Tom's estate. The second part of the novel is Tom's story, told in the first person, of his unsuccessful attempt, prior to entering college, to interest the Smithsonian in an ancient Indian mesa settlement, his discovery of which inspired in him the same "filial piety" experienced by Thea on her introduction to Indian art.

Despite obvious differences between St. Peter and Tom, their impracticality and devotion to history are plainly meant to mark them both as uncommon men. But Tom is not merely uncommon; he is well-nigh incredible, a fanciful embodiment of the lost glories of the West. (To Rosamond's husband, who never met him, Tom has become a "glittering idea.") St. Peter is more plausible, but one has trouble completely buying his feelings about Tom; part of the problem is that although they are seen together in flashback, we never encounter them *à deux* in intellectual communion. Yet there is something compelling about the book, and about Cather's unusual means of linking the tangible St. Peter with the ethereal Tom. By stirring fragments of one character, as it were, into the other, Cather creates an arresting protagonist out of highly atypical materials.

IF CATHER'S view of frontier life changed considerably over the years, so too did her attitude toward religion. Though her early novels treat sincere faith with respect, their view of religion itself is generally that of Dr. Archie in *The Song of the Lark,* who says that though "[a]ll religions are good," they speak of a "kindly Providence" when life is really ruled by "blind chance," and encourage passivity while the people who "really count" are those "who forge ahead and do something." A decided shift from Dr. Archie's view is evinced in *The Professor's House,* wherein Professor St. Peter belittles science for robbing mankind of sin: "We were better off when even the prosaic act of taking nourishment could have the magnificence of a sin. I don't think you help people by making their conduct of no importance – you impoverish them." Once upon a time, he argues, everyone was "a principal in a gorgeous drama with God. . . . And that's what makes men happy, believing in the mystery and importance of their own little individual lives. . . . Art and religion (they are the same thing, in the end, of course) have given man the only happiness he has ever had."

This view of religion is central to *Death Comes for the Archbishop* (1927) and *Shadows on the Rock* (1931), two novels about the early Catholic settlers of North America. The earlier novel is based on the true story of the first bishop of New Mexico and his vicar general. Bishop Jean Latour and Father Joseph Vaillant, as Cather calls them, form an interesting team, not unlike other pairs in her fiction. Latour, like Professor St. Peter and Jim Burden, was brought up in a relatively cultured, prosperous home, while Vaillant, like Tom Outland and Antonia, was raised to a life of physical activity and displays more of a common touch. The novel, set over several decades of the nineteenth century, is plotless and episodic, designed to demonstrate the quiet and unflashy heroism of the two priests. The prose, composed largely of simple declarative sentences, has an almost Biblical stateliness and authority; Cather requires but a few words to capture a character's temperament and imbue him with dimension and dignity. The book also has an almost Biblical sense of time. Years pass in a sentence; for the bishop to travel to and from a conference in Europe takes several months. By continually reminding us of the speed with which time advances, and of how "slight . . . but precious" (as she writes in *Shadows on the Rock*) a single life is, Cather underlines the folly of egoism and the importance of tradition. It is indicative of this book's somewhat different emphases, however, that when the Bishop speaks about the obligation of the present to the past, he makes reference not to the artistic heritage that so impressed Thea Kronborg and Tom Outland but to a bowl of soup prepared by Father Joseph. "[T]his is not the work of one man," the Bishop points out. "It is the result of a constantly refined tradition. There are nearly a thousand years of history in this soup."

Death Comes for the Archbishop has been accused of sentimentality; and, admittedly, a few of the book's minor figures reflect an overly sanguine authorial outlook. A young woman, rescued by the priests from a sociopathic husband, recovers all too easily; and Cather insists upon hailing Kit Carson as a noble frontiersman in the Tom Outland mold, a view that renders her helpless to account for his subsequent participation in a massacre of Indians. It does seem to be a valid complaint, moreover, that for all the people whose lives they touch, Latour and Vaillant are not seen interacting in any meaningful way with anyone but each other.

Other structural curiosities are a deliberate part of the book's thematic design. Though the prologue (set in Rome) seems to prepare us for a story about the dramatic spiritual transformation of the American Southwest, there is no suggestion that the aloof, erudite Latour effects any such change; late in the book, he wonders whether his talents would have better served the Church in a part of the world more civilized than the New Mexico diocese. Yet he concludes that "God had his reasons" and that perhaps "something would remain through all the years to come; some ideal, or memory, or legend." This, in Cather's view, appears to be the great value of this Bishop to New Mexico: not as a miracle worker but as a "glittering idea" (like Tom Outland) to inspire later generations. Perhaps it is for this reason that the book's title refers not to the Bishop's lifetime of commitment but to the death of the archbishop that he becomes in old age, a death that makes possible his magnification into a mythic figure.

Shadows on the Rock, which takes us to the other end of North America, likewise features a pioneering bishop, the retired Father Hector, whose "rare qualities" might, at first blush, seem wasted on the frontier. The novel, a meandering account of life in the "rock-set town" of Québec City during a single winter in the late seventeenth century, focuses largely on young Cécile Auclair and her pharmacist father, who, though "a natural city-dweller" and "not a man of action," is, in his devotion to sensible but unfashionable medical practices, a true pioneer. The novel is highly dexterous and evocative, but much of its interest derives from its similarities to its more formidable predecessor. Both books contain tales of miracles and atrocities: a story in *Shadows on the*

Rock, for example, concerns a Montréal woman who becomes a hermit and is visited by angels, while one in *Death Comes for the Archbishop* recounts the horrific punishment of a friar for his exploitative treatment of Indians. Many of these anecdotes are not a part of the main narrative but are rather part of local history or legend; they are, apparently, what the commonfolk in these places have instead of literature, and the joy of these people in hearing about miracles would seem to be, in Cather's view, the frontier equivalent of an aesthetic *frisson*. For in miracles, she writes in *Shadows on the Rock*, "the vague worship and devotion of the simple-hearted assumes a form. From being a shapeless longing, it becomes a beautiful image; a dumb rapture becomes a melody that can be remembered and repeated; and the experience of a moment, which might have been a lost ecstasy, is made an actual possession and can be bequeathed to another."

It is no coincidence that the protagonists of both *Death Comes for the Archbishop* and *Shadows on the Rock* are French. Since, to Cather, the French are the "most civilized people in Europe," their early experiences as New World settlers make for an especially striking contrast between civilization and wilderness, and can better illustrate the view, articulated in *Shadows on the Rock*, that "[w]hen an adventurer carries his gods with him into a remote and savage country, the colony he founds will, from the beginning, have graces, traditions, riches of the mind and spirit." Both novels are informed by the belief that the special hardships of the New World make for greater heroes and saints. Men like Latour and Vaillant, we are told, "threw themselves naked upon the heart of a country that was calculated to try the endurance of giants. . . . Surely these endured *Hunger, Thirst, Cold, Nakedness*, of a kind beyond any conception St. Paul and his brethren could have had." Likewise, Cécile contrasts the travails of European saints with those of North American martyrs: "To be thrown into the Rhone or the Moselle, to be decapitated at Lyon, – what was that to the tortures the Jesuit missionaries endured at the hands of the Iroquois, in those savage, interminable forests?"

COMPARED to their predecessors, Cather's last two novels are surprisingly bland and conventional. *Lucy Gayheart* (1935) reads like a shorter, paler version of *The Song of the Lark*. Set in the early years of this century, it is the story of a small-town midwestern girl who falls in love with a famous Chicago baritone for whom she works as a rehearsal pianist. When he dies in a boating accident, she leaves Chicago and, back home again, is slighted by her old boyfriend; after a period of grief, she finds herself being drawn to "Life itself" as to a sweetheart, and resolves to return to "a world that strove for excellence"; soon afterward, she perishes while attempting to skate on thin ice in the Platte River. The novel is an unsatisfying one: though it has the shape and concentration of a short story, its depiction of romance (a rare ingredient in a Cather novel) is highly unconvincing, as are the two accidents. Similar problems afflict *Sapphira and the Slave Girl* (1940), set during the 1850s in the Virginia country of Cather's early childhood. Sapphira, an aging plantation mistress, has developed such resentment toward Nancy, a young mulatto slave, that when the mistress's nephew presses his attentions upon the girl, Sapphira's daughter, fearing that her mother has encouraged him to seduce Nancy, helps the girl flee to Canada. Sapphira's family members all have a degree of moral complexity, and their relationships are convincing in their ambivalence; yet the story is never more than mildly interesting, and both major black characters are one-dimensional, with Nancy coming off as a vague (and non-tragic) gesture toward the stereotype of the tragic mulatto. It must be said, too, that both the catastrophic conclusion of *Lucy Gayheart* and the happy ending of *Sapphira and the Slave Girl* strike one as equally slick.

Yet these relatively slight novels are the exceptions in a deeply satisfying — and abundantly human — oeuvre. Cather can, of course, write beautifully about nature, and evinces a deep appreciation for the romance of the West; but to the mature Cather, nature is highly equivocal — both mundane and sublime, at once an adversary and a source of inspiration. And always more important to her than the essence of nature is its role in the drama of man's self-realization. She agrees with Tom Outland that "there is something stirring about finding evidences of human labour and care in the soil of an empty country," and with the priest in *The Professor's House* who says that "[w]herever humanity has made the hardest of all starts and lived itself out of mere brutality, is a sacred spot." In *O Pioneers!*, a rhapsodic description of Alexandra's farm, which "seemed beautiful to her, rich and strong and glorious," soon gives way to a consideration of how "the Genius of the Divide, the great, free spirit which breathes across it," has bent to Alexandra's will. "The history of every country," Cather writes, "begins in the heart of a man or a woman."

Cather's fascination with human endowment and potential pervades her fiction. She is a master at describing people, and the tender attentiveness of many of her descriptions – of, for instance, the old churchgoing woman in *The Song of the Lark* whose "face was brown, and worn away as rocks are worn by water" – recalls Mary Cassatt, with whom she shares an eye for the comeliness and dignity of people engaged in selfless and purposeful activity. Cather has a gift, too, for perceiving the essential points of similarity and difference between people, for delineating the subtle transformations that people undergo as the result of the passage of time and changes in location and circumstance, and for detailing the alterations in demeanor, carriage, and aspect that follow upon these transformations. Cather recognizes that it is a rare gift in people to be able to recognize rare gifts in others, and knows how much of life depends on chance; she has an appreciation for what Professor St. Peter calls "the fine, the almost imaginary obligations," and knows that the way in which people observe or fail to observe those obligations tells much about their characters. Yet she can also acknowledge the value of such vain and foolish women as Marian Forrester in *A Lost Lady* and Doña Isabella in *Death Comes for the Archbishop,* whose frailties of character are excusable because (as the Bishop says) they bring a touch of *"poésie"* to the frontier.

Yet there are serious shortcomings in Cather's portrayal of human experience. She is far better at developing individual characters, and at describing attachments that are not very close – or that involve children rather than grown-ups – than at convincingly depicting intimate and gratifying adult relationships. Her fiction contains very few love affairs and not many warm friendships; for the most part, she avoids depicting romance, and when she does, it is usually perfunctory (as in *One of Ours*) or unconvincing (as in *Lucy Gayheart*). Doubtless this failing is related to the fact that Cather regards romantic love and family ties as more of a hindrance and a distraction to uncommon people than a source of support. It cannot be denied that this is a serious – indeed, almost a crippling – weakness. Yet it is balanced, I think, by an abundance of strengths. What is remarkable, indeed, is not that Cather labored under such a deficiency, but that she managed in spite of it to produce fiction that exemplified, even as it celebrated, the ability of uncommon people to do magnificent things.

(SEPTEMBER 1990)

Race and Art:
James Baldwin

Hey Jimmy:
Ain't you heard?
RACE and ART
Are far apart.

— postcard from Langston Hughes to James Baldwin, 1962

By THE TIME of his death in 1987, James Baldwin had long since become that most tragic of literary figures: a major writer on the skids whose last few published books, painful in their lack of distinction, served only to remind discriminating readers of how far he had plummeted since his glory days. And glory days they had truly been: in the late fifties and early sixties he was not only one of America's most critically acclaimed authors, but, in the words of James Campbell – who has now published the second full biography of Baldwin – "practically the most famous writer in the land."[1] In later years, however, he spent less time writing, it seemed, than sitting in Paris cafés, giving interviews in which he spun out fraudulent, self-flattering versions of his personal history as well as glibly radical pronouncements upon American society and race relations. Indeed, as Campbell notes, Baldwin's genre of choice during his later years was not the novel, play, poem, essay, or short story – at all of which he had tried his hand – but the interview; and the more absurdly extremist his remarks, the more sorrowfully aware his sometime admirers were of how much distance he had placed not only

1. *Talking at the Gates: A Life of James Baldwin,* by James Campbell; Viking.

between himself and the literary interests of his youth, but between himself and the philosophy of race that he had communicated so eloquently in much of his early work.

It means nothing simply to know that an artist is black; it can be important, however, to know what being black means to him, to know the ideas about race on which he was raised. As anyone knows who has read "Notes of a Native Son" – one of the handful of autobiographical essays that form perhaps his most enduring achievement – Baldwin, born in Harlem in 1924, grew up in an atmosphere of racial hate. His father, David Baldwin, who died when the author was eighteen (and whom he afterward discovered, to his shock, to have been only his stepfather), was a proud, cruel, charming, remote, and physically abusive Pentecostal preacher from New Orleans whose love for God was matched only by his enmity for white people. He maintained that "none of them were to be trusted," an attitude that Baldwin could hardly regard as inexplicable, given his own early, deeply embittering experiences with racial discrimination, which, despite his close friendships with several white classmates, helped breed in his heart a malice toward whites not unlike his father's – and a malice, too, toward blacks, who along with whites had helped to create the bleak and violent Harlem that he knew. Yet the young Baldwin fought off the racist hate that had made his father "the most bitter man I have ever met": for "blackness and whiteness did not matter; to believe that they did was to acquiesce in one's own destruction. Hatred, which could destroy so much, never failed to destroy the man who hated and this was an immutable law." At fourteen, driven by an egotism no less formidable than his father's and by a desire to "break . . . his hold over me," the young Baldwin had himself become a preacher, in competition with his father; and he remained one till the end of high school, at which time, having already situated himself at the heart of a mostly white literary circle (including the future publisher Emile Capouya and the photographer-to-be Richard Avedon), he exchanged God for art and Harlem for Greenwich Village.

"The son must slay the father," Baldwin was fond of saying, and he applied the remark not only to his difficult relationship with David Baldwin but to his strange filial tie to Richard Wright. The author of *Native Son* was an early hero and mentor – helping Baldwin to win the fellow-

ship that paid for his move to Paris – but at age twenty-four Baldwin rebelled against him, arguing in the essay "Everybody's Protest Novel"
(an attack on *Uncle Tom's Cabin*) that Wright's story of Bigger Thomas,
like Stowe's slavery tale, fails to rise above the level of racial propaganda
to that of artistic truth. For truth, he writes,

> is meant to imply a devotion to the human being, his freedom and ful-
> fillment; freedom which cannot be legislated, fulfillment which can-
> not be charted. This is the prime concern, the frame of reference; it is
> not to be confused with a devotion to humanity which is too easily
> equated with a devotion to a Cause; and Causes, as we know, are no-
> toriously bloodthirsty. We have, as it seems to me, in this most me-
> chanical and interlocking of civilizations, attempted to lop this crea-
> ture down to the status of a time-saving invention. He is not, after all,
> merely a member of a Society or a Group or a deplorable conundrum
> to be explained by Science. He is – and how old-fashioned the words
> sound! – something more than that, something resolutely indefinable,
> unpredictable. In overlooking, denying, evading his complexity –
> which is nothing more than the disquieting complexity of ourselves –
> we are diminished and we perish; only within this web of ambiguity,
> paradox, this hunger, danger, darkness, can we find at once ourselves
> and the power that will free us from ourselves. It is this power of reve-
> lation which is the business of the novelist, this journey toward a
> more vast reality which must take precedence over all other claims.
> . . . The failure of the protest novel lies in its rejection of life, the
> human being, the denial of his beauty, dread, power, in its insistence
> that it is his categorization alone which is real and which cannot be
> transcended.

Two years later, in the essay "Many Thousands Gone," Baldwin
launched a full-scale attack on *Native Son,* arguing that novels, whether
about blacks or whites, should traffic not in political simplicities but in
human complexities, in "the heat and horror and pain of life itself where
all men are betrayed by greed and guilt and blood lust and where no
one's hands are clean." Wright was not pleased. Ridiculing Baldwin's
"art for art's sake crap," he maintained, Campbell tells us, "that all literature was protest. All literature may be protest, Baldwin replied, but not
all protest is literature." So strongly did Baldwin feel about such matters
that in Paris, according to the novelist Richard Gibson, he avoided a

café popular with other black American writers because "[h]e did not feel comfortable in the leftist atmosphere of the place." He excoriated Norman Mailer, whose romantic ideas about blacks in his essay "The White Negro" Baldwin saw as little more than a modern version of the "noble savage" stereotype. Campbell quotes an old friend of Baldwin's as saying that in those days he "was very insistent that he was not a black writer but an American one – indeed an English-language writer"; so eager was he to avoid a crude sense of racial partisanship in his writing that in his 1948 essay "The Harlem Ghetto" he speaks of "we" Americans and refers to Negroes as "they." "Relations between Negroes and whites," he asserted in an early review, "must be based on the assumption that there is one race and we are all part of it"; if he rejected Wright's protest fiction, he celebrated the artistry of Ralph Ellison, "the first Negro novelist I have ever read to utilize in language, and brilliantly, some of the ambiguity and irony of Negro life."

BALDWIN'S own most valiant attempt to capture the "ambiguity and irony of Negro life" was his first novel, *Go Tell It on the Mountain* (1953), which centers on a Harlem family not unlike his own. Like the Trinitarian God, the book is divided into three parts: John, who is the focus of the first and third parts (and who, like Baldwin, is known as "Frog Eyes"), is the stepson of Gabriel, a preacher who believes "that all white people [are] wicked, and that God [is] going to bring them low," and who feels that God has promised him a son to carry on his holy work; the second part, itself divided in three and consisting largely of flashbacks, outlines the earlier lives of Gabriel (who many years ago, we learn, had a mistress and an illegitimate son, both of whom died as a consequence of his refusal to acknowledge them), of Gabriel's sister Florence, and of his second wife, Elizabeth (whose ill-fated and fervently atheistic first lover, John's father, loved art as much as Gabriel loves God). Baldwin renders this family's inner history – the details of which John will probably never know, though it has profoundly influenced his own life – with both the tenderest sympathy and the harshest insight; he sees the life of faith from both inside and out, and by exploring the past through these several pairs of eyes not only conveys something of the richness and mystery of a family's life but reminds us that to understand is to forgive. And he does a remarkably vivid job of capturing the streets of New York as seen by a boy raised on Pentecostal sermons:

> And certainly perdition sucked at the feet of the people who walked there; and cried in the lights, in the gigantic towers; the marks of Satan could be found in the faces of the people who waited at the doors of movie houses; his words were printed on the great movie posters that invited people to sin. It was the roar of the damned that filled Broadway, where motor cars and buses and the hurrying people disputed every inch with death. *Broadway:* the way that led to death was broad, and many could be found thereon; but narrow was the way that led to life eternal, and few there were who found it.

The novel, whose style has something of the stateliness of the King James Bible and the music of black vernacular, splendidly evokes Harlem's sights and sounds, its frustrations and hypocrisies. Baldwin excels at small descriptive touches, as when Gabriel observes the "distant and angry compassion" in his illegitimate son's face. This is, as Campbell says, "Baldwin's most accomplished novel, technically, and his most disciplined," free of the "idealizations, the sentimentality, the jarring tones and overlong conversations, even the moral fervour, which, separately or all at once, were to mar, in part or whole, his later novels."

Yet Campbell is also right to call *Go Tell It on the Mountain* "somewhat stiff and formal." Though Baldwin aims for a natural-seeming lyricism (and though the novel does rise to beautiful lyrical heights), there is too often an air of contrivance about it. Like a sermon in a black church, the prose is sometimes poetic and inspired, sometimes windy, repetitious, bombastic. Baldwin hammers us relentlessly with biblical verses – and with good reason, for his purpose is to impress upon us the ubiquity of religion in John's family and his sense of being bound inextricably to God – but it doesn't take long before we're weary of it all and the verses seem like mere gimmickry. Many of the novel's more protracted sentences, too, which should sound fresh and musical – like hymns, say, with long melodic lines – strike one as rather too self-consciously constructed; and the frequent flashbacks – which were to become a familiar device in Baldwin's work, as if to suggest the immense history that lies behind even the most seemingly negligible occurence in black America – are less dramatically effective than they are confusing.

Go Tell It on the Mountain was written in Paris, to which Baldwin had relocated in 1948 – a move that to him "stank of betrayal" but that he felt compelled to make in order to "escape from the daily enormities of racism." Though he would spend years there in poverty, Paris was a place where he could safely live in a white neighborhood, eat in white restaurants, and take white lovers. Yet even there, he came to realize, he could not escape intolerance completely: in the essay "Equal in Paris," he recalls his arrest for possession of a stolen bedsheet, a crime of which he was acquitted but which made him the butt of laughter in court, a humiliation he would never forget. The people who laughed, he wrote, were representative of all those "who consider themselves to be at a safe remove from all the wretched, for whom the pain of living is not real. I had heard it [laughter] so often in my native land that I had resolved to find a place where I would never hear it anymore. In some deep, black, stony, and liberating way, my life, in my own eyes, began during that first year in Paris, when it was borne in on me that this laughter is universal and can never be stilled." This is doubtless true; yet it should perhaps be noted that people who feel "at a safe remove from all the wretched" don't generally find the misfortunes of others particularly hilarious; it is the unfortunate, not the privileged, who tend to entertain themselves by laughing at the even less fortunate – or, for that matter, by committing racist acts.

Paris provides the chief setting for Baldwin's second novel, *Giovanni's Room* (1956). This short, meticulously composed book is the story of David, a handsome and well-to-do young white American who, while his fiancée, Hella, vacations in Spain, is both thrilled and horrified to find himself falling in love with a young Italian waiter named Giovanni. They have an affair, conducted mainly in Giovanni's one-room flat, which "was not large enough for two"; David, who has an "offhand" relationship with his fiancée, experiences with Giovanni a passion such as he has never known. Yet he chooses to return to Hella. "What kind of life can we have in this room?" he demands of Giovanni, and proceeds to "cling [to Hella] for my very life." He finds his love for Giovanni constricting, a prison in which he has been locked away from the world he knows; yet by rejecting that love, he brings on tragedy for Giovanni (and perhaps his fiancée, too) and builds for himself a loveless prison, a cell for one rather than two. He eventually learns – a major theme throughout Baldwin – that love can turn into its opposite: "there opened in me a hatred for Giovanni which was as powerful as my love and which was nourished by the same roots." In one of the most powerful episodes in *Go Tell It on the Mountain*, Gabriel admits to Deborah, his first wife, that the devilish neighborhood boy Royal is his son; the parallel scene in *Giovanni's Room* is one in which David admits to his fiancée his love for Giovanni. Both scenes are about sin and confession, the sin being the denial and betrayal of a loving relationship by a man whose fear and self-loathing and sense of vulnerability render him incapable of bridging the gap between self and other. David learns what Giovanni knew all along: that the love they shared was not profane but virtuous, and that evil has issued only from his denial of it, which has twisted his love for Giovanni into hate, and Giovanni's innocence and self-respect into corruption and self-abasement.

The story, which David narrates in flashback, abounds in witty observations of Paris and its denizens and in details that suggest how much one can read in people's faces, gestures, and movements. It moves with great elegance and psychological plausibility, and with a fine sense of dramatic inevitability, from its opening pages to the point, at page 90 or thereabouts, at which David finally surrenders to his love for Giovanni, telling the reader that "[w]ith everything in me screaming *No!* yet the sum of me sighed *Yes*." There are vivid descriptions (Giovanni kisses David with a "strange insistent gentleness") and lyrical metaphors ("I felt myself flow toward him, as a river rushes when the ice breaks up"). The decorous, restrained tone and the fastidious qualifying phrases patently derive from Henry James, a great enthusiasm of Baldwin's at this time, while its deliberate simplicity and repetitiousness, and the frequent serial linkage of simple clauses with the word "and," betray a debt to Hemingway; like both writers, Baldwin is concerned here with the time-honored theme of Americans in Europe, with the clash of innocence and experience, of New World and Old World notions of sexual morality. Though its pacing might at times be faulted for being a bit too deliberate, its style for being a bit too self-consciously spare, and its periodic sentences for being a bit too impressed with their own stateliness, *Giovanni's Room* is wonderfully evocative both of its milieu and of David's inner conflict—a conflict that doubtless held great personal meaning for Baldwin but from which he manages, almost throughout, to distance himself successfully.

If David is very well drawn, however, perhaps the novel's weakest element is Giovanni. As Campbell points out, "Giovanni is the first of those intensely human, yet idealized, characters, with a touch of the saint about them, who were later to dominate Baldwin's fiction.... After Giovanni, they were mostly black." In fact, Giovanni is quite one-dimensional, an improbable embodiment of perfect affection, gentleness, probity, and fidelity. He is, in short, too good and loving to be true, and his climactic speech to David—"You want to leave Giovanni because he makes you stink. You want to despise Giovanni because he is not afraid of the stink of love. You want to *kill* him in the name of all your lying little moralities.... Is *this* what you should do to love?"—is completely ridiculous, making him sound like a cross between a Psych 101 student and the innocent little island girl who loved Lieutenant Cable in *South Pacific*. The novel is also marred by the melodramatic present-tense passages in which David, standing by a window in a Riviera château on the night before Giovanni's execution for murder, tries to imagine what Giovanni is seeing and feeling; and it is weakened, too, by the occasional manifest intrusion by Baldwin himself, who, Campbell notes, couldn't "keep his own opinions and tone of voice out of his characters' mouths" after *Go Tell It on the Mountain*. These opinions and this tone – a kind of intimate, smug, world-weary drawl – make their first appearance here.

Giovanni's Room also marks the first significant appearance in Baldwin's longer fiction of the theme of homosexuality, which was to figure prominently in most of his novels. One gathers that Baldwin accepted his homosexuality with relative ease; Campbell writes that no sooner did Baldwin discover his proclivities than he began to "confess" them to everyone:

> Baldwin urged himself to own up to it, to confess, confession being the spirit's cleansing operation.... Baldwin was determined not to

treat his homosexuality like a skeleton in the cupboard – if you can't be frank about that, then until it's in the open you can't be frank about anything else . . . By "going public" in this way, he pre-empted the shame which was usually attendant upon a homosexual life in those days. Baldwin had grown up to the shocking discovery that the colour of his skin stood between him and the possibility of life lived to its full potential – between him and life itself, in fact. He made up his mind not to allow his sexual orientation to fortify the barrier.

The logical connections here seem rather hazy. Surely Campbell cannot mean to say that Baldwin viewed homosexuality as something of which one must be spiritually cleansed; and even if such were the case, how did telling people about it effect such a "cleansing"? How did it "pre-empt shame"? And how did it make his sexuality less of a barrier? Campbell writes that Baldwin's "desire for women, or perhaps for the sense of normality and orthodoxy that relationships with women conferred, was not extinguished altogether." But heterosexual desire and a longing for "normality" are two utterly different things. If Baldwin slept with women for reasons other than sexual attraction, what does this say about his supposed lack of discomfort about his homosexuality?

BALDWIN's Paris years, in Campbell's words, mark his "heyday as an artist." Returning to America in 1957, he threw himself into the civil-rights movement, whereupon – finding himself in the American South for the first time in his life, embroiled in extremely dramatic confrontations and aligned with other people of color who did not hesitate to sketch in stark black and white a picture that he had always insisted upon painting in shades of gray – he lost control of that exquisite mechanism by which he had theretofore controlled his rage. "Baldwin's true subject," writes Campbell, "was his difficult history," and though his powerful and long-suppressed rage could be explained only by the complex circumstances of that personal history, he chose, in the sixties and thereafter, to regard that rage as his racial inheritance, pure and simple, as something he shared *tout à fait* with every other black American. The man who had written in *Notes of a Native Son* about his love of America now, in the early sixties, referred to Americans as "the most unattractive people on earth." And he began to rewrite his own history, claiming untruthfully in 1970 that his best friends in Paris had been "Algerians and Africans" and writing about Martin Luther King and other civil-rights leaders after their deaths in a way that suggested he'd been closer to them than he really had. Campbell offers the most sympathetic possible reading of all this: "If he inflated his importance within the top echelon of the black leadership, it was to help prop up a spirit that died each time a limb of that leadership was broken off." Perhaps. (And perhaps, to be less charitable about it, he was responding to the irony that he'd left the pulpit to join the mainstream culture, only to see a fellow preacher become the most celebrated black American of his time.) Underlying such prevarications, one imagines, must have been a profound and long-buried sense of guilt about consorting with whites – and a superego that spoke in the voice of his racist stepfather.

During this period Baldwin's elegant style deteriorated – some might say disappeared. Sent the galley proofs of his novel *Tell Me How Long the Train's Been Gone,* the once fastidious writer shocked his editors by not even bothering to return them: "Do what you like," he said. The writer who had identified with the classical tradition now described himself as a "blues singer" or a "jazz musician" in prose; the writer who had revered figures like Henry James and T. S. Eliot now claimed that Eliot was "not a poet" because he wrote from "culture" rather than experience; the writer who had denied "that the Negro has it worse than anybody else" now maintained precisely the opposite. One after another of his post-Paris writings promotes the idea that all blacks are victims, all whites oppressors. His 1964 play *Blues for Mr. Charlie* traffics in much the same sort of stereotyping that he had criticized in his early essays. "I fear you are becoming a 'NEGRO' writer – and a propaganda one, at that!" Langston Hughes wrote him in 1962. Alas, he was; and over the course of the sixties and seventies, his literary stock plunged dramatically.

To read about the *après*-Paris Baldwin is to notice striking parallels between his career and Mailer's. Baldwin set out to "beat" Richard Wright as Mailer set out to beat Hemingway; as Mailer rejected the "Jewish novelist" label, so Baldwin sought to avoid being pigeonholed as a Negro novelist. Both wrote first novels that were evocative but also rather conventional, unadventurous, and overstuffed; both wrote second novels that were spare, idiosyncratic, and populated with bohemians. Both became at least as well known for their controversial nonfiction as for their fiction; and it might be said of Mailer, as Campbell says of Baldwin, that "the intellect, not the imagination, was [his] strong suit," and the personal essay, not the novel, his natural territory. Both writers' heads were turned by the political events of the sixties, both tried to place themselves at the center of the action and to be identified with antiestablishment causes, and both tended to be seen by the leaders of the movements with which they associated themselves as naïve, frivolous, egocentric, and unreliable interlopers whose involvement might ultimately do the cause more harm than good. (According to Campbell, King kept his distance from Baldwin because he found his homosexuality offensive, saying that he would be "better qualified to lead a homosexual movement than a civil rights movement.") Yet while the turmoil of the sixties had no discernible effect on Mailer's attitude toward his Jewishness, and made it possible for him to write books that drew profitably upon his singular talents, Baldwin became fixated on racial issues, writing books and articles that often seemed resolutely antiliterary. One can only wonder whether Baldwin was punishing himself for his years of devotion to literature, his interracial friendships, and his magnificent success beyond the ghetto – a success that he may well have subconsciously regarded, thanks to his stepfather's conditioning, as a mark not of talent and perseverance but of betrayal.

This is not to suggest that Baldwin went over completely to the most radical elements in the Black Power movement. On the contrary, the distinctive mark of his work in the sixties and after is a bemusing mixture of liberality and racism, of love and hate, that seems to have been designed to please both black radicals and white liberals but succeeded in pleasing neither – for his language was too fancy and his politics too tame for one party and his sentences too sloppy and his rhetoric too hostile for the other. Consider, for example, the slack and highly personalized account of the Black Muslims that makes up most of his book *The Fire Next Time* (1963). On the one hand, he takes the Black Muslims seriously, handling their outrageously racist credo with kid gloves, and speaks of Elijah Muhammed (who was patently a father figure for him) with something close to affection; on the other hand, he makes a point of the fact that, after hearing Elijah and other Black Muslim leaders inveigh against the "white devils" (i.e., Caucasians), he went off to have drinks with some "white devils" who were friends of his. He concludes the first of the piece's three parts with a denunciation of religions that preach hate: "If the concept of God has any validity or any use, it can only be to make us larger, freer, and more loving. If God cannot do this, then it is time we got rid of Him"; likewise, after the book's publication, he acknowledged that the Black Muslims were "racists" who "batten[ed] on the despair of black men." Yet he would not attack individual blacks, refusing, when Eldridge Cleaver maligned him, to respond in kind; indeed, he was, in Campbell's words, "almost automatically loyal to black leadership," however irresponsible, managing to "skate over" the activists' Maoism, indoctrination programs, and advocacy of violence. So quick was he to equate black with good and white with evil, in fact, that when Malcolm X was killed by a black man, Baldwin blamed the crime on whites, telling a reporter that "[t]he hand that pulled the trigger did not buy the bullet. That bullet was forged in the crucible of the Western world." As if this were not enough, he spoke in 1968 of the imminent possibility of an antiblack holocaust in America.

This preoccupation with racial categories – a preoccupation that Baldwin had once deplored – is ubiquitous in the novels following *Giovanni's Room*. He embraces, for instance, the image of blacks as better lovers, as people who are more free-spirited and in touch with their bodies than whites – a stereotype he had once rebuked Mailer for propagating. As Campbell notes, these novels feature "too many bloodless characters, too neatly divided into goodies and baddies; too strong a dependence on colour as an indicator of virtue . . . ; too many rambling conversations and descriptions . . . ; too many rhetorical passages which belong not to the narrator but to James Baldwin." They also feature jeremiads about race, often hysterically antiwhite, and occasional horror stories about white injustices against blacks, some of them cropping up in anecdotes told by characters and some forming part of the main narrative. As in *Go Tell It on the Mountain*, lines from hymns are frequently interpolated without comment, in order to underscore one theme or another; but the device generally seems less appropriate to these books than to Baldwin's debut novel, and he employs it so often that it ends up seeming like little more than a contrivance, a bad habit. There are also quotations from jazz and blues and gospel lyrics – so many of them, indeed, in novels containing virtually no literary allusions, that one begins to get the impression that, in Baldwin's view, these lyrics occupy some unique cultural plane, illuminating black American life in a way the great authors of the Western tradition could never do. (What's more, the black characters in these later novels habitually drop the first names of such singers as Billie Holiday and Mahalia Jackson, as if their common skin color made them all sisters and brothers and thus entitled them to first-name familiarity.)

Plotless, repetitious, and self-indulgent, Baldwin's post-Paris novels abound in confusing flashbacks and in overlong conversations of a sort that one can imagine Baldwin having after midnight in some Paris bistro and being impressed with himself for having; stylistically, they are not far removed from the potboilers of an Irving Wallace or a Jerome Weidman. The usual best-seller themes – fame, money, show biz, sex – are almost invariably present, the notable difference being that much of the sex is gay or interracial (or both) and much of the conversation about race; the other recurrent story elements tend to divide into those that are reminiscent of *Go Tell It on the Mountain* (black preachers, Harlem) and those that recall *Giovanni's Room* (gay love affairs in France). Throughout these books various characters address one another as "baby" and refer to third parties as "cats," and, in general, sound like James Baldwin. In three of them, the protagonists – all black men, and all, like Baldwin, artists of some kind – either die young or survive early heart attacks, as if to suggest that the strain of trying to succeed as a black artist in America is too much for them; and everyone spends a lot of time in bars and restaurants and cafés, drinking and chatting and laughing, so that Baldwin's intended points about the agonies of black American life don't come across as powerfully as they might.

THE FIRST of these novels, *Another Country* (1962), introduces us to a young Harlem musician named Rufus, whom Baldwin, on the book's second page, describes melodramatically as "one of the fallen – for the weight of this city was murderous – one of those who had been

crushed on the day, which was every day, these towers fell." We are expected to understand that Rufus is a tragic case, a brilliant artist and sensitive soul destroyed by American racism. But we're not convinced; Rufus comes off simply as a messed-up young man full of hostility toward
"all those white sons of bitches out there." Torn between this rage and
his personal ties to individual whites – for, as it happens, his best friend,
Vivaldo, is white, as is his girlfriend, Leona – Rufus eventually jumps to
his death from the George Washington Bridge. Baldwin spends the rest
of the book bringing together Rufus's nearest and dearest so that they
can (a) pair off and have sex and (b) talk about love and race and the
meaning of Rufus's death. Vivaldo and Ida, Rufus's sister, become lovers, and she spends much of her time asserting that he and Rufus could
never *really* have been friends because of the color line: "Somewhere in
his heart the black boy hated the white boy because he was white. Somewhere in his heart Vivaldo had feared and hated Rufus because he was
black." Vivaldo, she says, doesn't know what it's like to be black (as if
blackness meant precisely the same thing to every black person), and
thus didn't know what it was like to be Rufus, and thus was unable to
save him. She comes off as a caricature of an Angry Black Woman, but
Baldwin plainly wants us to see her as tormented, wants us to recognize
and be moved by the truth of her claims; if once he had repudiated racial
divisions, here he seems to endorse a view of those divisions as absolute
and unbridgeable, and to subscribe to the notion that blacks, by virtue
of their skin color, are acquainted with certain things about which
whites can never so much as earn the right to have an opinion. Yet he
also seems to agree with the preacher at Rufus's funeral who says, "The
world's already bitter enough, we got to try to be better than the
world."

When not discussing race, the folks in *Another Country* wax poetic
about life and love. Bedding down Vivaldo, Rufus's ex-lover Eric wonders: "how old was this rite, this act of love, how deep? in impersonal
time, in the actors?" Afterward, he says: "Maybe, at this very moment,
while both of us are huddled here, hiding from things which frighten
us – maybe you love me and I love you as well as we'll ever love, or be
loved, in this world." (Where, one wonders, does all this leave Eric's
lover, who is to arrive from France within a few days? Baldwin doesn't

seem to care, and it doesn't seem to occur to him that *we* might; the important thing to him, apparently, is that there be sex scenes and portentous postcoital homilies.) There are, to be sure, some fine descriptive passages here. Baldwin is good on New York and its denizens, on Ida's singing (which derives its strength from "a sense of the self so profound and so powerful that it does not so much leap barriers as reduce them to atoms"), at capturing certain little things that happen between people. When Richard cuffs his son lightly on the head, for instance, the boy "always reacted . . . with a kind of surly, withdrawn delight; seeming to say to himself, each time, that he loved his father enough to overlook an occasional lapse of dignity."

Baldwin once described Leo Proudhammer, the hero and narrator of *Tell Me How Long the Train's Been Gone* (1968), as "Rufus qui n'est pas un suicide." Leo is America's greatest black actor, and the novel tells his rags-to-riches story, or, more accurately, presents a hodgepodge of memories upon which Leo reflects after surviving a heart attack at thirty-nine. Born in Harlem, he became an actor in order to rise above himself, his limitations, and his rage. Art is his means of deliverance, of self-transformation, and Baldwin (whom one friend described as "fundamentally an actor") devotes a considerable amount of self-dramatizing rhetoric to this theme. Upon achieving his first great theatrical success, Leo realizes that "[i]f I kept the faith, I could do for others what I felt had not been done for me, and if I could do that, if I could give, I could live." Art is for Leo, then, a matter of faith, of ministry; yet both Baldwin and Leo seem to confuse the artist's ministry with the very different ministry of the black leader or role model. The irony of Leo's life, and his abiding source of frustration, is that he will never be hired to play the great "white" roles – Hamlet, Lear – and will thus never achieve the level of artistic fulfillment of which he is capable; for all his wealth and fame, then, we are meant to see that he is not less of a victim than other blacks but rather a greater, more tragic victim, the very personification of his people's afflictions.

Needless to say, Baldwin's representation of Leo's predicament tells us much about his view óf himself; indeed, one frequently has the feeling that one is reading not about Leo, America's greatest black actor, but about Baldwin, America's most famous black writer. Lazily and playfully, Baldwin incorporates various autobiographical elements into the book, bequeathing to Leo his views on race and art, the tone of his voice, and the curve of his life. (Leo even shares one of Baldwin's friends, Marlon Brando, whose name he drops.) His implausibly loving, flawless, and uncomplicated relationship with a street boy much younger than hiself (who, Leo tells us, is "black in color, black in pride, black in rage" – but not so full of rage, apparently, as to interfere seriously with Leo's fun) comes across as a sketchy, romanticized version of some real-life liaison, rather than as a fully focused and integrated part of the fiction. Finally, the novel is so crammed with tacky bits relating to Hollywood, the Oscars, etc., that at times Baldwin appears to be as interested in the hardships that accompany movie stardom as in those that accompany negritude.

Its brevity, tidily developed plot, and unglamorous protagonists make *If Beale Street Could Talk* (1974) an exception among Baldwin's later novels. Set in Harlem, the story is simple, not dissimilar to many of the nightmare anecdotes of racial persecution in his other books. It focuses on a young couple, the pregnant nineteen-year-old Tish and her boyfriend, Fonny, who is wrongly arrested for rape. Contrasted with this beautiful and loving twosome are white Americans, whose only function here is to taunt and threaten (the one good Caucasian is an Italian immigrant who stands up for Fonny against a vicious white cop). Tish, supposedly a typical Harlem girl, tells her story in preposterously literary, even poetic, language; it's as if Baldwin had either lost touch with the vernacular or lost interest in reproducing it. Throughout the book, moreover, he puts racist talk in his characters' mouths and doesn't give us any reason to think he finds it excessive.

If *Another Country* centers on a musician and *Tell Me How Long the Train's Been Gone* on an actor, Baldwin's last and longest novel, *Just Above My Head* (1979), features a gospel singer named Arthur Montana who is billed as "THE SOUL EMPEROR" and who, as the novel opens, has just died in his early forties. Arthur's older brother and manager, Hall, serves as narrator, recalling, in a patchwork of flashbacks, their upbringing in Harlem, Arthur's rise to fame and discovery of his homosexuality, and the brothers' involvement in the civil-rights movement. The book represents little more than a reshuffling of the ingredients of the two aforementioned novels, from the references to the transcendent power of art to the big, empty pronouncements made by our narrator, who, like his author, has seen all, done all, and knows all, and appears to regard himself as a sage. At one point Hall reflects that the American pioneers "had brought to the savage an unprecedented savagery. The red-skinned tribes were right: the land is not to be bought or sold. The blacks were right: a man is not to be used as a thing. The tom-tom and the smoke signal and the talking drums are true, and the gods are many." That these reflections might pack more punch if Hall were not, at the moment, jetting comfortably across America, a cigarette in one hand and a magazine in the other, doesn't seem to have occurred to Baldwin: in these later novels, the bizarre spectacle of black characters at once condemning and living the American dream is not uncommon.

Of all Baldwin's novels, his last is perhaps his feeblest. To convey how deeply Hall misses his dead brother, Baldwin has him say that "I miss him, miss, miss, miss, miss him, miss him worse than you miss a toothache [?], worse than you miss the missing tooth, worse than you miss the missing leg, even worse than you miss the stillborn baby." So that we may hear about Arthur's sojourn in Paris, Hall is temporarily replaced by an omniscient narrator; later, his narrative voice gives way, without so much as a one-line break in the text, to Jimmy's. And no other Baldwin novel contains more pointless details and more perplexing attempts at humor: "Thousands and thousands of people at the airport, multitudes, multitudes, going where? Everywhere: and, furthermore, Everywhere is numbered. Flight 123 to Dayton, Flight 246 to Tucson, Flight 890 to Dallas, Flight 333 to Birmingham, Flight 679 to Denver, Flight 321 to Washington, three-four to Baltimore, five-six to Pick Up Sticks, three-four-five-six-seven, and all good niggers go to heaven."

BALDWIN never really settled down after his return to America. Instead, "a stranger everywhere," he spent the rest of his life as a self-styled "transatlantic commuter," now in New York, now in Paris, now in Istanbul. His later novels were written by a man too distracted by his public life to devote the necessary effort to his art, and too taken with the ideas of racial propagandists to be the artist that he had it in him to be. As a young man, he had recognized that what people share as children of God transcends what divides them, and that what does distinguish them as individuals – and makes them interesting and distinctive as human beings – has only partially, and in the most complex and ambiguous ways, to do with matters of race or ethnicity. He knew that the more fully one understands the intricacies of a given human situation, the less importance categories will have; he knew that to respond to hate with hate is self-destructive, and that to react to a tyrant's categorization of yourself by centering your identity (and basing your sense of pride) on that category is to capitulate to his vision of you, to cooperate in your own dehumanization. Baldwin is eloquent on this subject in his early essays. After his return from Europe, however, and the manifestation in his fiction of a rage that seems often to have been impossible to control, he began to identify that rage as a corollary of his status as a black American. But the particular circumstances of his upbringing – the pride that made him acutely conscious of his own smallness and plainness, the homosexuality that violated the fundamentalist faith on which he had been raised, the lifelong association of his tyrannical father with God, and the unsettling discovery that his father was not his father after all – all these factors certainly contributed mightily to his precarious sense of self, his inability to settle permanently in any one place or with any one person, and the overpowering fury that seemed, at times, to be that of a man who could not decide whether he was a native son or an outsider.

If there is a problem with Campbell's biography, it is that, in his admirable determination to focus on the development of Baldwin's literary career and not on the sensational details of his personal life, he doesn't come quite as close to the heart of these conflicts as one might desire. One emerges from this book with only the vaguest sense of what it felt like to be James Baldwin, and only the fuzziest images of the people who were closest to him. One might wish, too, that Campbell, a Scotsman, were more familiar with certain American figures and institutions that figure in this story: for instance, he misspells Sidney Hook's first name and doesn't seem aware of the hostility that existed between J. Edgar Hoover and Robert F. Kennedy (both of whom considered Baldwin a dangerous radical). But enough: these are minor cavils about an unusually intelligent, concise, and responsible study whose author knows politics from art, knows the good work from the bad, is capable of feeling sympathy and even affection for his subject while seeing him very clearly, and doesn't hesitate to pass severe judgments or to acknowledge that most of the later work is hopelessly disfigured by anger and bigotry. He recognizes, in short, that it does Baldwin no great service to pretend that his later writings are any better than they were; and he recognizes, too, that to acknowledge Baldwin's falling-off, and to try to understand how it came to pass, is to begin to appreciate how heroic an achievement his finest work really was.

(NOVEMBER 1991)

Peter Matthiessen,
Nature Boy

PETER MATTHIESSEN occupies a unique position in contemporary letters. In the more than three decades since the publication of his first book, a novel called *Race Rock* (1954), he has received a good deal of attention for his contributions to two seemingly very distinct literary genres. Some readers know him primarily for his fiction – especially for the two longest, most recent, and most accomplished of his five novels, *At Play in the Fields of the Lord* (1965) and *Far Tortuga* (1975) – while some are more familiar with his nonfiction writings on man and nature, a dozen-odd books with titles like *The Cold Forest, Under the Mountain Wall, The Tree Where Man Was Born,* and *The Snow Leopard.* His work in both genres has been awarded recognition at a high level: *At Play in the Fields of the Lord* and *The Tree Where Man Was Born* were each nominated for the National Book Award, and *The Snow Leopard* won it; in the past two years, moreover, Random House has done him the honor of reprinting all of his novels, and his most recent book of nonfiction, in a handsome, uniform series of Vintage paperbacks.[1] Patently, to even a cursory observer, this is an impressive, not to say a prepossessing, résumé: how many living American writers, after all, have distinguished themselves in two such disparate fields as natural history and the novel?

As one looks more closely at Matthiessen's oeuvre, however, these fields begin to seem less removed from one another; indeed, one comes to recognize that Matthiessen's two most estimable novels draw heavily upon his learning as a naturalist and anthropologist and his experience as an explorer. *At Play in the Fields of the Lord* is a beautifully shaped and elegantly written story of four ill-fated North American missionaries in

---

1. *Race Rock; Partisans; Raditzer; At Play in the Fields of the Lord; Far Tortuga; Men's Lives.*

the South American jungle; *Far Tortuga* is a formally innovative tale of an even more ill-fated Caribbean turtling expedition. Both novels are notable largely for Matthiessen's extremely convincing rendering of the sensibilities, dialogue, and folkways of, respectively, remote Niaruna tribesmen and Cayman Islands seamen; both are also distinguished by expert, evocative descriptions of land forms, tides, currents, flora, fauna, and sundry phenomena of nature. Conversely, such nonfiction volumes as *Men's Lives* (1986), an account of several generations of Long Island bass fishermen, rely strongly upon his considerable gifts for narrative, dialogue, and character development. It might fairly be said, as a matter of fact, that Matthiessen's singular quality as a writer resides essentially in his ability to combine his talents as a storyteller and a naturalist – something that he accomplishes, in his best books, in such an original and striking manner that they test the boundaries of whichever generic territory they happen to inhabit.

Yet if Matthiessen's finest novels and nonfiction share many of the same strengths, they also share – in varying degrees – substantial weaknesses. Probably the most significant of these weaknesses is Matthiessen's tendency to romanticize the lives, customs, and beliefs of people more primitive than himself; whom he all but reveres for their supposed oneness with nature and closeness to God, and to regard civilization – Western civilization especially, and American civilization most of all – not only as a departure from nature and God but as a wholesale assault upon them. In *At Play in the Fields of the Lord,* for instance, Matthiessen's principal purpose is to make us see that the four fictional American Protestant missionaries – Leslie and Andy Huben, and Martin and Hazel Quarrier – who think of themselves as bearing the light of God's truth and goodness into the pagan darkness of the jungle, are in fact the enemies of everything that is right and virtuous and godly in the reputedly savage Niaruna tribe. To the degree that they are wrapped up in their own culture and its assumptions and willfully ignorant of others, Matthiessen wants us to have contempt for the missionaries, to find them arrogant and pietistic and absurd. The worst offender is unquestionably Leslie Huben, the humorless, self-righteous leader of the mission. Huben – whose prudishness and parochialism, not to mention his outspoken anti-Romanism, are so pronounced as to strain one's credulity – is categorically incapable of understanding the Niaruna in the slightest: we are meant to understand that their nakedness, which he sees as obscene, has about it a purity that he cannot comprehend, and that their life in nature, which he imagines to be steeped in ignorance and superstition, has a harmony, and even a wisdom, that is utterly beyond his ken.

The other Americans in the book are intended to be admirable insofar as they come to respect the Niaruna ways and to reject their own culture and its assumptions. Lewis Moon, for instance, an educated United States citizen of American Indian stock who abandons the grubby, godless South American town of Madre de Dios for life among the Niaruna, admires the tribesmen inordinately on this account: "He had never envied anything so much as the identity of these people with their surroundings, nor realized quite so painfully how displaced he had always been." The white American who finds it easiest of all to communicate with the Indians is the Quarriers' son, Billy, the only Caucasian whom the Niaruna do not hold in contempt; indeed, the Indians speak to Billy "naturally," as if he were one of them – and in a sense he is, as far as Matthiessen is concerned, for in this author's mind primitivism and innocence are inextricably bound together.

One problem with the *Weltanschauung* of this novel is that a double standard lies at its center: Matthiessen manifestly regards the white Americans' ethnocentrism – their insistence upon judging other cultures by their own – as a weakness, a mark of naïveté and arrogance and corruption; in the Niaruna, however, the same ethnocentrism is a virtue, a sign of integrity. Another problem is that, for all the energy that Matthiessen devotes to assailing the hypocrisy of the Hubens and Quarriers, it seems more than a little hypocritical of this well-to-do fellow (who was born in New York City, prepped at Hotchkiss, and was graduated from Yale) to write and publish a novel whose purpose is, in large part, to condemn the very civilization that made possible the creation of such a work. For however much he may find to admire in primitive people, and however refreshing it may be for an affluent upper-middle-class American adventurer to go gallivanting in the wild occasionally, away from the telephone, the typewriter, and the general hubbub and complexity of civilized life, Matthiessen seems a tad too blithely oblivious of the fact that without the literary culture – not to mention the printing presses, distribution networks, and bookstores – which only a civilized society can provide, there would be no *At Play in the Fields of the Lord,* and he'd be a mute inglorious Matthiessen.

One wonders, furthermore, whether Matthiessen, for all his primitivist enthusiasm, would truly want someone he loves to exchange life in America for the sort of existence led by a typical member of a tribe like the Niaruna. In *At Play in the Fields of the Lord,* he symbolically makes clear his view of white Americans by having Andy Huben, through her carelessness, pass influenza on to the local Indians, who, having no resistance to the virus, start perishing from the disease in droves. Yet this is a grossly unfair way of representing Western civilization, especially in its relation to medical matters – for Western learning has made possible vaccines, treatments, and cures for ailments that force most people like the Niaruna (Matthiessen's starry-eyed romanticizing of them notwithstanding) to lead lives that are truly nasty, brutish, and short. Would Matthiessen, it seems fair to ask, want his family to live without the benefits of Western medicine? And what of Western freedoms? For it is worth noting that although Matthiessen ridicules the American missionaries – and, by implication, the United States and the West in general – for their smug intolerance of other cultures, tolerance is, in point of fact, a peculiarly Western virtue, far more prevalent among civilized Western societies than among primitive tribes like the Niaruna.

Yet these facts do not prevent Matthiessen from writing, in *At Play in the Fields of the Lord,* a novel that might well be described as both an elegy and an indictment: an elegy, that is, for the Niaruna, as well as for all primitive peoples whose way of life is gradually disappearing from the face of the earth; and an indictment of the Western world, particularly the United States. For it is on American culture that Matthiessen places the brunt of the blame for the fading of primitive, nature-centered cultures, and it is America whose people, he would like us to believe, are at a farther remove from the true, the good, and the beautiful than primitive folk could ever be. To Matthiessen, the steady eradication of primitive cultures is a major tragedy of our time, and America is the tragedy's principal villain.

MATTHIESSEN continues to lament this development in his novel *Far Tortuga,* which chronicles a 1968 turtling expedition – an expedition that turns out to be the last – of a schooner called the *Lillias Eden.* Though the seven Cayman Islands seamen who compose the bulk of the novel's *dramatis personae* are hardly as backward as the Niaruna, they too find their old ways to be in increasing danger of extinction. It is this extinction, as a matter of fact, for which the story of the *Lillias Eden*'s final voyage, and of the attrition of its nine-man crew, is plainly intended to be a metaphor. As Raib Avers, the ship's captain, observes,

> Well, good men hard to get now for de sailin boat – de work is harder, and dey work in de night and in de day. De times is changin. You fellas wantin dis goddom progress cause you are lazy. I never wanted it some way, but I got to get on with life so I make my peace with it.

The reply of Junior Bodden (Speedy), one of the ship's hands: "Dass de way de world go – modern time, mon." These words – "modern time, mon" – become something of a refrain in the novel, consistently invoked as an explanation for everything from laziness and cruelty to the use of plastic cups instead of "dem good old blue tin coffee cups." Taking note of someone's selfishness, for instance, Speedy comments, "Modern time, mon. Every mon for hisself. Learn dat from school days." And then there's this exchange (in which Matthiessen skips a space, instead of using quotation marks and indenting, to indicate a change of speakers) regarding the promiscuity of Camanian women:

> Modern time, mon. Girls gets knocked up before you gets dere....
>
> Well, Speedy, dey don't behave in dat manner in Caymans, I tellin you dat much – !
>
> Cause you in de back time, Doddy, de plenty of water between you and de world. But you just wait a while, you gone to see. Modern time, mon – dey ain't no place to hide.

Like the jungle lands of the Niaruna, the Cayman Islands are an outpost of relative primitivism whose primitive days are numbered. Although they are not highly educated in a contemporary Western sense, we are meant to recognize that the islanders on the *Lillias Eden,* like the members of the Niaruna tribe, know a great deal about the things that really matter to their lives – about the sea, about the islands, about the history of their people. The crewmen also know – or, at least, most of them do – who is most responsible for the modern ways that represent such a threat to their old ways: the United States. Although there are no Americans in *Far Tortuga,* America itself is a very strong presence in the book. The crewmen complain, for instance, that because of American "tourist boats foulin the sea," the fishing off Grand Cayman is not what it used to be: "an honest mon can't hardly find a fish no more along de island." The captain complains that most of his sons, lured by the money to be made in the States or in the American tourist trade, don't want to follow the family tradition and become turtlers: "dey like de big ships better. . . . dey all abandonin dere home, dey livin up dere in Tampa and Miami." To Matthiessen, it would seem, this exodus of young people is a tragic trend – the heirs of a magnificent local tradition, in his view, are being drawn away from their beautiful native island and their glorious customary ways by the false promises and cheap glitter of that environmentally unsound monster, America. But anyone with a modicum of respect for the common sense of these young Cayman Islanders, and (in particular) for their ability to make sensible decisions about their lives, has to recognize that there must be good reasons why these people packed up and removed to the United States. Wouldn't it be interesting, in fact, if instead of writing *Far Tortuga* (which was inspired, reportedly, by a Caribbean turtling expedition on which he tagged along), Matthiessen had looked up a few of those Cayman Islands emigrants, taken a serious look at their lives and choices, and written a novel about *that?*

To be sure, the complaints of the islanders in *Far Tortuga* about American tourist boats, and about young people "abandoning dere home," seem believable enough. But at times the men's remarks about America ring false, and one is aware of the presence of Matthiessen behind it all, pulling the strings, eager to magnify the United States into a symbol of fatuous, menacing power. Consider, for example, the following discussion of an American installation on Swan Island:

One time I was over to Swan Island; went up dere to de weather station. Couldn't come near, dem Yankees got so many bad dogs to keep you off.

Spies, mon. Got spies in Caymans, too, most likely.

What dey spy on at Swan Island? De sprat birds? Used to be de Glidden family raise plenty nice cattle over dere—now de Yankees in dere with bad dogs!

Bad dogs protect de spies, mon. One thing spies don't like, and dat is people spyin on dem. Oh, dey *hates* dat, mon!

Well, what dem Yankees doin is, dey broadcastin to Cuba—we heard all dem spies yellin at de time of de Bay of Pigs. Got dem bad dogs dere to keep people off while dey tellin de Cubans what de s'posed to be thinkin about Cuba. After dey gets done with dat, dey tell dem all about de land of de free and de home of de brave.

Elsewhere, Speedy complains that the captain of an American shrimp boat he once worked on called him a Communist for suggesting that he give away a quantity of unmarketable small shrimp to poor people. A fellow crewman named Vemon responds with a belligerent and rather pathetic tirade against communism, saying that "if *I* was de President of de United States of America, I'd give de order to bomb out every last one of dem goddom Cubans . . . make de world safe for democracy, goddom it! And *God!* . . . And dem dirty goddom commonists comin in dere and tellin me what I must do! *No* mon! Tellin a *free* mon what he must do? NO, mon." Matthiessen has the captain put Vemon in his place: "Free mon! Listen to dat idiot! . . . You a *stupid* mon, Vemon! You just de kind dem people need! Squawkin out everything dey tell you on de Yankee radio like some kind of a goddom parrot!" Clearly we're supposed to see the wisdom in the captain's reply; and, just as clearly, there aren't going to be any intelligent, articulate anticommunist voices raised in *this* forum. It is only when Matthiessen has his characters talk about such matters that their conversations sound less than genuine. For all his skill at conveying their sensibilities and capturing the sounds of their voices, Matthiessen apparently can't help using these men, from time to time, as mouthpieces for his own anti-Americanism.

For the most part, however, the dialogue in *Far Tortuga* convinces. As my quotations from the novel indicate, this dialogue does not take a conventional form; nor, for that matter, does the novel as a whole. Doubtless in an attempt to keep the American voice and sensibility as muted as possible, Matthiessen keeps the conventional narrative passages to a minimum, letting the all Caribbean cast speak for itself whenever feasible. Matthiessen intrudes mostly to provide us with objective data – the names and physical descriptions of characters, the time of day, the ship's position – and various details of local color ("New sun on a vermilion fence. Breadfruit and tamarind"). The novel is broken up not into paragraphs but into larger and smaller blocks of type – sentences, fragments, individual words – with varying amounts of white space between them. Matthiessen's narrative passages run, in conventional fashion, from margin to margin, while the characters' dialogue is indented at the left and ragged on the right; various individual words and crabbed phrases – the precise meaning and purpose of which are often obscure – appear every now and then, hovering in midpage or thereabouts, as do certain recurring graphics: small filled and unfilled circles to indicate night and noon respectively; an ink-splattered circle to indicate a death. A two-page spread early in the novel contains a blueprint of the *Lillias Eden;* another page consists of the ship's manifest; a third page contains nothing but the single word "horizon" and a faint horizontal line; several other pages contain nothing but rough pen strokes to indicate the rough waters of the Misteriosa Reefs. It must be said that, off-putting as all this may appear to a casual bookshelf browser, the unusual form of *Far Tortuga* is surprisingly successful, if in a rather limited way; though the novel does not add up to the powerful allegory that Matthiessen may have wished it to be, it does pass muster as a striking impressionistic work of a minor order, rich in discrete natural images and in the sounds of native voices.

DESPITE the diverse attractions and distractions of their respective styles and forms, however, one comes away from both *At Play in the*

Fields of the Lord and *Far Tortuga* thinking less about manner than about matter. One is, for instance, bemused by the powerful antagonisms that inform both of these novels: antagonisms toward America, toward Western civilization, toward the Christian God (or, at least, toward what Matthiessen thinks Christians in the West, and especially Protestants in the United States, have made of him – namely, a distant, austere First World boss-man). These same antagonisms, it should be noted, inform much of Matthiessen's nonfiction; behind one innocuous-sounding title after another there crouches an author itching to pounce on his prey. *Wildlife in America* (1959), for instance, proves to be a history of "the white man's effect on wildlife in North America, from the earliest records to the present day." (Hint: it's not a *good* effect.) *Indian Country* (1984) is aptly described in its jacket copy as an exploration of "ten important instances where the white man's encroachments upon the sacred grounds of Indian tribes show the tragic effects of a confrontation that is bound to harm both sides. . . ." Then there's *Nine-Headed Dragon River: Zen Journals 1969–1982* (1986), an exceedingly peculiar work in which Matthiessen attempts to explain how Zen has brought him the joy of enlightenment. Matthiessen carries on breathlessly about "mystical perception," "the beginningless potential of all things," "the eternal rising and perishing reality of the world," and the "realization of one's own Buddha-nature"; he tells us that "[i]n zazen, one is one's present self, what one was, and what one will be, all at once"; and he reverently quotes one after another of his Zen teachers: "'The sun is shining; the sun is *always* shining. The sun is enlightenment; *everything* is enlightenment!'" More than anything else he has written, the Zen journals vividly reflect the profundity and perverseness of Matthiessen's antagonism toward America, toward Western civilization, and toward the Christian idea of God; to read them is a tiresome and dismaying experience. Indeed, when one realizes that they recall nothing so much as Shirley MacLaine's goofy testament *Out on a Limb*, they strike one as truly pathetic: what can it be, one wonders, that led this genuinely intelligent and supremely well-educated man, this veritable scion of Western civilization, this Yale graduate, to reject the riches of Western philosophy, religion, and culture in so dramatic, so *desperate*, a manner? Could he truly have found that legacy so useless, so empty, so incapable of addressing his own questions about life, death, and the cosmos? Or was he driven to Zen – and to immersion in this whole range of non-Western cultural and social phenomena – by some more subjective need, some irrational private anguish?

Perhaps, perhaps not. But the more one reads Matthiessen, the more one cannot help connecting these antagonisms to one that – though I have not yet mentioned it – also figures prominently in *At Play in the Fields of the Lord* and *Far Tortuga*. I am speaking of an antagonism toward fathers. Though not manifested as explicitly in these novels as are the other antagonisms, this antagonism is, in both books, quite important thematically. Consider *At Play in the Fields of the Lord*, a father-son story in more ways than one. For instance, the novel tells the story of a son (Billy Quarrier) who proves to be much more in harmony with the Indians, with nature, and with God than his missionary father (Martin Quarrier). It is also the story of Lewis Moon and his mixed emotions about his Cheyenne father, whom he once taunted for serving in World War I and called a "mongrel white." *Far Tortuga* is likewise very much concerned with fathers and sons. Captain Raib carries aboard his ship not only his father, "Capn Andrew," but his seventeen-year-old son, Jim Eden (a.k.a. Buddy). As one of the crewmen observes, Buddy (who has never before served on a ship's crew) is an "old fashion boy" who "love his doddy" and who, unlike his many brothers, wants very much to follow in the old man's footsteps; however hard he tries to please his father, though, Captain Raib (who can't even remember his son's name) offers little in return but complaints and insults:

> Why you standin dere? Nothin to do? You know dat de bilges ain't been pumped dis mornin, and you ain't took Capn Andrew to de rails so he might ease hisself, and you know dere is ropes to splice and ends to whip up and down de ship (*his voice rises)* and you standin dere starin at me! (*points*) DEY MEN OUT DERE RISKIN DERE LIVES!

Noticing these parallels, one begins to wonder: is Matthiessen, in his two most recent novels, engaged in working out some sort of longstanding personal conflict regarding his own father? Do his antagonisms toward America, Western civilization, and the Christian God – all of them symbols of authority, equivalent in the subconscious mind with the father – represent instances of transference of this father-related conflict? Are his enthusiasms for Third World primitive cultures, for nature, and for Eastern religion, accordingly, a form of rebellion against the idea of the father, and against the very concept of fatherly authority?

This may be an audacious notion, but it is one that inevitably occurs to the alert reader of Matthiessen's most celebrated novels. And a perusal of Matthiessen's first three not-so-celebrated novels would seem to support the hypothesis. But the first thing to be said about these volumes – *Race Rock* (1954), *Partisans* (1955), and *Raditzer* (1961) – is that they hardly belong in the same discussion as *At Play* and *Far Tortuga*. They might, indeed, be categorized most accurately as apprentice works, as the creations of a young man who has yet to learn how – and how not – to draw upon his real-life emotions in the course of manufacturing full-length serious fictions. (It should be noted that Matthiessen, born in 1927, was still in his early thirties when his third novel was published.) To put it more bluntly, these are terrible books, in which Matthiessen's preoccupations are more baldly and crudely set forth than in *At Play* and *Far Tortuga*. But they do seem worth looking at, if only because of the harsher, less subtle light they shed on those preoccupations.

AND WHAT *is* Matthiessen preoccupied with in these early novels? Well, with a number of things: the passing of childhood, the nature of friendship, young love and its discontents. But at the center of each of these three books lies a single conflict: a privileged young man's antagonism toward his affluent and powerful father. In *Race Rock* the young man is George McConville, a New York stockbroker who, we learn, grew up in Manhattan (as did Matthiessen) as well as a New England village; there he became part of a small circle of young people, two of them (Sam Rubicam and Eve Murray) the children of well-heeled city folk, two (Daniel Barleyfield and Cady Shipman) the offspring of dirt-poor locals. The novel flashes back continually to the key episodes of these characters' shared childhood and early youth, from the perspective of what we are apparently meant to recognize – in the cases of George, Sam, and Eve, anyway – as a tragically jaded adulthood (even though they're all barely into their mid-twenties). The point of these flashbacks?

To underline these rich kids' lost innocence, their removal from the rural demesne that poor boys like Daniel and Cody continue to inhabit. (Matthiessen hammers away at this theme with breathtaking heavy-handedness: "childhood escaped them like a breath, and with it, innocence.") But it's impossible to care much about what George and company have lost, mainly because neither George nor Matthiessen has any perspective on the situation; we are plainly meant to view this loss as tragic, and to recognize that in some vague way George's wealthy father is responsible for it all. If George feels "unbearably oppressed," in other words, it is because he finds it "fatuous to work for *more* money . . . fatuous to fill the shoes of the man [George's father] who had crushed by his own example the incentive to do so." Poor kid!

Edwin (Barney) Sand, the young, Paris-based American reporter who is the protagonist of the slender novel *Partisans,* also has a powerful father. (Matthiessen, let it be noted, studied at the Sorbonne in 1948–49, and after his 1950 graduation from Yale returned to the French capital to help found the *Paris Review.*) Here, as in *Race Rock,* Matthiessen flashes back to the hero's childhood – specifically, to a day in 1938, when Sand's father, an American consul in Spain, took his wife and fourteen-year-old son out of that war-torn country into France, and a notorious Communist party leader named Jacobi hitched a ride. Now, fifteen years later, Jacobi having reportedly been expelled from the Party and confined somewhere in Paris by Party officials, Sand undergoes several bizarre, increasingly disordered days and nights in the homes of various agents and counter-agents, awaiting a reunion with Jacobi, whom he has not spoken with since that first meeting; like George McConville, he is "searching for . . . something-to-believe-in." We are expected to accept the notion that Sand's brief youthful encounter with Jacobi changed the boy's life, making him aware for the first time that he belonged to a wealthy minority, and that "his way of life, however innocent, was built on selfishness and wrong." As a result of this encounter, the boy learned to feel guilty about having servants, became a newspaperman instead of joining his dad in the foreign service, and took the regular-guy nickname of Barney (a name that his father refuses to acknowledge); indeed, Jacobi became a veritable father figure to Sand, to a large extent supplanting his real father, whom Sand continues to identify with the forces of "selfishness and wrong" and to blame for making him an unwilling part of it all.

None of this is any more believable than it sounds, and it doesn't help that, as in *Race Rock,* Matthiessen goes in for purple prose ("This was the hour of solitude, Sand thought, of ultimate reality"), muses insipidly about innocence ("the boy peered down at war, and, innocent, saw only the slow smoke of it, silent, without smell"), proffers corny dialogue ("'Love. . . . There are times when it seems as inevitable as air'"), and spells out his symbolism ("Rudi Gleize . . . represented the labyrinth beneath the desolate scene of postwar Europe"). As in *Race Rock,* too, Matthiessen behaves as if the protagonist's silly rich-boy problem is tragic in its dimensions and universal in its implications; it doesn't ever occur to him that a young man who has made a father image out of someone he met for a couple of hours at age fourteen is not a compelling symbol of postwar alienation and confusion but a pitiful case of arrested development.

In the slim novel *Raditzer,* the privileged young protagonist is Charlie Stark, who atones for his affluence – and escapes "his predestined future in his father's Portland law firm, a future as inexorable . . . as death" – by enlisting in the Navy. Like Sand, Charlie has had it out with his father (who is essentially a retread of George's philistine dad) over the issue of privilege; the outcome of the argument is a compromise: Charlie goes to college and studies art and prelaw simultaneously. (Not that he has a very strong interest in art; no, Matthiessen seems to take it for granted that we recognize, as he does, that one of the important functions of the arts is to provide a way for rich boys to rebel against their parents.) It is in 1945, on a Hawaii-bound troopship, that Charlie meets Raditzer, an enlisted man whom Matthiessen tries to build into a symbol of evil – unsuccessfully, for Raditzer, as depicted here, is not evil, merely sleazy and vulgar (and not nearly as interesting as Matthiessen seems to think). Oddly, Matthiessen also seems to regard Raditzer as an archetypal white American common man, a pendant to rich-boy Stark – thus positing an equation of evil and the American underclass that should give one pause. It is, we are apparently supposed to believe, the subtle influence of Raditzer that causes Charlie to cheat on his wife with an "unspoiled native girl" whose "animal warmth" he finds irresistible; on the heels of this liaison, Charlie returns to the mainland, knowing that his future with his wife "would be at best that compromise with life which, like death itself, happened only to other people."

Obviously, Matthiessen is altogether too quick, in these feeble early novels of his, to compare his protagonists' relatively minor woes with death. After all, the only problem that George McConville, Barney Sand, and Charlie Stark have, when you get right down to it, is that they don't really *have* any problems. Matthiessen almost admits as much himself, when discussing Charlie's reasons for joining the Navy:

> He [Charlie] had only wanted to go, to get away. What he wanted to flee, where he wished to go – these questions were much less clear, for his life was pleasant. There was really nothing to rebel against. Perhaps that was part of it, the fatness of it all, the comfortable assumptions, the infallibility of "good family."

Comfort, pleasantness, "good family": these, in sum, are the things that all the heroes of Matthiessen's early novels are rebelling against. Needless to say, there's something uncompelling about making use of this as a theme for an entire novel. Indeed, the self-fascination implicit in a novelist's choice of such a topic is itself downright offensive; these early novels depict a world in which everything is so wildly out of proportion that World War II (in *Raditzer*) and the Cold War (in *Partisans*) hardly seem to exist at all, except as they affect the trivial conflicts of Matthiessen's protagonists. Why does Stark join the Navy? To "get away," we're told, as if World War II were a fortnight's trip to the Riviera to escape Daddy for a bit. In fact, it hardly seems an exaggeration to say that, though these early novels are patently supposed to be meditations on privilege, the author's own unself-conscious narcissism itself provides a far more devastating, if inadvertent, commentary upon the privileged-boy mentality than Matthiessen could ever intentionally have mounted.

WHICH LEAVES only one question – namely, what happened, after the publication of these first three novels, to change the direction and scope of Matthiessen's fiction so dramatically? The answer is simple: he found (to borrow his own terminology) something to rebel against.

Or, more accurately, he discovered a more sophisticated and a less solipsistic means of drawing fiction out of his tirelessly persistent impulses toward filial rebellion. The chronology is revealing: it was in the late fifties that Matthiessen made the earliest of his many journeys into the wild, and it was in 1959 and 1961 – the same years in which *Partisans* and *Raditzer* appeared – that he published his first volumes of natural history. In these books Matthiessen celebrates his discovery of the noncivilized, non-American world. But, as one can see quite clearly in retrospect, he is doing something more: he is laying the foundation for a kind of novel that, while rejecting the civilized Western milieu of his first three novels and moving beyond their numbing preoccupation with the Oedipal conflicts of privileged young men, would draw its inspiration from the same emotions that informed the earlier books. In *At Play in the Fields of the Lord* and *Far Tortuga*, accordingly, the much-resented father became subsumed into America, into Western civilization, into the Christian God; and an uncritical reverence for nature – and for the supposed childlike innocence of those who live in it – took the place of his sometime absorption in an inordinately puerile self.

(JUNE 1988)

The Mysteries of
John Fowles

———————

CONTEMPORARY English novels, as a rule, are modest things – modest in their themes, their manner, their physical dimensions. If many an American, Continental, or Latin American novelist attempts, in each new book, to embody a startlingly original vision, to be formally innovative, to stage a linguistic fireworks display, and to make major statements about love, death, history, the nature of reality, man's life in society, and the function of art, the typical postwar English novelist seeks rather to relate a relatively unambitious story about the subtle pains and pleasures of a single unremarkable life. The characteristic virtues of the postwar English novel, accordingly, have been its exquisite restraint and delicacy of nuance, its ability to convey the significance of everyday reality, the simple beauty of even the most prosaic human soul.

For the past quarter century or so, the major exception to this rule has been John Fowles. He is the author of six novels – *The Collector, The Magus, The French Lieutenant's Woman, Daniel Martin, Mantissa,* and *A Maggot* – as well as of a poetry collection (*Poems*), a volume of short stories (*The Ebony Tower*), a philosophical treatise (*The Aristos*),[1] and the texts of numerous books of photographs. Though his novels are strikingly different from one another in plot and setting (and even exhibit an unusual variety of style and form), they are all strange and provocative, and – most important – share at bottom a consonance of theme and situation. "My chief concern," Fowles writes in his preface to the 1968 edition of *The Aristos*, "is to preserve the freedom of the individual against all those pressures-to-conform that threaten our century." Elsewhere he

———

1. All of these titles were published by Little, Brown with the exception of *Poems*, which was published by Ecco Press.

has been quoted as saying that the major theme of his work is "[f]ree-dom.... How you can achieve freedom. That obsesses me. All my books are about that."

But Fowles is also concerned with a number of other, related themes. The words *mystery* and *passion,* for instance, recur in his fiction, and time and again they are associated with escape from the confinement and conformity of civilization to the instructive "wild innocence" of some Edenic locale, usually a wood (from which, inevitably, Fowles's escapists must return to society to apply what they have learned to the conditions of life and love in the real world). Fowles's principal characters are usually confused and isolated men who are attracted to intelligent and spirited women; his novels are often constructed like Chinese boxes, with one mystery leading into another, one apparent epiphany giving way to another, and an expected sexual consummation interminably postponed; their climaxes often involve the male protagonist being forced to confront long-hidden truths, to make difficult judgments and to alter himself in some profound manner. References to specific paintings, and to mirrors, fill Fowles's novels. So do references to certain antitheses, among them innocence and experience, nature and civilization, the Victorian and the modern, paradise and prison, order and chaos, determinism and free will, action and impotence, duty and desire, possession and enjoyment, life and art, reality and illusion, history and fiction, the Many and the Few, the English and the foreign. Fowles possesses a mind that is at once didactic and dialectical; though he is almost constantly pressing some idea or another upon the reader, and holds certain beliefs very strongly – for example, that suffering is evil, and that possession should not be the purpose of life – he is sometimes not easy to pin down. Frequently he strikes one as congenitally self-contradictory; perhaps the most accurate way to put it is to say that, at his best, he is less interested in baldly promulgating ideas than in probing them, exploring them as if they were characters. He is at his weakest when he flat-out sermonizes and when he probes an idea to death, as he does at some point or another in each of his books. Thus Fowles's novels – though consistently elegant in their style – are by turns mesmerizing and tiresome, brilliant and inane; one is capable of finding his intellectual gamesmanship exhilarating on one page, infuriating on the next, and boring on the page after that. If at times, then, his love of ideas seems a definite asset, at other times – namely, when he allows it to undermine his narrative, and to obscure his very considerable gifts for language and storytelling and his innate sense of human character – his philosophical promiscuity seems by far his greatest liability.

On the subject of political philosophy, in particular, Fowles appears to contain multitudes. Like many Oxbridgeans (he was graduated from Oxford University in 1950), he manages to be both an elitist snob and a "democratic socialist"; also, he is at once an idealist and a relativist, a male chauvinist and a self-proclaimed feminist. But most of the time he does not come across as an extremist of any sort; on the contrary, when he is not being fervidly didactic, the Fowles of the novels and stories generally impresses one as a good Jeffersonian democrat who is honest enough to admit that the highest achievements of any civilized society are the work of an intelligent and gifted minority. Likewise, though he calls himself an existentialist and preaches on the subject every so often, his brand of existentialism seems much more palatable – because more sensible, moderate, intelligent, and humane – than most. He distinguishes, for example, between existential freedom and indulgence in escapist fantasy; indeed, most of his fiction is concerned, in large part, with drawing a clear distinction between the two.

IN EARLY FEBRUARY[2], American television viewers were provided with an introduction to Fowles in the form of an hour-long British dramatization of his 1974 novella "The Ebony Tower." The program – directed by Robert Knights and written by John Mortimer – was a presentation of the PBS *Great Performances* series. This novella may well be the best possible point of entry into the world according to Fowles. It offers both a representative example of his fictional method and a précis of his major philosophical interests; it also illustrates the gracefulness of his prose and the foolish didacticism into which he so often wanders. Fowles tells the story of a two-day visit by David Williams, an up-and-coming young English abstract painter and art critic, to Coëtminais

---

2. February 1987.

("monks' woods"), the rural French *manoir* of Henry Breasley, a legendary seventy-seven-year-old representational artist – and a notorious
womanizer and bohemian – who has spent most of his life in self-exile
from England. An English publisher is planning a volume of Breasley's
work, and David, to his surprise, has been recommended by Breasley to
supply the introduction; he has come to Coëtminais, which is located in
the heart of a dense wood, to meet the great man for the first time and to
interview him for the book.

In its focus upon youth and age and the artist's vocation, as well as in
its wistful tone and atmosphere of mystery, "The Ebony Tower" is
rather reminiscent of *Cakes and Ale, The Ghost Writer,* and other such
works. (It also recalls *The Aspern Papers.*) As in Maugham's and Roth's
novels, it is in the contrast – and the subtle conflict – between the young
artist and the old that much of the story's drama resides. Thirty-one-
year-old David, who counts Braque, De Stijl, and Ben Nicholson
among his influences, is a confirmed abstractionist; Breasley, whose
house is full of Bonnards, Dufys, and Ensors, and whose own darkly
sensuous canvases are in the direct line of descent from Uccello and
Goya, considers abstraction the "[g]reatest betrayal in the history of
art." As "Mouse," one of two enticing young women who live at Coëtminais and attend to Breasley's sexual and professional needs, explains
to David, "Henry feels that full abstraction represents a flight from human and social responsibility." Or, as Breasley himself puts it, art should
have "balls" – humanity, sensuousness – and abstract art doesn't; it represents the "triumph of the bloody eunuch," of "traitors" more concerned with "fundamentals" than "fundaments" – i.e., human bodies,
sex organs. Breasley: "That's reality. Not your piddling little theorems
and pansy colors. I know what you people are after, Williams. You're
afraid of the human body." David: "Perhaps simply more interested in
the mind than the genitals." Breasley: "God help your bloody wife
then." Breasley sums up the whole phenomenon of abstract art in a
single image: the ebony tower. As "Mouse" explains, the phrase refers
to "[a]nything he doesn't like about modern art. That he thinks is obscure because the artist is scared to be clear." Fowles's characterization
of the two men makes it obvious that he endorses Breasley's view of
things: David is quintessentially English, an extremely reserved, proper

young man who, as we learn at the story's end, is tragically repressed; Breasley, even in his declining years, is randy, outrageous, full of life, and marvelously capable of enjoying it.

But modern art is not the only subject of conflict between David and Breasley. There is also "Mouse," whose real name is Diana, and who proves to be a very fine artist and an admirer of David's work; looking over her drawings, David finds the representational ones rather cold and unoriginal – inferior imitations of Breasley – but finds the abstract drawings (which remind him of his own work) magnificent. He quickly develops a romantic attachment to her, and the feeling is mutual. Far from being the cold-blooded young tart he had first assumed her to be, Diana turns out to be shy, relatively inexperienced, and afraid of returning to the world outside Coëtminais. For her, the *manoir* has become at once a sensual paradise, where she can swim and sunbathe and frolic in the glorious altogether, and a monastic retreat where she can feel like a nun, free of the vulgar carnality of the outside world and "the effort of getting to know people." When David learns that Breasley has proposed marriage to her, and that she is considering the offer, he is shocked; left alone with her on the night before his departure, David (who is married) asks her to sleep with him, but she refuses. He senses that if he presses her, she will give in. But he doesn't press her, and she retires, leaving him alone with his regrets – upon which Fowles elaborates in a passage that is (to say the least) hyperbolic and unconvincing:

> He turned into his room and stood in its blackness in a rage of lost chance; made out his faint shape there in the old gilt-framed mirror. A ghost, a no-man. The horror was that he was still being plunged forward, still melting, still realizing; as there are rare psychic phenomena read of, imagined, yet missed when they finally happen. To one part of him – already desperate to diminish, to devaluate – it was merely a perverse refusal; and to another, an acute and overwhelming sense of loss, of being cleft, struck down, endlessly deprived . . . and deceived. He wanted with all his being – now it was too late; was seared unendurably by something that did not exist, racked by an emotion as extinct as the dodo. Even as he stood there he knew it was a far more than sexual experience, but a fragment of one that reversed all logic, process, that struck new suns, new evolutions, new universes out of nothingness. It was metaphysical: something far beyond the girl; an

anguish, a being bereft of a freedom whose true nature he had only just seen.

For the first time in his life he knew more than the fact of being; but the passion to exist.

The last five pages or so of the novella constitute a feverish and repetitious account of David's new realization about himself in the wake of his visit to Coëtminais. It is simply that he, unlike Breasley, has "a fear of challenge," a fear manifested in his attitude toward both art and sex. "One killed all risk, one refused all challenge, and so one became an artificial man." To Fowles, it is the lesson of art, not sex, that is patently more important at the end of the story: David's refusal to seduce Diana and to rescue her from Breasley is ultimately only a metaphor for his refusal to take the "existential chance" in his art the way Breasley does; his returning to his wife is only a metaphor for the "settled-for-the-safe" choice of abstractionism. "Coët had been a mirror," Fowles writes, a mirror wherein David, a captive of the ebony tower, had been allowed a view of "the old green freedom," "a glimpse of his lost true self." Yet David knows that this insight will not change him.

> . . . he would go on painting as before, he would forget this day, he would find reasons to interpret everything differently, as a transient losing his head, a self-indulgent folly. A scar would grow over it, then fade away, and the skin would be as if there had never been a wound. He was crippled by common sense, he had no ultimate belief in chance and its exploitation, the missed opportunity would become the finally sensible decision, the decent thing; the flame of deep fire that had singed him a dream, a moment's illusion; her reality just one more unpursued idea kept among old sketchbooks at the back of a studio cupboard.

It hardly needs to be said that for a writer who is foursquare against abstractionism in art, the hyperbolic ending of "The Ebony Tower" provides an astonishing example of literary abstraction and generalization gone haywire. It is difficult to see why anyone would consider this novella good material for a television program. After all, the story makes no sense without the two crucial passages from which I have quoted—the one in which David, for the first time in his life, knows "the passion to exist," and the concluding rant on abstract art – and it is not easy to imagine either of these passages being made dramatically effective. Even if it were possible to dramatize them, the novella would still have what is, to my mind, a critical structural flaw: namely, that one never has so much as a clue, before the story's climax, that David has never known "the passion to exist," or that his commitment to art is so shallow. Besides, can his marriage possibly be so loveless and banal that a stranger is capable, in the course of a weekend, of leading him to an emotional epiphany that he has never experienced in his thirty-one years? But then, Fowles is less interested here in telling a wholly believable realistic story than in presenting a parable.

John Mortimer and Robert Knights, the writer and director of the television adaptation of "The Ebony Tower," have avoided some of the story's inherent problems by focusing, at the denouement, on sex rather than art – by letting David's inability to take risks in his art function as a metaphor for his inability to take risks in his personal life, rather than the other way around. To be sure, some of David's final reflections on the hollowness of his vocation crop up, in slightly altered form, as lines of dialogue at various points in the film. For example, his recognition that he has been playing it safe by being an abstractionist becomes a line of dialogue spoken by Breasley (played by Laurence Olivier): "Don't be so *safe*, dear boy." And David's characterization of Coëtminais as a mirror becomes, in the film, a line spoken by Diana (Greta Scacchi) to David (Roger Rees) about Breasley: "He's like a mirror. You see exactly who you are – he cuts all your clever little triumphs down to scale."

But most of David's closing thoughts are scuttled by the producers, and the film, rather than ending with his feeble proposition to Diana, his introduction to "the passion to exist," and his sudden tragic awareness of his "fear of challenge," concludes with a series of brief scenes in which David – momentarily, at least – shakes off that fear. In the film, he offers Diana not only an evening of sex but an alternative to life with Breasley; apparently willing to desert his wife for her, he begs Diana to leave Coëtminais with him. She refuses. He then takes on Breasley, accuses him of being terrified of age and of change, of wanting "to marry Diana so that you can keep her here in chains." An unruffled Breasley entreats him to look closely at Pisanello's *St. George and the Princess* next time he visits the National Gallery. "The princess has got the dragon on a lead – her pet, her tame companion": Saint George, the would-be rescuer, is only making a fool of himself. At the fade-out, then, the television version of "The Ebony Tower" is not about the reasons for a young man's devotion to abstract art but about a young woman's unwillingness to leave an elderly artist to whom she is passionately devoted.

The film's shift of emphasis from art to sex works surprisingly well. But many of the smaller changes in the script are less effective. For some reason, John Mortimer has added some awfully stale lines. When Diana first compliments David, he says, "Flattery will get you everywhere"; when Breasley's forward manner stuns David into silence, the old man asks, "Cat got your tongue?"; and when David confronts Breasley about Diana, he says, "She has to lead her own life" and "Being a genius doesn't give you the right to ruin someone else's life." None of these lines appears in the novella. The casting is problematical, too: the viewer is plainly supposed to sympathize with David, to hope that he will overcome his priggery, throw caution to the winds, and leave Coëtminais with Diana in his arms. But Olivier's Breasley is so winning, and Roger Rees's David so utterly smug, humorless, and uncharismatic, that one finds oneself wanting Rees to get out of there as quickly as possible and to leave Lord Olivier and his women to their devices.

To FOLLOW a reading of "The Ebony Tower" (or even a viewing of the television adaptation) with a brief perusal of *The Aristos* (1965) is to recognize how many of Fowles's chief philosophical notions figure in the novella – as they do, I might add, throughout his works. *The Aristos,* originally subtitled "A Self-Portrait in Ideas," consists of several hundred related axioms that are organized into eleven chapters with titles like "The Universal Situation," "The Tensional Nature of Human Reality," and "The Importance of Art." The axioms, some of which consist of a single sentence and only one of which occupies so much as an entire page, are numbered chapter by chapter, like verses of the Bible. The book is nothing less than Fowles's answer to Plato's *Republic* – it represents his notion of what ideas on life, death, art, religion, politics, science, economics, education, and sex should govern a world run by superior men and women. And indeed his primary concern is with the superior individual, the *aristos*. The word is borrowed from Heraclitus, who, Fowles reminds us, "saw mankind divided into a moral and intellectual *élite* (the *aristoi,* the good ones, *not*–this is a later sense–the ones of noble birth) and an unthinking conforming mass – *hoi polloi,* the many." Fowles notes that Heraclitus has been condemned as "the grandfather of modern totalitarianism," but insists that

> in every field of human endeavour it is obvious that most of the achievements, most of the great steps forward, have come from individuals – whether they be scientific or artistic geniuses, saints, revolutionaries, what you will. And we do not need the evidence of intelligence testing to know conversely that the vast mass of mankind are not highly intelligent – or highly moral, or highly gifted artistically, or indeed highly qualified to carry out any of the nobler human activities.

Fowles thus divides mankind into two groups, the Few and the Many. Nonetheless he declares himself to be a socialist: "All my adult life I have believed that the only rational political doctrine one can hold is democratic socialism." His way of reconciling these two disparate views is to say that *"the dividing line between the Few and the Many must run through each individual, not between individuals.* In short, none of us are wholly perfect; and none wholly imperfect." Or, as he puts it at the end of the book, "We are all sometimes of the Many." If this is true, however, then why posit a "Few" and a "Many" in the first place?[3]

Fowles sees life in terms of process: to him, everything is ultimately unknowable, indefinite, mysterious. But, though we will never reach perfection of any kind, we can nonetheless strive for it ("We build towards nothing; we build" –1.33). And it is this endless striving that makes life worth living. "Our universe is the best possible because it can contain no Promised Land; no point where we could have all we imagine. We are designed to want: with nothing to want, we are like windmills in a world without wind" (1.34). What human beings need most of all in such a universe – and what David Williams so tragically lacks in "The Ebony Tower" – is freedom of will. It is "the highest human

---

3. That Fowles still maintains these two contrary postions is made clear in an interview that appears in the spring 1987 issue of *Boulevard.*

good" (1.64); to be true *aristoi*, men and women must overcome the "asphyxiating smog of opinions foisted on them by society," which forces ordinary people to "lose all independence of judgement, and all freedom of action" and to "see themselves increasingly . . . as parts of a machine" (3.29). We must, in short, commit existential acts – existentialism signifying, by his definition, "the revolt of the individual against all those systems of thought, theories of psychology, and social and political pressures that attempt to rob him of his individuality" (7.74). Fowles is not inciting mass revolution, though, for "existentialism is conspicuously unsuited to political or social subversion, since it is incapable of organized dogmatic resistance or formulations of resistance. It is capable only of one man's resistance; one personal expression of view; such as this book" (7.79). Fowles insists, moreover, on the importance of moral judgment, proclaiming that "[o]ur function is to judge, to choose between good and evil. If we refuse to do so, we cease to be human beings and revert to our basic state, of being matter" (5.45). As for risks, we need to take them in order to improve our lives and ourselves. "The purpose of hazard is to force us, and the rest of matter, to evolve" (2.61).

As "The Ebony Tower" demonstrates, the sort of freedom that usually figures most prominently in Fowles's fiction is sexual freedom. Fowles has a good deal to say about this subject in *The Aristos*. He speaks of the twentieth-century emergence of sex "from behind the curtains and crinolines of Victorian modesty and propriety" (9.97) and finds it necessary to say that "[s]exual attraction and the sexual act are in themselves innocent, neither intrinsically moral nor immoral. Sex is like all great forces: simply a force" (9.105). One has the feeling, after reading through Fowles's oeuvre, that his obsession with freedom has a great deal to do with his complicated feelings about sex; he often seems to be taking on an enemy – namely, the stifling sexual morality of the Victorian period – that no longer exists. Indeed, he has made reference, in several of his novels, to the Victorian notions of morality with which people of his generation were raised. "My contemporaries," notes the Fowles-like narrator of *Daniel Martin*, "were all brought up in some degree of the nineteenth century, since the twentieth did not begin till 1945."

A concept that is of central importance to Fowles is that of the "nemo," which Fowles defines as "a man's sense of his own futility and ephemerality; of his relativity, his comparativeness; of his virtual nothingness" (3.7). Fowles says that it is art, above all else, that "best conquers time, and therefore the nemo"; an art object is "as nearly immortal as an object in a cosmos without immortality can be." Fowles devotes much of his chapter on art to a description of the situation of the modern artist – a situation that, for all his criticism of Victorian vis-à-vis modern culture, he is not at all happy with. He deplores, for instance, "the tyranny of self-expression" (10.35); the narrowing of the artist's audience to "a literate few" (10.51); and the pressure on the artist to present "a mirror to the world around him" (10.36). He is disturbed by the rise of a type of intellectual that is interested mainly in "colour, shape, texture, pattern, setting, movement," rather than in "the properly intellectual (moral and socio-political) significance of events and objects" – more interested, in short, in style than in content, which to him is the single most woeful symptom of the modern temperament.

What *The Aristos* essentially amounts to, then, is a collection of opinions, some of which one agrees with, some of which one doesn't; there is much in it that is intelligent and thought-provoking, and much that is silly and wrongheaded. Fowles is often guilty of sentimental overgeneralization; in distinguishing between the craftsman and the genius, he says that the former "is very concerned with his contemporary success, his market value," while the latter "is indifferent to contemporary success." And Fowles can be unintentionally amusing while he is pretending to be objective about things that are close to him. For example, having decided that mankind should have a universal language, he arrives, by way of an elaborate and (he thinks) purely logical argument, at the conclusion that the language of choice should be – guess what? – English. Likewise, this man who chooses to identify himself at the beginning of the book as "a poet first; and then a scientist," determines – by means of an equally sophisticated and objective bit of dialectic – that "the great arts" are not equal, and that "[l]iterature, in particular poetry," is of all the arts "the most essential and the most valuable."

Despite such weaknesses, however, one cannot help but admire

Fowles for his intellectual seriousness, his acute sense of the artist's dignity as well as of his moral and social responsibility, and his attempt to express and to codify his way of seeing the world. It is rare and admirable for a contemporary British or American novelist to be as intensely and seriously concerned as John Fowles is with the relations between art and ideas, art and morality. But *The Aristos* is chiefly of interest not as a work of philosophy but as a catalogue raisonné, as it were, of many of the thematic preoccupations of Fowles's fiction.

THE FIRST of Fowles's novels, *The Collector* (1963), is in some ways the most uncharacteristic of his books — straightforward, lucid, and relatively short. The collector is a lower-class young English orphan named Ferdinand Clegg who, after striking it rich in the lottery, quits his job, kidnaps a beautiful young middle-class art student named Miranda whom he has long admired from afar, and locks her in his basement. In the first half of the book, Clegg narrates the story of her seven-week imprisonment; the second half consists of the diary that Miranda keeps during her ordeal. The book's title derives from the fact that Clegg is a butterfly collector; he has what Fowles thinks of as the collector's mentality, and comes in for much criticism from Miranda on this score: "I hate people who collect things, and classify things and give them names and then forget all about them. That's what people are always doing in art. They call a painter an impressionist or a cubist or something and then they put him in a drawer and don't see him as a living individual painter any more." "I know what I am," she writes. "A butterfly he has always wanted to catch."

The irony is that once Clegg has caught Miranda, he doesn't know what to do with her. He won't have sex with her, because he thinks that's dirty. Miranda needles him about that, too:

> You're the most beautiful specimen of petit bourgeois squareness I've ever met.... You despise the real bourgeois classes for all their snobbishness and their snobbish voices and ways.... Did you know that every great thing in the history of art and every beautiful thing in life is actually what you call nasty or has been caused by feelings you

would call nasty? By passion, by love, by hatred, by truth. . . . Why do you take all the life out of life? Why do you kill all the beauty?

Later in the story, Miranda cuddles up to Clegg; her purpose, as she explains to him (in a variation on axiom 9.105), is "to show you that sex – sex is just an activity, like anything else. It's not dirty, it's just two people playing with each other's bodies. Like dancing. Like a game." But Clegg doesn't understand; all he can see is that Miranda is a filthy-minded little trollop, not at all the nice girl he thought her to be.

The problem with Clegg, Fowles wants to convince us, is not that he's a screwball; on the contrary, as Miranda observes, he's "ordinary" – stupid, sluggish, unimaginative. Indeed, "he's so ordinary that he's extraordinary." Miranda spells it out to Clegg: "Everything free and decent in life is being locked away in filthy little cellars by beastly people who don't care." For Miranda, as she herself realizes, is a "special person," a budding *aristos* (though she doesn't use the word); she knows that "I am intelligent. . . that I am beginning to understand life much better than most people of my age." She wants not "to be clever or great or 'significant' or given all that clumsy masculine analysis," but rather "to *make* beauty," to paint the "essences" of things, "[n]ot the things themselves." In case we don't get the idea of all this, Fowles explains it in his 1968 preface to *The Aristos*: "My purpose in *The Collector* was to attempt to analyse, through a parable, some of the results of this confrontation [between the Few and the Many]." In kidnapping Miranda, Clegg commits an evil, "but I tried to show that his evil was largely, perhaps wholly, the result of a bad education, a mean environment, being orphaned: all factors over which he had no control." Thus he stands not only for the evil of the Many but for "the virtual *innocence* of the Many." Miranda is also the product of her environment: "she had well-to-do parents, good educational opportunity, inherited aptitude and intelligence."

Though *The Collector* is quite a powerful thriller, it doesn't work at all as a parable about the Few and the Many. For one thing, Miranda, with her forthright little opinions and her snobbish attitude toward ordinary people, is very unsympathetic. Fowles admits as much in his *Aristos* preface: she is "arrogant in her ideas, a prig, a liberal-humanist snob. . . .

Yet . . . she might have become something better, the kind of being humanity so desperately needs." But to my mind there is little indication,
in *The Collector*, that Miranda is anything more than just another spoiled
and obnoxious art-school type. As for Clegg, it is impossible to think of
him as an "ordinary man." Ordinary men don't kidnap girls and lock
them in cellars. Not that Clegg is an unconvincing character; on the
contrary, Fowles's portrait of him is chillingly believable. Certainly it is
possible to imagine a character – particularly an emotionally disturbed
kidnapper of young women – who is so antipathetic to sex and so unfamiliar with sexual passion. (In this regard, of course, Clegg is similar to
David Williams of "The Ebony Tower.") But how can Fowles possibly
use such a figure as a symbol of the ordinary man? It simply doesn't
wash. And it's offensive, as well: does Fowles really think that somewhere in every working-class soul there lurks a desperately sick kidnapper? Does he really think that human evil is primarily the result of
"poor education" and "mean environment," and that aptitude and
intelligence are to be found exclusively, or even primarily, in the privileged classes? Furthermore, the second half of the book is a good deal
weaker than the first – partly because Clegg is a more interesting character than Miranda, partly because the first half is relatively free of symbol-
mongering, and partly because the second half forces us to go over
ground we've already covered. But – to put it mildly – Fowles has never
worried overmuch about seeming redundant.

The Magus (1965) is as long and expansive as *The Collector* is short and
claustrophobic. Like Ferdinand Clegg, Nicholas Urfe, the narrator and
protagonist of *The Magus*, is an *isolato*, an orphaned young man with
time on his hands. Though Nicholas, unlike Clegg, is an Oxford graduate and a self-styled poet with a good deal of sexual experience, he shares
Clegg's emotional detachment; he sees love as an ephemeral thing, and
likes it that way. "You've built your life so that nothing could ever reach
you," complains his latest lover, Alison Kelly, an Australian stewardess
who genuinely loves him. Nicholas sees himself as a lone wolf, a rebel.
Disgusted with the "mass-produced middle-class boys" that he is forced
to teach in an undistinguished East Anglian public school, Nicholas de-

cides in the spring of 1953 to leave smug, predictable old England – and Alison – for a year's stint at the Lord Byron School on the Greek island of Phraxos. (The school is based upon Anargyrios College on the island of Spetsai, where Fowles taught in 1951 and met his wife, Elizabeth.) Once there, feeling alone and directionless, Nicholas prepares to kill himself, but does not; he lacks the freedom of will to do so, and realizes that he is, "in existentialist terms, unauthentic. I knew I would never kill myself, I knew I would always want to go on living with myself, however hollow I became, however diseased."

It is then that Nicholas is drawn to Bourani, a wooded estate that is inhabited by a highly cultured and strongly opinionated old man named Maurice Conchis. The house is full of Modiglianis, Rodins, Giacomettis, and the like; Conchis – who will prove to be the magus (magician, sorcerer) of the title – is full of views on art, history, and society. He sounds as if he's memorized *The Aristos:* he hates collecting, believes that "destiny is hazard" and "[l]ife is an eternal wanting more," divides mankind into "the many" and "the few" (or "the elect"), proclaims the essential isolation of each individual, and rhapsodizes about "the passion to exist." During one of Nicholas's weekend visits, Conchis hypnotizes him into a state of mind wherein (as Nicholas explains in a feverish eight-hundred-word passage reminiscent of "The Ebony Tower") he is intensely "aware of existing," aware "that reality [is] endless interaction," aware that there is "no meaning, only being." Suddenly, the "endless solitude of the one, its total enislement from all else, [seems] the same thing as the total interrelationship of all," and he is possessed of an "enormous and vertiginous sense of the innumerability of the universe; an innumerability in which transience and unchangingness [seem] integral, essential and uncontradictory."

Odd things begin to happen. Exotic figures – Greek gods one weekend, Nazi soldiers the next – appear on the grounds at Bourani, enacting a pagan masque of sorts with an extremely baffled Nicholas as both actor and audience. One of the players is Lily, an innocent and beautiful young Englishwoman who claims to be Conchis's long-dead love. Conchis tells Nicholas that she's a schizophrenic; she confides to Nicholas that she's an actress named Julie Holmes who has been hired by Conchis to play Lily. (Is this getting complicated enough?) Nicholas and Julie fall in love – which, she tells him, is precisely what Conchis wants: he's conducting an "experiment in mystification" and is leading Nicholas into "a . . . sort of trap." And so he is. When Nicholas takes Julie to a hotel room to consummate their love, she flings the door open at the last minute, crying, "There is no Julie," and admits Conchis and two members of his repertory company, who subdue and narcotize Nicholas. Several days later he is led into a courtroom where Conchis, Julie, and other actors from the masque identify themselves as experimental psychologists, explain to Nicholas that he has been the subject of some behavioral research, and proceed (in a very funny episode) to read their humiliating, jargon-ridden "analyses" of his personality. After refusing the opportunity to whip Julie (who now identifies herself as Dr. Vanessa Maxwell), Nicholas is taken to a room to watch her perform a live sex act with a huge black man. Conchis then tells a totally humiliated Nicholas that he has made it into the "elect," and sets him free. "Intolerably alone," Nicholas returns to England. There – after several months of rejection, and a few more twists of Conchis's plot, which he learns is called "the godgame" – he again faces Alison. Fowles leaves open the question of whether they are reunited.[4]

Of course, the story of *The Magus* is completely ludicrous; as with *The Collector,* Fowles means the book to be read as an allegory, a lesson in love and in the proper uses of freedom. But what is the lesson? What has Nicholas learned from his harrowing experience at the hands of Conchis and company; what has happened to earn him entry into the elite? The answer, presumably, is that, having been made to recognize Lily/Julie as an unrealistic projection of his own childish fantasies (fantasies not unlike Ferdinand Clegg's illusions about Miranda), Nicholas has learned to love, and to accept love from, a real woman like Alison. Allegory or not, however, there is much about the novel that is truly disturbing. With every new twist in Conchis's systematic humiliation of Nicholas, one finds oneself saying, "This is *sick.*" Yes, the story is absurd, but one's awareness of its absurdity does not prevent one from being

---

4. In an extensively revised edition of *The Magus,* published in Britain in 1977 and in America a year later, Fowles made Nicholas and Alison's chances for happiness at the end a bit brighter.

outraged all the same by the cruel and unusual punishments, both emotional and physical, that Conchis devises for Nicholas. These acts would seem unwarranted and indefensible whatever their purpose, but since Conchis's aim is apparently to teach Nicholas a lesson about love and freedom, they come across as particularly horrible. There is something tyrannical about Conchis's assumption that he has a right to change Nicholas, to brainwash him into his own way of seeing things. For this is what *The Magus* amounts to: the fantastic story of a brainwashing.

The more one thinks about it, the more Ferdinand Clegg and Maurice Conchis, the title figures of Fowles's first two novels, seem two of a kind. Though to Fowles there is indubitably a great difference between them – Clegg is an agent of evil, Conchis an agent of good – both are sadists, tyrants, god-players. And so, in his own way, is Fowles. Reading *The Collector*, one sometimes feels like a prisoner oneself, with Fowles as the jailer; reading *The Magus*, one finds oneself identifying with Nicholas Urfe's confusion and helplessness, and begins to regard Fowles with the same paradoxical combination of wonder, resentment, respect, and hostility with which Nicholas regards Conchis. *The Magus* is, indeed, largely about the author as magus; Fowles is, in a sense, Maurice Conchis, and every reader of *The Magus* is Nicholas Urfe, being led through the paces of the godgame toward enlightenment – or Fowles's version of it, anyway.

FOWLES's finest novel, *The French Lieutenant's Woman* (1969), is set in the late 1860s, primarily in the Dorset coastal town of Lyme Regis (in which Fowles has lived since 1966). The protagonist is Charles Smithson, a thirty-two-year-old London gentleman who, like Nicholas Urfe, is an "intelligent idler" (he collects sand dollars), a self-styled poet, and a man of the world; like Nicholas, Charles finds "English society too hidebound, English solemnity too solemn, English thought too moralistic, English religion too bigoted." Though engaged to marry the conventional Ernestina Freeman, Charles finds himself drawn to a mysterious young woman named Sarah Woodruff, whom he first glimpses at the gray, windy seaside while he and Ernestina are in Lyme Regis visiting her aunt. Sarah, a creature of "passion and imagination" who surprises Charles by speaking to him as if she were his intellectual equal, is notorious for her recent scandalous affair with a French lieutenant who, it is said, promised to marry her, took her virtue, and ran away; instead of attempting to make a new life for herself in another part of the country, Sarah has chosen to stay in Lyme Regis – where she is known to everyone as "the French lieutenant's whore" – and to live with the severely proper Mrs. Poulteney, to whom Sarah is little more than the embodiment of terrible carnal sin. Why has she chosen such a life? Desperate to explain her position to someone who will understand, Sarah persuades Charles to meet her secretly in a large wood (and a lovers' rendezvous) called the Ware Commons; there she explains that remaining in Lyme Regis and moving in with Mrs. Poulteney was "a kind of suicide," an "act of despair" that she performed in order to avoid literally killing herself.

On the advice of Charles, who has fallen in love with her, Sarah moves to Exeter; soon afterward, while journeying from London to Lyme Regis, he makes a monumental decision: he will stop in Exeter and spend the night with her. The "moment of choice" (as Fowles calls it) excites him enormously. "He had not the benefit of existential terminology," writes Fowles; "but what he felt was really a very clear case of the anxiety of freedom – that is, the realization that one *is* free and the realization that being free is a situation of terror." Charles also experiences anxiety when, after taking Sarah to bed, he discovers that he has stolen her virginity. Unable to comprehend why she has posed as a fallen woman – or why she has slept with him, an engaged man – Charles speaks to an enlightened doctor, who presents him with a French book of case histories in sexual hysteria. Charles is shocked; the book opens his eyes to a whole world of "perversions" ("and in the pure and sacred sex"!) whose existence the repressed and hypocritical Victorian age could not so much as acknowledge. What Charles has been confronted with in Sarah is the modern era, with its sexual openness, sexual equality, and freedom – an era whose fundamental assumptions and characteristic attitudes were just beginning to emerge at the time of *The French Lieutenant's Woman*. The modern era is also, to Fowles, that of the existential man, and Fowles's novel is, in essence, the story of the gradual emergence of the existential man – the man of passion and freedom and "existentialist terror" – that has been hidden behind Charles Smithson's proper Victorian façade.

To be sure, Fowles does not paint the contrast between the Victorian and the modern in black and white; *The French Lieutenant's Woman* is a dialectical novel, an attempt to see both worlds more clearly, to understand them more fully, and to condemn neither outright. It should not come as a surprise that in some respects Fowles finds the Victorian age far more congenial than our own. It was, for instance, "a world without the tyranny of specialization"; it was also a world without the tyranny of the Many, a world in which the elect still held their own against the hoi polloi. But the modern world was on its way, and majority rule with it; just as Sarah gives Charles a foretaste of modern sexual equality, so his would-be father-in-law Mr. Freeman, and Charles's servant Sam, give him a foretaste of modern equality of the classes. What Mr. Freeman does is to suggest that Charles go into business with him; Charles decides to reject the offer, and Fowles wants us to admire him for it. "To be sure," Fowles admits, "there was something base in his rejection – a mere snobbism."

> But there was one noble element in his rejection: a sense that the pursuit of money was an insufficient purpose in life. . . . [H]e gained a queer sort of momentary self-respect in his nothingness, a sense that choosing to be nothing . . . was the last saving grace of a gentleman; his last freedom, almost.

Fowles admires Charles for feeling this way, and for feeling that if he ever sets foot in Mr. Freeman's store he is "done for"; Fowles explains that "every culture, however undemocratic, or however egalitarian, needs a kind of self-questioning, ethical elite" that rejects "the notion of *possession* as the purpose of life." Apparently to Fowles's way of thinking it's all right to *possess,* the way Charles does; it's just not all right to *want* to possess.

At any rate, it is Mr. Freeman's unseemly offer, in part, that prompts Charles – who is beginning to realize that Ernestina may not be right for him – to spend the night in Exeter. And it is Sam's urge to possess that plays the key role in the next twist of the novel's plot. Charles, after his night with Sarah, hands Sam a letter to take to her, explaining that he will break off his engagement and marry her; but Sam, wanting Charles to marry Ernestina (whose father can help get Sam started in business) does not deliver it. Consequently, when Charles returns to Exeter for Sarah she is gone; and it is not until almost two years later that Charles finds her. He discovers that Sarah has become a "New Woman," a member of the bohemian Rossetti circle—which, like Coëtminais and Bourani, is "a community of honorable endeavor, of noble purpose." But she shows him no affection, remarking coolly that she treasures her independence too much to marry anyone. She has become the complete modern woman, "a spirit prepared to sacrifice everything but itself— ready to surrender truth, feeling, perhaps even all womanly modesty in order to save its own integrity." Charles perceives his superiority to her, a superiority "not of birth or education, not of intelligence, not of sex, but of an ability to give that was also an inability to compromise." Charles is truly free; Sarah, unwilling to take risks or to love, is not.

The French Lieutenant's Woman is a wonderful cross between a Victorian and a modern novel, and its effectiveness is doubtless due in large part to Fowles's obvious sympathy with the period. For once his delight in moral and philosophical generalization does not feel at all out of place; after all, the practice of digressing from the plot to offer a few authorial observations is quintessentially Victorian. Fowles, keenly aware of the differences between the Victorian and modern conceptions of the author, plays games with the reader, behaving one minute like Trollope, the next like Roland Barthes. Having ended chapter 12 by asking, "Who is Sarah? Out of what shadows does she come?", Fowles begins chapter 13 by saying that he does not *know* who Sarah is; his story and characters are imaginary, and if he has pretended to know their minds, it is simply because "I am writing in . . . a convention universally accepted at the time of my story: that the novelist stands next to God." Rather than puncture the fictional illusion, however, these interruptions foster in the reader that existential anxiety, that constant feeling of being off balance, which one has to experience in order to see the world through Fowles's eyes. Indeed, Fowles goes so far as to offer alternate conclusions to *The French Lieutenant's Woman*. In one Charles never sleeps with Sarah and marries Ernestina; in the other his final confrontation with Sarah ends in an embrace. Perhaps the chief virtues of the novel, however, are altogether conventional ones: it is beautifully written, with an elegance and fluency that *The Magus* (vivid and energetic though it is) often lacks; it is extremely well paced; and it is a tour de force of imaginative reconstruction, not only of Victorian sensibilities but of the cities and landscape of nineteenth-century England. Some of Fowles's descriptions of the Dorset countryside and seascape are as evocative as impressionistic paintings.

In *Daniel Martin* (1977), Fowles returns to the contemporary scene. The novel (his longest) has many strengths, but is terribly rambling and prolix, and – when compared to its predecessor – seems the work of a weary and self-obsessed imagination. The eponymous narrator and protagonist – who sometimes refers to himself in the first person, sometimes in the third ("Dan") – is a successful middle-aged English playwright and screenwriter, the son of a Devonshire preacher, and (like Nicholas Urfe) an Oxford graduate, self-exile, and ladies' man. He is wrapping up a film in Los Angeles while Jane Mallory, the twin sister of his ex-wife, Nell, summons him to Oxford for a last meeting with her dying husband, Anthony, a philosophy don. At university, the four of them – Dan, Nell, Anthony, and Jane – were inseparable friends who shared a "false paradise," but Dan has not spoken to Anthony and Jane in years, and has seen Nell only to discuss their daughter, Caroline, who is now about twenty years old. Those happy Oxford days seem very distant now to Dan; directionless and unsatisfied, he finds the film industry every bit as corrupt and degrading as Charles Smithson finds Mr. Freeman's business in *The French Lieutenant's Woman*. He tells his mistress, a young English actress named Jenny McNeil, that he has been "creat-[ing] other people" for so long that he feels as if he's "been taken over by someone else." He wants to write a novel, but claims to be too much of a perfectionist; Jenny shares with him a friend's observation that "being a perfectionist and being scared are often the same thing."

As for his personal life, he has always – shades of Ferdinand Clegg – looked upon women as "specimens"; they are mirrors in which he can "see himself reflected." His relationship with Jenny is less than passionate; though he is "in love with both her body and her independence," he feels that "only too frequently 'I love you' is a euphemism for 'I want to own you,'" and he would prefer not to be "intolerably possessive."

He sincerely wants, he says, "to leave Jenny in the public gallery of her own freedom." But he also admits that he prefers not to feel responsible to her in any profound way. He is a member of a generation that was "brought up in some degree of the nineteenth century," and that in shedding "unnecessary guilt, irrational respect, and emotional dependence" has in effect sterilized itself, much as Sarah has sterilized herself by the end of *The French Lieutenant's Woman*.

When Jane asks him to come to Oxford, Dan is faced with what he recognizes to be a major decision, a "moment of will." In one of several flashbacks to his student days, he describes another fateful day when he and Jane, both already engaged to be married, declared their mutual love and, "surrender[ing] to existentialism," slept together. But they didn't follow through, and two unfortunate mismatches took place: Jane married the dry-as-dust Anthony, while Dan married the conventional Nell. If Dan's marriage eroded so quickly, it was because, happy though they had been at Oxford, Dan and Nell were incapable of living happily together in the "real" world. As for Jane and Anthony, they have stayed together in what Dan has always assumed to be a good marriage. It is not until Dan arrives at Oxford that he learns, from a cool, remote Jane, that it hasn't been good at all; Anthony agrees, admitting that over the years he's taken the life out of her, and asks that Dan help Jane to discover her old self. That night, Anthony kills himself, and when Dan invites Jane to join him on a Nile cruise, it is clear that something will develop between them.

In the meantime, however, Fowles offers some of his dullest, most discursive prose – and some of his most offensive polemics. The situation is unfortunate: Jane, as it happens, is both a Communist and a terrible snob; Dan seems at times to be only a bit less extreme in both directions; and Fowles, alas, has the opportunity – in the form of their slow, uneventful cruise – to write a number of long shipboard conversations between the two of them about their lives, ideas, and politics. Some of these passages are so rich with illogic – reminiscent of the worst of *The Aristos* – that one can hardly believe they are not intended as a grotesque parody of a certain type of blinkered upperclass English leftist. For instance, Jane declares her belief in the need for revolutionary social change, but says, "I think certain intellectual climates also have to be preserved. Disciplines. Knowledges. Even pleasures. For when the revolution's over." And for *her*, naturally. What a wonderfully convenient version of Marxism – Marxism with a loophole for intellectual writers and their inquisitive sisters-in-law!

The Nile cruise also gives Fowles a chance to expose Dan and Jane to American tourists – particularly a friendly young scientist named Mitch Hooper and his wife Marcia – and to present us with their opinions on the breed. Mitch makes the mistake of not sharing Dan and Jane's intellectual interests, and of employing too little subtlety and understatement in his conversation; Jane can barely get through their first conversation without cutting him dead, and afterward she says to Dan, "I used to hate my mother, she used to be so cutting to them [Americans, that is] sometimes. But I don't know if it isn't more honest than playing games." Dan's reply: "You mustn't expect subtlety from the backwoods of Illinois." (They're from Joliet.) And Dan and Jane proceed to note how the Hoopers disprove "the ridiculous notion that advanced technology produces richer human beings." Throughout all of this, it is clear that Fowles is using Dan and Jane as mouthpieces; we're supposed to share their contempt for the Hoopers, supposed to go along with their characterization of Americans as "the most culturally deprived people in the advanced West." What snobs these Marxists be!

The plain and unfortunate truth is that in *Daniel Martin*, more than in any of his previous books, Fowles lets his mania for ideas – especially bad ones – get away from him. The fact that he incorporates into the novel extensive quotations from both Antonio Gramsci and Georg Lukács leads one to suspect that he was under the spell of one or both of these philosophers while writing the book. Who but John Fowles would quote sentences such as the following (from Gramsci) in a novel: *"The philosophy of praxis is consciousness full of contradictions, in which the philosopher himself, understood both individually and as an entire social group, not merely grasps the contradictions, but posits himself as an element of the contradiction and elevates this element to a principle of knowledge and therefore of action."* So intent is Fowles on having his characters yammer endlessly at each other about such things that, when news comes of Anthony's suicide, Dan and Jane pause for only a moment, it seems, to express their shock and grief before resuming their witty dialectic. A remark that Anthony makes to Dan sums up the tone of the novel perfectly: "Perhaps the most profound breach in our marriage has been over the question of whether we have some control over our lives or not." Who but Fowles could write such a sentence with a straight face?

Since *Daniel Martin*, Fowles has published two additional novels, *Mantissa* (1982) and *A Maggot* (1985). Both of these books represent an appreciable falling off in quality from the level of his previous work. In both, Fowles experiments radically with form—and he does so, I think, at the expense of style and content. Significantly, whereas the titles of his earlier novels all refer to characters, the titles of these two novels describe the books themselves—and in neither case very flatteringly. A mantissa, as Fowles coyly explains in a footnote toward the end of the first book, quoting from the *Oxford English Dictionary*, is an "addition of comparatively small importance, especially to a literary effort or discourse." As for the word *maggot*, he tells us in the second book's prologue that it describes "the larval stage of a winged creature," has the obsolete meaning of "whim or quirk," and in the late seventeenth and early eighteenth centuries was used in the titles of "dance-tunes and airs," such as "Mr. Beveridge's Maggot." The titles of both of these later Fowles novels seem designed, then, to indicate that they are admittedly less substantial than their predecessors, that they are *jeux d'esprit* rather than full-fledged serious novels in the manner of *The Magus*, *The French Lieutenant's Woman*, and *Daniel Martin*.

By a considerable margin, *Mantissa* is the shortest of all Fowles's novels. The back cover of the paperback edition describes it as "teasingly enigmatic," and that it is—but indulgently, rather than interestingly, so. Feverish, inchoate, otherworldly, it is a cousin to such books as *Naked Lunch* and *Why Are We in Vietnam?* It begins with a page or so of obscure, convoluted prose in which a character comes to consciousness; he is then told that he is in a hospital room, is addressed as Mr. Green, and spends much of the rest of the novel being sexually abused by a female doctor and nurse, who tell him they are engaged in a serious course of medical treatment and that their function is to provide him with "a source of erotic arousal." But though they offer to do anything he wants—"we can offer most of [the positions] in the Kama Sutra, Aretino, the Hokuwata Monosaki, Kinsey, Sjostrom"—they show no feeling whatsoever, and take notes while speaking constantly in medical and psychoanalytic jargon. The book contains the usual references to many of Fowles's pet topics, but it feels shapeless and unfocused; it reads like a narcotics-induced revision of the most odious and sadistic portions of *The Magus*.

Like *The French Lieutenant's Woman*, *A Maggot*, set in eighteenth-century England, brings together the past and the present, the era of society and the age of the self. A young gentleman and his three companions disappear while on a journey; the book consists primarily of lengthy transcripts of the court inquiry into the matter. The key witness is a "wench" named Rebecca Lee, who tells a fantastic tale of being led by the young gentleman to a cavern in a wood, where she was taken on board a spacecraft of sorts (she describes it as resembling a giant maggot) and shown films of an ideal futuristic world. She says that the young gentleman and his companions were divinities, and that they and their craft disappeared into the heavens. At the end of the book, Rebecca, having slept with one of the missing men, is delivered of a baby, who turns out to be Ann Lee. Since many readers may not know who Ann Lee is, Fowles, in an epilogue, explains that she was the founder of the Shakers, whom he admires because in the eighteenth century "[u]n-orthodox religion was the only vehicle by which the vast majority, who were neither philosophers nor artists, could express this painful breaking of the seed of the self from the hard soil of an irrational and tradition-bound society." Ann Lee was, in other words, an existentialist.

To read *A Maggot* in conjunction with Fowles's earlier novels is a sad experience. The bluntly intrusive authorial remarks about free will and determinism, the Few and the Many, Godhead and authorship assure one that the book is the work of John Fowles, but most of the qualities that make his fiction memorable and his philosophy palatable are absent. Gone are the rich language, the evocative descriptions, the subtly etched characters of, say, *The French Lieutenant's Woman*. One has the feeling that Fowles – who has been quoted as saying that he would rather be a good philosopher or poet than a good novelist – has finally grown bored with the fictional way of truth and would rather just come out and say what he has to say. This book makes one realize that perhaps another Fowlesian antithesis should be added to the list at the beginning of this essay – namely, that of philosopher and novelist. For the struggle that each of Fowles's novels most assuredly dramatizes is the one between these two poles of his professional identity. There is nothing wrong, of course, with a novelist holding strong opinions; the trouble in Fowles's case is that he focuses so intently upon the beliefs his characters hold and the philosophical concepts they represent that he often seems in danger of reducing the characters to these beliefs and concepts. Fowles has come very close, in his career, to writing a first-rate novel, but one cannot be a truly first-rate novelist without a comprehensive gift for curiosity and empathy, an ability to examine individuals in isolation from their ideas – or at least an ability to recognize, for example, that one man's existentialism is not the same as another's.

For all his virtues and accomplishments, Fowles is the best possible illustration of why it was complimentary for Eliot to say of Henry James that he had a mind so fine that no idea could violate it. By closing his mind, as it were, to ideas, James opened it to insight, sympathy, understanding. Fowles, when he wants to be, is a wonderfully perceptive observer of human behavior; but all too often, he takes a promising character and – rather than allow him to develop, to take on dimension, to speak in a fresh and distinctive voice – Fowles leads him once more into the woods, puts him through the paces of yet another Fowlesian godgame, and forces him to utter axioms on mystery, passion, and the need to act. In *The French Lieutenant's Woman*, Fowles notes critically that the Victorians "were not the people for existentialist moments, but for chains of cause and effect; for positive all-explaining theories, carefully studied and studiously applied." Fowles is, in large part, correct to view himself as different from the Victorians he describes. Yet in their own way, his constantly recurring themes and archetypes are as stifling and tyrannical as the most stiff-necked sort of Victorian rationalism; in *Mantissa* and *A Maggot*, the enlightened tyranny of the earlier novels has grown capricious and repressive. Fowles's philosophy has, in short, held him and his fiction in its increasingly deleterious sway for a quarter of a century now; plainly the time has come for Fowles to be a real-life existential hero and to throw it over once and for all.

(APRIL 1987)

The Long Journey of
Doris Lessing

In the constellation of post-World War II fiction, Doris Lessing shines with a most peculiar light. To describe her as a novelist and short-story writer (and occasional essayist, playwright, scenarist, and poet) seems, somehow, to be misleading; like Ayn Rand, she is an author many of whose most fervent devotees have been drawn less by the plangency of her prose or the charm of her characters than by the unabashed fervor with which she has polemicized on behalf of an idea. Precisely what that idea is, however, has been a subject of widespread misconception since the publication in 1950 of her first novel, *The Grass Is Singing* (the story of a white African woman's murder by a black houseboy), and particularly since the appearance of her sixth and most celebrated novel, *The Golden Notebook,* in 1962. That, of course, was the book that made Lessing a popular prophet: liberation-minded women on both sides of the Atlantic clutched it to their bosoms, proclaimed it their Bible, declared Lessing their Voice. To their minds, her message was, unmistakably, that in the Western world it's hard to be a woman – however gifted, however loved, however privileged. Though Lessing, a strong feminist, sympathized with these women, she disapproved of their reading of her magnum opus. *The Golden Notebook,* she complained in a 1971 introduction to a new edition of the novel, is not "a tract about the sex war." Broadly speaking, this is true; for what most of her eighteen novels have really been about, *The Golden Notebook* included, is Lessing's lifelong desire for "freedom" from bourgeois conformity. It is a desire that has caused her to walk many of the social, political, and mystical paths less traveled by in contemporary Western society, and that has occasioned behavior (much of it described self-flatteringly in her work) that, all too often, can only be characterized as egocentric to the point of irresponsibility. The appearance of a new Lessing novel, *The Good Terrorist*[1] – which, with its two immediate predecessors, seems to indicate a shift away from the programmatic intransigence of her earlier years – provides an excellent opportunity to examine this much celebrated but widely misunderstood novelistic career.

D o r i s   L e s s i n g ' s rebellion against middle-class values began in her early youth. Born Doris May Tayler in 1919 in the Persian city of Kermanshah, and raised mostly in British-controlled Southern Rhodesia (now Zimbabwe), she was, even in her childhood, a rebel in search of a cause. She did not, however, want for anything to rebel against: from the start, her chief antagonist was her mother, Emily Tayler, whose modest middle-class ambitions – primarily, to maintain a civilized English-style household on the African veld, and to provide her children with a good education – earned her Doris's resentment. In fact, as Lessing herself has admitted, it was mainly as a reaction against her conventionally minded mother that Doris, at the age of fourteen, dropped out of the Girls' High School in Salisbury, never to return. Thenceforth she took the autodidactic route, reading haphazardly – if industriously – in the classics. To this day she considers her decision to leave school a sound one. "I am grateful for a lucky escape," she has written. Though she has registered some reasonable complaints about the conventional education with which the Rhodesian authorities attempted to provide her, it is clear that Lessing's principal objection to that education, then and now, is simply that it was, indeed, conventional, and therefore by definition an encroachment upon her right to self-fulfillment. Even at fourteen, then, Lessing was an adversary of conformity of any sort, whose single article of faith was that Mother and Western civilization were in league to prevent her from finding herself.

In this connection, the first four novels of Lessing's *Children of Violence* series are especially revealing. They compose a slightly fictionalized record of her life in Africa, from her teens to age thirty, with emphasis upon her unmoderated self-regard. Lessing appears (with charac-

1. *The Good Terrorist*, by Doris Lessing; Knopf.

teristic lack of subtlety) as "Martha Quest," who, in the eponymous first volume of the series (1952), spends her days enjoying the beauty of the African veld and her nights partying with the smart upper-middle-class younger crowd, dreaming all the while of being freed from her torment. What torment? Why, the torment of living in a century that is dominated by violence, in an outpost of Empire (" Zambesia") that is ruled by racism, in a superficial society that forces a serious, sensitive Martha to present herself as a frivolous, fun-loving "Matty." Never mind that she is herself white, privileged, thousands of miles from the battle lines; Martha is the kind of girl who sits in her backyard, sipping a cool drink and reading about atrocities a continent and a half away, and whines, "Oh, dear, why does this have to happen to *me?*" How she suffers! Going out with a beau, she is thrilled at being "set free" from "her parents who destroyed her." She dreams of someone handing her a hundred pounds and saying, "'Here, Martha Quest, you deserve this, this is to set you free.'" It's awfully funny – and the funniest thing of all is that Lessing doesn't find it funny. Unlike many another self-adoring novelist, she has absolutely no sense of humor about herself, or about protagonists who are her near-perfect reflections. On this score, she puts even Philip Roth in the shade; for some part of Roth, at least, is always aware of his egomania, and laughs at it, as if to say: "I know I'm obnoxious, but I can't help it." Not so Lessing. The saga of Martha Quest is, to her mind, an utterly serious affair; Martha is nothing less than a prisoner of Western ways and means, shaking the bars of her cage, yearning to breathe free.

What makes Martha's puerile rebelliousness easier for Lessing to pass off as sympathetic, even admirable, is that Martha's mother (like Lessing's own) is a racist – an ignorant woman, in the manner of most Rhodesian whites of her time, who sees blacks and Jews as inferior. This gives Martha (as it did Doris) the opportunity to engage in symbolic, seemingly principled, acts of defiance: for example, she dates a Jewish man in whom she has absolutely no romantic interest, and with whom she would otherwise never have associated. Lessing recognizes that this act is patronizing and self-serving, that Martha is taking advantage of the man in order to slap her mother in the face; but this doesn't bother her. To her mind, Martha is manifestly a beacon of moral commitment:

something that, as Lessing portrays it, is characterized neither by acute crises of conscience nor by brave and challenging acts of self-abnegation, but, on the contrary, by a "driving individualism" – than which, we are to understand, there is hardly anything more wonderful.

In *A Proper Marriage* (1954), Martha seeks freedom by marrying one Douglas Knowell. (In real life, his name was Frank Charles Wisdom.) Since her "first fierce tenet in life" is "hatred for the tyranny of the family" (she's a student of Engels's *Origin of the Family*), her intention is to have not a traditional marriage, in which the partners are chained to one another, but a union that is "sensible," unsullied by belief "in jealousy or even fidelity." (*Sensible,* interestingly, is also the word used by the heroine of Lessing's most famous story, "To Room Nineteen," to describe the marriage that will eventually drive her mad.) To Lessing's way of thinking, this sort of progressive marriage is a good idea in theory, but it just doesn't work – because jealousies *do* arise, babies get born, and next thing you know you're stuck in a tyrannical bourgeois marriage. This, at least, is what happens to Martha. After a brief shining moment of freedom she is incarcerated by the most vicious of all jailers: pregnancy (described in "To Room Nineteen" as a period of "cold storage"). She has a daughter, Caroline, and switches as soon as possible from breast- to bottle-feeding in order to be "free again." But she's not free for long. Bringing up Caroline, she is "sucked into the [domestic] pattern"; three years after the child's birth, she recognizes that "her female self [is] sharply demanding that she should start the cycle of life again," and knows that if she had another baby, "she would be committed to staying here; she would live in the pattern till she died." There's only one thing to do, and she does it: she deserts Douglas and Caroline (as Lessing, at age twenty-four, left Frank Wisdom, who retained custody of their two children, John and Jean). "You'll be perfectly free, Caroline," Martha tells her baby. "I'm setting you free" – meaning that her refusal to stay with her family and play Mummy will keep Caroline from despising her the way Martha despises *her* mother.

For all this lack of responsibility, these first two volumes of *Children of Violence* are among Lessing's least didactic books – and are, in parts, even charming. Like *The Grass Is Singing* and those of her early stories that are set in Africa – and that have been collected in such volumes as

This Was the Old Chief's Country (1951), *The Habit of Loving* (1957), and *African Stories* (1964) – these novels are admirable above all for their exquisite and loving evocation of the veld. Also, though Martha's tireless self-absorption is usually a bit much on the nerves, many of the supporting players, such as Martha's suave but sexless boyfriend Donovan, are affectingly drawn. (What makes this achievement all the more remarkable is that, most of the time, Lessing clearly has quite the opposite effect in mind – that is, we are supposed to be touched to the core by her unruly heroine, and irritated by these conventional dullards who stand in the way of her independence.) At times we even feel for Martha; in *A Proper Marriage,* for example, the description of her pregnancy and confinement, and of her mixed reactions to childbirth, is so rich, natural, and unforced that one cannot help being moved.

The third and fourth volumes of the series, however, are rather less human and much drearier. Martha's "driving individualism" has led her, in *A Proper Marriage,* to the same place it led Lessing in 1942 – namely, into local Communist politics. Consequently, *A Ripple from the Storm* (1958) and *Landlocked* (1965) are more or less obsessed with Martha's adventures in a cabal of Zambesian comrades, where she learns how to express her hatred for convention and her passion for personhood in numbingly conventional and impersonal Marxist rhetoric (which, at times, disfigures our narrator's prose as well – something a traveler through Lessingland had better get accustomed to fast). She marries a German named Anton Hesse (in real life: Gottfried Anton Lessing) who seems, at first, to be a perfect Communist, above those petty personal attachments and jealousies that shackle the middle-class mind. But he eventually disappoints her, for beneath that Marxian mind beats a bourgeois heart. Disenchanted with both Anton and the whole idea of organized radical activism (it's hard to be an individual when you have to go to meetings all the time), Martha once again jumps ship – leaving husband, comrades, and Africa (as Lessing did in 1949 with her two-year-old son, Peter Lessing), for England. What she's "learned" is summed up by critic Mona Knapp: "individuality cannot thrive in the ritualistic affiliation with society's institutions and counterinstitutions." And individuality is, without a doubt, the bottom line with Lessing. This is why she does not consider Martha's Communist adventure, however politically unproductive she may recognize it to be, to have been a waste of time. For to Lessing's way of thinking, whether Martha's leftist activities actually have had an influence upon the way people in her nation live – and whether that influence has been positive or negative – hardly matters; what is important is whether Marxism has been a "useful experience" for Martha, personal-growth-wise. And that it has been.

Lı k e *Landlocked, The Golden Notebook* is a leaving-the-comrades story. Whereas the former novel is based upon Lessing's Marxist activities in Southern Rhodesia during the forties, the latter derives from her involvement with the British Communist party in the fifties. Structurally, it is more complex than the four early *Children of Violence* books. Its principal component is a novel-within-a-novel called "Free Women," set in 1957, in which Lessing presents herself as Anna Wulf, a middle-aged London novelist in crisis, who, though buoyed by her friendship with an actress and socialist named Molly, has been failed by her men (they keep going back to their wives), by her Muse (she's suffering from writer's block), by her ten-year-old daughter Janet (who's decided that Mummy's beloved world of "disorder [and] experiment" is not for her), and, most important of all, by her politics (she's a disenchanted member of the Soviet-dominated British Communist party, which refuses to admit the truth about Stalin or to protest the recent invasion of Hungary). The novel covers a period of several months during which Anna – to whom life without the ideals represented by the Communist party, and the hopes symbolized by Stalin, seems frighteningly chaotic and meaningless – deconstructs herself, as she has been doing for several years now, in four notebooks containing memoirs, notes, clippings, journals. The black notebook (much of which rehearses the materials of *Children of Violence*) relates to her early years in Africa and to the publication of her novel of Africa, *Frontiers of War*; the red one pertains to her life as a Communist; the blue one records current news events and romances; and the yellow one contains a novel in progress entitled *The Shadow of the Third* whose protagonist, Ella, shares Anna's preoccupations and (with, we are to understand, only slight variations) lives out a romance Anna had a couple of years earlier. (And, in turn, writes her *own* novel.) If in "Free Women" we read about Anna's troubled present, the notebooks, printed between the sections of "Free Women," give us glimpses, from different angles, of its roots in her political, sexual, and literary past; and then, in a fifth gold-colored notebook, we watch her crack up, put herself together with the help of a schizophrenic American named Saul Green, resign from the Party (as Lessing herself did in that year), and march, head high, alone – but with a sense of her spiritual interconnectedness with all living things – into the future.

Though many critics have complained justifiably that there is less purpose to *The Golden Notebook*'s complex construction than Lessing would have us believe, the structure is largely responsible for this novel's being a good deal more interesting than most of her longer fiction. For once, rather than merely talking about herself, Lessing shows us what it is like to talk about herself, tries to suggest why she is so preoccupied with talking about herself. In short, though it is unarguably a tour de force of narcissism, of mirror-gazing (for Anna is obviously a reflection of Lessing, and Ella, in turn, a reflection of Anna), *The Golden Notebook* is also an apologia of sorts for her entire oeuvre; and it is – as so many contemporary novels try to be – a novel about the making of fictions and the nature of fictional truth.

Yet *The Golden Notebook* is infuriating. For Anna's life, like Martha Quest's, centers upon her need to be "free" from bourgeois conformity. If the conflict at the heart of the novel is her crisis over whether to leave the Party, it is because communism is at the heart of her self-image as a "free woman." Having joined the Party in 1950 because she was disgusted with the "prissy, maiden-auntish" London literary world and was impressed by the Party's "atmosphere of friendliness, of people working for a common goal," she is clearly in the habit of looking upon her Party affiliation less as a serious commitment to an international movement – a movement, moreover, whose actions are liable to have deadly serious consequences – than as a means of rebelling against the sort of people Lessing refers to elsewhere as "the conforming, the average, the obedient." In a typical encounter, Anna reveals her communism to a conforming, average, and obedient American woman because "I wanted to shock her," and the woman reacts according to plan, sputtering that Anna doesn't strike her as the Red type; a disgusted Anna confides to a notebook: "Better to be a communist, and at almost any cost, better to be in touch than to be so cut off from any reality that one can make a remark as stupid as that." The rationale here is fascinating; it's 1957, Anna is still a Soviet hireling, and we're supposed to see her as being "in touch"!

It's very offensive. For Anna *knows* what the Soviets are guilty of. But she prefers to wrap those troubles in dreams – to escape into the simplistic illusion that, gulags or no gulags, Communism is synonymous with "a dedicated faith in humanity," a "belie[f] in something," and may yet prove to be the great hope of mankind. She knows that to leave the Party would be to leave behind "murder, cynicism, horror, betrayal," but, as a friend tells her – and we are obviously supposed to love her for this – she remains in the fold because she is "full of faith." Indeed, she's a regular Marxist Joan of Arc. "Although I am quite prepared to believe that he [Stalin] is mad and a murderer," reads a characteristic notebook entry of the early fifties, "I like to hear people use that tone of simple, friendly respect for him. Because if that tone were to be thrown aside, something very important would go with it, paradoxically enough, a faith in the possibility of democracy, of decency. A dream would be dead – for our time, at least." Yes, a misplaced faith, and a misbegotten dream, without which we would all be a good deal better off. Anna's is a politics of idealism in the worst sense of the word; and we are supposed to admire her for it.

Even when Anna does leave the Communist party, she is hardly contrite about her years of working against the best interests of Western freedoms, in favor of a murderous tyranny. After all, her admission that the Soviet Union is indeed little better than a concentration camp and that Britain is "safe, comfortable, prosperous" should, by rights, go hand-in-hand with an acknowledgment that her whole political career has been foolish and irresponsible. But Anna doesn't see things in this way, and neither does Lessing. At the end of the novel she wants us to perceive Anna in the same way that Anna perceives Anna: as a Sisyphean "boulder-pusher" on the mountain of "human stupidity," a selfless life-long worker toward that great day "when the world [will be] full of people who don't hate and fear and murder." This is, of course, major-league self-delusion. What makes it particularly difficult to tolerate is that, long after her departure from the Communist party, Lessing continued to speak and write as if the greatest villain of the fifties was not Stalin but McCarthy, and to endorse radical activism as a means of achieving "freedom" from dull conformity. In a 1970 interview, for instance, when asked about campus riots, she declared that "in the 1960s the youth have had a great deal of freedom. It has been a wonderful moment in history." Predictably, as in *Children of Violence,* this infatuation with irresponsibility is the bottom line in *The Golden Notebook.* To Lessing, once again, what ultimately matters about our heroine's Communist adventure is not whether it has served mankind well or ill, but whether it has benefited our heroine's personal development. And, bless her, it has. "I was a communist," Anna says near the end of the novel. "On the whole, a mistake. A useful experience though, and one can never have too many of those."

Nor, to Anna's mind, can one have too many men. Since she is, as she sees it, "a completely new type of woman," wisely wary of liaisons that might lead to formal commitments ("Neither of us," as Anna boasts to her similarly disposed friend Molly, "were [sic] prepared to get married simply to give our children fathers"), she generally confines herself to brief encounters with married men – some of them out-of-town businessmen, some of them casual acquaintances. She is attracted to what she calls *"real men"* (and the term means to her exactly what it does to the author of *Real Men Don't Eat Quiche*) and, in particular, to the cruel, bellicose, and mentally disturbed. She likes tension, craziness, sees madness as a sign of adventurous individualism ("People stay sane by blocking off, by limiting themselves"). Saul Green (under whose alternately loving and malicious eye she breaks down and puts herself back together) is schizophrenic, at times "a madman full of hate." She finds this aphrodisiacal, as she does the sexual partner who comes right out and says: "I enjoy a society where women are second-class citizens, I enjoy being boss and being flattered." Her response: "Good. . . . Because in a society where not one man in ten thousand begins to understand the ways in which women are second-class citizens, we have to rely for company on the men who are at least not hypocrites."

Anna's got it all figured out. But when the evening's over, she can't understand it: why was it so unfulfilling? Why are men (for she feels free to generalize about the entire sex on the basis of these specimens) so obtuse, possessive, vain, impersonal, insulting? Why are they so uninterested in or unaware of how to please a woman in bed? Why are they so quick to be on their way in the morning? Why, just when she starts to get attached, do they cheat on her, make her jealous, undermine her hard-won freedom? And why do they keep saying that she's "castrating"? (This is a sore point with Lessing, who complains in her introduction that most "women are . . . cowards" who "will run like little dogs with stones thrown at them when a man says: You are unfeminine, aggressive, you are unmanning me. It is my belief that any woman who marries or takes seriously in any way at all a man who uses this threat, deserves everything she gets. For such a man is a bully. . . . ignorant . . . a coward.") Anna could, of course, try to find herself a "good man," but she doesn't want one. In her notebooks, she quotes a book reviewer's observation that "women, even the nicest of them, tend to fall in love with men quite unworthy of them." "This review, of course," notes Anna, "[was] written by a man. The truth is that when 'nice women' fall in love with 'unworthy men' it is always either because these men have 'named' them, or because they have an ambiguous uncreated quality impossible to the 'good' or 'nice' men. The normal, the good men, are finished and completed and without potentialities."

Lessing-Anna-Ella's attitude toward the enslaving sex, then, is much the same as her attitude toward governments: the dangerous, mysterious ones, the ones with "potentialities," exert an insuperable attraction upon her, and the "good" ones she despises. Perhaps the most telling male-female relationship in the book, in this respect, is that between Anna and her young homosexual boarder, Ivor. He is probably the only good man in all of *The Golden Notebook,* but Anna has only contempt for him because, in her eyes, "he's not a man." Why? Because "with 'a real man' there would be a whole area of tension, of wry understanding that there can't be with Ivor; there would be a whole dimension there isn't now. . . ." If a real man shared her flat, her daughter Janet (who loves Ivor) "would resent him, would have to accept him, have to come to terms." There would be *tension,* and Anna—who loves tension, whose whole life is an exercise in the creation of tension between herself and her environment – wants it for her daughter too. Thinking this through, Anna hears Ivor reading Janet a story about a girls' school, his voice (Anna decides) tinged with a tyrannical male mockery that is "aimed at the world of the girls' school, at the feminine world." "Well, my poor girl," she muses, "you'd better get used to it early, because you're going to have to live in a world full of it." What a switch! One minute Anna is full of contempt for Ivor as a less-than-real man, not intimidating enough for her; the next minute he is a supermale tyrant. It's inane. And Lessing doesn't realize it; she just doesn't see it. Nor does she intend any irony when, in the next paragraph, Anna worries that Ivor and his boy-friend will "corrupt" Janet, but concludes that "my influence, the healthy female influence, is strong enough to outweigh theirs" – the "healthy influence," of course, being that of a middle-aged adventuress who keeps bringing loosely wrapped men in off the street to spend the night.

A N N A ' S breakdown is occasioned by her disenchantment with the Communist party. Could it be that the rampantness of mental distur-bance in the novels that follow *The Golden Notebook* is, similarly, due to the loss of Soviet communism as a foundation for Lessing's rebellious self-image? The more one reads these later novels, the more one is per-suaded that, with the Communist party and the idea of Stalin no longer available as a means of justifying her systematic intractability to herself and to the world, Lessing was at sea. Without a *Weltanschauung* handy, the world was, for her, suddenly bereft of logic, plunged into chaos. This seems to be the *raison d'être,* in any case, of *The Four-Gated City* (1969), the fifth and last novel in *Children of Violence.* This book – more dense, dark, and chattily capacious than its predecessors – is more a symbolic than a realistic representation of Lessing's own life. It follows Martha Quest through twenty dull years in a gray, Kafkaesque London, during which she lives with and keeps house for a well-to-do family of Communists, Labourites, neurotics, kleptomaniacs, and a psy-chotic named Lynda. The supporting cast carries on at length about McCarthyism, the Korean War, the atomic bomb, and other preoccupa-tions familiar to readers of *The Golden Notebook,* and our narrator describes with admiration such events as a Knightsbridge rally of anarchists, Communists, and pacifists, whom she praises as the "small...number" on whom "depend[s] the belief in saying no." Martha herself keeps a low political profile, of course, having lost her faith in the efficacy of organized radicalism way back in *Landlocked*. But she finds something wonderful to take its place: madness. Observing Lynda, she comes to recognize, *à la* R. D. Laing, that the insane are not really insane; it's our *society* that's insane, and therefore the insane are the sanest of us all. Perhaps, then, madness is the road to truth? *Eureka!* Before we know it, Martha is hearing voices, breaking down, foreseeing the future. *(Anything* to avoid being conventional!) And then, in 1968 or thereabouts, a nuclear holocaust takes place, and in the brief epistolary "appendix," we are suddenly in the realm of apocalyptic fiction. We learn that in the months preceding the holocaust, the already fascistically inclined governments of Britain and the United States clamped down on freedom; in Britain, "order, self-discipline, formal religion, conformity, authority" were the rule, while America experienced a "new age of 'piety and iron'" during which Dr. Spock was "sentenced for unconformity." This "bland, insular conformity" soon gave way to violence, social collapse, and, ultimately, nuclear nightmare – after which radiation-mutated children began to develop telepathic and visionary powers, leading to hopes of a humbled, less authoritarian world united by extrasensory perception, where a psychotic like Lynda is no longer regarded as a psychotic but, in Martha's words, is valued as "a first-class 'listener,' a first-class 'seer.'" In the future, according to Lessing, it is upon such hopes of better living through psychochemistry, as it were, that the fate of mankind precariously rests.

The strange and marvelous powers of the human mind, the fecundity of madness: *Briefing for a Descent into Hell* (1971), which reads like the swiftly churned-out record of a narcotics trip, picks up these themes and contemplates them obsessively. Charles Watkins, the first male protagonist in a Lessing novel, loses his mind on the gray, dreary streets of London – or, rather, finds it; for, asleep for weeks on end in his hospital bed, he journeys through a beautiful dream world where he experiences "the mind of humanity... not at all to be separated from the animal mind which married and fused with it everywhere"; he "watche[s] a pulsing swirl of all being, continually changing, moving, dancing, a controlled impelled lava"; he finds the "strand of humanity [to be] part of the shimmering web of fluid joyful being." And so forth. Such pseudo-poetry forms the bulk of this novel. "Humanity," we learn, is "a pulse in the light of the sun," part of a "Cosmic Harmony," in which "individuals [do] not matter, because an individual [can] only be important insofar as he or she [is] a pledge for the future...." This is not to suggest that Lessing has parted from her raging egoism; on the contrary, she's merely taken it one step further, to the cosmic level, like Whitman or Ginsberg. She's become a seer, a container of multitudes, a visionary.

If this sounds like Eastern mysticism at its dippiest, it is because *Briefing for a Descent into Hell,* like *Landlocked* and *The Four-Gated City* before it, was written under the influence of Sufism, a form of Islamic mysticism of which Lessing first became aware when she reviewed Idries Shah's book *The Sufis* in 1964. Suggestive at times of Neoplatonism, Transcendentalism, and Jungian psychology, the Sufist philosophy is based largely upon the doctrine of "Oneness of Being," which (according to *What Is Sufism?* by Martin Lings) "means that what the eye sees and the mind records is an illusion, and that every apparently separate and finite thing is in Truth the Presence of the One Infinite." The physical world is nothing; spirit and mind are all:

> the primordial soul is a unified multiple harmony suspended as it were between the next world and this world, that is, between the Inward and the Outward, in such a way that there is a perfect balance between the pull of the inward signs – the Heart and beyond it the Spirit – and the *signs on the horizons....* But in the fallen soul, where the attraction of the Heart is more or less imperceptible, the balance is broken and the scales are heavily weighted in favour of the outer world.
>
> To ask how the true balance can be restored is one way of asking "What is Sufism?" And the first part of the answer is that an inward movement must be set up in the soul to counteract the pull of the outer world so that the lost harmony can be regained.

It is not surprising that Lessing's most significant ideological act, after leaving the Communist party, was not to move toward a more moderate and sensible political position, but rather to throw herself into a nonpolitical ideology that was equally immoderate. It is, furthermore, clear why Lessing found the doctrines of Sufism, in particular, so allur-ing. Here, after all, was a system of thought that, like Communism, of-fered her an established means of being an antiestablishment Utopian idealist – and yet that was decidedly *not* a form of organized religion or politics. On the contrary, it was, with its emphasis upon inner truth, the perfect ideology for an individualist. Sufism spoke in terms of universes, but the self was always at the center; it thus represented a magnificent perspective from which to envision (in *The Four-Gated City* and later in *Memoirs of a Survivor*) the disintegration of civilization as a reflection of her own confusion and mental collapse. Sufism also was ideally suited to an ex-Communist party type like herself, for it explained exactly what was wrong with her. The years as a Party functionary had thrown her off balance: her scales had been too heavily weighted in favor of the outer world. The solution was to restore true balance, to set up an "inward movement." This is the guiding idea in *Briefing*, which features, in place of an epigraph, the words "CATEGORY: INNER-SPACE FICTION/ *For there is never anywhere to go but in.*" Lessing has loaded her dice here: Watkins is a supremely earthbound professor of classics, a veritable sym-bol of classicism, order, tradition – everything Lessing despises. His madness is, of course, a reaction to his classically ordered life – a healthy reaction, we are supposed to feel, that puts him in touch with his true, abundant inner self. We are expected to resent his dull, faceless doctors (whom Lessing identifies only as X and Y) for referring to his dream world as "religious delusions" and for, at the end, curing him and re-turning him to his waking life, to his family and career, the memory of the dream world erased forever.

Like *Briefing*, *Memoirs of a Survivor* (1975) is an exercise in mystical monomania; like the "appendix" of *The Four-Gated City*, it is the story of life in a primitive, chaotic world of the near future in which – at first, anyway – people "[live] on, adjusting our lives as if nothing fundamen-tal [is] happening." In a grim pseudo-London, the absence of order is at first a nuisance for our Lessing-like protagonist but eventually gives way to a Sufistic vision in which the young man, girl, and dog with whom she has spent these dark days are led away by a mysterious, beautiful she-figure – "the one person I had been looking for all this time." The book ends as follows (the ellipsis is Lessing's):

Both [the girl and dog] walked quickly behind that One who went ahead showing them the way out of this collapsed little world into another order of world altogether. Both, just for an instant, turned their faces as they passed that other threshold. They smiled. . . . Seeing those faces, [the young man] was drawn after them, but still he hesitated in a fearful conflict, looking back and around, while the brilliant fragments whirled around him. And then, at the very last moment, they came, his children came running, clinging to his hands and his clothes, and they all followed quickly on after the others as the last walls dissolved.

Memoirs was, so to speak, only prologue. In 1979 Lessing began publishing her infamous science-fiction series entitled *Canopus in Argos: Archives,* an apparent attempt at some sort of postmodern Pentateuch. The novels followed one another rapidly; the first, *Shikasta. Re: Colonised Planet 5,* was soon joined by *The Marriage between Zones Three, Four, and Five. As Narrated by the Chroniclers of Zone Three* (1980), *The Sirian Experiments. The Report by Ambien II, of the Five* (1981); *The Making of the Representative for Planet 8* (1982); and *Documents Relating to the Sentimental Agents in the Volyen Empire* (1983). The novels are, alas, as graceless and clotted as their titles. In presenting them as a series of documents, Lessing was only demonstrating an interest in unorthodox forms that she had exhibited earlier, in the notebooks of *The Golden Notebook* and the correspondence-filled "appendix" of *The Four-Gated City;* it is difficult not to see this predilection as the result of Lessing's growing impatience with both the traditional form of the novel and its stylistic requirements. Lessing had, after all, never been celebrated as a stylist, and to open a volume of the *Canopus* series at random is to be convinced that she had at last grown tired of sifting her increasingly intense and recondite vision through the mesh of art – had, in other words, left the necessity of fine-tuning her prose, the responsibility for finding *le mot juste,* and most of the other requisites of the literary art far behind her.

She did not, unfortunately, leave behind a single one of her familiar themes, doctrines, and type-scenes; they are all here, jumbled together in a febrile galactic mishmash. As in *The Golden Notebook,* there are diatribes against the United States as the warmonger and capitalistic raper of continents, the greatest evil on Earth (which is known here as the planet Shikasta); as in *The Four-Gated City,* there is a nuclear holocaust in the near future, after which the hope is that life can be good again, thanks to the primitive pleasures of some pseudo-Sufistic entity known as SOWF (Substance-of-We-Feeling). As in *Children of Violence,* there is racial tension in Africa and the "lesson" that both institutions and counterinstitutions are worthless. There are humans and aliens, and lives that last hundreds of years. At the center of it all is a vision of a Utopian universe governed by the Sufist idea of collective consciousness, the sharing of a single mind and soul by all living beings; though Lessing clearly believes that Sufism has taught her the foolishness of self-centeredness, she just as clearly has made use of that philosophy, in these books, to build her self-fascination into an egomania of galactic proportions. The following excerpts from a speech by a character named Doeg in *The Making of the Representative* offer a fair representation of this pseudoholistic egomania at work:

> I remember how the thought came into me that I, Doeg, was in the shape I am, with the features I have, because of a choice among multitudes. I set in front of myself a mirror, and I looked at my features. . . . I imagined . . . slight modifications of me, some very similar indeed, some hardly at all. I filled a town with these variations of myself, then a city, then, in my mind, whole landscapes. Doeg, Doeg, Doeg again. . . . I said to them: Look, here you are, in me . . . for the feeling of me, of I, that feeling *I am here, Doeg,* would have been your feeling had the chances of the genes fallen differently, and if you, your particular shape and mould, had been born instead of me. What was born, then, to those repositories of a million years of the dicing of the genes, was a *feeling,* a consciousness, was the self-awareness: *here I am.* And this awareness was given the name Doeg—though I have used many names in my life. . . . it is true, it must be true, that this precious thing, what I hold on to when I say: *I am here, Doeg,* this is the feeling I am, and have, and what I recognise in sleep, and will recognise as myself when I die, leaving all this behind . . . all that there is of this little feeling, *here I am,* the feeling of *me*—and yet it is not mine at all, but is shared, it must be, for how can it be possible that there are as many shades and degrees of me-ness as there are individuals on this planet of ours? [Two pages later:] . . . my loneliness is softened when I reflect that in saying *I, here I am, here is what I am,* this feeling or sensa-

tion or taste of *me* – I speak for . . . but I do not know how many. For others, that is certain. In that feeling of me-ness is, must be, a sharing, must be a companionship. I shall never wake from the deep sleep . . . without thinking . . . *Here I am, here is the consciousness of me,* of those others, who are I, are myself, though I do not know who they are, nor they me. . . .

And so on, through the millennia.

THE LAST THING one might have expected, after these ponderous cosmic excursions, was that Lessing would come gently down to earth and proceed to write a pair of novels whose taut structure, restrained prose, relative indifference to ideology, and penetrating attention to human character would cause her to be compared with Barbara Pym. But that (for reasons I shall discuss presently) was precisely what happened. The two novels were *The Diary of a Good Neighbour* (1983) and *If the Old Could . . .* (1984). Reading these graceful and touching books, one could not help feeling that, in the bizarre *Canopus* series, Lessing had been deliberately purging her soul, not only of the last tattered vestiges of communism and Sufism but of the egocentric rebelliousness that had drawn her to them in the first place.

In these novels, both written in diary form, Lessing was born again as Jane ("Janna") Somers, who, at the beginning of the first novel, is a stylish, fiftyish London women's-magazine editor with no children and no strong personal attachments or obligations, even to her husband, Freddie; she is a woman who "likes the freedom of being alone in a crowd. I like being alone. Period." Her sister Georgie (who lives in "exactly the house my parents lived in always. . . . country-suburban, comfortable, conventional, conservative") considers Janna "the irresponsible one" in the family, guilty of "selfish childlessness," and has nothing but contempt for her "glamorous goings-on." When Freddie becomes ill, Janna thinks it "unfair to me"; when he dies, she takes in her mother, who has been living for years with Georgie's family, and whom Janna has "always found embarrassing. . . . When I was out with her I used to think, no one would believe I could be her daughter, two worlds, heavy suburban respectable – and me." After a year, though, her mother develops cancer, and since Janna cannot face the necessity of making prolonged visits to the hospital, Georgie does it instead. We learn that, years earlier, Janna behaved even more abominably during her grandmother's last illness: "I simply behaved as if Granny being ill had nothing to do with me. Not my affair!"

But soon after her mother dies, everything changes. Janna meets a poor, lonely, cantankerous old working-class woman named Maudie Fowler, and finds herself gradually becoming Maudie's best friend, her daily companion and helpmeet. Now Janna is able to see herself plain. She tells Georgie: "It has only recently occurred to me that I never lifted a finger all the time Granny was dying." She realizes that she misses having talked to Granny, to Mother, to Freddie. Why didn't she talk to them when they were alive? She knows the answer immediately: "I didn't want to, that is the answer. *I didn't want to know.*"

It is a breakthrough, a moving one – and the reader who is a veteran of the windy narcissism of Lessing's previous novels (and, particularly, of Martha Quest's rebellion against her conventional mother) cannot help being especially moved. For suddenly Janna – in whom, despite some significant differences in background, we can see the contours of earlier Lessing heroines – knows what she has been, and wants to change; she *wants* responsibility, wants to care, to be attached, to comprehend (as best she can) what it is like to be someone other than herself. To this end she devotes several pages of her diary to a sensitive description of "Maudie's day" as she imagines it – and later in the novel does the same for other unfortunates whom she has met. To be sure, Janna's interest in Maudie is, at first anyway, unconsciously self-serving; it's a way of appeasing her guilt. But she *does* learn to be responsible, in a quiet, efficient, very English way (these are, I think, the most "English" of Lessing's novels); and the friendship that develops between the two women is precisely, believably evoked and extremely affecting.

Nor does Lessing ruin it all by canonizing Janna for her newfound selflessness or by turning her self-sacrificing heroine into yet another suffering victim of responsibility. Quite the contrary; *The Diary of a Good Neighbour* is a work of conspicuous proportion, in which, at last, a Lessing heroine is not a self-obsessed, offbeat ideologue at war with the white male capitalist hegemony, but a sympathetic, truly believable human being, untainted by fanatical political allegiances or by goofy mystical beliefs, whose unexceptional life is made luminous by her creator's patience, perception, and humor. The reader familiar with Lessing's previous works cannot but take grateful notice of the scorn with which Janna regards her niece Jill's entanglement with fashionable radicals ("The thing is, poor creatures, they don't know it's their social lives, they really believe it's politics"), her definition of madness as "losing touch with reality," and her use – more than once – of the word *sensible* as a special compliment. Likewise, in *If the Old Could...*, an almost equally fine (if more meandering and less moving) achievement that picks our heroine up where we left her and sees her through an affair with a problematic married man, Janna is dismayed when her beloved expresses the desire to avoid "the entrance into responsibility." Among the responsibilities Janna takes on in the latter novel is the care of her troubled niece Kate, who associates with some young revolutionary types living at a "squat" – and for whose "persecuted minority" pose Janna has little patience.

The themes that these two novels share – responsibility, rebellion, sanity, sensibleness – are certainly recognizable from Lessing's previous work; it is the perspective upon them that has changed, changed utterly. In fact, so far removed is all this, in its "sensible" point of view, from the earlier novels that one cannot help but wonder if both of these books are some sort of joke or charade or *jeu d'esprit* in which Lessing is playing the part of a very different sort of woman from herself simply to see what it would be like to be responsible and selfless. Or, perhaps, do these novels represent yet another utterly solemn attempt to "free" herself – this time, paradoxically enough, from the very strain of rebellious egocentrism that drives her to seek "freedom" in the first place? That, in one way or another, Lessing was indeed trying, in these novels, to free herself from *herself* would seem to be supported by the fact that they were originally published not under Lessing's own name, but under the name of Jane Somers, who was identified as "a well-known woman journalist," her real identity being known to only a few editors. Lessing revealed last year that she was the novels' true author, and the impression given by the newspaper reports was that she had used a pseudonym primarily to demonstrate how badly the work of unknown first novelists fares in Britain and America; but, when the novels were reissued last year in a single paperback volume bearing Lessing's own name and the collective title *The Diaries of Jane Somers,* Lessing added an introduction that made it clear that her real motives were rather more personal. If the Jane Somers novels indeed sound like the work of a novelist with a changed sensibility, this introduction is most definitely the product of the old (humorless, ego-happy, freedom-obsessed) Lessing. She explains how irritating it is to have been pigeonholed by reviewers over the years – who have categorized her, in turn, as a writer about race, communism, sex, mysticism – and says that, the *Canopus* series having "set [her] free to write in ways [she] had not used before," she "wondered if there would be a similar liberation if I were to write in the first person in a different character. . . . And it did turn out that as Jane Somers I wrote in ways that Doris Lessing cannot. . . . Jane Somers knew nothing about a kind of dryness, like a conscience, that monitors Doris Lessing whatever she writes and in whatever style." "Some," she goes on to suggest, "may think this [*The Diaries*] is a detached way to write about Doris Lessing"; but who is Doris Lessing? Like Doeg in *The Making of the Representative,* she proceeds to discuss the question of identity, and to contemplate the various names she has had in her life. "I sometimes wonder what my real name is; surely I must have one?" Could it be Jane Somers? One influence, she says, upon her conception of Jane Somers was

> reflections about what my mother would be like if she lived now: that practical, efficient, energetic woman, by temperament conservative, a little sentimental, and only with difficulty (and a lot of practice at it) able to understand weakness and failure, though always kind. No, Jane Somers is not my mother, but thoughts of women like my mother did feed Jane Somers.

Thoughts of women like her mother fed the despised May Quest too, of course. One comes away from Lessing's introduction suspecting that the key to the whole Jane Somers phenomenon is that, whether permanently or temporarily, the Lessing of the *Diaries* essentially reversed her position on her mother, and that this change made all the difference – caused selfishness to turn to self-effacement, blind individualism to a firm appreciation of the value of personal attachments and responsibilities.

IN *The Good Terrorist,* Lessing's most recent novel, we are no longer in Jane Somers territory. But we have not come all the way back to Lessingland, either. To be sure, our heroine – a thirty-six-year-old Communist named Alice Mellings – has a good deal in common with Martha Quest. Like Martha, she is spoiled, resents her bourgeois mother, belongs to a small-time Marxist organization (the "Communist Centre Union"). But the difference is that Lessing depicts her much the way Jane Somers might do. As the novel opens, Alice is, with her sleazy homosexual friend Jasper, taking up residence in a large condemned house (a "squat," as in If *the Old Could*...) on the outskirts of London; she proceeds to set it in magnificent order and to fill it with other young radicals, for whom she becomes (as Martha does in *The Four-Gated City*) a happy little cook and housekeeper. She also becomes an enthusiastic participant in her housemates' bizarre visions of the revolution they will lead against British capitalism; and she listens uneasily – not quite able to bring herself to protest – when they plot to explode a bomb at a nearby hotel.

In many ways, this situation is reminiscent of Joseph Conrad's *The Secret Agent,* wherein a cadre of revolutionaries similarly share a shabby London house, call each other "comrade," endure the watchful attentions of the local police, and plan a terrorist bombing. Lessing's conspirators, like Conrad's, perceive their bombing as a powerful revolutionary statement; but, as in Conrad's novel, any sane person could recognize the planned act of terrorism as purely destructive, with no possible positive ends – in Conrad's words, an "act of madness and despair." The pathetic pointlessness of the enterprise is underscored in *The Good Terrorist,* as in *The Secret Agent,* by the fact that the bomb ends up blowing one of the major characters to bits. In Lessing, as in Conrad, the aim of all this is to probe the "impenetrable mystery" of the revolutionary sensibility – and, more broadly, to examine the human capacity for illogic, moral slovenliness, and destructiveness.

Yet, at heart, Lessing's novel is a world away from Conrad's. If his book is a powerful exploration of certain ambiguities of the human soul, hers is, in the end, a rather contrived and unnecessary demonstration that young English terrorists are likely to be irresponsible, deluded misfits, who act primarily out of jealousy for the stable and happy and well-to-do, and who are all too content to be supported by the society of which they consider themselves enemies. This is, of course, hardly news. But one can see nonetheless why Lessing is so concerned with telling it to us, and why she seems so convinced that she has a strong and controversial point to make: for, though she resigned from the British Communist party decades ago, it is clear that the Marxist collective still remains a force in her psyche, one that she takes quite seriously, continues to be strongly drawn to, perhaps even feels threatened by. Reading this book, consequently, one is not fascinated (as Lessing wishes one to be) by her portrait of a revolutionary squat, so much as one is irritated that, after all these years, and whatever her attitude toward it, Lessing is still so fascinated by the phenomenon of radical activism. In a way, one senses, this novel is not intended for the lay reader so much as it is the judgment of an "old Red" (as she calls herself elsewhere) upon the pursuits of a corps of much younger Reds. More than anything else, it is a case of Doris Lessing talking to herself – doing her damnedest, that is, to prove something that most of her audience already takes for granted.

At the center of all this is the portrait of Alice – the radical whose greatest joy is keeping house, the self-proclaimed "worker" who was born into the middle classes and has never held a job. As we gradually learn, she (as well as Jasper) has been living with that conventional mother of hers for years, joyfully running the house for her; now her mother has been forced to move into a tiny, run-down flat, and Alice – in the manner of a stubborn, threatened five-year-old – cannot understand it, accept it, or even remember it from one minute to the next. Her mother explains: "I can't afford to live here. I'll have trouble paying my own bills. Do you understand, Alice ?" No, she doesn't. How can her mother *do* this to her? Her only recourse is to abuse her mother with Marxist rhetoric: "Don't you see that your world is finished? The day of the rich selfish bourgeoisie is over. You are doomed. . . ." Later she visits her mother's house, finds it empty, and can't figure it out: "Where was her mother . . . ? Did she imagine she could run away from Alice, just like that? Was she mad? Well, she must be, not telling Alice and Jasper. . . . Here somewhere deep in her mind a thought began tugging and nagging, that her mother had told her. Well, if so, not in such a way that Alice could take it in." When Alice finally locates her mother's new flat in Hampstead, she is confused by her mother's poverty, and disturbed that her mother is living among working-class women (one of whom Alice, on an earlier reconnaissance of the building, has befriended *à la* Janna Somers). Alice's mother (who is surprised at Alice's confusion) reminds Alice that she helped sell the house. Alice doesn't remember.

Is she supposed to be insane? Not quite: that would ruin Lessing's point. For it seems that to Lessing's mind, Alice is, as her mother, Dorothy, complains, simply immature, like other members of her generation. "You've all had it so easy all your lives, you simply do not understand. If you want something, then you take it for granted you can have it. . . . You're all spoiled rotten." As Lessing puts it in the last sentence of the book, Alice is a "poor baby" — a girl who never grew up, a 1980s Martha Quest who stayed too long at the fair. But could emotional immaturity alone account for Alice's extremely bizarre behavior? It seems unlikely. One thing, at any rate, is for certain: whatever the explanation for their behavior, it is impossible, after a certain point, to care about Alice or any of her cohorts, who, even when they do come to life, do so in a very limited way, having little to offer aside from their mindless, megalomaniacal rantings about the need "to put an end to this shitty fucking filthy lying cruel hypocritical system." When the bomb goes off and kills one of them, the reader is supposed to be anguished, enlightened; but one's dominant feeling is regret that the bomb failed to dispatch the whole sick crew.

The characters with whom Lessing patently sympathizes more than any other are Dorothy and her longtime friend Zoë, whom it is possible to see as Anna and Molly of *The Golden Notebook,* thirty years later. Both are ex-radicals, but whereas Zoë has remained left-wing, Dorothy — whom we are clearly intended to recognize as the most intelligent, sensible, and well-adjusted person in the book — has changed her tune. In their single confrontation, Dorothy's position unarguably comes out ahead. "The next thing," says Zoë, "you'll be supporting Reagan's and Thatcher's foreign policies." "I've been wondering whether I shouldn't," Dorothy replies. "After all, forty years ago it wasn't fascist to fight for the bad against the worse. Why is it now?" Is Lessing becoming a Tory? Will this first post-Jane Somers novel initiate a series of conservative tracts in the manner of the later Dos Passos? Perhaps; yet one would guess otherwise. It is, of course, regrettable that Lessing has returned in this novel to the drab little community of radical activism, and that, once again, she is at least as preoccupied with politics as with human character. But one suspects that, after the Jane Somers affair, she may have felt compelled to return to her old Communist stomping ground one more time – to look it over, as it were, from her new perspective – before proceeding, in subsequent novels, to other, less obsessively political matters. Let us hope, at least, that this is the case. For Lessing has demonstrated adroitly that – when freed from the foolish, crippling systems of thought that have been her true jailers for all too many years – she is capable of creating works of fiction that are not only intellectually responsible but stylish, affecting, and truly artful.

(SEPTEMBER 1985)

Ford Madox Ford,
Man of Letters

THERE ARE great authors whose lifework one could read in an afternoon. In the case of Ford Madox Ford – even assuming that one could gather his essays, reviews, editorials, and all eighty-odd of his books in one place – it would take at least a day simply to sort through them and to begin working out some sense of the shape of his career. To be sure, one need not go to such trouble in order to read Ford's best writings: for virtually everybody who has written about him since his death in 1939 has noted that the highlights of his oeuvre are *The Good Soldier* (1915) – which is not only Ford's best novel but one of the major English novels of the twentieth century – and the splendid tetralogy *Parade's End* (1924–28). Yet even these achievements, despite the high regard in which they are held in some quarters, have never been as familiar to serious readers as they ought to be; and one cannot help thinking that Ford's sheer productivity, his longtime reputation as a literary jack-of-all-trades, is at least partly to blame for this relative neglect. Certainly, for a fervent admirer of *The Good Soldier,* the profoundly dispiriting experience of sitting in a library and paging one's way through the mediocre books that make up the bulk of Ford's legacy can help one to understand why his contemporaries might well have had the notion of him as a literary hack so firmly fixed in their minds that it was simply impossible for them to conceive of his writing a masterpiece.

And yet he did write at least one masterpiece. Indeed, one of the most remarkable things about Ford was that if he was among the century's most indefatigable manufacturers of middlebrow fiction, he was also among its most eloquent exponents and gifted practitioners of high literary art, a man whose gods were Turgenev, Flaubert, and Maupassant. One might describe his devotion to art as a birthright: born Ford

Madox Hueffer in 1873 (he changed his surname in 1919), he was the son of the German-born composer and music critic Francis Hueffer, a grandson of the Pre-Raphaelite artist Ford Madox Brown (who had been born in France), and a nephew of Dante Gabriel Rossetti (in his twenties he would publish biographical studies of both Brown and Rossetti), and was raised, as he once explained, "to believe that humanity divided itself into two classes – those who were creative artists and those who were merely the stuff to fill graveyards." (The maxim found its way into several of his books.) Indeed, as the English critic Alan Judd writes in his new biography,[1] Ford and his cousins "were intended for artistic and literary genius and were not supposed to be content with anything else."

From an early age, accordingly, Ford – who considered his childhood "moral torture," who grew up despising "the middle Victorian... bearded Great," and whose immense productivity may owe something to an overachiever mentality induced by his family's partiality to his older brother, Oliver – set about creating. When his classmates at the Praetorius School in Folkestone proceeded to university, Ford began publishing his first books: a fairy story at seventeen, a novel at eighteen, a collection of poems at nineteen. By age twenty, he had published five volumes. Not that his life was all writing: at twenty he married one Elsie Martindale, by whom he fathered two daughters, and with whom he lived for a dozen-odd years in Kent (where his friends and neighbors included Henry James, H. G. Wells, Stephen Crane, and Joseph Conrad), then in Sussex and London (where he suffered a nervous breakdown and, in 1908–9, edited the short-lived *English Review*); in 1910, estranged from Elsie, he moved for a time to Germany, where he secured an invalid divorce and an equally invalid marriage to his mistress, the writer Violet Hunt (who, in a highly publicized case, was sued by Elsie for using Ford's name), and became involved, during the months before the First World War, in the Imagist movement. Shell-shocked in the Battle of the Somme, he was separated from Violet and in the years *entre deux guerres* lived with one Stella Bowen (by whom he had a third daughter), conducted an affair with the writer Jean Rhys, and then

1. *Ford Madox Ford*, by Alan Judd; Harvard University Press.

began a long-term relationship with the artist Janice Biala, with whom he lived during the twenties in Toulon and Paris (where he edited the *transatlantic review* in 1924 – 25) and during the thirties in both France and America, becoming a writer in residence and then an honorary professor at Michigan's Olivet College.

It was a crowded and colorful life, during which Ford – a large, stocky man noted for his sensitivity, sentimentality, snobbishness, generosity, and Francophilia – lived for decades at the center of the literary world, taking walks in the Kentish countryside with James, sitting in Paris cafés with Hemingway, and exchanging witty letters with Pound (who addressed him as "Old Fordie" and "Gruberroruntopus"). But his principal activity was always writing: throughout his life he was a veritable book factory, churning out everything from art-critical monographs like *Hans Holbein* and *The Pre-Raphaelite Brotherhood* to literary-critical omnibuses with such titles as *The English Novel: From the Earliest Days to Joseph Conrad* and *The March of Literature from Confucius' Day to Our Own*, from historical romances like *The Portrait* (which takes place during the reign of George I) and *A Little Less Than Gods* (which is set in Napoleonic times) to such modern-dress novels as *Mr. Fleight* (a political satire that at times recalls Trollope's *Phineas Finn*), *A Call* (a high-society confection in pseudo-Jamesian prose), and *Vive le Roy* (a thriller whose broadly sardonic treatment of its American-in-Paris protagonist reminds one of Sinclair Lewis). During the first decade of the century, moreover, Ford collaborated with Conrad – whom he revered, and from whom he claimed to have "learned all I know of Literature" – on two light novels, *The Inheritors* and *Romance* (a third, *The Nature of a Crime,* composed during the same period, was not published as a book until 1924), and during the next decade collaborated on two nonfiction books, *The Desirable Alien* and *Zeppelin Nights,* with Violet Hunt.

Ford wrote so many now-forgotten novels, indeed, that one approaches them with the thought that somewhere in so large a body of work by a man capable of writing *The Good Soldier* and *Parade's End* must be an undiscovered treasure. Unfortunately, this does not appear to be the case. Most of these novels, whether historical or contemporary, are run-of-the-mill specimens of the popular fiction of the day, the characters slickly conceived, the prose merely serviceable, the vision routine. The most remarkable thing about them is that a man who wrote one of the most extraordinary novels of the century could have written so many downright ordinary ones. Among the many things an American reader, anyway, takes note of is that, while *The Good Soldier*'s narrator is a thoroughly convincing Philadelphian, several of Ford's other novels feature less plausible stateside characters who speak largely in slangy Americanisms. (A few lines of dialogue on a single page of *When the Wicked Man,* for instance, contain the following locutions: "swell," "darned," "lousy," "kid," "No, siree!", "the works," "a mighty long offing," and "hired dicks.")

Some of Ford's minor novels, to be sure, have their champions. But his most accomplished work of fiction, other than *The Good Soldier* and *Parade's End,* may be his trilogy *The Fifth Queen* (1906−8), which centers on Henry VIII's penultimate wife, Katharine Howard, and which Conrad called "the swan song of historical romance." Ford did not choose this subject lightly: he had long been interested in Henry VIII, whose reign he saw as marking the start of the modern world and of whom he once intended to write a biography; it was during the reign of Henry VIII, he argued in his book *The Spirit of the People,* that England was transformed from Europe's "laughingstock" into its "arbiter." Ford's entire literary career might be understood as an attempt to understand the meaning of the words *modern* and *English,* and in the Katharine Howard trilogy he plainly attempts to imagine some of the human drama behind the founding of modern England; it is not surprising, therefore, that the trilogy is considerably more serious and substantial than most of his other historical efforts. If a later Tudor-era novel, *The Young Lovell* (1913), reads like a bad imitation of Sir Walter Scott − its action improbable, its characters (among them a witch with a crutch) ludicrously picturesque, and its attempt at period language clumsy, self-conscious, and artificial − *The Fifth Queen* and its successors, *Privy Seal* and *The Fifth Queen Crowned,* are composed in a rich, fastidious style that effectively but undistractingly suggests the English of the day, and contain a number of compelling characters. Chief among them is Henry's Privy Seal, Thomas Cromwell, whom Ford considered "the great man" of the Tudor period, and who in his view "wedded England into one formidable whole" and instituted the pragmatic methods of government that the men under Queen Elizabeth would successfully follow. The trilogy offers arresting glimpses of England on the verge of modernity, with Catholic patterns of thought giving way to Protestant ones and an old man's reverence for the knightly code of honor giving way to the Machiavellian thinking of younger men.

Yet the trilogy has a major failing, and it lies in the heroine herself – a flat character who sees moral issues in black and white, who tends to react rather than to act, and whose intense allegiance to the Old Faith (which supposedly motivates her every action) doesn't convince. Ford's queen is rather difficult to square with the historical record: though the real Katharine was the aristocratic niece of Thomas Howard, Duke of Norfolk, and was probably guilty of the debauchery for which she was beheaded, Ford sees her as an exceedingly pious, naïve, and saintly country girl who is taken aback by the intrigues at court and especially by the sneaky behavior of the cleric, Bishop Stephen Gardiner, whom she has long revered. Strangely enough, however, Ford also sees her as cocky, hot-tempered, scheming, and murderous – and the two sides don't quite fit together. If Katharine is very aware of social station, moreover, referring to Cromwell scornfully as a "brewer's son," she is also weirdly indifferent to the rank of the king and his handlers. Reading *The Fifth Queen,* one wonders about one thing after another: Why does Katharine, of all people, become a focus of conspiracy for everyone immediately upon her arrival at court? What, given all that her fellow Catholics have suffered during Henry's reign, is going through her head when she speaks recklessly to the king's men, and why does she take so long to realize that to behave impudently with them is to play with fire? What, when she agrees to urge Princess Mary to write a controversial letter to her cousin the emperor, are Katharine's motives? Admiration for the king? Her Catholic faith? Her enmity for Cromwell? The answer is far from clear. The king, on the other hand, is complex and convincing, and Ford does a fine job, especially in Henry's case, of showing how the "hard world" drives essentially good natures to harsh deeds. Though the plot of *The Fifth Queen* is, ultimately, no less silly and contrived than that of many of Ford's historical romances, it often rises considerably above the level of those books.

PERHAPS FORD's least familiar writing is his poetry, several collections of which appeared over the years; volumes entitled *Collected Poems* were published in 1913 and 1936. Ford was far from a great poet, but the clarity, directness, and precision of his best prose and verse strongly influenced the doctrines of Imagism, which in turn played a pivotal role in the development of modern poetry. "I would rather talk about poetry with Ford Madox Hueffer than with any man in London," said Pound, who credited Ford with the Imagist principle that "poetry must be *as well written as prose.*" Ford's own attitude toward his verse is elucidated in the preface to his earlier *Collected Poems:*

> the writing of verse hardly appears to me to be a matter of work: it is a process, as far as I am concerned, too uncontrollable. From time to time words in verse have come into my head and I have written them down, quite powerlessly and without much interest, under the stress of certain emotions.

This is not, shall we say, a deeply serious poet speaking. Given Ford's nonchalance in these matters, however, it is surprising that some of his poems are as good as they are. Ford's poems range from a few lines to several pages in length, and take a variety of forms: there are sonnets, *vers libre* dialogues, Yeatsian "songs" in multiple voices, lyrics of love and war. These poems tend toward the loose and talky, and are most often gentle, civilized, and rather sad, the most characteristic tone being a sort of worldly wistfulness. Even Ford's war verse, as illustrated by these lines from *Poems Written on Active Service* about a troop-train ride through the English countryside, is rarely bitter or cynical:

> Running between the green and the grain
> Something like the peace of God
> Descended over the hum and the drone
> Of the wheels and the wine and the buzz of the talk.
> And one thought:
> "In two days' time we enter the Unknown,
> And this is what we die for!"

For what do we die? For what do we live? These questions are not far from the surface of many a Ford poem, including "On Heaven," which at several pages' length envisions paradise (which he situates in Provence). Time and again, Ford ponders the purpose of life's struggle, now with a Kiplingesque muscularity ("Yes, what's the use of striving on? / And what's to show all is done?") and now with a Hardyesque homeliness: "better / To lie for ever, a warm slug-a-bed / Or to rise up and bide by Fate and Chance, / The rawness of the morning...?" Perhaps Ford's poetry is best read alongside typical examples of the minor late-Victorian verse against which he and his Imagist cronies were rebelling; to see it in such a context is to appreciate the freshness of his language and the naturalness of his rhythms.

On the whole, Ford's nonfiction books have probably held up better than his fiction and poetry. Some, to be sure, are as lackluster as any of his novels: *Henry James* (1914), for instance, is a textbook example of slapdash writing by a man who, despite his veneration of the Master, would seem to have had little to say about him. But Ford also wrote some fine nonfiction books, and some that, though less than fine, are intermittently interesting and well written. (As Ezra Pound once lamented, much of Ford's best writing is buried here and there in books no one reads.) Some of the finest of these volumes are about places Ford knew and enjoyed, from southern England (*The Cinque Ports*) and southern France (*Provence*) to parts of the eastern United States (*New York Is Not America*). Though these books vary considerably in approach and quality, they all contain evocative descriptions of town and/or country and interesting (if often factitious) historical details and anecdotes about the natives. In all these books Ford conveys his genuine affection for these places, and also communicates a fervent desire to come off as a man of the world, a fellow who would feel at home in a Paris café, a Sussex alehouse, or a Tennessee plantation manse, and who is fluent in the more important modern languages. Often, alas, Ford's tireless attempts to establish his worldliness succeed only in demonstrating the opposite. In his memoir *Return to Yesterday* (1931), for instance, he makes simple mistakes in Spanish and German; just as some of his novels, moreover, go overboard on Americanisms, so his nonfiction books have more than their share of glib generalizations about the States, and of broad, highly debatable Anglo-American contrasts: "In England it is the land that counts first: in America, it has seemed to me it was the people."

Reading in a book like *The Great Trade Route* (1937) – an astonishingly quirky grab bag of observations about Western civilization that takes as its *point d'appui* a 1934–35 transatlantic journey by Ford and Janice Biala – one can hardly imagine anyone other than Ford writing such a thing: like much of his work, it is both elegant and effusive, charming and outrageously self-indulgent. Perhaps more typical of Ford's better nonfiction, however, are three books that appeared in America as one volume entitled *England and the English*. Leisurely and engaging, low on careful research and fact-checking and high on personality and personal impressions, the books read like a series of ladies' club monologues by a garrulous Edwardian man of letters. If *The Soul of London* (1905) seeks, by means of descriptions of trams and tramps and of quotations from bus drivers, to convey the feel of the British metropolis, *The Heart of the Country* (1906) meticulously evokes the picturesque English countryside and the conversation of rustic folk. Perhaps the most interesting volume of the three is *The Spirit of the People* (1907), wherein Ford seeks to define the nature of the English character. The Englishman's foremost virtue, Ford notes in these pages, is his "general good nature" – his tolerance, optimism, respect for the law, lack of vengefulness; "in no other nature," Ford writes, "are so many of the civic and the practical virtues so worked into the mystical code of life." The Englishman's "great defect," meanwhile, is his "want of sympathetic imagination." These ideas about the English would find their way into both *The Good Soldier* and *Parade's End*.

Particularly worth noting, in light of the role of religion in Ford's best fiction, are his remarks about the Englishman's relation to God. "The English official Deity," he writes, "is a just God. But . . . just in the sense only that He rewards the good. The evil He lets slip by him, as the Englishman, remarking 'poor devil,' would let most impotent sinners escape punishment." Ford, who joined the Roman Catholic Church at seventeen – because, said his friend Olive Garnett, he "found poetry in it" and sought "relief from the gospel of perfect indifference to everything" – and who identified himself sometimes as a Catholic and sometimes as an agnostic, is of course talking here about members of the Church of England (as Christopher Tietjens observes in *Parade's End,* Roman Catholics in England are "not quite English"); he even goes so far as to state that Anglicans share a frame of mind and not a religion . . . in which, though the ethical basis of Christianity is more or less excellently preserved, the theological conditions remain in a very fragmentary condition. . . . [T]he Englishman is hardly religious at all, since it is not so much the supernatural as the human side of the Deity that has a daily significance for him.

Ford's focus here is less on Anglicanism, *per se*, than on the English attitude toward religion that helped to shape the national church and that has in turn been partly shaped by it; he aims, in other words, not to denigrate a faith but to understand the psychology of a people. Ford—who was often accused of being more sympathetic to France or Germany than to England, and who professed in a memoir never to have "had a very strong sense of nationality at all," though many of his books reflect a preoccupation with the idea of national identity—quite rightly saw Anglicanism as a clue to the character of his native land. The differences between Anglicanism and Roman Catholicism figure significantly in his novels: *The Fifth Queen, The Good Soldier,* and *Parade's End* all feature married couples in which the husband is an Anglican and the wife a Roman Catholic, the sectarian distinctions in each case reflecting, among other things, a certain divergence of mind and spirit between the two parties.

I F A C H I E F M E R I T of Ford's nonfiction is his ability to convey vivid impressions of people and places, one of its great defects is his casual way with factual detail. Ford had little regard for facts, which he routinely denigrated at the expense of subjective impressions. In his later years, he wrote several books of reminiscence—notably *Return to Yesterday* (1931) and *It Was the Nightingale* (1933)—and sometimes combined reminiscence with criticism and biography, as in *Joseph Conrad: A Personal Remembrance* (1924). Manifestly, Ford's goal in each of these books is not to record objective historical data for posterity but to capture, page by page, the feel of various events and encounters. To read a book like *It Was the Nightingale* is to recognize how much Ford influenced Hemingway; for here, as in *A Moveable Feast,* one enters the author's life and consciousness *in medias res* and meanders with him, as it were, through the streets of 1920s Paris, dropping in with him at sundry cafés and ateliers and listening in on his conversations with artists and writers. The style is graceful, the tone intimate and chatty; it is assumed that we are familiar with the lineaments of Ford's career, that we know he lived in such-and-such a place at such-and-such a time, and that he associated with certain immortals of art and literature (whom he generally introduces by their surnames).

There is a good deal of braggadocio in these books: Ford takes pains to let us know how familiar he was with the luminaries and hot spots of the day, to inform us that he gave Conrad the idea for *The Secret Agent* and wrote part of *Nostromo*, and to convince us that he was more famous than he really was. But his egoism is balanced by a willingness to tell stories on himself, by a real interest in other creative folk, and by a deep reverence for the literary art: "The only human activity that has always been of extreme importance to the world is imaginative literature. It is of supreme importance because it is the only means by which humanity can express at once emotions and ideas." Science? "I have always entertained the most vivid distrust for the scientific mind." Politics? "I never took any stock in politics." As for politics in literature, "Galsworthy believed that humanity could be benefited by propaganda for virtue of a Christian order whereas I believed that humanity can only be brought to ameliorate itself if life as it is is presented in terms of an art. And the business of art is not to elevate humanity but to render." Among those writers who rendered to Ford's satisfaction were James and Conrad; but his gallery of admired writers also includes some names less familiar today, among them W. H. Hudson, Miss Braddon (the author of *East Lynne*), and George Moore.

Ford's memoirs are notorious for their factual unreliability, but this characteristic doubtless owes much to his readiness to alter details so that an anecdote might convey, by his lights, a more authentic impression. As Horace Gregory and Marya Zaturenska once wrote, Ford's recollections "must not be accepted for their literal truth but for their flashes of an essential, one might almost say poetic, validity." On one occasion, for instance, Ford remarked that his latest book had sold twelve thousand copies when it had sold only twelve hundred; he afterward explained the prevarication by saying that his interlocutor had known little about publishing, and would not appreciate precisely what a success the book had been unless the sales figure were multiplied by ten. The point: facts have their place, but in order to impart to an audience the character of a person, the dimensions of an object, or the flavor of an experience – in order, that is, to capture the *truth* – it is often necessary to alter the mere facts; such, indeed, is the essence of art. As Alan Judd says, "Ford's eye is on the right effect, not the right fact. . . . [He was] always prepared to create in order to get the right effect." (That it might not be ethically defensible to treat facts this way in a casual conversation as if it were a work of art, in which the creator's right to deceive is tacitly accepted by both parties, does not seem to have bothered Ford overmuch.)

Though it is intended as a serious critical history, Ford's baggy valedictory volume, *The March of Literature* (1938), has much in common with his impressionistic memoirs. Crammed with dubious literary anecdotes and gratuitous autobiographical references (the only difference is that Ford speaks not of "I" or "me" but of "this writer"), this chatty 878-page tome is nonetheless largely redeemed by Ford's real passion for the writers he discusses, by the liveliness of his prose, by the soundness of much of his critical commentary, and by his willingness to express and defend his strong and often idiosyncratic views. (Sample: "Except perhaps for Jane Austen, [Trollope] is the greatest of all specifically English novelists. He is less of an artist than she but he is male, and that counts.") Throughout these pages, Ford comes off as a "village explainer" in the Pound mold, quirky and tangent-happy, a bit condescending, perhaps, toward his intended audience of common readers but sincere in his zeal to acquaint them with the transcendent works of world literature. (Ford was never a critic, really, so much as he was a promoter of things he liked, who could explain sensitively and intelligently why he liked them.) Less self-indulgent – but also less compelling – is Ford's posthumous *A History of Our Own Times* (1988), the first of three projected volumes that covers the years 1870–95, charting such developments as the rise of American industry and the partition of Africa. Why did Ford choose to write about such matters? "We seek," he explains, "to know not only the state of our world in our own time but how it has arrived at the state in which it finds itself." Yet even this book begins with a personal impression: "mention to me the British Raj . . . in India and I will at once see myself being a small boy dragged along unwillingly by an irresistible nurse's hand – I will still see a poster that I was not allowed to look at for long enough because of my nurse's impatience. It represented a fat man in a fez, falling to the ground, his feet above his head. He was Arabi Pasha."

IT IS SAID that a writer is as good as his best book, but Ford did not get off lightly for writing so many mediocre ones. Generous though he was to writers whose talent he respected, many of those whom he most admired did not take him very seriously as an author. In *Henry James*, Ford lauded James as "the greatest of living writers and in consequence, for me, the greatest of living men," but James never even bothered to read the book. Conrad, whose genius Ford tirelessly trumpeted, mocked the seriousness with which he took their collaborations. And Hemingway repaid Ford (who had employed him as assistant editor of the *transatlantic review*) by describing him in *A Moveable Feast* as a rather preposterous literary snob who, in his physical grossness, resembled "a well-clothed, up-ended hogshead." Yet that hogshead was the author of a greater novel than Hemingway would ever write. *The Good Soldier*, first published in 1915 and set in Germany, does not even mention the First World War; yet in the sense that it is about estrangement and betrayal, about barriers that can never be crossed, and about the ways in which people destroy themselves and others, it might fairly be described as a "war novel." The book centers on the nine-year friendship of two well-to-do middle-aged couples who live in Europe and spend part of every year in the German resort city of Nauheim. John Dowell, a Philadelphia Quaker, and his wife, the former Florence Hurlbird of Massachusetts, stay in the city, famous for its salt springs, because Florence has a "heart" (that is, cardiac problems); their friends, Captain Edward Ashburnham, an English Anglican, and his wife Leonora (née Powys), an Irish Catholic, come to Nauheim because Edward too has a "heart." Dowell, the book's narrator, describes the friendship as "a young middle-aged affair" between two couples of "quite quiet dispositions"; the four of them were "quite good people," he says, and together they shared "nine years of uninterrupted tranquillity."

Those years of tranquility, however, ended in Florence's and Edward's suicides, and it is Dowell's aim, writing during the months following those deaths, to try to make sense of them. This is not easy, for when he thinks about the Ashburnhams now, he realizes (as he admits on the novel's first page) that in a sense he "knew nothing at all about them." Indeed, four pages later he acknowledges further that "I know nothing—nothing in the world of the hearts of men." Twenty-nine pages after this he is asserting that such ignorance is general: "After forty-five years of mixing with one's kind, one ought to have acquired the habit of being able to know something about one's fellow beings. But one doesn't." And he repeats this contention again and again. On page 155: "Who in the world knows anything of any other heart—or of his own?" On page 203: "the human heart is a very mysterious thing." Needless to say, the human heart does not figure here only as a circulatory organ. Its mystery is one of Ford's constant themes (in a poem entitled "Old Man's Evensong," he laments that "I shall never utter the uttermost secrets aright, / They lie so deep"), and it is clear that he agrees with Dowell that the heart's congenital unknowability is aggravated by "the modern civilized habit—the modern English habit—of taking everyone for granted," a habit that afflicts certain civilized Americans of English ancestry, like the Dowells, as surely as it does the English themselves. People like himself and Edward, Dowell says, peg each other on first sight as "good people," and fail to look much further; it is for this reason, he suggests, that he was able to remain friends with the Ashburnhams for nine years without realizing that Florence, whose allegedly weak heart had supposedly prevented the consummation of their marriage, was all the time deceiving him about her health (which was, in fact, fine) and was, as Leonora knew, having an affair with Edward—who was also perfectly healthy, and whose affair with Florence was bookended by infatuations with other women.

Yet Ford signals to us constantly that, for all the validity of Dowell's observations about the heart's mystery, there may well be more to this story than meets Dowell's eye—or, more precisely, than he is willing to see. To be sure, the novel can be read "straight," and Dowell's version of events accepted (as it is by Ford's biographer Arthur Mizener) as the truth, the whole truth, and nothing but the truth. But as one reads along, one begins to suspect otherwise – to suspect, that is, that Dowell is an unreliable narrator, unreliable less by virtue of any conscious desire to deceive the reader than by virtue of an unconscious desire to deceive himself. Ford seems to be throwing out plenty of hints that Dowell is working with a world-class set of defense mechanisms: after going on about Florence for pages, Dowell insists that he has "never given her another thought" since her death; of his nine years with her and the Ashburnhams, he says "I don't know how we put in our time." His repeated references to "poor Leonora," "poor Florence," and "poor Edward" suggest that he needs desperately to insist upon the other characters' piteousness in order to keep from feeling unbearably pathetic himself; and his contention that Florence hid an earlier affair from him only because a honeymoon tantrum made her fear his temper is hard not to read as a cuckold's feeble bid at salvaging a little self-respect. The book, Dowell informs us, is several months in the writing, and over the course of that period his testimony undergoes a discernible shift: in the opening pages he says of Florence that "I don't believe that for one minute she was out of my sight, except when she was safely tucked up in bed"; later, though, he corrects himself: Florence was, he now realizes, out of his sight "most of the time." He can even contradict himself from one page to the next: immediately after describing life with the Ashburnhams as tranquil, he describes it as "a prison full of screaming hysterics."

What did Dowell know and when did he know it? He insists that it was not until after Florence's death that he learned about her affair with Edward; and indeed he consoles himself with the thought that the real truth of the matter lay not in the disagreeable facts that were unknown to him but in his far more pleasant, if mistaken, impression: "If for nine years I have possessed a goodly apple that is rotten at the core and discover its rottenness only in nine years and six months less four days, isn't it true to say that for nine years I possessed a goodly apple?" Yet one gradually comes to suspect that, on some level, Dowell knew for a long time about Florence's infidelity. Consider the visit to Marburg that the two couples take early in the friendship. During the visit, Dowell says, Leonora became visibly upset, which frightened him; he assumed, he says, that Leonora was jealous of Florence and Edward, and he was much relieved when, seemingly about to reveal something to him, she proved to be upset about something else. The reader can conclude only that what Dowell feared was being confronted with facts about Florence and Edward that he didn't want to acknowledge to himself or to have to deal with.

This is not to say that Dowell has absolutely no self-knowledge: his awareness that his subconscious mind has kept certain things hidden from him is indicated by his reference, at one point, to the "inner self" or "dual personality" that "had realized long before that Florence was a personality of paper." Nor does Ford mean to single Dowell out or ridicule him; on the contrary, we are meant to understand that Dowell differs from the rest of us only in degree, not in kind, and that, as even Dowell himself notes in passing, certain "delusions are necessary to keep us going." Defense mechanisms exist for a reason, after all, and self-deception is not necessarily a bad thing: in a sense, the truth is what one's conscious mind thinks it sees, rather than the objective reality to which it is blind. In any event, Ford's purpose here is not to pass some kind of rudimentary moral judgment on his narrator but to *render*. And his method of rendering is a highly impressionistic one; Dowell rambles back and forth in time as one event reminds him of another or inspires comment, and returns to certain events again and again, often changing his testimony. As he says, "when one discusses an affair – a long, sad affair – one goes back, one goes forward. One remembers points that one has forgotten and one explains them all the more minutely since one recognizes that one has forgotten to mention them in their proper places and that one may have given, by omitting them, a false impression." Certainly Ford's selection of such a narrative technique for *The Good Soldier* would appear to point to the fact that the operation of Dowell's mind is very much a principal theme of the book, and that one of the things Ford seeks to render here is the complexity of the human psyche. That one can know and not know something; that, on one level of the mind, one can discover and be devastated by something that one has long known about on another level; that the hearts even of those whom one thinks one knows intimately can be such a mystery that one can discover essential facts about them that shake one to one's very core; and that even when one has confronted and supposedly accepted certain facts, one can continue to deceive oneself, to play subconscious interpretive games: these are among the aspects of human psychology that lie at the heart of *The Good Soldier*. One might almost say that in its preoccupation with the obstacles to human knowledge the novel is a deconstructionist's dream, except that it could not be further in spirit from the romantic nihilism of Derrida and his disciples: implicit on every page is the notion that people matter, that their feelings matter, and that, however formidable a task it may seem, one ought never to cease striving earnestly for meaning and for a more nearly perfect communion with one's fellow man.

ALL OF WHICH rather begs the question: if Dowell blinded himself to Florence's infidelity, why did he do so? There are no unequivocal answers to this question – indeed, Ford doesn't offer the reader any more certainty about the ultimate psychological facts of the case than he offers Dowell – but there is much here to ponder. When Dowell first knew her, for instance, Florence "faintly hinted" that "she did not want much physical passion" in marriage, and her aunts hinted (less faintly) that she was no fit match for "a good young man." Yet Dowell gives no indication of having hesitated to marry her. Why? Did he want a wife who would make no sexual demands and/or betray him? The first suggestion that she had a "heart" came during the Atlantic crossing on their honeymoon, when she feigned cardiac pains and Dowell became her uncomplaining nurse: "in the retaining of her in this world I had my occupation, my career, my ambition." (Yet later he claims that "What I wanted mostly was to cease being a nurse-attendant.") Was he, in some odd way, using Florence just as she was using him? He boasts of "the cleanness of my thoughts and the absolute chastity of my life." Did he marry Florence so that he could lead a sexless existence and experience passion vicariously? If so, what does this say about his feelings toward Edward? For surely one of the most striking things about the novel is the contrast between how Dowell speaks of Florence and how he speaks of Edward. For her he shows little affection: "Florence was vulgar; Florence was a common flirt." To be sure, he says of her and the Ashburnhams that "I cannot think any of them wicked," and reflects that she and Edward "were only poor wretches creeping over this earth in the shadow of an eternal wrath." Yet a page later he is vicious: "I hate Florence. I hate Florence with such a hatred that I would not spare her an eternity of loneliness." Only once, in a very curious passage, does he speak of passionate love for a woman: "the real fierceness of desire, the real heat of a passion long continued and withering up the soul of a man, is the craving for identity with the woman that he loves. He desires to see with the same eyes, to touch with the same sense of touch, to hear with the same ears, to lose his identity, to be enveloped, to be supported."

If Dowell had touched with Florence's hands, of course, he would have touched Edward – who is, as it happens, the object of far more affection than anyone else in the book. Edward had, Dowell tells us, "all the virtues that are usually accounted English": he was "a splendid fellow . . . upright, honest, fair-dealing, fair-thinking," who "carried himself well, was moderate at the table, and led a regular life." He had the English failings also, the principal one being that "there was too much of the sentimentalist about him " – though this fact doesn't diminish our narrator's devotion to his memory, for Dowell (himself an imitation Englishman) is sentimental as well. On the contrary, Dowell's affection for Edward is "so intense that even to this day I cannot think of Edward without sighing" (a remark one recalls later when Dowell, professing to have loved a young woman called Nancy, adds that "I don't mean to say that I sighed about her or groaned" but rather that "I wanted to marry her as some people want to go to Carcassonne"). Are we meant to gather from all this that Dowell's feelings for Edward fall under the category of the love that dare not speak its name? I think not; more likely, we are meant to recognize that serious bonds between human beings take all forms, and that sexuality, in some cases, is largely beside the point. As Dowell himself says: "Of the question of the sex instinct I know very little and I do not think that it counts for very much in a really great passion." One cannot but be reminded of Ford's own life: apparently all his romantic partners were women, but accounts by intimates have suggested that his friendships with certain men, notably Conrad, were as important to him as his marriage or affairs, and that given a choice between sexual and verbal intercourse he would have chosen the latter. "[T]alk," Alan Judd writes, "was to him the final communion of souls." (One suspects that he felt similarly about literary collaboration.) It might be said, indeed, that one of the subjects of this novel is the relation of sexuality to true human intimacy; and there can be little question but that Ford was considerably more interested in the latter than the former.

One of the exceptional things about *The Good Soldier* is the way its sad story hovers at the brink of absurdity without ever crossing it. Push Dowell a bit further and he turns from a man of great interest and sympathy into a caricature of an otiose, imperturbable Edwardian cuckold. Nor is he the book's only near-absurdity. "It's odd," says someone in Ford's novel *An English Girl* (1907), "how absurd coincidences – silly synchronisations – get into one's life." *The Good Soldier* contains a set of "synchronisations" that are, objectively speaking, highly improbable: over the years between 1899 and 1913, we learn, many key events in Florence's life occurred on her birthday, the fourth of August (which, though Dowell never mentions it, was the date in 1914 on which Britain declared war on Germany). Yet these synchronizations exert a dramatic force that has something, at least, to do with the date's reminder that it is not only for Dowell that life is a matter of tragic detonations lying in wait, of moments in which years are shattered and long ties sundered. Also effective is the book's German setting, which provides a foreign backdrop for Ford's portrayal of the English (and Anglo-American) character in action, and, with war imminent, underlines how quickly friendly turf can become enemy territory.

What's more, Germany is the birthplace of Protestantism, whose breach with Rome Leonora pronounces the "cause of . . . the whole sorrow of the world." It is at Marburg, Dowell reminds us, that "the Reformer [Luther] and his friends met for the first time under the protection of the gentleman that had three wives at once [the landgrave of Hesse] and formed an alliance with the gentleman that had six wives, one after the other [Henry VIII]." It is no coincidence that there is a tacit parallel here between Henry VIII and Edward (an Englishman who has had several extramarital sweethearts in a row) and between the landgrave and Dowell (a Quaker with Pennsylvania Dutch ties who says he would like to be a polygamist). The mention of Henry VIII is especially germane, for Ford sees a significant irony in the fact that modern England and the modern English church – which are personified here by the high-minded, womanizing Edward Ashburnham – had their origin in a high-minded, womanizing king, at once brilliant, devout, and brutal, who wanted a divorce. To Ford, there is a continuum between the psychological and moral complexities of Henry VIII and those of the modern English gentleman, the principled, pietistic, and empire-building "good soldier" who believes in marriage and discreet philandering, who honors his wife and expects the same in return, and who accepts hypocrisy as one of the prices of civilization. (In *Parade's End,* Tietjens says of "good people" in England that "We're always, as it were, committing adultery . . . with the name of Heaven on our lips.") No wonder, then, that Leonora laments the Reformation: in an England more like Catholic Europe, Dowell observes, a woman in her position would secure a divorce "for two hundred dollars paid in the right quarter" and Edward would eventually become a tramp or marry a barmaid.

The Good Soldier has often been viewed as social criticism, and interpreted as an indictment of the "modern" English sensibility embodied by Edward on the brink of the war that would finish it off and make it seem distinctly old-fashioned. Yet it is more accurate, I think, to speak of the novel as a critical consideration of that sensibility which recognizes both its good and bad qualities. For, his criticisms of modern England and Anglicanism notwithstanding, Ford's fiction never seems polemical on the subject. On the contrary, the modern English sensibility comes across throughout as profoundly complex in its morality; the tragedy of *The Good Soldier,* indeed, is that Edward really did manifest many sterling (and distinctively English) qualities, and that they were well-nigh inseparable from those distinctively English failings wherein lay the seeds of his destruction. On a higher level, furthermore, the novel is not merely about the social upheavals of a particular historical moment, or even about the English national character, but about the abiding paradoxes of the human mind and human relations; it is a novel in which the Reformation becomes a striking emblem of the painful divisions that Dowell is lamenting when he says: "We are all so afraid, we are all so alone, we all so need from the outside the assurance of our own worthiness to exist." It is, indeed, a wonder of a novel, whose shape, pace, and tone are right on target: like a virtuoso actor in a role he was born to play, Ford creates a narrator whose every gesture and comment, and every leap from one time frame to another, strikes one as totally authentic, and whose voice, perfect in pitch and rhythm, Ford finds in his first sentence and never loses. Ford is a master here at the impressionistic ordering of effects: throughout the book one feels that one is inside not merely another world but another consciousness, and Ford generates interest and builds suspense by peeling away the layers of that consciousness.

Parade's End is also notable for its impressionistic ordering, though the general movement in all four novels is conventionally linear. Most impressive in this regard is the first volume, *Some Do Not . . .* (1924), whose third-person narration shifts its focus from one individual to another and digresses from the main story line into the characters' musings or memories and back again with the fluidity and stateliness of a classical symphony. The characters' consciousnesses are richly rendered and beautifully differentiated, their relations to and impressions of each other convincingly set forth, and their upper-class, prewar milieu evoked with remarkable effectiveness and economy, so that, even as the story is developing and the tension rising, the reader obtains a wonderfully rich sense of the protagonist and the world he inhabits. That protagonist is Christopher Tietjens, the very model of an English gentleman, gallant and generous, temperate and proper, his mind "a perfect encyclopaedia of exact material knowledge," his character exceptionally free of envy and rancor (though he has the usual prejudices of his time and class); the youngest son of a Yorkshire gentleman, he has "never lied or [done] a dishonorable thing in his life." He belongs to the "class [that] administer[s] the world": when the tetralogy begins in 1912, he is a bright and promising twenty-six-year-old official in the Imperial Department of Statistics ("He was without ambition, but these things would come to him as they do in England") and is headed for Germany to retrieve his beautiful and selfish wife, Sylvia, who has run off with another man. It is Tietjens's very near-perfection that drove Sylvia to adultery; he is too Christ-like for her (it is no coincidence that his name means "bearer of Christ"), and she is rankled by his readiness to forgive: "there is only one man from whom a woman could take 'Neither I condemn thee' and not hate him more than she hates the fiend! . . ." Such resentment of rectitude helps to explain why, in the ensuing months and years, Tietjens becomes "overwhelmed by foul and baseless rumours" that depict him as the lover of a young suffragette named Valentine Wannop and Sylvia as an injured wife. As Ford observes: "It is, in fact, asking for trouble if you are more altruist than the society that surrounds you." (Just ask his Katharine Howard.)

It is a society that is embarrassed by emotion, a society where one is known by the whiskey one serves and judged by which Oxford or Cambridge college one attended, a society where one's reputation can be ruined by a single bounced check. Ford does a magnificent job of steering Tietjens through this world – introducing him, in turn, into the company of artistic, political, religious, and military figures – and showing how his marital situation affects his membership in what his friend Macmaster calls "the circumspect classes." Underscoring the distance between the supposedly lofty moral code of these classes and the base values and motives that really govern their actions (and that make it possible for a guileful mediocrity like Macmaster to win a knighthood), the novel also makes it clear that what sets Tietjens apart – and makes him at times, for all his intelligence and nobility, seem maddeningly foolish and naïve – is that he actually takes the code seriously, and tries, in his sober, literal-minded way, to live according to its precepts. The title *Some Do Not . . .* points to these qualities of character: when Tietjens exerts himself to save a carriage horse after an accident, the driver says he'd never do that "for no beast . . . Some do and some . . . do not"; likewise, when war comes and Tietjens, after being gravely wounded, tells a superior officer that he wants to be sent back to the front lines, the officer replies: "Some do. Some do not." As if to suggest, moreover, that the smart and upright Valentine, despite her scorn for Tietjens's Toryism (she calls him "a regular Admirable Crichton"), is a woman after his own heart, an old man on the street, spying her, says: "That's women! . . . Some do! . . . Some do not!"

One might call Tietjens a good soldier, and there are indeed a number of parallels between *Some Do Not . . .* and Ford's earlier novel. Here, as in *The Good Soldier,* Ford emphasizes the distance that exists between even close friends: though they have been mates for years, Macmaster knows "next to nothing" of Tietjens's feelings. (Sylvia's position on the subject, meanwhile, is that "To know everything about a person is to be bored . . . bored . . . bored!") If, like Dowell, Tietjens is a cuckold,

like Edward Ashburnham he is an Anglican whose soul is "at bottom
...perfectly direct, simple, and sentimental," and whose wife is a
rather frosty Roman Catholic of "good stock." Yet there are ways in
which Tietjens, unlike Edward, is less a modern Englishman than a medieval knight: at times, indeed, he seems at once too beleaguered, too
saintly, and too good-natured under fire to be easily believed, as if Ford
had not drawn him from life but from the list of manly virtues enumer-
ated in Kipling's "If" and from his own robust sense of being under-
appreciated by those around him. (Certainly the latter, and little else,
would seem to explain why so exemplary a man as Tietjens should have
such a shallow wife and best friend.) Nor does one believe in Tietjens's
love for Sylvia's son, who carries his name but is apparently not really
his.

In the remaining novels of the tetralogy, Ford spends more time
reading the characters' minds, and does it to rather less productive effect. Since he restricts himself more – centering in *No More Parades* on a
wartime encounter between Tietjens and Sylvia in Rouen, and in *A
Man Could Stand Up* on Tietjens and Valentine's 1918 romantic epiphany in London – these books seem less varied than *Some Do Not . . .*, the
minuetlike dance of perspectives in the initial volume, with its precise,
complex, and beautifully elaborated tensions and its vividly conveyed
impression of a broad and populous world, giving way here to succes-
sions of long, often slack and ellipsis-crowded passages in which the
reader feels immured in a character's mind, sometimes to absorbing and
sometimes to claustrophobic effect. Absent is the constant sense of psychological discovery that is such a remarkable feature of *The Good
Soldier.* Yet if one finds oneself feeling on occasion that one already
knows all there is to know about Tietjens, there is also much here of interest, especially in *No More Parades,* which offers a discerning look at
the paradoxical brew of emotions – hate and affection, contempt and
adulation – that can exist within a long-standing marriage, and at the
mysteries that can persist in such a relationship even after years of the utmost intimacy; a particular merit of this novel is that in its pages Sylvia
grows into a rounder and richer character, capable of passion, loyalty,
even love, a woman both poignant and utterly credible in her contradictions. The third and fourth books of the tetralogy represent a bit of a
falling-off: *A Man Could Stand Up* – suffers from the relative dullness of

Valentine as a character, and *The Last Post* (which is set in a country cottage during a few hours in the late twenties, and relates what became of Tietjens's marriage and his romance with Valentine) from a feeling that Ford is tying up loose ends with one hand and beating a dead horse with the other. Yet *Parade's End* as a whole is a marvelous achievement, a penetrating depiction of Tietjens's gradual adjustment – though not his capitulation – to the moral climate of the world he lives in. To read it is to take note of qualities that are rare in the flat, minimalistic fictions of our time: a fascination with the workings of the human mind, an intense awareness of the intricacy and mystery of human relations, and a passionate sense of the importance of moral character.

ALAN JUDD's biography of Ford is written in a chummy plain style that recalls one of Ford's own books of reminiscence. Indeed, there are many respects in which one is reminded of those books: now elegant, now glibly offhand ("Ford's failings are well known and have been reheated and served up many times"), Judd plunges into his material *in medias res*, proffering jaunty generalizations that show how worldly he is ("every Georgian in Paris was a prince in those days") and making a reader feel as if he has joined a circle of friends in midstory at a smart cosmopolitan cocktail party. Unlike Arthur Mizener, whose view of Ford's life is indicated by the title (*The Saddest Story*) of his bulky 1971 biography, Judd sees Ford's life as a tale of "the rich in spirit." Though he calls Mizener's book "thorough," Judd pointedly reminds us that Ford "hated academic biographies, feeling that they put in everything but what was important," and he doubtless thinks Ford would have liked his book better. He's probably right. He calls Ford's memoirs "a great rich unreliable tapestry which gives an impression of his life that no biographer could hope to equal," and his own book is an impressionistic tapestry that, while presumably more reliable, derives its value not from critical objectivity but from a forthrightly Fordian subjectivity that affords the reader an opportunity to view Ford from a new angle.

Ford was, Judd tells us, a "good club man," "a realist who wants to be an idealist," a "deeply unconventional" man who was also "a respecter of proprieties," a lover of good writing who was "prepared to worship" good writers, a man whom sixteen or seventeen doctors mysteriously diagnosed as suffering from "sexual abnormalities." Judd quotes Allen Tate on Ford's memory: "He said then that he had the entire novel [*The Good Soldier*] – every sentence – in his head before he began to write it in 1913. He had the most prodigious memory I have ever encountered in any man." Judd makes a number of percipient observations about the distinctive attributes of Ford's work and about the gifts and qualities of character that made the best of it possible. He points out, for instance, that Ford prefers not to deal directly with either sex or death, and suggests that Ford's avoidance of action scenes "may be symptomatic of Ford's own horror of 'scenes.'" He relates an anecdote that shows the novelist's sense of character in action: "Towards the end of their affair, Violet Hunt told him she had spent time at her cottage in Selsey with another man. Ford listened and then quietly re-created the conversation Violet had had with her admirer – according to her, almost word for word – on the basis of his knowledge of them both." Judd stresses the war's role in Ford's development, saying that after it "there was no longer any question as to the nature of his existence on earth. He had been through the fire and everything inessential had been burned off." He praises *The Good Soldier* but doesn't say much about it; he notes that *Parade's End* was supposedly inspired by Proust's funeral and draws an interesting parallel between Ford's tetralogy and Proust's masterwork. His main purpose would apparently be to draw attention to novels like *The Rash Act* (1933) and the autobiographical war story *No Enemy* (1929), both of which he considers very underrated, and to Ford's poems (several of which he quotes in their entirety, including the thirteen-page "On Heaven"), but he doesn't make a very convincing case for them. What Judd is best at, really, is the sort of sharp, nonacademic observation that would probably have pleased his subject. After quoting a passage from *The Fifth Queen,* for instance, he comments: "If you were an actor you would know from that scene how to play Henry." Above all, Judd's sense of Ford seems right on the money, and his admiration for Ford as both man and writer no less clear-eyed for being fervent. His book is a welcome homage to an artist who deserves a far larger audience than he has.

(MARCH 1991)

Baseless Dreaming:
the Novels of Graham Greene

In the firmament of contemporary international letters, there are a few select names that seem to trail clouds of glory everywhere they go. For literate folk around the world – even for literate folk who have never read a word of their writings – the names of such authors as Calvino and Borges have much the same iconic quality that names like Garbo and Gable continue to have for old-movie enthusiasts. As in the case of Hollywood stardom, furthermore, the extraordinary fame of these writers often has as much to do with nonaesthetic factors – among them personality, politics, public relations, and sheer serendipity – as with the actual breadth of their talents and the artistic value of their achievements.

In the English-speaking world, there is no one who belongs to this exclusive circle of authors more surely than Graham Greene; and that he, of all the English-language writers in his generation, should have achieved such eminence can only be described as remarkable. Now in his mid-eighties, Greene first attained a degree of celebrity, more than half a century ago, as an author of best-selling thrillers, if he was respected at all, it was not for his artistry but for his productivity, his ability to concoct entertaining light narratives, and his impressive sales figures. The story of how this young author of thrillers; developed an international reputation as one of the great writers of his time cannot help being a most instructive one – instructive, that is, in what it can tell us about the twentieth-century art of literary-career management, and (by extension) in what it can tell us about the peculiar values of Western literary culture in our time. As it happens, this is an especially appropriate time for a thoughtful consideration of Greene's literary career, for the Viking Press has recently published the capacious first volume of an authorized two-part biography of Greene, which takes him from his birth in 1904 to the outbreak of World War II; the book is by Norman Sherry, the writer of several studies of Joseph Conrad, Jane Austen, and the Brontës.[1]

Sherry is, indeed, such a splendid example of the sort of commentator who has helped to raise Greene's reputation to its present heights that it would be useful, I think, to examine his biography in some detail before proceeding to a discussion of Greene's career. Not that the casual bookstore browser need scrutinize this volume for long before deciding whether to buy it: on the contrary, he'll get a pretty good idea of what's coming from the very first paragraph. For the biography's main text begins with a highly unpromising agglomeration of detail about – what else? – the day of Greene's birth in 1904. "The second of October," Sherry informs us, "was a Sunday; the weather, after a cold and cloudy September, was fair; and according to his mother's entry in a sixpenny booklet entitled 'All About Baby' (produced by Steedman's of Walworth, Surrey, who manufactured soothing powders for children cutting their teeth, and illustrated with line drawings of some plump and rather sinister-looking young children), the boy was born at 10:20 a.m. and weighed 7½ lbs." Seven and a half pounds – got that? And so it goes: in the next few pages, Sherry provides for posterity the dates on which Greene wore his first short clothes, cut his first tooth, and so forth; the reader who looks forward to seven-hundred-odd pages of this sort of niggling detail will, alas, not be disappointed.

How was Sherry, of all people, recruited for this momentous project? In a chatty preface, he informs us proudly that he was chosen by Greene himself – and chosen not by reason of his superior wisdom or insight or style but rather because Greene admired the way he'd researched his books on Conrad (one of Greene's favorite authors): instead of poring through criticism and such, he'd "vacated the library" and reverently retraced Conrad's footsteps, exploring the places around the world that the author of *Heart of Darkness* had known and used as settings for his fiction. In researching the Greene biography, Sherry followed much the same procedure, journeying to remote villages in Mexico and West Africa that had found their way into such novels as *The Heart of the Matter*

1. *The Life of Graham Greene.* Volume I: 1904–1939. Viking.

and *The Power and the Glory,* and interviewing some of the people on whom Greene had modeled his characters. It is not necessarily a bad idea, to be sure, for a biographer to devote much of his time to this sort of traveling; but in the course of reading Sherry's book one finds oneself wishing that for every week he spent on arduous expeditions to Third World backwaters he had devoted an hour or so in an easy chair to concentrated reflection about the verities that were right under his nose.

What, one wonders, really lies behind Greene's choice of this man as his Ellmann, his Edel? Possibly there was an element of identification: Sherry's *modus operandi,* after all, strongly resembles Greene's own longtime practice of sojourning for weeks on end in exotic and dangerous places in order to soak up atmosphere for his novels. Or could it be that the solitary and secretive Greene, in selecting the peripatetic Sherry as his official biographer, deliberately chose someone who he knew would spend more time accumulating innocuous facts than investigating bothersome truths, someone who would be more interested in pointing out trivial inconsistencies of date and place in his interviewees' half-century-old recollections than in pondering the deep moral and intellectual contradictions that are part of the very fabric of Greene's life and art? Any reader who is aware of Greene's penchant for practical jokes may be excused for concluding that his selection of the vapid, literal-minded Sherry as his biographer may well have been something of a joke on all of us.

In the event, if Greene wanted to be the subject of a dull, undiscerning hagiography, he could hardly have done better than Sherry. His book is a treasure trove of wonderfully inane remarks: "At University he did not go to church, understandably since he was an atheist." At the end of part one ("Childhood"): "Graham's potentiality as demonstrated at school was almost nil and has become almost infinite." Sherry's credulity, moreover, is beyond belief—an especially unfortunate characteristic in a biographer of Greene, given the subject's tendency to tell striking yet unsubstantiated anecdotes about himself, to offer highly dubious and glib explanations of queer behavior on his part, and to dismiss patently significant formative events as trifles. Sherry borrows heavily from Greene's memoirs, *A Sort of Life* (1971) and *Ways of Escape* (1980), as well as from his other nonfiction books, and (with a few exceptions) tends to buy Greene's testimony wholesale. He accepts without question, for instance, Greene's claims that as a young man he played Russian roulette (by himself) several times, and that after his boyhood psychoanalysis "he could no longer take an aesthetic interest in any visual thing – staring at a sight that others assured him was beautiful, he would feel nothing."

How SILLY is this book? Here's how silly it is: Sherry finds it necessary to tell us that the title *Goodnight Sweet Ladies* "is from *Hamlet* (Act IV, Scene 5)" and that "Professor Cedric Watts has suggested that the pseudonym Kolley Kibber [used by a character in *Brighton Rock*] is adapted from the eighteenth-century actor-manager and Poet Laureate Colley Cibber." No kidding! He places great emphasis, too, on the correction of minor factual errors in Greene's autobiographical writings (even as he manages to overlook more momentous, if nonfactual, lapses). When Greene refers, for instance, to a theater poster advertising *The Private Secretary,* Sherry records triumphantly that the poster could not have been advertising that movie because "it was not playing in Nottingham during Christmas 1925." His air is that of a Biblical scholar discovering heretofore unrecognized historical errors in the Gospels.

Vigilant though he is about such picayune matters, however, Sherry is altogether too quick to try to explain away anything that makes Greene look less than honorable. When confronted with frank acknowledgments by the Master himself of ignominious thoughts or deeds, Sherry tends to downplay the admissions themselves as much as possible and instead often takes the opportunity to commend Greene for his honesty. For instance, Greene writes in *A Sort of Life* that when as a youth he spurned the attractions of Parisian trollops, it was because of his timidity: "It was certainly no sense of morality which restrained me. Morality comes with the sad wisdom of age, when the curiosity has withered." Sherry quotes this remark – which, as the testimony of someone widely considered a major contemporary moralist, must be considered outrageous – but chooses not to comment at all on it, except to praise its "characteristic honesty." Likewise, in his travel book *The Law-*

less Roads (1939), Greene admits that he first took up the study of Catholicism for two reasons: one, because he was marrying a member of the Church and felt an obligation to know something about the faith; two, because "it would kill the time." Sherry's bizarre gloss on this colossal flippancy: "Greene's honesty is so pronounced it would be irresponsible to ignore these statements, even though made so many years after conversion. Killing time has been an important activity for him."

In other instances, Sherry tries to turn Greene's vices themselves into virtues by citing them as examples of a relentless intellectual curiosity. Here's Sherry, for instance, letting Greene off the hook for his prodigal whoring: "Greene has such a curiosity about all things in life, that it was inevitable that he would be attracted to profane love." Yet while he is eager to absolve Greene of any serious character flaws (however overwhelming the evidence to the contrary), Sherry routinely comes to unfair, unsubstantiated conclusions about Greene's supporting cast, none of whom seems to have any importance (or even reality) for Sherry.

As for Sherry's prose, he is something less than a world-class stylist. The biography is full of crude redundancies, awkward phrasings that would be quite easy to put right ("Trollope was administrator of the Cathedral but was deeply dissatisfied with the thought of any future which could be represented as a success"), and classic errors of construction: "Trevor Wilson, at one time British Consul in Hanoi and who provided Greene with some insight into the conditions in Vietnam for *The Quiet American,* called on Marion Greene very late in her life." Sherry doesn't appear to be aware of the difference between a restrictive and a nonrestrictive clause, or to know about the proper use of hyphens in group modifiers or of colons preceding quotations. Participles dangle all over the place:

> A very sensitive boy, the fact that his physical awkwardness could not be hidden and therefore was obvious to others, filled him with intense shame.

Many sentences, meanwhile, read like sets of rough notes that Sherry has neglected to turn into finished prose:

Another aspect of his schizophrenic life at this time was his urge to become a successful writer, though he complained to his mother of not having time to do anything during that final autumn term at Oxford, he had begun a novel and was concerned about publishing his first book of verse.

Above all, Sherry is a master of the long, messy run-on: "From this point of view his adventure with Russian roulette and later his incessant travelling to inaccessible and often dangerous places, is not simply the desire to test himself (the uninspired weakling on the playing fields of Berkhamsted becomes the inspired adventurer off them) but to escape from a depressed condition: '& the bubble gets bigger, & bigger & I want, oh God, how I want to be dead, or asleep or blind drunk . . . so that I can't think.'" Ask yourself: could that sentence be any worse?

EVEN IF SHERRY is, in short, a skilled collector of information, he doesn't set it forth with much elegance, and almost invariably misses the point of it all. Yet if one reads between the lines of this biography – or, for that matter, if one skips the biography entirely and reads *A Sort of Life* – one gets a sense, readily enough, of what's truly important here. Plainly, one of the most salient facts is that Greene spent his entire childhood on the grounds of a public school, the Berkhamsted School in Surrey, where his father, Charles Henry Greene, was first a housemaster and then (beginning in 1910) the headmaster – a position in which he remained throughout Greene's own student days at the school. (Greene was graduated from Berkhamsted in 1922.) From his earliest childhood, in short, the Berkhamsted School was Greene's entire universe; its canons and customs, its manners and mores, its ideals and ideas about life, were the only ones – the only establishment-approved ones, anyway – that he knew. If other boys came to this environment fresh from conventional homes (where, naturally, the reigning values and daily routines were quite different from the school's) and were therefore able to put life at Berkhamsted into some sort of context, Greene seems to have grown up viewing the world only from the schoolyard – with the result that the school's way of looking at the world had a more potent, more concentrated influence upon him than it had upon other boys. That the school's way was, by definition, his father's way can only have intensified this influence.

The enduring effect of Berkhamsted on Greene is testified to, in a funny way, by the fact that a number of characters in his novels are themselves preoccupied with their public-school past. One thinks, for instance, of the hapless "old Lancaster boy" in *Brighton Rock,* whose life seems to have gone straight to hell since his school days; of Harris, in *The Heart of the Matter,* who lingers over a copy of his alumni bulletin; and of the way in which the unspeakable perfidy of his best prep-school friend, Harry Lime, leads Rollo Martins, in *The Third Man,* to lose faith in everything that the old school represented to him. Then there is the pathetic journalist Minty in *England Made Me,* with his well-nigh pathological attachment to old Harrow: "The school and he were joined by a painful reluctant coition, a passionless coition that leaves everything to regret, nothing to love, everything to hate, but cannot destroy the idea: we are one body." Greene himself has explicitly acknowledged the centrality of Berkhamsted's impact upon his adult character. "Everything one was to become must have been there, for better or worse," he writes in *A Sort of Life.* "One's future might have been prophesied from the shape of the houses as from the lines of the hand.... For twenty years it was to be almost the only scene of happiness, misery, first love, the attempt to write."

It was also the place where Greene first learned about sex – a subject on which his gentle, unworldly father held fanatically Victorian opinions. Although Sherry usually doesn't seem to recognize it, these opinions, and the school policies that Greene's father instituted because of them during his headmastership, shed a great deal of light on almost every aspect of Greene's adult life and work. One of his relatives recalls that Greene *père* – a devotee of Charles Kingsley's "muscular Christianity" – was "bewildered by sex," and was fixated on the idea of its sinfulness. One Berkhamsted alumnus recalls that the headmaster's last advice to him was "to be faithful to your future wife"; another remembers being told by the old man to "come to your future wife clean." Gentle though he may have been, we are told that the novelist's father dealt severely with boys caught at the slightest carnal offense, whether it be innocuous kissing or solitary masturbation. According to Claud Cockburn, who was a friend and fellow student of Greene's at Berkhamsted, Greene's father "believed sincerely" that if any two boys were allowed to be alone together for twenty minutes, "sin would occur"; so it was that he imposed on the boys a rigorously organized daily schedule that ensured that none of them would be left idle for a moment – a fact that may help to explain Greene's lifelong restlessness, his seemingly desperate need for travel.

What's more, the zealously reiterated paternal lesson that intimacy leads to sin must have played a large role in the development of Greene's lifelong unease around other people, his profound sense of detachment from the rest of humanity (he is, in Sherry's words, "squeamish about too much intimacy with others"); and the fact that Berkhamsted's masters and prefects were encouraged to spy on boys – and that boys were required to inform on each other when crimes of onanism and the like had been committed – must certainly account in large part for Greene's lifelong interest in espionage, betrayal, loyalty.

It has sometimes been said that Greene tends to write only about the grubbiest of people and the seediest of places. But it is more nearly correct to say that, to Greene's way of thinking, the earth hardly consists of anything else: to him the world is steeped in grubbiness, in seediness – in sin. To read about his father's preoccupation with the filthiness of sex is to begin to understand the origins of this grim *Weltanschauung*. Greene was, after all, taught that sex is the ultimate transgression. And yet sex brings people together; it perpetuates the species. It permeates life – which means, therefore, that *sin* permeates life. If Greene writes about the world as if it were suffused with evil, it is because, to someone who regards sex as the ultimate transgression, the world *is* suffused with evil; and if he creates protagonists who are drawn strongly to great sins, it is because, if sex is considered the ultimate transgression, all men *are* drawn strongly to great sins. (As Mr. Surrogate reflects in *It's a Battlefield,* "Man is a beast, a lecherous beast. He may mate above him, but presently he finds his proper level.") As for Greene's own lack of ethical rigor – for example, his patronization of prostitutes both shortly before and shortly after his marriage – it can, I think, be explained by a fatalistic attitude on Greene's part toward this perceived state of affairs: a feeling, namely, that if one is unable to sublimate one's sexual drives, one is already a prodigious sinner; that there is consequently no point in trying to be virtuous in other ways; and that, on the contrary, an impassioned dedication to and joy in iniquity may in fact prove to be one's only consolation, or (at least) a form of revenge upon the cosmos. Reading through Greene's biography, one sees evidence of such a moral fatalism in operation time and again.

Interestingly enough, moreover, this interpretation pretty much sums up the psychology of one of Greene's most monstrous protagonists: Pinkie, the psychopathic teenage gangster at the center of *Brighton Rock*. During the course of the novel, we learn that Pinkie was raised as a Catholic and was taught that sex is evil. Consequently he is at once a virgin and a murderer: feeling a "prick of sexual desire" for a woman "disturbed him like a sickness. Was there no escape – anywhere – for anyone? It was worth murdering a world." Pinkie's way of coping with the world's wickedness, in short, is not to succumb to his agony over the wickedness, but to glory in it, and to contribute to it himself as fully as possible. Now Graham Greene, as a boy, was not quite a murderer, but neither was he completely unlike Pinkie. Even in his childhood, according to Peter Quennell, "his talk had an exuberantly sceptical and blithely pessimistic turn, and his contemplation of the horrors of human life appeared to cause him unaffected pleasure. . . . At each fresh insight into human absurdity or wickedness, his pallid, faintly woebegone face would assume an air of solemn glee."

THERE IS no getting around the fact, though Sherry somehow manages to do so, that Quennell's account (which Sherry quotes from a memoir, *The Marble Foot*) paints a portrait of a very sick boy. Even the sketchiest chronicle of his late childhood and early youth makes it clear that Greene was most dreadfully disturbed: during his teens, he claims, he attempted suicide a number of times by various means; at sixteen, he suffered a nervous breakdown and underwent the aforementioned psychoanalysis (the treatment left him no less detached, but, it is said, considerably more self-assured); at twenty, while a student at Balliol College, Oxford, he went to a dentist and, "to escape the 'oppression of boredom,'" pretended to be suffering from an abscess and had a perfectly good tooth extracted.

It was during the same period – on six different occasions within half a year – that Greene supposedly engaged in his now-famous series of suicide attempts, holding a loaded revolver to his head and pulling the trigger. Sherry completely credits this story, and accepts Greene's explanation that it was part of "a life-long war against boredom"; by pointing a gun at his head, Greene later explained, he sought "to escape boredom... to get more out of life." This may well be true, but it begs the question: why should a talented, well-heeled, relatively intelligent young man be so bored? Boredom on such a scale is pathological – a sign of deep psychological disturbance, of an enduring immaturity and selfishness, of a disquieting lack of consideration for one's family and friends. It also contains an element of outright snobbery; for to complain about boredom is, after all, the prerogative of the spoiled child, and to air such a grievance is almost a way of bragging about one's advantages. Indeed, though Sherry dutifully records every bit of Greene's aberrant adolescent behavior, he seems not to realize quite how aberrant it is; nor does he acknowledge how profound an influence the abnormal psychology of the boy has had upon the literary *oeuvre* of the man, whose novels are swarming with characters who commit, contemplate, or at least talk about suicide. (One of the things that are most unsettling about the alleged Russian-roulette episode, alas, is that Greene himself, who is willing enough to discuss it, has to this day given no indication of being unsettled by it.)

In similar fashion, Sherry writes about Greene's undergraduate flirtation with espionage as if it were perfectly natural – or, at least, spunky and harmlessly amusing. It happened this way: in 1924, during an outbreak of unrest between the French and Germans in the Ruhr, the nineteen-year-old Greene contacted the first secretary of the German embassy in London and proposed an arrangement. If the Germans would provide covert financing for a journey by him to the Ruhr, he would write, on his return, pro-German articles for the newspapers at heavily pro-French Oxford. The Germans liked the idea, and the deal was struck. Sherry doesn't seem at all to recognize the questionableness of Greene's clandestine association with a recent enemy power. Nor, though Sherry finds Greene's escapade "daring," and admires him for his "appreciation of [the] futility" of the Germans' elaborate secrecy, does he remark on the manifest elitist cockiness of the enterprise. Yet it is hard not to recognize this episode as a crucial one in the history of Greene's moral evolution or lack thereof. Claud Cockburn describes the nineteen-year-old Greene as "the greatest case of arrested development he had ever met" – and the fact is that Greene's dealings with the German government bespeak a level of indifference to ethical considerations that can be described only as infantile. This incident would seem to be one of the earliest examples of Greene's moral fatalism at work – his cynical feeling, in other words, that, man being as beastly as he is, one might as well join the fun; and one suspects that its manifestation in such a frivolous and sophomoric form can be attributed to a boyhood spent exclusively in a public school – in an environment, that is, that predisposed the teenager to view everything (except, of course, sex) as a game, and in which he must have considered himself a sort of court favorite, a specially privileged being, exempt from the usual punishments.

Much the same sort of thinking would seem to be behind Greene's enrollment in the Communist party in 1925. At the time, he told a friend that communism was "the only future," but Sherry says now that the enlistment was only "another student escapade," a "ruse to allow Greene to visit Paris and the Communist headquarters there." If this is true, Greene's action again shows the ease with which he could adopt positions on international affairs to serve his most shallow private whims. Sherry doesn't touch on this point. Nor does he have much to say about Greene's quite un-Communistic service, during the General Strike of 1926, as a strike-breaker and special constable, duties that Greene claims to have accepted "[m]ore from curiosity than from any wish to support the Establishment." In neither of these instances does Greene seem to have shown a commitment to anything beyond his own immediate pleasure.

Greene's complaints of boredom – and his supposed attraction to suicide – did not disappear after the Russian roulette incidents. On the heels of his graduation from Oxford, he took a job with the British American Tobacco Company which (had he not resigned at the last minute) would have taken him to China for several years. His letters to his then-fiancée, Vivien, characterize the job as a form of suicide. "China," he writes, "would he a splendid sort of suicide-without-scandal-touch. And I agree with you that one doesn't want to go on much longer." Similarly, he suggests in a subsequent letter that "the only thing worth doing at the moment seems to be to go & get killed somehow in an exciting manner." Sherry doesn't get far beneath the surface of this sort of remark, which seems to speak volumes about the irresponsible motives behind his life long globe-trotting, and especially behind his attraction to trouble spots.

In much the same vein, and far more offensive, are some comments in yet another missive Greene wrote during this period: "One can't help envying the people of my age in 1914. Everything at any rate was absolutely settled for them. Nothing they could do could alter their fate. They were either going to die or live, & they could just drift with the crowd. I should like the Germans better than ever, if only they'd start a show [i.e., a war] now again." And, as if one needed any further evidence of Greene's coldheartedness, a chilling illustration is provided by a couple of letters relating to the demise of his favorite uncle. The first was written just before the event: "I shall hear tomorrow whether my uncle's pulled through. . . . What annoys me most is that it should have come & spoilt my mother's holiday." The second was written immediately afterwards: "I don't feel much cut up. It must be pretty beastly for my mother, as he was her only brother." Greene may sound like an eight-year-old here, but he's actually twenty-two. "There is a splinter of ice in the heart of a writer," he has written; in his case it would seem to be something considerably larger than a splinter.

Greene has given no indication, to this day, that he feels any differently than he did when he expressed these less-than-attractive sentiments about suicide, war, and a relative's death. That he did express such sentiments is of more than passing importance, of course, because Greene is not just any famous novelist: he is a writer who has long been celebrated – and, in many quarters, revered – for his left-wing politics. These early documents, however, suggest strongly that Greene's politics owe little or nothing to any natural sympathy for the masses; on the contrary, the enthusiasm implied in these letters for diversion at any cost – even if that cost be a suicide that leaves his loved ones in emotional torment, or a global conflict that leaves millions dead, mutilated, or homeless – could exist only in someone utterly devoid of compassion. To some Marxists, the human catastrophes that have been brought about by their social philosophy may seem a good reason to give up the faith; to a man like Greene, eager to witness the bloody "show" that a Marxist revolution and its aftermath would furnish, those catastrophes would seem to be as good a reason as any to adopt the faith. Greene himself admits as much in a 1984 interview with *Literaturnaya Gazeta* (in the last sentence of which he makes a sharp turn from frivolousness into a pretense of serious radicalism): "I was always drawn to those countries where the political situation involved a game of life and death. . . . I was always interested in turning-points and found them in Asia and Africa, in Central and Latin America. Literature, you know, helps the fight against dictatorial regimes and I did what I could to contribute to this fight."

The more one reads about Greene's life, in fact, the more one recognizes that his leftism is anything but serious; it is the leftism not of a man of the people but of a man of privilege, ever alert to his privileges – one of which is the freedom to take absurd, cynical, and self-righteous political positions without suffering at all on their account. His are, one might say, the politics of the headmaster's son who, in a very real sense, has never left the schoolyard; they are the politics of the Balliol student who never received the slightest punishment for his callous flirtation with the German embassy and the Communist party.

Certainly class snobbery has always been a key component of Greene's sensibility. From Nottingham Park, where he lived for several months in a poor neighborhood after throwing over the position with British American Tobacco, he complained in a letter to Vivien that "[o]ne sees absolutely no one here of one's own class." Time and again in this biography, he shows himself to be virtually incapable of communicating with ordinary people. As a matter of fact, what is often characterized as his contempt for the living conditions of the poverty-ridden – whether in England or the Third World – would appear in reality to be a sublimated contempt for indigent folk themselves. During his first trip to Mexico, Greene wrote about "the hideous inexpressiveness of brown eyes. . . . If Spain is like this, I can understand the temptation to massacre." In one Mexican town, he was delighted to meet a Norwegian woman and her two blonde daughters, whom he found "startlingly beautiful in a land where you grow weary of black and oily hair and brown sentimental eyes." Greene's criticisms, in his memoirs and travel books, of the mediocre food, shabby lodgings, and medieval plumbing in such places remind one less of the social outrage of a Jacob August Riis than of the imperious whinings of a pampered Oxbridgean on a slumming tour. Greene often seems to be holding up to ridicule the very idea that the people who live in such places might really *matter*—that they might lead meaningful, even happy, lives. If his novels are full of killers and spies, it's partly because he's incapable of finding the world of common people anything other than a dreary joke, something to patronize, to place in facile ironic contrast to the fear and terror with which secret agents and murderers typically live.

H IS EARLY TWENTIES were important years for Greene: he married a young woman named Vivien Dayrell-Browning, converted to Catholicism (about which more presently), and worked as a subeditor on the *Nottingham Journal* and the London *Times*. He also wrote and published the first of his twenty-six novels. Set in nineteenth-century England, *The Man Within* (1929) is far from his best work (the title derives from Sir Thomas Browne: "There's another man within me that's angry with me"), but it is worth examining in some detail—partly because it introduces many of his most familiar themes and motifs, and partly because it illuminates Greene's feelings about his father in a way that none of his later books would do.

The protagonist of *The Man Within* is a very young man named Andrews, who as the novel opens has been working for three years as a smuggler along the Sussex coast. Now, having informed on his confederates—six of whom have been arrested—and having been pursued through the countryside by the three other gang members who remain at large, he finds refuge in a humble cottage with a nineteen-year-old stranger named Elizabeth. As in many a Greene novel to come, our hero promptly falls for this young lady whom fate has thrown in his path, and she returns the favor. Fortunately, not only is Elizabeth altogether perfect – impossibly wise, loving, and beautiful – but her stepfather has just died (his body, laid out in Elizabeth's house, is the first of many un-subtle *memento mori* in Greene's work) and she is therefore, quite conve-niently, in need of a man. Greene, it should be said, never quite brings Elizabeth to life; she's more a young man's romantic conception – a boys' school ideal of womanhood – than a real person: though provin-cial, friendless, and innocent, she is nonetheless preternaturally astute, and when Andrews's former partners in crime catch up with him she proves totally fearless. She ultimately becomes, moreover, the first of many Greene characters to be drawn – by chance or error – into a haz-ardous affair not of their making, and to perish as a result.

Why did Andrews turn his fellows in? Interestingly, the answer cen-ters on Andrews's feelings about his father. The senior Andrews, we learn, was a successful smuggler, revered by his colleagues as brave, ad-venturous, and loyal; yet Andrews, as a boy, knew – and hated – him as a conceited, ignorant wife-beater. When his father died, Andrews was re-moved from his Devonshire school by Carlyon, one of his father's asso-ciates, and was (so to speak) taken into the firm; there his resentment of his late father grew, for, unlike the old man, the timid, sensitive An-drews was not a born smuggler: "I could do nothing which was not weighed up with my father and found wanting." Yet he found a substi-tute father in Carlyon, who is as much of a boys'-school conception as Elizabeth; bold and manly though he is, Carlyon also (like Andrews's mother) loves poetry and music, is deeply intelligent and goodhearted, and has "a voice as near to music as any voice I've ever heard." Carlyon, indeed, became for Andrews the focus both of a newfound devotion and of his transferred hostility towards his real father; Andrews hardly knew "whether the twisted feeling at his heart when he uttered the name [of Carlyon] was love or hate." It was out of this jumble of emotions that his betrayal grew. Andrews double-crossed his comrades, he explains, because "I had a father whom I hated and he was always being put be-fore me as a model. It made me mad. And I'm a coward. . . . I was afraid of being hurt and I hated the sea and the noise and the danger. And un-less I did something it would have gone on for always and always. And I wanted to show those men that I was someone to be considered, that I had the power to smash all their plans." He wanted, too, to prove that he was Carlyon's match: "Haven't I outwitted the fool now?...I've shown them that I'm of importance now."

Like the protagonists of many Greene novels to come, Andrews is two men in one. He knows he's "made up of...the sentimental, bullying, desiring child and another more stern critic." Like many Greene heroes, moreover, Andrews is preoccupied with the idea that he's "a coward and altogether despicable." Like those other heroes, he lives in a grim world of chaos and mistrust, and wonders whether he will ever know "peace from pursuit"; peace, we are told, "was a sanity which he did not believe that he had ever known." What's more, Andrews has faced a predicament that confronts many a Greene protagonist: the conflict between personal loyalty and some more or less worthy motive, which may be anything from the confused Freudian impulses that rack Andrews's heart to the desire of the hero in *The Third Man* to bring his best friend to justice.

Another moral predicament familiar to readers of Greene is that posed by sex. The distinctive position on this subject that Greene communicates in his later novels – and which clearly has its origin in his father's austere teachings on the subject – makes its first blunt appearance here. Even someone who knew nothing about Greene's life would be able to conclude, from *The Man Within*, that its young author suffered from what is essentially a severe virgin/whore complex – a conviction that fornication is sinful, that the truest and purest sort of romantic love should thus be free of the taint of sexual attraction, and that consequently (man being concupiscent by nature) the betrayal of one's beloved is inevitable. Elizabeth, in Andrews's eyes, has "mystery," "a kind of sanctity which blurred and obscured his desire with love"; with a prostitute, however (into whose bed he falls at the first opportunity), there's "no love and no reverence. The animal in him could ponder her beauty crudely and lustfully." It's not just the young Andrews, moreover, who feels this way about women; the worldly Carlyon shares the same philosophy, remarking to Elizabeth that she's "full of disgusting physical needs. You'll never find a man who will love you for anything but a bare, unfilled-in outline of yourself.... Only a woman can love a real person." Romantic love is one thing, physical desire another: succumbing to the trollop's modest charms, Andrews "had turned a deaf ear to what his heart . . . had asked of him, but he had capitulated at the first hungry wail his dirty, lusting body had uttered." Greene does not hesitate to give this conflict a religious foundation. "Are you a devil as well as a harlot?" Andrews asks the puzzled whore (who hadn't counted on a philosophical discussion); although he doesn't fear death, he has "a terror of life, of going on soiling himself and repenting and soiling himself again."

Like many later Greene heroes, then, Andrews is attracted to the idea of death as an eternal sanctuary from danger and from the possibility of sin. (If life, he reflects, "were barren of desire and of the need of any action how sweet [it] would be.") Yet he fears extinction because "I am all that I have, I'm afraid of losing that." To the author of *The Man Within,* God is not a manifestation of, or an explanation for, our sense of closeness to others, but a force that works in opposition to an attraction to others, and that occupies the void that other people fail to fill. As in most of Greene's other novels, Christian imagery proliferates here: Carlyon is described as a Christ figure and Andrews as "a sort of Judas" who denies Carlyon (and Elizabeth as well) several times. (For good measure, he introduces himself at one point as "Absalom.")

There are many other characteristics that *The Man Within* shares with Greene's later novels: the ironic conjunction of comfortable and terrorized lives; the image of a desperate fugitive arriving (often incognito) in an unfamiliar place and falling for a strange woman; a concern with the themes of flight and pursuit, good and evil, love and loyalty, courage and cowardice, justice and injustice, the longing for peace and the necessity of action; the distinct implication that the protagonist's alienation, huntedness, need for disguise, and desire for escape are a satisfactory metaphor for the human condition; and the notion that man is best ruled by his heart, not his mind. In this book, moreover, Greene establishes his sentimental – and, ultimately, self-serving – enthusiasm for what he calls "baseless dreaming": "Suppose that after all a man . . . chose his dreams whether they were to be good or evil. Then, even though he were untrue to them, some credit was owing simply to the baseless dreaming. They were potentialities, aspects, and no man could tell whether suddenly and without warning they might not take control and turn the coward for one instant into the hero."

Like Greene's later books, too, *The Man Within* profits from a vigorous style, a strong narrative sense, and a meticulous attention to atmospheric detail. Yet, like many of its successors, it abounds in hyperbolic rhetoric. Elizabeth's dead stepfather has "the peace of God in his face"; at his burial, "the falling clods were a measurement of time, recording the vanishing moments of his peace." Time, in fact, "was here in the cottage. Clocks ticked and hands went round as everywhere else in the world. He [Andrews] had a sense of time rushing past him, rushing like a Gadarene swine to destruction."

The best thing one can say about *The Man Within* is that it's an elegant contrivance – a fastidiously well-made novel whose restrictions of time, place, and number of characters are thoroughly intentional, and whose author's patent naïveté is largely compensated for by his impressive sense of pacing and of dramatic shape. Yet it is that naïveté, alas, which leaves the most lasting impression: the characters' endless chatter about God, conscience, cowardice, and so forth serves only to remind one, on virtually every page, of the narrow boundaries of the author's immature and self-romanticizing view of life. Greene emerges as a callow, narcissistic young man raised on an equation of sex and sin, accustomed to self-indulgence, to the guilt that follows, and to the self-indulgent pleasure of confession that follows that. Even Greene recognizes – to some extent, anyway – the book's deficiencies: the Penguin paperback reprint is prefaced with an apologetic Author's Note, added a couple of decades after the book's publication, in which Greene acknowledges its "embarrassingly romantic" tone and "derivative" style but asks that he be allowed, by its reissuance, "one sentimental gesture towards his own past, the period of ambition and hope." (An interesting comment, by the way, given that much of Greene's fiction is fundamentally a sentimental gesture.)

The Man Within won a wide readership, and Greene went on to write two more historical romances: *The Name of Action* (1930) and *Rumour at Nightfall* (1931). Both books, however, were failures (neither has been in print for decades), and Greene – who had quit his *Times* job on the strength of his first novel's success – decided to shift genres dramatically. The result was *Stamboul Train* (1932), issued in the United States as *Orient Express;* a best-seller on both sides of the Atlantic, it inaugurated a series of fictions – most of them melodramatic, a few farcical – that Greene would later classify as "entertainments" as a way of distinguishing them from his more serious novels. And certainly there is nothing serious about *Stamboul Train.* Its characters – all of them passengers on the Orient Express from Ostend to Constantinople – are essentially caricatures who can be adequately described in five or six words apiece. Like the *dramatis personae* of many a Greene novel, they compose a motley crew: Carleton Myatt, a good-hearted Jewish bachelor in the currant business (one of many Jews, often ashamedly hiding behind Gentile-sounding names, who may be found in Greene's fiction); Coral Musker, a lonely, insecure young English dancer; Mabel Warren, a tough, ruthless lesbian journalist; Janet Pardoe, her lovely but fickle young protégée; Quin Savory, a vulgar, social-climbing Cockney novelist; Mr. Opie, a fatuous Anglican cleric; and Dr. Czinner, a gallant socialist insurgent headed for Belgrade (incognito, naturally) to take part in a revolution.

But one doesn't read such entertainments in order to acquaint oneself with towering, full-blooded characters; one reads them for the reason one reads any thriller, to see how the story will come out. Will Coral end up with Myatt? Will Janet leave Mabel? Will Myatt's crucial negotiations in Constantinople be resolved to his satisfaction? And how will they all be affected by the unstable political situation in Yugoslavia? In bringing together these frankly one-dimensional characters, Greene makes abundant use of the melodramatist's book of tricks: coincidences and improbabilities proliferate, romances spring up out of nowhere, lives are reshuffled as swiftly and gracefully as a deck of cards. And yet his painstaking use of realistic atmospheric details lends the far-fetched story a certain transient plausibility; in many ways – its economical but vivid establishment of settings, its brisk cutting from one set of characters to another, its unflagging sense of movement – the book is almost aggressively cinematic. A great deal happens here, and none of it means anything: it's entertainment, pure and simple. Yes, the characters do exchange ideas about religion and politics, but these ideas are there not for their own sake but to establish character, to explain motivations, to set an urbane tone; to Greene the entertainer, no idea matters as much as the forward movement of the story. As he writes of another entertainment, *The Third Man*, "[r]eality . . . was only a background to a fairy tale."

This generalization holds true for all of the entertainments that Greene published in the wake of *Stamboul Train*. The earliest of these is *A Gun for Sale* (1936), the story of a European political crisis whose chief players are a hired assassin, a munitions king, a war minister, a female hostage, and a detective named Mather. Then there's *The Confidential Agent* (1939), wherein a secret agent known only as D. travels to England to secure a contract for the delivery of coal to his civil-war-torn homeland. As is typical in a Greene entertainment, D. unknowingly meets Rose Cullen, the daughter of the British coal baron Lord Benditch, on the Channel crossing and falls quickly in love; and, after checking into a London rooming house, he just as rapidly wins the undying loyalty of Else, a fourteen-year-old serving-girl. His ensuing cat-and-mouse game with an enemy agent – who's out to thwart D.'s deal with Lord Benditch – occasions both amusing episodes and a plethora of appropriately bleak assertions about the difficulty of moral choice and the impossibility of perfect trust. Part of what makes this book entertaining, indeed, is its insistent, calculatedly cynical depiction of a world of "treachery and dependence," a world in which God is a "joker," in which "[t]he dead were to be envied" because "[i]t was the living who had to suffer from loneliness and distrust," a world in which the hero's "territory was death: he could love the dead and the dying better than the living, [who] were robbed of reality by their complacent safety." Such passages serve much the same atmosphere-setting function here that a hard-bitten Bogart hero's misanthropic *mots* serve in a movie like *Casablanca* or *Key Largo*. The book's logic, meanwhile, operates according to classic Hitchcock-movie rules: the characters flirt and trade quips even though their lives are in immediate peril; the mundane regularly appears alongside the life-or-death (e.g., an endangered D. finds himself in a room where "Hints to the Young Housewife" is playing on the radio).

Greene follows the same solemnity-and-suspense formula in several of his other entertainments. Take, for instance, *The Ministry of Fear*

(1943), the Blitz-era story of a man who pines for his lost childhood only to fall victim to a bomb that destroys his memory of the last twenty years and thus ironically effects his escape from adulthood's "savage country." Or *The Third Man* (1950), in which Rollo Martins, investigating the death of his old school friend Harry Lime in postwar Vienna, discovers that Harry's not dead but in hiding from the police; he's been selling impure blackmarket penicillin and thus ensuring the deaths of innumerable hospitalized children. Martins is forced to choose between loyalty to a friend and larger, more abstract allegiances. (If the book reads like a film treatment rather than a novel or an entertainment – strong on action, that is, but slapdash in style – it's because it *is* a film treatment; as Greene himself admits in his preface, Carol Reed's famous motion picture "is better than the story because it is in this case the finished state of the story.")[2] Then there's *Our Man in Havana* (1958), wherein a divorced Englishman named Wormold, the owner of a less-than-flourishing vacuum-cleaner outlet in Havana, is approached by a mysterious representative of MI6; since he can use the money, he agrees to be the Foreign Office's man in Havana, and proceeds to recruit fictitious subagents and to file utterly fabricated accounts of enemy espionage activity (including specious Soviet atomic-weapons plans that he has in fact based on vacuum-cleaner designs). His reports win praise from his superiors in London – but then the game turns deadly as the real people with whose names he has christened his subagents start being liquidated. Though it's a one-gag story, the joke is played out amusingly enough (at least throughout the first half of the book); the problem is that the outrageous humor is accompanied by an incongruously bleak mise en scène and by mordant pronouncements that, while no darker than those found in *The Confidential Agent* and *The Third Man*, seem utterly at odds with the farcical story.

Greene's last two entertainments are considerably less gloomy. The exceedingly brief *Loser Takes All* (1955), which he describes in his dedication as a "frivolity," relates the whimsical but slight story of an unad-

---

2. Greene's equally slapdash book, *The Tenth Man*, written in 1944 but first issued only in 1985, was likewise composed not as a novel but as a film story for Metro-Goldwyn-Mayer.

venturous assistant accountant who strikes it rich in Monte Carlo while on his honeymoon. And *Travels with My Aunt* (1969) details, with ample charm and occasional hilarity, the adventures of a similarly drab retired banker named Henry Pulling, who, after his mother's death, is plucked from his quiet bachelor life in suburban London by his vivacious, globe-trotting seventy-five-year-old Aunt Augusta. His aunt, whom he hasn't met in a half-century, takes Henry under her wing, spiriting him to Paris, Istanbul, and Paraguay, introducing him to a wide variety of idiosyncratic phenomena (not the least of which is her large young African lover, Wordsworth), and drawing him into what turns out to be a trafficking scheme.

Though perhaps the merriest of all Greene's books, *Travels with My Aunt* nonetheless touches upon many of the themes of his more serious novels. Most important, it dramatizes – in the encounter between Pulling and his aunt – the key Greenian conflict between innocence and experience. As ever, Greene strongly favors the latter, implying that Aunt Augusta's experience – even her criminality – is preferable to Pulling's innocence, that her ethical imperfection has given her a more sophisticated moral understanding than her nephew. But Greene doesn't push these notions down our throats; he keeps things light, making sure that all the references to religion are funny ("I sometimes believe in a Higher Power," says Aunt Augusta, "even though I am a Catholic") and making the coincidences even more fantastic than usual (Pulling, for instance, meets an American girl named Tooley on the Orient Express, and later runs into her father – a CIA man – in Argentina).

Stamboul Train was not only the first of Greene's entertainments; it also gave rise to three other books whose intentions seem – at times, anyway – to be more serious than those of the entertainments. The desire to tell a diverting story is not Greene's sole, or even his primary, aim in these books: Greene the storyteller shares control with Greene the social philosopher and metaphysician, whose objective is to essay an indictment of English statecraft and/or soulcraft. To be sure, as in *Stamboul Train* and the other entertainments, atmospheric detail is important in these three novels; the difference here is that Greene seems to make calculated use of his command of this detail to make himself appear equally authoritative in regard to other matters, in particular political situations and religious verities. Yet all three of these books are conspicuously unsuccessful; it is as if Greene thought that all he needed to do, in order to write first-rate serious novels rather than light thrillers, was to plug away more insistently at the grim atmosphere and at the fatalistic commentary about highfalutin (and often capitalized) abstractions – Faith, Justice, Guilt, Love, Hate – while keeping the characters as flat (and, in most cases, less colorful and distinctive) and the fatalism every bit as facile as in the entertainments. Needless to say, Greene was badly mistaken in this regard; all three of these novels are notable for their pretentiousness, contrivance, rhetorical excess, and downright dullness.

The first of these books, *It's a Battlefield* (1934), concerns the swirl of events surrounding the sentencing to death of Jim Drover, a London bus driver. Drover, an active member of the British Communist party, has been found guilty of the unpremeditated murder of a policeman, who (he thought) was about to strike Drover's wife, Milly, during a Communist riot. On the heels of the sentencing, the Assistant Commissioner of Police – who is known throughout the novel only by that title – is requested by a Cabinet minister's secretary to look into the possible political benefits of a reprieve for Drover. Meanwhile Drover's brother, Conrad, does his best to effect the reduction of Drover's sentence to a long term of imprisonment; a wealthy, virtuous aristocrat named Lady Caroline Bury (another *memento-mori* monicker) works toward the same end on purely humanitarian grounds; and Mr. Surrogate, a Communist party leader, is less interested in saving Drover's skin than in making use of him as a public-relations tool, a symbol.

The novel's ultimate point is clear: to demonstrate that the English system of justice is capricious and inequitable, that well-meaning citizens are impotent to change it, and that the remainder are all too willing to cooperate cynically with it for their own selfish purposes. Or, as Greene puts it: "The world . . . was run by the whims of a few men, the whims of a politician, a journalist, a bishop and a policeman. They hanged this man and pardoned that; one embezzler was in prison, but other men of the same kind were sent to Parliament." Even the Assistant Commissioner, a relatively decent man, survives only by distancing himself, as much as he can, from the unfair criteria that lie behind the decisions it is his job to enforce; he lives, in other words, according to a philosophy of narrowly defined duty not to justice but to Scotland Yard. The unmarried journalist Conder, meanwhile, deals with the narrowness of his own life by leading a fantasy life in which he is a husband and father. If there is anything here that Greene wants us to admire, it's Lady Caroline's faith – a faith not in the system or in any religion but a faith nonetheless which "perhaps . . . was unshakable because of its vagueness."

Like Conrad's *The Secret Agent*, a book that Greene greatly admires, *It's a Battlefield* is rich with gray urban detail, much of it superbly rendered. But Greene gets much too heavy-handed, including in one chapter a description of a prison whose inmates work – depending on the level of their skills – in either Block A, B, or C, and in the next chapter a description of an equally cheerless factory run on precisely the same system. (Get it? An English factory is a prison, too.) And Conder's overly reiterated need of a fantasy life, far from being touching, comes off as implausible and ridiculous; one cannot possibly take it seriously as a symbol of man's need to escape a horrible and lonely world. ("[E]very word, every phrase, every fake image [of Conder's invented life] was an indictment . . . against life, life without children or wife or home.") Like many other novels written in the 1930s, *It's a Battlefield* too often suffers from the bitter, synthetic taste of socialist realism.

England Made Me (1935) offers another dose of anti-capitalist message-mongering. The setting this time is Stockholm, although most of the principal characters are English. They include Erik Krogh, an extraordinarily rich Swedish industrialist whose involvement in a risky, unscrupulous business transaction could, if publicized, ruin him; Kate Farrant, Krogh's young, well-born English mistress (and the novel's part-time narrator) who loves her brother more than she does Krogh; Anthony Farrant, her ungrateful, ne'er-do-well sibling, for whom Kate arranges a job that places him at Krogh's right hand; and Minty, a scruffy, puerile English journalist who is willing to pay handsomely for information about Krogh. From early in the book, one can see the developments coming (sluggishly) across the Baltic. Meanwhile almost everything one is expected to believe is utterly unbelievable: one is told that Krogh is the richest man in the world, that Anthony and Kate have a deep-seated, all-enduring love for each other (which may, it's hinted, cross the line into incestuous lust), that the most trivial news about Krogh's life is of extreme interest to local journalists – and none of it rings true. Hardest of all to swallow is the subplot involving Andersson, a laborer in Krogh's factory who, possessed of a grievance, shows up in his workman's uniform at a fancy-dress affair attended by Krogh and finds himself brutally ejected; this episode, intended to demonstrate the ruthless exploitation of the lower classes by the upper, reads like bad Upton Sinclair. The switches between first- and third-person narrative, moreover, seem all but pointless. Padded and empty, with more than its share of abortive attempts at cleverness, this novel feels bogus from beginning to end.

Three years later, Greene published *Brighton Rock,* a novel whose immense reputation doubtless stems largely from the fact that it was his most "serious" book to date. Set in the English beach resort town of Brighton, it centers on Pinkie, a ruthless seventeen-year-old gang leader who, on a beautiful summer day, murders Charles Hale, a shabby newspaper hireling who has incurred his wrath. It's a perfect crime, except for one thing: Ida Arnold, a young lady who happened to meet Hale during his last hours and who doesn't accept the police conclusion that he died a natural death, has chosen to investigate on her own. Her persistent inquiries cause the inhumanly vicious Pinkie to take further action, committing more murders and marrying an uncommonly virtuous waitress named Rose – who witnessed a pivotal event on the day of Hale's murder – in order to prevent her from testifying against him. (Greene had made earlier use of this gimmick, by the way, in *England Made Me.*)

Not a bad plot for a Graham Greene entertainment. As the story proceeds, however, one comes to realize that Greene's principal motive in these pages is not to divert but to impart some extremely unusual ideas about good and evil. Accordingly, the novel's thrillerlike elements increasingly give way to bizarre – and even repugnant – lines of dialogue and bits of narrative. Pinkie, we learn, was raised as a Roman Catholic, was instructed by priests in the immorality of sex, and is consequently a virgin whose butchery we are apparently meant to understand as the response of an anguished soul to the world's depravity. (He had, we are told, "held intimacy back as long as he could at the end of a razor blade.") Whatever its origin, however, Pinkie's evil, in Greene's view, brings him nearer to God than those of us who have not murdered in cold blood. (Experience over innocence, you see.) As Charles Péguy writes in a passage that serves as the epigraph to *The Heart of the Matter,* "The sinner is at the heart of Christianity. No one is as competent as the sinner in the matter of Christianity. No one, if he is not a saint." *Brighton Rock* is, quite simply, about Pinkie's competence in the matter of Christianity. It is a competence he shares with the devout Rose – who, like him, was reared a Catholic – but not with Ida, a mere Anglican. Pinkie's evil, as a matter of fact, is drawn magnetlike to Rose's virtue; Greene writes of Pinkie and Rose that "[w]hat was most evil in him needed her: it couldn't get along without goodness." Ida, on the other hand, is "as far from either of them as she was from Hell – or Heaven."

There's something else that Pinkie and Rose share: the odd conviction that their sexual congress, married or not, constitutes a mortal sin. It's a view with which Greene plainly means for us to sympathize. By the same token, he wants us to disdain Ida for her easy virtue. "I like doing what's right," Ida declares at one point – only to add, when reminded that she has slept with men, "Oh, that. That's not wrong. That does no one any harm. That's not like murder." Ha! The point of Greene's irony is that fornication *is* like murder, a fact of which Pinkie and Rose are aware and of which Ida is not. But sex isn't the only front on which Ida, to Greene's way of thinking, deserves disparagement. "It's fun to be alive," she continually proclaims, and to Greene this kind of earthbound gaiety is an offense; as someone says in *The Heart of the Matter,* "Point me out the happy man and I will point you out either egotism, selfishness, evil – or else an absolute ignorance." (It is no accident, of course, that the action of *Brighton Rock* takes place against the ironic backdrop of a beach resort's temporal pleasures, and that more than one *memento mori* is on the scene – including, incidentally, a horse named Memento Mori.) Rose worries about confession and repentance; Ida counters, "That's just religion. . . . Believe me, it's the world we got to deal with."

No, Greene is saying, it's *not* just the world we've got to deal with. But his attempt to press upon the reader the importance of spiritual matters is infinitely complicated by the eccentricity of his understanding of these matters. His view of God and man, in other words, is an exceedingly perverse one, and he communicates it in a perverse way. Both Pinkie and Rose (whose willingness to marry him, even though she fully believes that it ensures her eternal damnation, is utterly baffling) are preposterous characters, their behavior untrue to the nature of normal human psychology, the workings of their minds virtually inaccessible; their tendency to chatter perpetually about theological abstractions would seem unlikely in a Catholic intellectual, let alone in a gangster and a waitress from Brighton. We're expected to sympathize with Pinkie's emotional torment, but his obsessiveness about sin seems merely psychopathic; and the details about his childhood – which are supposed to help us to understand his evil – feel altogether spurious. This information, moreover, is only told to us; we're never given a chance to *see* Pinkie's sensibility *in utero*, to see how Catholicism helped to make him what he is today.

Near the end of the book, an old priest tells Rose a story about a certain Frenchman: "He was a good man, a holy man, and he lived in sin all through his life, because he couldn't bear the idea that any soul could suffer damnation. . . . This man decided that if any soul was going to be damned, he would be damned too. He never took the sacraments, he never married his wife in church. I don't know, my child, but some people think he was – well, a saint. I think he died in what we are told is mortal sin – I'm not sure; it was in the war; perhaps. . . . You can't conceive, my child, nor can I or anyone – the . . . appalling . . . strangeness of the mercy of God." The implication here – that Pinkie may be, in some sense, a saint – is one that it is impossible to accept sincerely; this sort of thinking represents an offense against the genuinely good, the true saints.

It is a sort of thinking, however, that informs not only *Brighton Rock* but several of the novels that succeed it: *The Power and the Glory* (1940), *The Heart of the Matter* (1948), *The End of the Affair* (1951), and *A Burnt-Out Case* (1961). These so-called Catholic novels are widely considered to be Greene's pivotal works; and together with the more explicitly political novels that followed – *The Quiet American* (1956), *The Comedians* (1966), *The Honorary Consul* (1973), and *The Human Fac-*

tor (1978) – they are generally viewed as the core of Greene's oeuvre. Most of these books were set in places Greene had visited during decades of traveling, whether as an independent writer, a foreign correspondent, or (during World War II) as an agent of Britain's Secret Service. For the most part, indeed, the story of his adult life – which Sherry gets underway in his first volume and which Greene recounts in *Ways of Escape* – is a catalogue not only of novels, plays, and film scripts written, but also of lengthy sojourns in such places as Mexico, Sierra Leone, Argentina, French Indochina, Malaya, Kenya, the Belgian Congo, Papa Doc's Haiti, and Stalinist Poland.

The Catholic and political novels that grew out of these travels represent something of an apotheosis of the Greenian sensibility – a consummation, as it were, of a bizarre approach to religion and morality that can be traced clearly to Greene's boyhood on the grounds of Berkhamsted. In order to understand as fully as possible how Greene came to write these novels, it is first necessary to attend to the history of his involvement with Catholicism, to which he converted in his early twenties, and with which he has had an enigmatic relationship ever since.

CONSIDERING that Graham Greene is one of the world's most respected Catholic writers, the story of his introduction to the Roman Catholic faith is somewhat less than inspiring. In 1925 Greene met and fell in love with a Catholic girl named Vivien Dayrell-Browning, who declared that she would not marry him unless he converted to her faith. He did so within the year, although Sherry's account shows no evidence of a real conversion, and Greene (in his memoir *A Sort of Life*) is oddly vague and noncommittal: "I can only remember that in January 1926 I became convinced of the probable existence of something we call God, though I now dislike the word with all its anthropomorphic associations and prefer Chardin's 'Omega Point.'" Greene's references to Catholicism in his letters of the period are flippant, as is his reminiscence of his Catholic instruction: "Now it occurred to me, during the long empty mornings, that if I were to marry a Catholic I ought at least to learn the nature and limits of the beliefs she held. It was only fair, since she knew what I believed – in nothing supernatural. Besides, I thought, it would kill the time." For the most part, then, Greene seems to have looked upon his conversion to Catholicism in the same way that he looked upon his youthful association with the German embassy and his entry into the Communist party – namely, as a means to other ends, in this case marriage to Vivien.

Though the time came when Greene found it useful to place Catholic doctrines and characters at the center of his work, true Catholic piety and reflectiveness have continued to seem alien to him. He has often described himself, paradoxically, as a "Catholic-agnostic." Certainly he has never made any bones about his distrust of orthodox Catholic theology, his utter lack of curiosity about the intellectual underpinnings of the Church. One cannot help but connect him, in this regard, with Henry Pulling's dotty, lawless Aunt Augusta in *Travels with My Aunt* who, upon being asked if she is really a Roman Catholic, replies, "Yes, my dear, only I just don't believe in all the things they believe in." For Greene, intellectual assent to a set of doctrines prescribed by somebody else has little or nothing to do with being a Catholic; he has always felt free to accept or discard various elements of Roman dogma as he sees fit, and to contort Catholic precepts beyond recognition in order to suit his own psychological needs.

At times, indeed, Greene seems to have disposed of so much of Catholicism that there would appear to be no particular reason to call it Catholicism and not something else. Like Maurice, his protagonist in *The End of the Affair,* he "find[s] it hard to conceive of any God who is not as simple as a perfect equation, as clear as air." Greene much prefers a primitive religion to a doctrinaire, over-intellectualized one; he obviously shares the feeling of Dr. Colin, the African-based leprosy specialist in *A Burnt-Out Case,* when he comments that "it's a strange Christianity we have here, but I wonder whether the Apostles would find it as difficult to recognize as the collected works of Thomas Aquinas. If Peter could have understood those, it would have been an even greater miracle than Pentecost, don't you think? Even the Nicaean Creed – it has the flavour of higher mathematics to me." At one point Querry, the book's protagonist, goes so far as to say that "it would be a good thing for all of us if we were even more superficial."

In this connection, it should be observed that Catholicism served

Greene for many years as the locus – the essentially arbitrary locus – of something that he called "faith." A remark that Greene made in a 1986 interview with the *Literaturnaya Gazeta* is of interest. In the interview, he nonchalantly politicized the story of his conversion for the Soviet editors: "The nearer fascism came to us, and the more it spread all over the world, the more necessary it was to oppose it by building moral obstacles to it in the consciousness of the masses. It is here that I opted for faith. . . . I felt it necessary to make faith the symbol of resistance." Patently dishonest though this antifascist version of Greene's conversion may be, there is a truth at its center: namely, that Catholicism has generally functioned, in Greene's personal metaphysics, as a sort of escape hatch from the cold-eyed realism of which he is so proud; despite his professed loathing of romanticism, and his much-vaunted "realistic" attitude toward the Western world, the capitalistic system, and the United States, Greene's "faith" has provided him with a means of holding what are basically romantic views of certain aspects of life – in particular of Marxist ideas, exploits, and leaders. As the narrator remarks in *The Heart of the Matter,* "[I]f romance is what one lives by, one must never be cured of it. The world has too many spoilt priests of this faith or that: better surely to pretend a belief than wander in that vicious vacuum of cruelty and despair."

In its emphasis on faith, on the individual's personal relationship with God, and on a vigorous suspicion of prescribed doctrine, Greene's personal version of Christianity might seem to some observers more Protestant (if anything) than Catholic. Yet time and again Greene has gone out of his way to belittle Protestantism in general and the Anglicanism of his birth in particular. At times, indeed, he writes as if it were agreed by the whole world that Catholicism were the only real religion – the only one, that is to say, that can truly inhabit a soul and bring a communicant closer to God – and Anglicanism nothing more than a social club, a collection of pompous empty rituals whose participants give no thought to virtue or sin or the deity. "You are an Englishman," a Portuguese captain says to Scobie, a colonial policeman, in *The Heart of the Matter.* "You wouldn't believe in prayer." Scobie counters, "I'm a Catholic, too." Later in the novel, Scobie reflects that his mistress, Helen, has it good: since she's not a Catholic, "[s]he's lucky. She's free." The implication here – and elsewhere in Greene's *oeuvre* – is that non-Catholics are innocents of a sort, bound by no moral code and free of the dark and difficult knowledge that Catholics share. Catholicism, in short, is serious; Anglicanism is vain and frivolous. And yet Greene's easy dismissal of orthodox Catholic thought, his audacious distortion of its precepts to suit his own purposes, and his facile fictional use of such concepts as eternal damnation may well strike some readers – Catholic, Anglican, or otherwise – as the very height of vanity and frivolity.

How DID a young man brought up in the Church of England end up being such a fervent – if iconoclastic – Catholic? The question brings us back, I think, to Greene's childhood at the Berkhamsted School and to his headmaster father's stern sexual precepts; for the more closely one examines Greene's attitude toward religion, the more strongly one feels that conversion to Catholicism must have seemed, to the young Greene, a perfect way of rejecting his Anglican father, even while, in a sense, he was (consciously or not) perpetuating the old man's moral domination over him. For however much of Catholic doctrine Greene chose to leave out of his personal version of the religion, he certainly retained – and, it might be argued, blew out of all proportion – Catholicism's strict views on sex and marriage. In the process he managed to make of the Catholic Church (at least in terms of its sexual teachings) a veritable replica of the Berkhamsted of his youth. The Catholic protagonists in several of his novels, after all, agonize over the sin of fornication in a way that would have been far more familiar to a tormented Victorian (or, in Greene's case, Georgian) public-school boy than it would be to even an unusually devout modern-day Catholic. And so many of his autobiographical protagonists prove to have been educated at seminaries or Jesuit schools that one gets the impression Greene regards such institutions as rough equivalents of Berkhamsted – at least, that is, when it comes to the attitudes toward sex and sin that these schools have inculcated into the souls of their alumni. It is almost as if the young Greene, feeling irrationally guilty as he broke his childhood ties to family and school, found it necessary to replace Berkhamsted with the Catholic Church, and his father with God – and, in the process, also found it necessary to make certain adjustments in Catholicism so that it might more nearly approximate, in temper and teachings, the institution in which he been raised.

There are other likely reasons for his attraction to Catholicism. Given the fact that Greene, even in his early youth, was a master of suicidal boredom and misanthropic despair, he must surely have seen Roman Catholicism, with its reverence for suffering, as a way of legitimizing his veritable fetishization of misery. Time and again, his Catholic novels equate suffering with life, seriousness, wisdom. "As long as one suffers," he writes in *The End of the Affair*, "one lives." And in *The Heart of the Matter:* "Despair is the price one pays for setting oneself an impossible aim. It is, one is told, the unforgivable sin, but it is a sin the corrupt or evil man never practices. He always has hope. He never reaches the freezing point of knowing absolute failure. Only the man of good will carries always in his heart this capacity for damnation." The epigraph to *The End of the Affair* is from Léon Bloy: "Man has places in his heart which do not yet exist, and into them enters suffering in order that they may have existence." Too often, alas, Greene's fixation on suffering seems masochistic, morbid; certainly the notion that religion should be nothing but suffering is as distasteful as the notion that it should be nothing but sweetness and light.

There is one additional factor in Greene's attraction to Catholicism whose importance cannot be underestimated. Sherry's biography mentions only one aspect of Catholicism that genuinely appealed to Greene at the time of his conversion: the belief in hell. As Greene said at the time, "It gives something hard, nonsentimental and exciting." Hard, nonsentimental, and exciting: he might, one cannot but notice, be describing one of his own entertainments. And indeed it seems to have been not so much hell itself but the *melodrama* of hell, and of Catholicism in general, that captivated the young man. To the thoroughly English Greene, Catholicism must have seemed exotic and Latin, must have appealed not only to his personal sense of alienation but to the thrillermeister's love of the sensational. His Catholic novels, in any event, make it clear that Greene cherishes the drama of sin and eternal damnation; one thinks, for example, of the scene in *The Heart of the Matter* in which Scobie, taking communion in a state of mortal sin, is

"aware of the pale papery taste of his eternal sentence on the tongue."
What other religion could provide higher drama?

Traces of Greene's distinctive view of Catholicism – or of its development – appear in virtually all of Greene's novels. But it reaches its
apotheosis in four of them: *The Power and the Glory, The Heart of the
Matter, The End of the Affair,* and *A Burnt-Out Case.* Taken together,
these books almost seem to have been designed as a set of Greenian Articles of Faith. The chief tenets of this faith – among them the notion of
experience as the road to metaphysical knowledge, of prodigious sin as
the path to saintliness – are explored tirelessly in these books; if various
other Greene novels convey the idea that it is important to have some
kind of faith or to take a stand on one side or the other of a given con-
test, these four novels spell out Greene's specific brand of faith with considerable precision. Each of them contains a major character who is a
sinner, whose central conflict is his struggle with faith, and whose struggle ends in death; invariably, the assumptions upon which the conflict
takes place, the terms in which it is presented, and the conclusions that
are drawn from its outcome derive entirely from Greene's own iconoclastic version of Catholicism.

For instance, *The Power and the Glory* (1940), set in socialist Mexico
in the 1930s, takes as its protagonist a cowardly alcoholic priest who
has married one woman and fathered a child by another. This "whiskey
priest" (whose name we never learn) is the last Roman Catholic cleric
remaining in a province where it's been declared a crime to say Mass;
like many a Greene hero, he spends much of the book on the lam from
the authorities. This simply structured novel is dense with evocations of
rural poverty and with pronouncements about various spiritual topics –
good and evil, love and lust, experience and innocence – from which
Greene typically doesn't distance himself at all. "[O]ur sins have so
much beauty," the whiskey priest declares at one point. "I'm a bad
priest, you see. I know – from experience – how much beauty Satan carried down with him when He fell. Nobody ever said the fallen angels
were the ugly ones." It is his corruption, the priest says, that has
brought him close to God: as a "comparatively innocent" young man,

he was "unbearable." (In Greene's novels, of course, innocent men are invariably unbearable.) And indeed we are meant to understand, at the book's conclusion, that for all his sin the priest may well be something of a saint.

Though Greene does not depart radically here from the brisk, lucid manner of his early novels and entertainments, he does – rather like Hemingway in *For Whom the Bell Tolls* – attempt to modify his characteristic precision and simplicity in the direction of a certain austere stateliness, and thereby to give his "whiskey priest" a magnitude, and even a kind of coarse nobility, that his previous heroes didn't have. As in Hemingway's novel, however, the results of this stylistic modification are questionable. For one thing, the frequent appearance of colons between strings of independent clauses ("The squad of police made their way back to the station: they walked raggedly with rifles slung anyhow: ends of cotton where buttons should have been: a puttee slipping down over the ankle: small men with black secret Indian eyes") seems to have no *raison d'être* other than the author's affectation; for another, the novel's plainness of style ("He hustled them out: one by one they picked their way across the clearing towards the hut: and the old man set off down the path toward the river to take the place of the boy who watched the ford for soldiers") feels strained and phony in the way of the most self-parodic Hemingway.

Patently, Greene seeks to convey in this novel a solemn, intense vision of the human condition – a vision in which there would appear to be little room for the humor that helps (occasionally, at least) to relieve the darkness of his earlier books. But it's less a vision, really, than a contrivance, a repetitive and deliberate hammering away at the irony of the priest's position as "a damned man putting God into the mouths of men." The priest constantly flagellates himself, and we're plainly meant to be moved by his distress; but because that supposed distress is, for the most part, simply reiterated, rather than being reflected in a serious effort to change his ways, it's hard to take it very seriously. It's hard, for that matter, to believe that *Greene* takes it seriously: for the novel shows every sign of having been built less upon a passionate devotion to the idea of God than upon a view – at once glib, sentimental, patronizing, and upper-crust-Protestant – of swarthy, dirt-poor, Romance-language-speaking Catholics as close to the earth and, *ipso facto,* close to the Almighty.

The sinner at the heart of *The Heart of the Matter* (1948), which takes place during World War II, is Major Scobie, the middle-aged assistant police commissioner in a British colonial town on the West African coast. Described by his superior as "Scobie the Just," by a Syrian trader as "a just man," by a local MI5 agent named Wilson as "too damned honest to live," and by his wife, Louise, as "the typical second man [t]he one who always does the work," Scobie has been stationed in this town for fifteen years – "too long to go," as he puts it – and he has a rare understanding of and compassion for the natives. He is also a Catholic (he married into the faith) and a loyal husband, and has the sort of less-than-rosy outlook of which Greene approves: "It seemed to Scobie that life was immeasurably long. Couldn't the test of man have been carried out in fewer years? Couldn't we have committed our first major sin at seven, have ruined ourselves for love or hate at ten, have clutched at redemption on a fifteen-year-old death bed?"

Love, sin, and redemption are, as it happens, the principal concerns here; and the first intimation of peril comes when Wilson becomes infatuated with Louise. But Scobie's true downfall begins when he encounters a boatful of shipwreck survivors, falls swiftly in love with one of them – a young widow named Helen Rolt – and commences to break his marital vows while Louise is away: "God can wait, he thought: how can one love God at the expense of one of his creatures?" During his affair with Helen, Scobie is insufferable – although Greene doesn't seem to *intend* for him to be insufferable – about the threat of perdition hanging over his head. "If you believe in hell," Helen asks him, "why are you with me now?" Good question. And after Louise's return, Scobie finds himself in a spiritual bind: if he doesn't take communion with Louise, she'll know he committed a mortal sin; if he does take it with the taint of his adultery on his soul, he will (he believes) be irredeemably damned. In the end, he chooses the latter; and, after taking communion ("O God, I offer up my damnation to you"), whining to Helen about it ("I'm damned for all eternity. . . . what I've done is far worse than murder"), and wallowing for a while in self-pity ("This was what human love had done to him – it had robbed him of love for eternity"), he commits suicide – which, we've been told, "puts a man outside mercy." For those who haven't caught the irony here, Greene has already spelled it out: "Only the man of good will carries always in his heart this capacity for damnation."

With its solemn (if often highly dubious) aphorisms about love, damnation, and eternity, its consistently elevated tone, its sweltering and exotic African setting (whose purpose is perhaps to suggest at once the intensity of Scobie's passions, the extremity of his spiritual crisis, and the torment of hell), and its unyielding focus upon a man's relentless march toward his own everlasting doom, this novel seems to insist, with every sentence, on its own greatness. And many readers, over the years, have agreed that it *is* great. But is it? For a man who believes that adultery is a path to hell, Scobie certainly doesn't seem to put up much of a struggle against temptation – which makes it hard to take all the rhetoric about God and sin and damnation very seriously. Nor does he try very hard to escape his doom after sleeping with Helen; he presents himself in the confessional, to be sure, but since he can't promise to avoid seeing Helen, the priest can't guarantee a valid absolution. It's absurd: if Scobie truly believes his soul is on the line, why doesn't he do everything in his power to avoid Helen? Or at least, for heaven's sake, skip communion till the romance blows over? His behavior is so irrational, so preposterously gentlemanly, so *English;* to read about his fate is to feel that a real Catholic could never have invented such a character, a man who would sacrifice his eternal soul to avoid creating a scene.

What Greene has manufactured here is a public-school heroic fantasy that has no relevance whatsoever to the real world, Catholic or otherwise; in the person of Scobie, Greene brings together a rigid Catholic faith (which might be found in a certain kind of man) with a readiness to commit adultery (which might be characteristic of another, very different sort of man); combining the two traits, however, results not in a portrait of a complex, full-blooded individual but in an unbelievable concoction that reflects only its creator's obsessions. It may be that the only way one can easily understand Scobie, in real-world terms, is as a man who has for years been waiting for a good reason to kill himself. Certainly his thoughts are full of the subject: he ponders the fact that "[d]eath never comes when one desires it most"; he reflects of his long deceased daughter that she "was safe now, for ever" (like many Greene characters, he considers death a sanctuary).[3] If *The Heart of the Matter* is effective, it is largely as a demonstration of the ability of emotionally disturbed individuals to twist religion into a tool of self-destruction.

*T*he *End of the Affair* (1951), like *The Heart of the Matter*, depicts a fatal romantic triangle. Set in London and its environs, the novel is described by its narrator and protagonist, a writer named Maurice Bendrix, as "a record of hate far more than of love." As the novel opens in January of 1946, Bendrix learns from his friend Henry Miles, a high-ranking member of the government, that Henry's wife, Sarah, may be having an affair; Bendrix is hurt, for unbeknownst to Henry, he had enjoyed a three-year liaison with Sarah himself until, a year and a half earlier, she broke it off inexplicably and Bendrix "began quite seriously to think of suicide." Now, desperate to know the truth, Bendrix engages a detective; the man pinches Sarah's diary, and it is from this document that Bendrix learns why she separated from him. One day, thinking him dead in an air raid, she had prayed to God: "Let him be alive, and I *will* believe. . . . I'll give him up for ever, only let him be alive." When Bendrix indeed proved to be alive, Sarah kept her word to God, and ever since has been engaged in a struggle with the idea of God, resenting Him, seeking advice from a fanatical antireligionist, and pouring her heart into her diary: "I want Maurice. I want ordinary corrupt human love. Dear God, you know I want to want Your pain, but I don't want it now." Bendrix refuses to take God seriously as a rival, and seeks to revive their affair. But he succeeds only (through an unfortunate happenstance) in bringing about Sarah's death – and learns afterward that she had been taking instruction in Catholicism, a faith into which (though she never knew it) she had been baptized as a child.

In many ways *The End of the Affair* is one of Greene's best books. It is exquisitely shaped and paced, the people and their relationships seem

---

3. Interestingly, Scobie's suicide is foreshadowed by that of another British officer, whose note contains a sentence reminiscent of Greene's own early missives: *"It's a pity I'm not in the army because then I might be killed."*

real, and both the passion and the bitterness ring true; though plenty of abstractions are brought into play, one does not constantly have the feeling that the characters serve merely as symbolic tokens. Yet, reading Sarah's diary account of her discovery of faith, one does want to ask the question: why Catholicism and not Anglicanism? Why must belief in a Creator necessarily lead, in the world according to Greene, to belief – as Sarah puts it – in "the whole bag of tricks" of the Catholic Church? The revelation of Sarah's childhood Catholicism suggests that Greene wants us to see her recent enthusiasm for the faith as some sort of mystical event, a reclaiming of Sarah, as it were, by God; but this reading, it seems to me, cheapens the book, turns it into a kind of religious thriller. (Do even pious Catholics believe that God plays such games?) One prefers to think that Sarah chooses Catholicism because it is the one Christian faith that would flatly forbid her to divorce Henry and marry Maurice – an act against which her sense of guilt about the affair rebels. To posit such a reading is not to deny the sublimity of religious faith, but merely to acknowledge the importance – to life, to literature, and even perhaps to God – of human character and psychology; what makes *The End of the Affair* more successful than *The Power and the Glory* and *The Heart of the Matter* is its greater appreciation of that importance.

A Burnt-Out Case (1961), the last of Greene's explicitly Catholic books, is in some ways a departure from its predecessors. It begins with the mysterious arrival of Querry, a world-famous church architect, at a small Central African leper hospital on a remote tributary of the Congo. Querry has come to the hospital – which is run by Catholic priests and by one Dr. Colin, and which is crowded with "burnt-out cases" (patients, many of them disfigured and impaired, from whose systems the leprosy infection has totally disappeared) – to finish out his life away from civilization. Why? Because in his own way Querry is a burnt-out case, too; or so, at least, he tells everyone who's ready to listen. Yes, he's perfectly scrupulous, well-functioning: "You are a whole man as far as one can see," says Parkinson, a sleazy reporter who tracks him down to the hospital. But Querry knows better: he's lost his faith. In contrast to his parents' simple, instinctive religion, he had constructed an edifice of logical proofs of the existence of God; but his realization that he didn't truly accept those proofs has caused an emotional crisis. He realizes he's been deceiving himself: he's never really loved ("Perhaps it's true that you can't believe in a god without loving a human being or love a human being without believing in a god"), never built a church for love of anything but himself ("To build a church when you don't believe in a god seems a little indecent, doesn't it?"). He'd always thought himself dedicated to God, but knows now that "anything he had ever done must have been done for love of himself." If Sarah, in *The End of the Affair,* longs for the suffering that will mark her as a true Christian, Querry is past all that: "I suffer from nothing. I no longer know what suffering is. I have come to an end of all that...." (One of the novel's epigraphs comes from Dante: "I did not die, yet nothing of life remained.")

Over the next few months, Querry assists the priests and helps them plan a new hospital. Ironically, when he saves a man's life he is celebrated as a saint by the ignoble Parkinson, the innocent Father Thomas, and the intellectual M. Rycker (a local factory manager and former seminarian); yet when he is falsely accused of having an affair with Mme. Rycker, those who declared him a saint are the first to condemn him. Interestingly – in what seems to be something of a move away from Greene's earlier concentration on faith, and toward a doctrine of good works – Querry's staunchest ally (and the most sympathetic and level-headed character in the book) is Dr. Colin, who "had long ago . . . lost faith in any god that a priest would have recognized," but who, despite his atheism, we are manifestly supposed to admire for his tireless dedication to the sick. Likewise, we're supposed to admire the priests (except for Father Thomas), who "would much prefer to talk about turbines" than about canon law, and who are "too busy to bother themselves with what the Church considered sin (moral theology was the subject they were least concerned with)."

And we *do* admire them. But it's hard to admire Querry. Though he's a decent enough chap, his enthusiasm for his own suffering is wearisome in the extreme; it comes across as the manifestation not of a crisis of faith (as Greene would have us believe) but of severe neurosis. Querry keeps insisting upon his inability to love and to believe, but it's all just words, words, words: his torment is never dramatized, just endlessly proclaimed. And to a large extent, it's simply too weird and too abstract to identify with: he can't make love anymore, he says, because sex should be an enacting of God's love for his people and he can no longer believe in God. We're apparently meant to see all this soul-searching as part of a sacred struggle, but for the most part it seems merely solipsistic, selfish; and it seems especially so because at the *léproserie* he is surrounded by people – among them many small children – who have a much more visible reason than he does to bewail their fates. Yet not even the sight of armless babies can take Querry out of himself for very long, and Greene doesn't seem to intend the irony: to him, as to Querry, the leprosy patients are basically set decoration, their physical disfigurement a metaphor for Querry's spiritual mutilation. Likewise, when Querry compares his own late, lamented intellectual Catholicism with his parents' "simple and uncomplex heart[s]," Greene doesn't seem to want us to find him arrogant – but of course we do. Even Dr. Colin regards Querry as a privileged character; when a priest suggests that publicity for the hospital might attract funds that could help hundreds of lepers, Dr. Colin rejects the idea because it wouldn't be good for Querry. "Limelight," he says, "is not very good for the mutilated."

There are logical problems with the book, too. The idea of a church architect as celebrity is a bit difficult to buy. And then there are certain questions of motivation: Querry claims to have come to the *léproserie* in order to escape the world, the Church, *la bête humaine;* yet, if this is the case, how did he happen to end up as a veritable social worker in a part of Central Africa that seems to contain more Catholics than the Vatican? And why, if he didn't want reporters to track him down, did he give everyone along the way his real name? Greene shows no sign of doubting Querry's motives. Then, as in *The Heart of the Matter,* there's the suicide angle. "A man can't live with nothing but himself," Dr. Colin says; "[s]ooner or later he would kill himself." Yes, Querry replies, "[i]f he had enough interest." Like Scobie, he seems essentially to be a suicide in search of a catalyst.

F OR THE MOST PART, indeed, all of Greene's so-called Catholic novels seem ultimately to have less to do with religion, *per se,* than with psychopathology – and, one might add, with melodramatic artifice; as

I've suggested in connection with *The End of the Affair,* it might even be more nearly correct to call them religious thrillers. To be sure, they have been treated very respectfully by critics and readers, and it is true that their deeply afflicted protagonists, their solemn metaphysical utterances, their grand abstractions, their richly symbolic settings, and their tragic endings tend to enforce the impression that Greene is a serious – perhaps even a profound – laborer in the fields of spiritual allegory. Yet to read these books in sequence is to become increasingly aware of the overly manipulated characters, the windy rhetoric, the author's glib misreading of the human heart. There are so many immense abstractions planted so closely together here that few of them have room to grow into life; but then it would be virtually impossible for *any* story to bear the weight of meaning that Greene seeks to impose on these tales. All four books, furthermore, are informed not only by the extreme notion – as expressed in the Charles Péguy quotation that Greene used as an epigraph to *The Heart of the Matter* – that "[t]he sinner is at the heart of Christianity," but also by Greene's even more extreme corollary that the greater one's sins are, the closer one is to God, and the more likely one is to be a saint. While this may sound like clever theology, in practice it's simply offensive: if we are to believe such things, then how are we to feel about Hitler? In this and other such pronouncements by Greene, one hears the voice not of a serious moral philosopher but of the melodramatist, the author of thrillers out for sheer effect.

POLITICS have always figured conspicuously in Graham Greene's fiction. Of all Greene's novels, however, the ones that probably come to mind most readily when the word *politics* is mentioned – or, at least, those in which his political notions find their most memorable expression – are *The Quiet American, The Comedians, The Honorary Consul,* and *The Human Factor.* If in Greene's political novels of the thirties his principal object of ridicule is Great Britain, in these later novels – which appeared between 1955 and 1978 – the repellent figure in the carpet is consistently the United States; while the protagonists are invariably competent, seasoned Britishers (or at least half-Brits) who know how complex and morally equivocal realpolitik can be, the forces of evil tend to be either credulous, sanctimonious Yanks (who, fools that they are, take words like *democracy* and *individuality* seriously) or their fascist lackeys.

These novels can, then, be shrill, and many a character overdetermined; what's good about them, however, is that they generally have the virtues of top-notch thrillers: superb pacing, picturesque minor characters, fine local color (not overdone, as in many of Greene's earlier books), and a convincing air of danger. In each of them, an apathetic but basically good man finds himself drawn by friendship or love into a dangerous, politically charged situation; invariably, the results are disastrous, and are meant to illustrate the tragic necessity of commitment. Catholicism – which is thematically central to such novels as *The Power and the Glory* and *The Heart of the Matter* – does not disappear from the scene, to be sure, but the struggles with faith that take place are depicted in broader, more secular terms; some of the concepts, moreover, that Greene might previously have represented in spiritual terms take on, in these novels, a more distinctly political coloring.

Take *The Quiet American* (1955), for example. Whereas in *A Burnt-Out Case* Greene chooses to embody innocence in the young and impercipient priest Father Thomas, in this novel innocence is personified by an American who, on the surface, seems to be the very incarnation of his native virtues. The book's setting is Saigon, and its protagonist-cum-narrator is Thomas Fowler, a world-weary, middle-aged English reporter who knows all the angles and whose credo is not to get involved; the man who finally gets him involved is the newly arrived U.S. economic envoy Alden Pyle, a young Harvard graduate, devout Christian, and probable virgin who befriends Fowler, and who is "determined... to do good, not to any individual person, but to a country, a continent, a world." He is also determined – in the most honorable fashion – to win the hand of Fowler's teenage Vietnamese mistress, Phuong, whom Fowler cannot marry because his Catholic wife in England won't give him a divorce. But Pyle's very innocence makes him a sucker for evil, causing him to sponsor the murderous General Thé, for whom he holds a misguided hope as a so-called Third Force solution to the current French-Vietnamese standoff; it is after one of Thé's bombs kills a number of women and children that Fowler rouses himself to action – and inadvertently brings about Pyle's demise.

Greene's command of cultural and atmospheric detail is particularly impressive here: Fowler discourses self-assuredly on the effects of opium, makes apparent sense of the confusion of mid-fifties Indo-chinese politics, and brings to life the "Low Country landscape where young green rice shoots and golden harvests take the place of tulips." Fowler's authoritativeness in regard to all things Annamese is impor-tant to the book, for it lends his strong opinions about the Vietnam situ-ation an air of validity. It also encourages us – for a while, anyway – to see Americans the way he does: as "big, noisy, boyish and middle-aged" oafs who swill Coca-Cola and drive big cars, who have taken degrees in "those subjects Americans can take degrees in," and who inhabit "a psy-chological world of great simplicity." As is typical of his countrymen, Pyle's only crime is his credulity; he has no business in Vietnam, Fowler insists, and should be "reading the Sunday supplements at home and following the baseball . . . safe with a standardized American girl who subscribed to a book club."

It's all quite clever. But a little America-bashing goes a long way, and eventually it's hard not to see Greene's prejudices – for these are clearly not just Fowler's opinions but his author's – as the puerile manifestation of a certain type of Englishman's irrational postwar resentment. The subtext of all these anti-American digs, in short, is that it's not an En-glish world anymore but an American one. "We used to speak of ster-ling qualities," Fowler says. "Have we got to talk now of a dollar love?" And he notes sardonically that at the American Legation, "[e]ven their lavatories were air-conditioned, and presently the temperature tem-pered air dried my tears as it dries the spit in your mouth and the seed in your body." What more revealing symbol could there be for Britain's emasculation by America?

Here, as in all of his later political novels, a fundamental part of Greene's hard-bitten-realist pose is a scornful attitude toward what he calls "isms" and "ocracies," which he contrasts unfavorably with "facts." "As for liberty," Fowler says, "I don't know what it means." Ditto for individuality. Only someone as naïve as an American, he implies, would take such concepts seriously. Needless to say, for a writer as individualis-tic as Greene – and as dependent as he is on Western freedoms – to as-sign such sentiments to a character who plainly speaks for him in such matters is unadulterated hypocrisy. And the character himself, meanwhile, represents the sheerest sort of self-flattery: while Pyle is at times almost inconceivably ingenuous, Fowler is just a bit too savvy to be believed, his eleventh-hour resolution a little too formulaic, his quips in the face of death a shade too reminiscent of a Bogart movie hero's.

Much the same is true of Brown, the British, Monaco-born, Jesuit-educated hotel owner who is the narrator and hero of *The Comedians* (1966). The setting is Haiti, which under the dictator "Papa Doc" Duvalier and his "bogey-men," the vicious Tontons Macoute, has become a police state. Like Fowler, Brown is an apathetic foreigner who knows this chaotic place inside out, but who—because of the subversive actions of a sleazy profiteer named Jones, who may or may not be American—ends up getting involved anyway. As in the case of Fowler, Brown's initial insistence that he had long ago "lost completely the capacity to be concerned" feels more like a thriller device than a genuine character trait; the same holds for his repeatedly proclaimed perception of those around him as "comedians" —as people who escape commitment, that is, by various forms of sentimentality and pretense.

The book is revealing—to put it mildly—for the parallels Greene draws between Catholicism and communism. Brown claims not to be a Communist, but when his German mistress tells him he speaks like one, he says, "Sometimes I wish I were," and declares his envy for the communism of his friend Dr. Magiot: "He's lucky to believe. I left all such absolutes behind me in the chapel of the Visitation." The novel concludes with Dr. Magiot's astonishing, anti-rational apologia for communism which, he says,

> is more than Marxism, just as Catholicism. . . is more than the Roman Curia. There is a *mystique* as well as a *politique*. We are humanists, you and I. Catholics and Communists have committed great crimes, but at least they have not stood aside, like an established society, and been indifferent. I would rather have blood on my hands than water like Pilate. . . . If you have abandoned one faith, do not abandon all faith. There is always an alternative to the faith we lose. Or is it the same faith under another mask?

We are plainly expected to read this paean without irony, to see it as wise and noble and heartfelt. Not only is this speech extremely ineffective in dramatic terms, however – its sentiments don't follow at all from the novel's story – but it would seem to confirm that Greene's leftist politics are no more a product of rational, responsible thought than is his peculiarly constituted Catholicism; as with Catholicism, it is largely the *mystique* of communism that appeals to him. Notwithstanding his much-vaunted disapproval of sentimentality and pretense, Greene's fondness for the false gods of communism (and it matters little, really, whether he calls himself a Communist or not) certainly seems the height of self-deceiving sentimentality.

THE THOMAS HARDY epigraph to *The Honorary Consul* (1973) would appear, by its placement in such a context, to reiterate Dr. Magiot's parallel between Catholicism and communism: "All things merge in one another – good into evil, generosity into justice, religion into politics." The dictatorship of choice this time around is Paraguay, the homeland of half-English physician Eduardo Plarr, who has lived since boyhood in an Argentinian border city and whose father – a well-known "idealist" – may or may not still be alive in a Paraguayan jail. It is on the off chance of helping to free his father that the aloof, apolitical Plarr lends a hand to Leon Rivas, a revolutionary ex-priest who seeks to gain the release of Paraguayan political prisoners by taking the British ambassador hostage. But someone blunders, and Rivas ends up in possession of Plarr's small-fry friend Charley Fortnum, who holds the empty title of British honorary consul, and about whom the London government could not care less. It is, Plarr feels, up to him to try to set things right.

Here again, the suspense is nicely managed, but the ideas that propel it are ludicrous. For one thing, with his distinctly early-seventies take on Greenian isolato-talk ("I know how to fuck – I don't know how to love"), Plarr sometimes sounds as if he'd be more at home in Marin County than in South America. And though the book was very well received at the time, one wonders how its sympathetic view of terrorist hostage-taking ("Perhaps it was love of a kind," Fortnum says afterward of his kidnapping by Rivas) would go over in the wake of the past decade's hostage crises in Iran and Lebanon. As in the cases of Fowler and Brown, moreover, Plarr's estrangement from his fellow man is presented from the beginning as a *fait accompli*, his background filled in like a laundry list. One doesn't believe deeply in (or feel deeply about) such a character's initial detachment, because one isn't shown how he came to be this way. And one senses that it simply wouldn't occur to Greene that such detachment has to be accounted for in dramatic terms, because this attitude toward life comes altogether too easily to him.

If *The Human Factor* (1978) is the most successful of Greene's later novels in terms of evading this problem, it is partly because its protagonist, the thirty-year British Foreign Office veteran Maurice Castle, faces a somewhat different emotional predicament than Fowler, Brown, and Plarr: instead of being pulled from an unconvincing political aloofness into a facile political engagement, he finds himself positioned between two strongly conflicting loyalties. One of them is to his beautiful Bantu wife, Sarah (notice how the names match those in Greene's 1951 novel *The End of the Affair*), whom he met several years before while stationed in Pretoria; the other is to his superiors, who regard him as highly reliable ("[d]ullish man . . . it's generally the brilliant and ambitious who are dangerous"). As we eventually discover, however, these two loyalties are in secret conflict: for several years now, Castle has been covertly supplying confidential information to the Communist agent who helped Sarah escape from South Africa. And just when he feels he should close up shop – for his higher-ups are beginning to suspect him – something comes along that he simply *has* to share with the enemy: a joint U.S.–British–South African operation called Uncle Remus, whose purpose is to perpetuate apartheid through the deployment (by South Africa) of atomic weapons. Castle's only hope of thwarting the implementation of this sinister plan is to leak word to his Communist contact – whatever the risk to his own life.

Greene's plot has holes in it. One need not be a Pollyanna to have trouble buying the premise that the United States and Britain would concoct something quite as extreme as Uncle Remus (or, for that matter, that they'd come up with that name for it). This is a significant flaw, for the book doesn't work unless one sympathizes, to some extent, with

Castle's treachery, and that sympathy depends largely upon one's ability to believe in the existence of Uncle Remus. Equally hard to buy is the rubout of Castle's partner, Davis, whom their superiors suspect of being the leak. Would the British Secret Service, one finds oneself wondering, really liquidate one of its own so quickly, and on so little evidence? And would their suspicions – under circumstances such as those detailed in the book – rest on Davis (whose only crime would seem to be his youth and negligence) and not on Castle, whose indebtedness to a Communist agent for his wife's safety is well known to them?

These problems alone do not necessarily cripple the book's effectiveness. But perhaps just as disabling to its credibility is the venomous attitude that Greene expresses toward America and everything it represents. Snide remarks about the United States are assigned to a number of characters, including Castle, who observes of the patrons of a pornographic bookstore that "they are not clean young Americans doing their duty like the napalm bombers [in Vietnam] were." Plausible though they may otherwise be, the characters come across only as authorial mouthpieces when they say this sort of thing. What's more, they refer to democracy only in sarcastic or dismissive terms, or else ignore its existence altogether, as does one of Castle's superiors when he remarks that "[t]hirty years ago when I was a student I rather fancied myself as a kind of Communist. Now . . . ? Who is the traitor – me or Davis? I really believed in internationalism, and now I'm fighting an underground war for nationalism." Finally, Greene makes irresponsible use of the fiction of Uncle Remus – which, of course, proves to be not an MI6 but a CIA brainchild – to score political points about the real world; Castle, for instance, says that the Soviet Union's "worst crimes are always in the past, and the future hasn't arrived yet. I can't go on parroting, 'Remember Prague! Remember Budapest!' – they were years ago. One has to be concerned about the present, and the present is Uncle Remus."

The unfortunate thing about all these failings is that *The Human Factor* is really a first-class thriller – its characters sharply drawn, its plot elegantly structured, its style crisp and serviceable. If one can allow oneself to accept, for dramatic purposes and for the duration of the novel, Greene's picture of the global situation, it makes for a very entertaining read. For a book that seeks to be regarded not just as a thriller, however, but as a serious novel, his warped representation of reality constitutes a major weakness. Greene has confessed that *The Human Factor* was "inspired" by his friend, the famous traitor Kim Philby, whom he has lauded for "the consistency with which he came to his new [Communist] convictions and defended them in the struggle against fascism"; the same deluded worldview that informs this outlandish remark is at the heart of *The Human Factor*.

After the publication of *The Human Factor*, Greene reportedly thought that he had written his last novel. And in a sense he had. The books that followed are odd, cryptic, rather underwhelming little fables: episodic and meandering, they are weak on plot and character, with a wispy, almost ultramundane tone not unlike that of Shakespeare's romances. Though they explore many of the same themes as his earlier novels, they do so in a manner at once dimmer and more indiscreet; with each book, the chapters get shorter and the margins wider. Each is essentially a character portrait of an eccentric – and either deific or diabolic – authority figure: a doctor, a monsignor, a captain. *Dr. Fischer of Geneva, or The Bomb Party* (1980) recounts the cruel and unusual behavior of the narrator's proud, evil millionaire father-in-law, Dr. Fischer (we know Dr. Fischer is evil because he finds theology "an amusing intellectual game"); *Monsignor Quixote* (1982), the tale of a modern-day village priest who travels across Spain with his Communist friend Sancho Zancas, apparently seeks to embody a sort of symbolic alliance of communism and Catholicism.

As for Greene's most recent novel, *The Captain and the Enemy* (1988), its premise bears an interesting resemblance to that of his first. Like Andrews (the protagonist of *The Man Within*), Victor (later Jim) Baxter is adopted by a charismatic, widely traveled friend of his father's who takes him away forever from his stern public school. This happens, however, not because he has been orphaned (as is the case with Andrews, who goes on to become an apprentice smuggler on the Sussex coast), but because his father has lost him in a game – maybe backgammon, maybe chess – to a mysterious gunrunner known as the Captain. After all this has transpired, alas, the tale grows slack and flat-footed, ultimately wandering into polemical territory with a slim, improbable story line involving the Panama Canal Treaty, the Somoza regime, and

Salvadoran death squads. The novel reads like the feverish dream of an old man possessed by an unreasoned hatred for the United States – a nation that is transformed, in this book, into a veritable symbol of supreme, unexceptioned evil – and by a mindless fascination with Latin American revolutionaries. If *The Man Within,* then, offers an uncommonly revealing glimpse into the Freudian preoccupations of a very young and ingenuous author, *The Captain and the Enemy* provides an equally candid insight into the sociopolitical obsessions of the same novelist sixty-odd years later – a man far older but, alas, not much wiser. In more than one way, then, *The Captain and the Enemy* brings Greene full circle.

ALL OF WHICH leaves us with one question: how did Graham Greene – an author who, as we have seen, has never quite shaken off the devices of a thriller writer – ever manage to acquire and maintain an international reputation as one of the most distinguished literary figures of his time? Undoubtedly this reputation owes much to the conspicuous role that Catholicism and leftist politics have played in Greene's most widely admired books. Certainly if he had spent his entire career writing straightforward thrillers along the lines of *Stamboul Train* and *The Confidential Agent,* Greene would have remained at most a peripheral figure on the literary scene; for, in those precincts where literary performances are evaluated and authorial ranks assigned, it is widely understood (if not universally accepted) that a thriller, however accomplished, represents an achievement of a different kind than a serious literary novel. But something odd happens, in a certain sort of critical mind, when religion or politics enters the picture. Religion is serious; politics are serious. For many critics, therefore, a novelist who purports to address religious or political questions is a novelist to be taken seriously – no matter how unserious the manner in which he engages those topics, and no matter how strongly the impact of his fiction may prove to depend upon the modalities of melodrama and the stylistic mannerisms of the thriller.

During the last twenty-five years or so, moreover – the period during which three of Greene's four later political novels were published – a conspicuous attraction to radical-left politics has become one way for a writer to ensure not only that he will be taken seriously but that he will be looked upon favorably by a number of influential literary critics; for to many such critics, as we know, the aesthetic value of a work of fiction is of less importance than its politics. And surely nothing could have been more appealing to leftist intellectuals from China to Peru during this period than the sort of anti-Americanism that figures in Greene's later political novels. Even less radically inclined commentators have often felt honor-bound, it would seem, to congratulate the outspoken, left-leaning Greene for his supposed courage and political commitment.

Yet how could any intelligent reader who considers himself socially responsible smile on the notion of political commitment that is typically reflected in Greene's later novels? And how, for that matter, could any devout and thoughtful Catholic not be made uncomfortable by Greene's singular view of Catholicism? For his Catholic novels and his later political novels make it clear that Greene looks upon both religion and politics, to a remarkable degree, not as means by which one may commit oneself to specific understandings of reality but as means of identifying oneself with certain ideals – ideals which one may well frankly accept as fanciful, illusory, and contrary to logic. Far from constituting rational, intellectual responses to the world, in other words, Greene's religion and politics more often seem attractive to him precisely because he regards them as forms of rebellion *against* intellect and reason, as ways of escape *from* the world. (Indeed, Sherry quotes a sister-in-law of Greene's as saying that he "was not a logical man. . . . He was not logical about politics, he was not logical about his religion.") Time and again, Greene approves of characters who pointedly dissociate their belief – whether religious or political – from reality. He patently wants us to admire Sarah, for instance, when she remarks in *The End of the Affair* that "[t]hey could dig up records that proved Christ had been invented by Pilate to get himself promoted and I'd believe just the same." (Here and in Greene's other Catholic novels, he makes it clear that the important thing is not to believe in God, in any conventional sense, but to love God – to cherish, that is, an idea of God.) Likewise, though communism may have had disastrous consequences in the real world, Greene wants us to cheer Dr. Magiot's loyalty to it as a romantic dream – his loyalty to, in Magiot's phrase, communism's *"mystique."*

(As Carlyon observes wistfully in *The Man Within,* "A dream is often all there is to a man.")

To many a reader, it may seem that Magiot's continued faith in the mystique of communism prevents him from becoming responsibly involved in the real world; to Greene, however, this *is* involvement. In Greene's paradoxical view, that is to say, mystique *is* realpolitik, and it is altogether proper to respond to real-world problems by dedicating oneself to an alluring absolute. Never mind that communism has had far bloodier consequences than Western democracy: the important thing is not that democracy has done better by humanity, but that communism has greater charisma. One of the unintended ironies of Greene's *oeuvre* is that, whereas he implicitly criticizes the innocence of many of his characters – among them Father Thomas in *A Burnt-Out Case* and Alden Pyle in *The Quiet American* – because it leads them to unwise judgments or disastrous associations, Greene's own broad experience of the world has patently not prevented him from making choices and forging alliances that are at least as ill-advised and calamitous.

Highly enlightening in this regard is *Getting to Know the General,* Greene's 1984 memoir of his friendship with the Marxist dictator of Panama, General Omar Torrijos Herrera, who had died three years earlier. Torrijos had first invited Greene to Panama in 1976, and over the succeeding years acted as his host during several visits (which seem to have provided the background for some of the later episodes in *The Captain and the Enemy*). Subtitled *The Story of an Involvement,* the memoir is an incredible document, an unintentionally devastating self-portrait in irresponsibility, egotism, and fatuity. It is also a portrait of General Torrijos, and no press agent ever wrote a more flattering one. For Greene – who was himself plainly flattered by the dictator's attentions – judges Torrijos not by his accomplishments but by his professed dreams, his utterly impracticable "plans" for everything from the elimination of slums to the construction of "a pleasure park for the poor." Another factor in Greene's admiration is that Torrijos proved to be a man after Greene's own heart, a man who loathed America, whose "romanticism was balanced by a streak of cynical wisdom" (this is clearly also Greene's view of himself), who was "not the kind of man to be sexually faithful to one woman" but who was "faithful above all to friendship." It means a lot to Greene when Torrijos tells him, "You and I are both self-destructive." Greene's comment: "It was like a friend speaking who knew me better than I knew myself."

Manifestly, *friend* and *friendship* are the key words here. There can be little question but that Torrijos's feelings of amity for him outweigh, in Greene's mind, the general's tyranny and thuggery. So it is that, in praising the Torrijos government early in the book, Greene manages to avoid mentioning that the general had imposed a ban on opposition political parties. (He finally mentions the ban much later on, when Torrijos lifts it – an act to which Greene can refer approvingly.) And so it is, too, that when Torrijos offers to send a hit man to France to rub out an enemy of Greene's, the author looks upon the proposal not as further evidence that Torrijos is a thug, but as a delightful confirmation of the general's friendship: imagine, the man likes him so much that he would have somebody killed for him! "I have never lost as good a friend as Omar Torrijos," Greene writes sincerely, apropos of Torrijos's offer – and from a man who has barely advanced beyond schoolyard values, this is supreme praise. Not surprisingly, Greene reserves his calumny in these pages almost exclusively for *norteamericanos,* waxing derisive, at one point, about the comfortable living conditions of Americans in Panama – conditions which, one suspects, hardly compare to the luxury that Greene enjoys in Antibes. (And this derision comes, moreover, from a man who, elsewhere in the book, without a trace of irony, complains about the lack of cheese on the Concorde on the way home!)

The fact that emerges conclusively from both his novels and memoirs is that Greene doesn't understand the meaning of the term social involvement. By all indications, the sometime public-school boy who avoided his fellows for fear of contamination by the evil of sex has remained detached, incapable of a truly selfless allegiance, a rationally founded devotion. In his view, it would seem, only love or pity or enthrallment by some kind of *mystique* is capable of drawing one into a commitment to either God or man. And such commitment is by its nature self-destructive, he believes, because it brings one into intimacy with "the odour of human meanness and injustice" (to quote Greene in *The Heart of the Matter*), and because (as Scobie reflects) "no human being can really understand another." As Joseph Conrad writes in a passage that Greene borrowed for the epigraph to *The Human Factor,* "I only know that he who forms a tie is lost. The germ of corruption has entered into his soul." The intended irony at the heart of Greene's fiction is that ideals – which are sublime at least in part because they exist forever apart from physical reality, incapable of being translated to it, realized in it, or corrupted by it – can cause a formerly aloof person to become embroiled in, and therefore corrupted by, the world around him.

Yet the cardinal failing of Greene's most celebrated novels is that the ideals – religious and political – that play so dominant a role in them are too often bizarre, their sincere espousal by sane, sober, and well-educated twentieth-century individuals hard to imagine and even harder to countenance. If his entertainments are on the whole more effective than his Catholic novels, it is because in the former he routinely distances himself from his protagonists, while in the latter he saddles his protagonists with some variation on his own perverse notion of faith; thus, as a rule, the heroes of the Catholic novels are motivated by ideas that the average intelligent reader – Catholic, Protestant, Jewish, agnostic, or otherwise – cannot take seriously, and that are so thematically pivotal that it is likewise virtually impossible to take the books themselves seriously. And if Greene's later political novels are (to varying degrees) successful as thrillers, they too are well-nigh irredeemably marred by the fatuous politics that figure importantly in their plots.

How, then, can Greene legitimately be called a great writer? Among other things, a great writer helps us to understand what it means – and why it is (or is not) worthwhile – to be human and to be alive. To examine Greene's novels thoughtfully is to be confronted, in quite dramatic fashion, with the plain fact that his dedication to the ideas supposedly central to his own life is ultimately so cursory, so self-contentedly shallow, that he cannot possibly have anything of importance to convey to us about such matters. Greene has, to be sure, a facility for narrative, an eye for atmosphere, a gift for publicity, and (to borrow Noel Coward's phrase) "a talent to amuse," sometimes when he least intends to do so – but he is, most assuredly, far from being the literary master that countless people who have read little or none of his work suppose him to be.

(SEPTEMBER–NOVEMBER 1989)

States of Grace:
William Maxwell

The simplest things are often not what they seem.
—WILLIAM MAXWELL, *The Château*

. . . who knows what oversensitive is, considering all there is to be sensitive to.
—WILLIAM MAXWELL, *So Long, See You Tomorrow*

IN AN AGE when editors of literary fiction increasingly prefer the sensationally modish to the quietly accomplished, when tastemakers at glossy magazines look upon twenty-eight-year-old first novelists as superannuated, and when supposedly serious critics neglect distinctive new novels in order to gush over the latest well-nigh interchangeable specimens of Brat Pack minimalism—in such an age, what could be more *démodé* than a thoroughgoing enthusiasm for William Maxwell?[1] For over half a century, Maxwell—now in his ninth decade—has gone his serene and unsplashy way, producing a new book every five years or so, all the while steadily accumulating one of the most admirable *oeuvres* in contemporary American letters. Though he could hardly be described as an unknown, Maxwell—who was born in 1908, and grew up in the Illinois town of Lincoln and in Chicago—has never enjoyed the fame of such contemporaries as, say, Richard Wright (b. 1908), Eudora Welty (b. 1909), or Mary McCarthy (b. 1912). Maxwell's fellow novelists

---

1. Maxwell's latest book is *The Outermost Dream: Essays and Reviews* (Knopf). All of the other Maxwell books mentioned in this essay are available in paperback reprints from David R. Godine, with the following exceptions: *Bright Center of Heaven* (Harper & Brothers, 1934); *Stories* (with Jean Stafford, John Cheever, and Daniel Fuchs; Farrar, Straus and Cudahy, 1956); and *So Long, See You Tomorrow* (available in Ballantine paperback).

and short story writers (many of whom benefited from his decades of editorial service at the *New Yorker*) have sung his praises melodiously among themselves – indeed, he is a near textbook case of a "writer's writer" – but he has been accorded little attention in the prominent literary journals, and even less in the halls of academe.

This is hardly surprising, for Maxwell is nobody's idea of an academic novelist. He has always been indifferent to literary trends, impervious to the influence of his more noted colleagues; implicit in his writings is a conviction that there is nothing new under the sun. His sentences don't cry out for explication: on the contrary, Maxwell has always written a luminously direct, clear, and matter-of-fact prose, never indulging in stylistic exhibitionism or willful obscurity. His primary aim in his work is a Flaubertian one: to evoke the texture of human experience, and to do so with precision, elegance, and sensitivity. A faithful recorder of the thousand and one passing moods, small embarrassments, and petty discomforts that flesh is heir to, he is never in too much of a hurry to do justice to phenomena that don't make it into most novels – for instance the way that one can fall in love with a stranger on a train whom one doesn't speak to and will never see again. Maxwell is unafraid of sheer feeling.

In his novel *The Château* (1961), he describes a pair of American tourists in France as follows: "They saw (as if seeing were an art and the end that everything is working toward) a barn with a sign painted on it: *Rasurel.*" To read Maxwell at any length is to find oneself deciding that seeing *is* an art, and Maxwell one of its unexampled masters. He is blessed with a rare sense of wonder: his books constantly remind us that life, love, friendship, youth, and a sense of beauty are mysterious gifts, things to marvel at. "Life," as one of his characters insists, "is something more than we believe it to be." Maxwell himself has commented: "So strange, life is. Why people do not go around in a continual state of surprise is beyond me." Yet he does not pretend to be able to penetrate life's mysteries in any lasting and conclusive way; as he observes in *The Château,* "When you explain a mystery, all you do is make room for another." He is acutely aware that man falls far short of omniscience; and he knows, too, that though we may sometimes think of ourselves as gods – as masters, that is, of the natural world – we are in reality a part of nature, subject to its laws and rhythms, its pleasures and perils, as helpless and vulnerable as all the other scurrying fauna.

Despite his depth of feeling, Maxwell is no sentimentalist: in fact, he is a good deal less of a romantic than his fellow midwesterners Fitzgerald and Hemingway (both of whom were his elders by a decade or so). He remains more of a midwesterner than they did, too: though he has written a novel about Americans in Europe, and a number of short stories about well-to-do New Yorkers, the emotional center of the bulk of his fiction has always been in the Midwest – specifically, in the World War I–era Illinois of his childhood and youth. Likewise, the guiding sensibility of his fiction has always been rather premodern. Maxwell employs irony sparingly, doesn't find angst any more fascinating than he does affection, and values sensibleness, hard work, generosity, tenderheartedness, and family loyalty. He also respects, in their place, both wildness and tameness; though we are all nature's children (a circumstance reflected in the names of such boy characters as Thorn and Spud), and though it is natural for the young to revel innocently in this circumstance, we also need civilization and its rituals – particularly as we grow older and take on responsibilities to one another.

Most of Maxwell's fiction, furthermore, obviously contains a strong autobiographical strain. In large part, this can probably be attributed to the fact that, at the age of eight, Maxwell lost his mother in the influenza epidemic of 1918; the memory of this devastating and irrevocable loss reverberates through much of his fiction. Though one rarely has the impression, to be sure, that a given Maxwell novel or story consists of pure, unadulterated memory, one nearly always senses that many of its characters are based upon the author's family members or friends, and that its settings derive from places that have figured importantly in his life; certainly it is impossible not to notice the proliferation of sensitive, artistic boy-heroes who live in Lincoln or Chicago, Illinois. For all this, however, few writers seem so free of self-indulgence, egocentrism, and narcissism, so naturally empathic. It is as if, to Maxwell, memory is a moral and an aesthetic act, and literary creation a means, as it were, of improving upon the shortcomings of photography and capturing moments in time. (He complains in *So Long, See You Tomorrow,* for example, that "love, even of the most ardent and soul-destroying kind, is never caught by the lens of the camera. One would almost think it didn't exist.") His sympathetic powers are prodigious: in setting innocence against experience, outsider against insider, brain against brawn – as he does in various novels – his purpose is not to exalt one type of person at the expense of another, but to examine the ways in which people of extremely different backgrounds get along with one another, or fail to. In his books, difficulties between people typically arise not from the malicious intentions of one or the other party, but rather from divergences in background, in cultural assumptions, and in ways of life. This is not to suggest that Maxwell has a Pollyanna-ish view of life, seeing innocence wherever he looks; on the contrary, he recognizes the blindness of most people to virtue, and the role of gossip as a community's means of compelling uniformity. Yet if, at its grimmest, Maxwell's fiction deplores forced uniformity as earnestly as it laments the barriers that separate people (and peoples) from one another, at its brightest it celebrates the genuine bonds that connect people – celebrates, that is, the ability of human beings to understand and care about and be kind to one another, in spite of (and, in some instances, because of) their differences.

A CASE IN POINT is Maxwell's flawed but interesting first book, *Bright Center of Heaven* (1934). Set in and around Meadowland, a boardinghouse in the Wisconsin countryside, the novel gives a detailed account of a single day in the lives of the house's residents and guests. The proprietor is Susan West, a high-toned, good-hearted, but rather scatterbrained and debt-ridden widow who is described by one of her boarders as "very much alive – more so than any woman I've ever known." Living with Mrs. West are her two teenage sons, Thorn and Whitey; among those also in residence, as the novel opens, are a painter, a pianist, and a pair of lovers named Paul and Nigel (a young lady). (This contemplative account of a country house populated by artists and intellectuals, and presided over by a benevolent matriarch, is vaguely reminiscent of *To the Lighthouse*.) Much of the day is spent in anticipation of the arrival of yet another boarder, Jefferson Carter, a well-educated black man who is a friend of Mrs. West's and whom no one else at the house has ever met. With some justice, Paul looks upon Mrs. West's invitation to Carter as a "sociological experiment" – for it is clear that at least one or two of the guests will not take kindly to his presence.

While we're waiting for Mr. Carter to arrive, Maxwell offers us glimpses into the minds of the other characters, several of whom experience, in isolation, a sense of grace. For instance, Josefa, the pianist, finds that a great piano piece is a "testimony, left by others, of something more than mind – of a moment of Grace which came upon them. . . . And what they remembered they wrote down in succession and re-arranged and made orderly, so that for other people there was something almost like a moment of Grace, though not Grace itself." Yet all is not harmony here. Mrs. West's cook, Johanna, has a private torment: her mother is ill in Germany. "Day and night for seven months, while her body was in domestic bondage to the Wests, her mind had been with her mother, in the mountains of another continent, with a wide sea between." In a way, everyone at Meadowland occupies a separate world. When it begins to rain during a midday picnic, Maxwell observes that "the same rain fell on them all, yet to each one it was a different thing": Susan sings, Whitey leaps in pretended fear, Thorn strolls along serenely, Johanna clucks in protest, Paul walks absently, Nigel runs "like a deer." As the artist Cynthia says, in explaining why she paints not people but oranges, "People are much too complex. . . . Once you begin to look at them, you discover too much that is individual."

For the most part, Maxwell limns these singular characters and their solitary worlds with considerable delicacy and wit. But the book does occasionally feel forced, the natural setting rather stylized. And when the most foreign character of all, Jefferson Carter, appears on the scene, Maxwell's vision seriously falters. There are several problems with Carter. First, it seems unlikely that an intelligent black man who is very active as "a lecturer and teacher and as a leader of the Negro race" would accept an invitation to a place like Meadowland. Second, for a man who has moved among white bigots all his life, and who patently would not have gotten to where he is if he hadn't kept his cool time and again in the face of their unreasoning hostility, Carter seems much too easily enraged by the outspoken prejudices of his dinner-table partners at Mrs. West's. Finally, while the white folks at Meadowland come across as flesh-and-blood characters, Carter seems a bit too much of a period stereotype – an Educated Negro, proud and dignified and devoted to the betterment of his people, thoroughly unobjectionable because thoroughly unindividuated. Since Carter's appearance – and his abrupt nocturnal departure – are the novel's climactic events, these failings are especially damaging. Clearly, Maxwell's primary thematic concern here is with the communion and estrangement not of races but of individuals (of whatever color, and for whatever reason). Yet the emphasis on Carter's race distorts this theme, and steers the book into the territory of the thirties social-problem novel – not necessarily a bad territory, but one whose language Maxwell simply doesn't speak.

Nonetheless, *Bright Center of Heaven* provides a useful introduction to the Maxwell oeuvre. The novel nicely communicates its author's high regard for love and compassion, his preoccupation with both the destructive and curative powers of time, his raw horror of death, his affection for nature and humanity, and his unwavering sense of the value of life. When the Wests' pet dog kills a beloved frog that has made its home in the goldfish pond, the point is made that the proliferation of seemingly identical frogs doesn't make any individual frog's life worth less; likewise, despite Cynthia's observation that similar patterns keep turning up on leaves and flowers ("as if the Lord lacked inventive powers and had to repeat himself frequently"), and despite a character's remark that people "repeat themselves just the way plants do," Maxwell emphasizes that humanity constitutes an infinite yet wondrously unified spectrum of tiny differences. Like Cynthia's painting, his first book aspires to be a "study in form," a study of the "relationship that exists throughout natural forms" – the natural forms in this instance, of course, being human individuals.

In MAXWELL'S next two novels, the canvas is considerably smaller – and the brushwork far more dexterous – than in *Bright Center of Heaven*. Or, to put it more precisely, the number of principal characters diminishes in these books while the time frame expands. Whereas *Bright Center of Heaven* explores the minds and hearts of a dozen or so people, mostly adults and mostly strangers to one another, over the space of one day, his second book closely examines the four members of a midwestern family over a period of a few weeks, while his third focuses intently upon the intimate friendship of two teenage boys, the choppy course of whose mutual enthrallment it follows through several years. It is plain that both of these novels derive, to a considerable extent, from the author's own emotion-packed childhood and youth; certainly both books feel a great deal more personal, and less programmatic, than their predecessor.

The earlier of these two books, *They Came Like Swallows* (1937), is a short novel about a single family – the Morisons of Logan, Illinois (a town that is about one hundred and fifty miles south of Maxwell's native Logan County) – and about the tragedy that befalls them in the final weeks of the year 1918. Instead of leaping every four or five pages from one character's point of view to another's, as in *Bright Center of Heaven,* Maxwell divides this novel into three sections, each of which confines itself to the perspective of a single member of the family. "Whose Angel Child" takes us inside the mind of the youngest Morison, the bright eight-year-old Peter, who is called Bunny and who is profoundly attached to his adoring (and pregnant) mother. Fifty-seven of the section's sixty pages are devoted to a painstaking evocation of a typical Sunday in the Morisons' home as experienced by Bunny; the section's final three pages, by contrast, offer an unsettlingly brief glimpse of the following morning, on which normality is forever shattered by an ironic combination of events: World War I finally ends (for this Monday happens to be the eleventh of November, 1918), and the devastating, much-discussed epidemic of so-called Spanish influenza finally touches the Morison family. Sections two ("Robert") and three ("Upon a Compass Point") continue the story of the Morisons' encounter with the disease – up to the inevitable, horrifying death in the family and its nightmarish aftermath – from the respective points of view of Bunny's thirteen-year-old brother, Robert, and the boys' distant and tormented father, James.

They Came Like Swallows is an impressive book, not least for Maxwell's expert use of foreshadowing and suspense, for his rendering of the gradually darkening mood of the Morison home, and for the way in which he captures the protagonists' feelings of love and loss without descending into bathos. Like James Agee in *A Death in the Family,* Max-

well proffers a number of false leads regarding who in the family is going to die – the point being that any of these people actually *could* die,
that death itself is arbitrary, capricious. Foretokenings of mortality –
falling leaves, a child's macabre song, a playmate's illness – abound from
the opening pages. Every visitor comes to seem a threat, a possible
source of contamination; even the ticking of the big clock in the hall
takes on a certain ominousness. The book's most unforgettable image is
the one alluded to in the title: a swallow flies into the sickroom – an
event that, we have been told, is a legendary harbinger of death – and
family members attempt to drive it out. Yet they cannot drive out death:
eventually, the epidemic takes its victim, and the Morisons' happy home
becomes a memory. Especially given the novel's tacit identification of
the epidemic with the chaotic, ravaging modern world that was ushered
in by the Great War, it would seem significant that Maxwell borrowed
the title of this novel from a line in the poem "Coole Park, 1929" by
William Butler Yeats; for Yeats's poem, it will be remembered, also
commemorates a household – that of Lady Gregory – that represented
premodern grace, and that, as a target of land-reform confiscation, was
destined to perish at the hands of the modern age as surely as the Morison home.

Fastidious yet piercing, *They Came Like Swallows* ponders the ways in
which people matter to each other, reminding us how strongly the unity
of a family – or of any group of people who share one another's lives –
can rely on the contribution of a single member. Here, as elsewhere in
Maxwell's fiction, a family – precious, precarious, and alarmingly
mutable – serves as the chief symbol of the fragile interdependence of
human lives. Maxwell's use of father-and-son protagonists, moreover,
provides him with an opportunity to demonstrate that many an adult is
no less baffled than a child is by the thornier vicissitudes of life – and
that, indeed, beneath the civilized surfaces there are fewer differences
between adults and children than meet the eye. Most of all, Maxwell's
second novel underlines how skilled Maxwell is with young characters.
Unlike many writers of fiction, he seems never to have forgotten how a
child's mind works, and the long sections he devotes to Bunny and Robert give us ample time to settle into the distinctive tones and rhythms of
these boys' lives. To be sure, Maxwell's employment of three distinct

centers of consciousness has its disadvantages: not only does the tripartite structure weaken the sense of focus but the fact is that in the latter part of the book we quite simple miss Bunny's perspective, which is more charming and affecting than that of his father. But this is a quibble about a book that should perhaps be counted among the minor classics of its time.

Maxwell's third – and, in many ways, his finest – novel, *The Folded Leaf* (1945), was published eight years after *They Came Like Swallows*, and takes place in the mid-1920s, from five to nine years after the action of *Swallows*. Once again we are in Illinois, and in the company of boys; indeed, the novel's teenage protagonist, Lymie Peters, bears more than a passing resemblance to the eight-year-old Bunny. As the novel opens in October of 1923, Lymie is a slight, sensitive, and intelligent fifteen-year-old; his mother has been dead for several years, during which he and his father, an emotionally undemonstrative stationery salesman, have lived in cheap hotels and gloomy furnished apartments and taken their meals in diners. Spud Latham is the new boy in Lymie's grade at school. Strong and athletic, and as combative as Lymie is gentle, Spud sorely misses the comfortable Wisconsin home that he, his parents, and his older sister have left behind, and despises the dark little big-city house into which his newly glum father's business reversals have forced the family to move.

Different as they are from each other, Lymie and Spud seem to have at least two things in common: both are neglected by their fathers and alienated from most of their schoolmates. It is not altogether surprising, then, that the fragile, awkward boy (who has never had a friend before) and the athlete with a chip on his shoulder become best buddies. Enhancing Lymie's attraction to Spud, moreover, are his envy of Spud's masculine build and cocky attitude, and his discovery in the Lathams of a surrogate family (whose ready and wholehearted acceptance of him as one of their own brings him immense joy). As for Spud, Lymie seems to be the only boy in school who doesn't strike him as a threat; even more important, he enjoys being admired. But there is a simpler explanation for the boys' interest in each other. At a classmate's home, Lymie ob-

serves a beautiful Chinese lacquer screen; on one side of it are images of
fierce armed warriors, and on the other side are white flowers. A professor explicates it for him: "The mutual attraction of gentleness and violence, don't you see, Mr. Peters? The brutal body and the calm philo-
sophic mind."

The first three-eighths of the novel chart the gradual development of
Lymie and Spud's friendship over the course of a high-school year. This
process is marked by a couple of highly dramatic, intimate, and enigmatic events. First, the boys initially encounter each other—naked—
during a water polo game in the school swimming pool; a panicky
Lymie, refusing to let go of the ball, is pushed underwater by several
classmates, and Spud saves him from drowning. Some weeks later
Lymie returns the favor, after a fashion: following a scarifying initiation
into a high-school boys' club, Spud discovers that his urine is green, and
it is Lymie who explains to him that he's not dying but simply voiding
some substance ingested during the hazing. It is in the wake of this bizarre incident that the boys begin to experience the intense mutual
awareness that will characterize their friendship for years to come:

> The door of Room 211 stood open, and high-pitched voices were
> swarming out of it. Spud and Lymie walked in together and down
> separate aisles. In spite of the babel and the steady tramping outside in
> the corridor, each of them heard the other's footsteps; heard them as
> distinctly as if the sound were made by a man walking late at night in
> an empty street.

Before long, the rhythms of Lymie's and Spud's lives have fallen into
step with one another. The last barrier to wholehearted devotion, on
Lymie's part, collapses on a rainy afternoon in the Latham house when
Spud tries to remove Lymie's wet clothes. Lymie surprises Spud—and
himself—by putting up a struggle; and he fights every step of the way,
"like a country defending itself against an invader," as Spud removes
one item of clothing after another. Then, suddenly, Lymie stops struggling: "Something had burst inside him, something more important
than any organ, and there was a flowing which was like blood. Though
he kept on breathing and his heart after a while pounded less violently,
there it was all the same, an underground river which went on and on

and was bound to keep on like that for years probably, never stopping, never once running dry." This description of a neglected, motherless boy's initial resistance to and ultimate acceptance of his love for another human being is brilliantly done: few writers could manage such an episode without stumbling headlong into sentimentality, or, on the other hand, without making the whole thing seem merely a carnal encounter.

That Lymie and Spud's friendship is a complex and not entirely salutary affair becomes increasingly clear during the latter part of the novel, which picks up Lymie at age nineteen (four years into his friendship with Spud) and follows him through a year at an unnamed midwestern college where he is Spud's roommate, bedmate (of a platonic variety), and helpmate. Lymie's manner with the insensitive Spud – who has become a boxer and acquired a girlfriend named Sally – is thoroughly devoted, self-abnegating; his day-to-day life is bound to Spud's as surely as any wife's to her husband's. Yet his feelings for Spud, and Spud's for him – feelings that the boys seem never to have examined, and that they have certainly never mentioned to each other – contain elements of resentment, jealousy, even hatred. We are told, for instance, that during their struggle on the Lathams' floor, Lymie's expression "was almost but not quite hate"; a classmate at college informs Lymie that Spud "talks for an hour at a time about how much he hates you."

What is afflicting this friendship? Maxwell's answer, in four words: paternal neglect, Freudian projection. The narrator – who is far more discursive here than in Maxwell's previous novels – has some surprisingly stern things to say about a society whose fathers force their sons to find their own way through adolescence to manhood. Apropos of the initiation ceremony of the boys' high-school club, which takes place at a Chicago hotel, the narrator expatiates upon the rites of puberty: "The world is wonderfully large and capable of infinite repetition. At no time is it necessary to restrict the eye in search of truth to one particular scene. Torture is to be found in many places besides the Hotel Balmoral, and if it is the rites of puberty that you are interested in, you can watch the same thing (or better) in New Guinea or New South Wales." If Western puberty rites are less satisfactory than those of the New Guinea savages, it is because fathers are not involved: "The rites of puberty allow the father to punish the son, the son to murder his father, without actual harm to either. If Mr. Latham had been present and had taken part in the initiation, he might have been able to release Spud forever from the basis of all his hostilities." And Mr. Peters might have done the same for Lymie. But Western initiations don't work that way. "Now instead of being freed of his childhood, Lymie will have to go on smearing his face up with taffy-apples of one kind or another and being stopped by every plaster pig that he encounters, for years to come."

One may not agree with the narrator that the interests of youth are better served by primitive rites of puberty than by Western civilization's substitutes, but he does present a rather convincing case that Lymie and Spud's extraordinary mutual attachment and antipathy are manifestations of, respectively, a lack of paternal attention and a deep-seated resentment thereof. In any event, Maxwell's interpretation of the boys' attachment to each other as the consequence of parental mismanagement does not gainsay his genuine regard for the attachment itself. For *The Folded Leaf* is ultimately a study not of neurosis but of love. The book is crowded with small, affecting, and utterly credible moments, all of them fondly observed; no reader can soon forget, for instance, Lymie's astonishment at Mrs. Latham's simple kindness to him, or his happiness at her pronouncement that he is a "member of the family." Whatever their genesis, the joy, comfort, and serenity that Lymie derives from his friendship with Spud are very real, and Maxwell does a magnificent job of bringing these feelings to life, and of making palpable their connection to the daily routines that Lymie cherishes so deeply. To read *The Folded Leaf,* indeed, is to see most other celebrated novels of adolescence as false, stylized, and riddled with cheap sentiment and nostalgia. Certainly this is one of the best American novels of its time.

MAXWELL's fourth and fifth novels represent a moderate shifting of gears. In these books the boy protagonists of *They Came Like Swallows* and *The Folded Leaf* are replaced by adults; concision gives way to a surprising expansiveness; and the almost lapidary structure of the earlier books is supplanted by a markedly looser, freer sense of form. Indeed, the reader of *Time Will Darken It* and *The Château,* which are Maxwell's longest novels by far, may well feel at times that there is no form at all to either of them – and it is this impression that Maxwell plainly seeks to foster. For his principal aim here is to mimic, as closely as possible, the patterns and textures and rhythms of real life – to make both novels feel, line for line, like valid renderings of reality. To some extent, of course, this is his purpose throughout his fiction – and, for that matter, the purpose of most novelists – but it has special priority in these two books. Though admirers of *They Came Like Swallows* and *The Folded Leaf* may find *Time Will Darken It* and *The Château* somewhat flat, arbitrary, and overlong, it must be said that, judged in terms of their implicit literary aims, they are really quite successful. To read each of these novels is to feel that one is experiencing life on the level on which it is actually lived; it is to feel as if one is watching relationships develop at a natural pace. In this connection, a passage from *Time Will Darken It* seems relevant: "Most people, when they are describing a friend or telling a story, make the mistake of editing, of leaving things out. Fearing that their audience will grow restless, they rush ahead to the point, get there too soon, have to go back and explain, and in the end, the quality of experience is not conveyed." Maxwell might as well be making an observation not about inexpert conversationalists but about the failings of his fellow novelists. Conveying the quality of an experience: that is clearly the chief goal of *Time Will Darken It* and *The Château,* and if the action sometimes meanders, if one or two plot threads are left hanging, and if a few conversations drag on a bit longer than they should – well (one imagines Maxwell explaining), that's the way life is, and the enormous gain in fidelity makes the trade-off more than worthwhile.

This is not to suggest that either of these novels is lacking in artfulness. As Joseph Conrad knew, to make a reader hear, feel, and see reality before him is a far from simple task. Yet at their best both of these books have the ultimate effect of making other, more high-profile contemporary novelists seem out of touch with reality – distant from it, false to it, their proportions wrong, their characters crude approximations. As in *Bright Center of Heaven,* the canvases of both *Time Will Darken It* and *The Château* are good-sized; each features a married couple who occupy the center of a large and complicated network of relationships. While Maxwell's focus, as always, is on individuals and not groups, sectional identity plays a key role in one of the novels, as does national identity in the other; and both books begin with the arrival of summer sojourners in a part of the world they consider foreign.

The couple in *Time Will Darken It* (1948) are Austin and Martha King of Draperville, Illinois. Austin is a lawyer, honest and unobtrusive, a solid citizen who has "taken very good care that people shouldn't know anything about him"; Martha is loving and insecure, "a beautiful woman who [can't] believe in her own beauty or accept love without casting every conceivable doubt on it." During the summer of 1912, they are visited by a Mr. and Mrs. Potter of Mississippi and their courting-age children, the plain but upright Nora and the handsome but irresponsible Randolph. A number of events ensue, the most important being that Nora falls in love with Austin and decides to remain in Draperville, where she helps two local spinsters, Alice and Lucy Beach, to set up a kindergarten. Though Austin doesn't return her love or encourage it, the town's gossipmongers find him guilty of adultery, and his career is severely damaged; Nora, meanwhile, sustains some damage herself in a freak accident, and is obliged to return to Mississippi.

Such is the novel's principal story line. But there are numerous other things going on here as well. During his visit to Draperville, for instance, Potter talks several of Austin's friends into a bad investment that Austin feels obliged to make good on; Mary Caroline, a homely neighbor girl, develops a crush on Randolph; Rachel, the Kings' servant, has man problems and leaves town; Austin's aging friend Bud Ellis makes a play for Nora. If in *The Folded Leaf* a pair of fathers are too neglectful of their growing sons, here two mothers (Mrs. Potter and Mrs. Beach) are overly possessive of their grown daughters, effectively denying them lives of their own. At its best, *Time Will Darken It* seems a rich tapestry of poignant images (of Mary Caroline, for instance, waiting patiently on her front porch for a glimpse of Randolph), of memorable dialogue (forty-seven-year-old Lucy Beach wonders aloud "why people don't tell you when you're young that life is tiring"), and of blunt maxims: "The world is not a nice place." (Maxwell even has a maxim about maxims: "Most maxims are lies, or at any rate misleading. A rolling stone gathers moss. A stitch in time doesn't save nine.") Maxwell is not afraid to make forthright statements about fundamental things. Nor does he shrink from the temptation to promulgate *outré* conceits; this novel contains curtains, baskets, and bassinets that "talk": *"There will be other summer nights,* the sundial said, *nights almost like this, but this night won't ever come again. Take it while you have it."*

One temptation that Maxwell does not succumb to, however, is the impulse to exploit the easy dramatic possibilities of his material. Though Austin and Martha have marital problems, they don't separate; though his solemn, untrusting senior partner, Mr. Hobey, suggests that Austin's position is in jeopardy because of the gossip about him and Nora, Austin doesn't get fired; though Martha has an exceptionally difficult pregnancy, she doesn't die in childbirth. During her residency in Draperville, Nora lives next door to the Kings, and her constant proximity – of which Austin (as well as the reader) is acutely aware – causes one to suspect that eventually Austin will succumb to her blandishments; but he never does. Maxwell's conspicuous setting forth of all these options, and his equally conspicuous refusal to take advantage of them, seem part of a deliberate attempt to demonstrate that serious fiction doesn't require such drastic contingencies in order to be compelling. Does he prove his point? On the whole, yes. The novel does have its slow stretches, and an occasional feeling of directionlessness; but it nicely captures the milieu it has chosen to examine, and the character portraits have great veracity and charm. Indeed, the book resonates with nobility and life, with an ardent love for the innocent and irrecoverable past, and with a mature awareness that there are many different ways to seize the day.

The *carpe diem* theme (as well as the talking furniture) crops up too in *The Château,* which chronicles the visit of a youngish American couple, Harold and Barbara Rhodes, to France in 1948. Harold is exceedingly reminiscent of Lymie Peters: during his midwestern childhood, we are told, "he would have liked to be somebody else – an athlete, broad-shouldered, blond, unworried, and popular." These days, he is a friendly, curious, and unworldly young man with a good enough job at an engraving firm. Barbara – who is often taken for Harold's sister – is beautiful, more perceptive than her husband, and somewhat more fluent in French. The Rhodeses have no children; if Spud serves as a sort of father substitute for Lymie, so the Rhodeses' French vacation is, in a strange way, a child substitute for them, and the ardor that they lavish on the country and its people is as breathless as that of parents for a newborn infant. As with Lymie's affection for Spud, however, Maxwell does not undervalue this ardor merely because he understands its mechanism. Nor, though many of their observations about France betray (by turns) naïveté, romanticism, and world-class insecurity, does he want us to regard Harold and Barbara as objects of ridicule.

The château of the novel's title is near Blois; it is during an extended stay there that the Rhodeses gather many of their lasting impressions of France. Like Susan West in *Bright Center of Heaven*, Mme. Viénot, the lady of the manor, is a high-born but impoverished widow whose home, now a boardinghouse, is occupied largely by intellectual types and nonpaying relatives. The Rhodeses spend much of their time worrying – about their French, about making a *faux pas*, about whether the other guests like them – and undergoing the exhilarating, exhausting task of meeting lots and lots of new people. There are the usual blisses and disappointments: they are attracted to certain people but never grow close to them, begin to form friendships only to have them collapse inexplicably, and wind up on intimate terms with certain individuals – an unattached and rather dotty old lady, an amiable young waiter – whose counterparts back home they would never have the occasion or inclination to befriend. A reader conditioned by other kinds of novels keeps expecting dramatic things to happen: an affair between Barbara and Mme. Viénot's handsome Canadian boarder? A devastating revelation about the delightful but contrary young couple Eugene and Alix? But nothing remarkable occurs – or, rather, *everything* remarkable occurs; for *The Château* is a celebration of the remarkableness of the ordinary, the mystery in the everyday. One of the book's lessons is that to visit a foreign country is not necessarily to discover exotic things; it is to discover the ordinary in exotic garb – to experience small talk, for instance, in a foreign tongue (Maxwell incorporates numerous passages in Basic French) – and thereby to learn anew to appreciate the mysteries with which one lives day by day.

A word should be added about the narratorial question-and-answer sessions in *The Château*. Though Maxwell adheres mostly to conventional narrative form, he departs from it briefly, about sixty pages into the story, in order to allow an unnamed interlocutor to query the narrator about Harold and Barbara's childhoods, employment histories, and reasons for being in Europe; the narrator proceeds to shed what light he can on these subjects. This curious dialogue resumes in"Some Explanations," a forty-six-page section at the end of the book, wherein the interlocutor expresses impatience with *The Château*'s lack of closure. "Is that all?" the interlocutor demands at the section's outset. He wants answers to the questions that the novel has left hanging. The narrator challenges him:

> I don't know that any of these things very much matters. They are details. You don't enjoy drawing your own conclusions about them?
> *Yes, but then I like to know if the conclusions I have come to are the right ones.*
> How can they not be when everything that happens happens for so many different reasons?

The narrator proceeds to satisfy his interlocutor on some points, but not on others. Is the *reader* satisfied? Yes and no. The section is at once provocative and irksome – sardonic one moment, slack the next, its very existence a seeming betrayal of the book's spirit. It does, however, add up to a cogent commentary upon the fact that readers of fiction have been trained to expect artificially tidy endings; Maxwell's implicit argument is that a novel should not pretend to solve insoluble riddles, but should instead provide some testimony of human feeling that may touch the hearts of its readers and cushion them somewhat against life's unfathomable cruelties. So it is that in the closing paragraph of the novel Mme. Viénot picks up a book – the memoirs of a priest – and "puts what happened to him, his harsh but beautifully dedicated life, between her and all silences, all creaking noises, all failures, all searching for answers that cannot be found."

After *The Château*, Maxwell did not publish another novel for almost two decades. The three books that did appear during these years represent a variety of genres. *The Old Man at the Railroad Crossing and Other Tales* (1966) is an odd volume of twenty-nine short fables, five or six pages apiece, which typically begin with the words "once upon a time" and have such titles as "The Industrious Tailor" and "The Old Man

Who Was Afraid of Falling" and "The Kingdom Where Straight-forward, Logical Thinking Was Admired Over Every Other Kind"; the tales have serious points to make, but they seem designed to appeal to a decidedly minority taste for whimsy, and those who do not share this taste are very likely to find them overly cute and (when taken in bulk) monotonous. *Ancestors* (1971), a long, affectionate history of several generations of Maxwell's forebears, attests admirably to his continued fascination with his family and its past; yet though he chronicles his ancestors' lives with a well-nigh heroic diligence, he fails to evoke them as vividly as he does the characters in his best fiction, and the relentlessly compiled details are in the end rather tedious. Finally, *Over by the River* (1977) is a volume of finely tuned, precisely detailed short stories set in New York, New England, Illinois, and France; while there is some good work here – notably the title story, which charts an Upper East Side family's day-to-day anxieties – most of the stories are appreciably slicker than Maxwell's novels, and the characters and situations too often give the impression of having been pulled off the *New Yorker* rack. (In 1956, Maxwell had published several of these pieces in *Stories,* a joint collection with Jean Stafford, John Cheever, and Daniel Fuchs.)

N OT UNTIL 1980 did Maxwell publish his sixth (and, to date, his last) novel, *So Long, See You Tomorrow.* This intense, dreamlike little work – in which he returns to the Lincoln, Illinois, of his childhood to tell of a tenuous friendship terminated by an act of violence – represents a triumphant consummation of its author's art. Though in theme and setting and dramatis personae it is vintage Maxwell, the book marks a sharp shift in tone and scale from his previous novels, and especially from its immediate predecessors. One-third the length of *Time Will Darken It* and *The Château,* it lacks those novels' sense of immediacy, their generosity of color, their genial inclusiveness; in place of those attributes, Maxwell offers a black-and-white, Ingmar Bergman-like austerity, an enigmatic spareness. The book has the quality of a fable, a reverie; it is as if, over the decades of his life, Maxwell's memories of childhood had undergone the same process – of shaping, heightening, purging of ancillary detail – by which a culture turns its early history into myth. In this regard, the novel is a close relative of the stories in *The Old Man at the Railroad Crossing and Other Tales.*

So Long, See You Tomorrow is Maxwell's only novel to be written in the first person, and throughout the book the identity of the aged, mannerly, bleak-minded narrator – who agrees with Ortega y Gasset that life is "in itself and forever shipwreck" – seems ambiguous: is he supposed to be William Maxwell, or only a fictional approximation? As far as one can tell, his personal history jibes with Maxwell's: in the early 1920s, when the story is set, he was twelve years old, living in Lincoln with his insurance-salesman father (who represented authority, and therefore "could not also represent understanding") and a new stepmother; his real mother had died a few years earlier, an event after which "there were no more disasters. The worst that could happen had happened." The nearest thing the boy had to a friend was Cletus Smith, a farmer's son with whom he would walk on the scaffolding of the unfinished house that his father and new stepmother were having built. Every evening the boys would part casually, saying "So long" and "See you tomorrow" – until one day when Cletus's father killed a neighbor (and former best friend) who had stolen his wife, and then committed suicide. Cletus was never called to testify in the case, and promptly left town with his mother for parts unknown; when our narrator moved to Chicago some time afterward, he was surprised to find his eyes meeting Cletus's in the school hallway.

Decades later, he still feels guilty about his failure to speak to Cletus on that occasion. Since he has no idea where Cletus is now, or even whether he is alive, "the one possibility of my making some connection with him seems to lie not in the present but in the past – in my trying to reconstruct the testimony that he was never called upon to give." So it is that the second half of the novel consists of an elaborate, meticulously worked-out imaginative reconstruction of the events in the lives of the Smiths and their friend that led up to the murder. While the narrator's recollections of his friendship are true, in other words – at least within the context of the book – his reconstruction is a "mixture of truth and fiction." Yet it has a kind of validity, he implies, because in inventing it he has drawn upon his long-standing familiarity with farm people and their lives. Besides, he observes, truth is a slippery thing in the best of cases: "The unsupported word of a witness who was not present except in imagination would not be acceptable in a court of law, but . . . the sworn testimony of the witness who was present is not trustworthy either."

Why does Maxwell choose to place his story of Cletus's family on such a slippery epistemological foundation? For one thing, the story's status as a question mark within a question mark enhances its mythic quality. For another, Maxwell's emphasis upon the fact that the story is a creation invites us to contemplate the boundary between memory and imagination – a boundary that Maxwell's novels have poignantly straddled time and again. Finally, the book is a means of communicating – at least in a metaphysical sense – with Cletus, whom our narrator has long since lost track of, and who may well have passed away decades ago. If imagination can be a form of sympathy, this novel represents a belated offering of consolation to Cletus, as well as an expression of compassion for all children who labor under the ingenuous delusion that there will always be a tomorrow, that time – which Maxwell memorably describes in *The Château* as "the relentless thieving that nobody pays any attention to" – will not someday make off with that which they hold most precious, and change their lives forever. The novel – which may well be Maxwell's best, aside from *The Folded Leaf* – brings to mind a remark from John Updike's recently published memoirs: "a writer's self-consciousness, for which he is much scorned, is really a mode of interestedness, that inevitably turns outward." It might be said that in *So Long, See You Tomorrow,* Maxwell turns outward from the anguish of his own childhood to that of another, even more tormented individual – a virtual stranger whose life touched his, lightly and fleetingly, or who may indeed be entirely a product of his imagination. The ultimate point is that it does not matter whether Cletus ever really existed, or whether our narrator is actually Maxwell: *So Long* is archetypally true, the story of everyone who knows what it means to have to live with one's past.

In his introductory note to his newest book, *The Outermost Dream: Essays and Reviews* – a collection of nonfiction that reaches the bookstore shelves fifty-five years after the publication of his first novel – Maxwell states, by implication, his criterion for good fiction: it must have "the breath of life." There hardly seems a more appropriate phrase than this with which to describe the supreme virtue of Maxwell's novels. At a time when many respected American authors fixate passionlessly upon banal domestic details, or twist reality out of recognition in service to this or that nonliterary purpose, or produce one enigmatic volume after another of words that are about nothing but themselves, one can only be grateful for a novelist whose particulars are thoughtfully and tellingly chosen, who never treats an idea as if it existed apart from human character, and who understands that the transcendent value of words in a work of fiction is their ability – in the hands of an artist – to capture things far beyond themselves: to mimic the rhythms and contours of life, to conjure up images and sensations preserved from oblivion. Maxwell understands, too, that such transfiguration doesn't come easily – that the truth, neither simple nor straightforward, "masquerades in inversions and paradoxes, is easier to get at in a lie than in an honest statement. If pursued, the truth withdraws, puts on one false face after another, and finally goes underground, where it can only be got at in the complex, agonizing absurdity of dreams." He is that splendid paradox: a commanding writer of conspicuous humility, a man of mature sensibility who has never ceased to apprehend this world as a cherished home, at once peril-ridden and rich with promise, in which we are all, in some sense, motherless children.

(MAY 1989)

Jean Stafford's Triumph

I F T H E R E I S one thing that David Roberts's new biography of the novelist and short-story writer Jean Stafford makes abundantly clear, it is that an essay about her should probably begin with her parents, her family, and her strangely tormented childhood.[1] She was born in Covina, California, in 1915, the youngest of four children. Her father, John Stafford, was himself a writer of sorts – a genuine obsessive whose career peaked early with the publication of an obscure hack Western novel, *When Cattle Kingdom Fell.* From there it was straight downhill: selling his Covina walnut ranch in 1921, he promptly lost the proceeds in the stock market and moved his family to Colorado, where he spent the last forty years of his life writing and rewriting a bizarre magnum opus designed, in Roberts's words, to "set the world straight" on the perils of the American economy. His wife, Ethel, was the practical-minded one, a pleasant former schoolteacher whom Jean resented for her conventional domestic preoccupations, and who, once the increasingly destitute family had found its way to the city of Boulder, earned her daughter's resentment for taking in her sorority-girl classmates as boarders.

Stafford's life with this hapless couple – and with her beloved brother, Dick, and her remoter sisters, Marjorie and Mary Lee – had deep and lasting effects. As Roberts observes, after the move to Colorado "Stafford would never again know a day free of the fear of poverty and of social inferiority." Forever after, her feelings about both her parents would be a heady compound of love and shame, pity and resentment; and many of her actions, during her undergraduate years at the

---

1. *Jean Stafford: A Biography,* by David Roberts; Little, Brown.

University of Colorado and thereafter, strike one primarily as desperate attempts to remove herself from the world of her parents, and to forge a distinctive identity. For instance, the young Stafford – universally described as fragile, shy, and sexually naïve – shocked her fellow students by becoming the nude model for a life drawing class, and by idolizing, befriending, and moving in with Lucy and Andrew Cooke, a notorious artsy couple. The Cookes seem to have symbolized sex and freedom to Stafford, but their wild, bohemian demimonde was shattered when Lucy committed suicide during Jean's senior year; long afterward, a still-devastated Stafford remarked of Lucy's suicide that "I am almost ready to write about it, although I have really written about nothing else ever." Indeed, though she never published anything explicitly based on her life with the Cookes, Stafford did give the names Lucy and Andrew to major characters in two of her novels, and dealt with her friends' memory in various subtler ways throughout her fiction.

Lucy's death did not put an end to Stafford's search for a separate identity. After her graduation from college, she studied philology for a year at Heidelberg, and had barely returned home before she began writing bitterly condescending letters about her parents and country. "I *can't* stay in America next year," she wrote a friend, "unless I completely repudiate the whole past and live in some foreign quarter." She didn't belong here, she insisted: "I have realized suddenly to my horror that I'm an artist + have to be with my fellow beings." Roberts describes how Stafford transcribed an affectionate letter from her mother, "underlined what she considered the more egregious Americanisms, and mailed it to her friends in Paris, moralizing, 'Well, all I can say is, it shore is a pity that Pa ever got hitched up with those fat McKillop girls.'" That Stafford would commit such a heartless act – an act so offensive that it's pathetic – points to a profound insecurity about her own independent identity; so little sense did she have of herself apart from her family – even after college, the Cookes, and Heidelberg – that she felt it necessary to insist, in this brutal manner, upon her distinction from her mother.

Roberts's book is replete with evidence of the young Stafford's deficient sense of self (though Roberts himself seems mostly not to notice). During her time in Heidelberg, for instance, Stafford was mesmerized

by the Nazis: "I was swept along on the tide of this well-organized collective conniption fit. . . . If a recruiter had come by and asked me to
pledge myself for the rest of my life to the [Nazi party], in all likelihood
I would have done so." A psychology professor at Boulder noted that
Stafford was the most "suggestible" hypnotic subject he'd ever had. The
principal reason why she didn't want to marry, she explained to an early
beau, was that marriage would turn her into a conventional wife, a philistine: "eventually we would be Mother and Dad." So unsure was she,
in short, of her identity as Jean Stafford, writer, that the only consequence of marriage she was able to envision was a gradual metamorphosis into a version of Ethel McKillop Stafford, housewife.

And yet when Stafford did take a husband, in 1940, she assumed the
role of thankless helpmeet almost immediately. Of the man in question – Robert Lowell – she wrote that he "does what I have always
needed to have done to me and that is that he dominates me." Lowell, of
course, was not just any domineering man; the prep-school educated
scion of a distinguished Boston family, he was the very personification
of wealth, breeding, and Easternness, all of which intimidated her. He
was also, alas, spoiled, irresponsible, and mentally unbalanced. In the
spring of 1938, with Stafford in the passenger seat of his car and a
quantity of alcohol in his blood, Lowell plowed into a wall at the end of
a road in Cambridge, Massachusetts; while he escaped unscathed, Stafford's face suffered extraordinary damage. By all accounts, Lowell was
less than remorseful over the incident; according to a friend, he regarded it as "just an accident, and he didn't feel responsible particularly.
He looked up, there was a dead end. It was not his fault." Yet the accident was a crucial event in Stafford's life; though surgeons managed to
restore her to relatively normal appearance, the accident had done permanent damage to both her looks and her health, and the fact of it hovered tragically over the eight-year marriage to Lowell.

That marriage was, from the start, an ambiguous enterprise. Once
Stafford and Lowell had set up house together – first in Baton Rouge
(where Lowell attended graduate school at LSU), then in New York,
Tennessee, and Maine – she apparently lost no time in becoming, like
her mother, the subservient spouse of an obsessive artist. While Lowell
wrote poems, Stafford performed secretarial work and housekeeping

chores; a fanatical convert to Catholicism, Lowell insisted, during their stay in New York, that she also do "Catholic work," and so she spent much of her free time folding papers at the offices of the *Catholic Woker*. (Lowell himself had a job – as a copy editor at Sheed and Ward – for a total of nine months during the marriage.) Even when she did find a few moments to sit at her typewriter, she often had to spend it typing Lowell's work rather than writing her own. "Lowell expected his wife to type up his poems as soon as he had written them," notes Roberts. "If on rereading he changed a single word, she had to type the poem over again."

In sum, Stafford seems to have given a great deal in her marriage and received very little in return. It is hard to escape the conclusion that, in marrying such a man as Lowell and in maintaining so self-abnegating a spousal role, she was essentially forsaking, for the time being at least, the hope of an independent identity, and capitulating to her own seemingly unshakable inner sense of identity with her much-despised mother.

IT WAS IN 1944 that Stafford – who before that year had published only one short story – became a best-selling novelist. *Boston Adventure* was not her first attempt at a novel; over the years she had worked on several different manuscripts, some of which she had abandoned, and some of which had been turned down by various editors. To any reader familiar with Stafford's later, superior fiction, her graceful, charming, but thoroughly stylized first novel reads like an out-and-out capitulation to the demands of the marketplace. It reads, as a matter of fact, like the work of someone with a weak sense of authorial identity, someone afraid to reveal a distinctive sensibility. Roberts suggests interesting parallels with Proust, James, and "the great Russian novels" (one might also mention Wharton) But to mention such names without qualification is ultimately misleading. In essence, *Boston Adventure* is one of those capacious, old-fashioned, atmosphere-heavy affairs, mostly decorous but with perhaps a touch of the risqué, that used to be written for respectable middlebrow ladies by such authors as Anya Seton, Margaret Goudge, Daphne du Maurier, and Nancy Hale; the chief difference is that Stafford is a far more stylish and intelligent writer than most of these women.

Like many novels of its kind, *Boston Adventure* concerns the dramatically improving fortunes, over a period of years, of an attractive young female – in this case, Sonie Marburg. The smart, well-read, endlessly put-upon daughter of a poor Chichester, Massachusetts, immigrant couple, Sonie spends her childhood and early youth working in a hotel and entertaining a secret pipe dream – that she might one day live with Miss Lucy Pride, a wealthy Boston lady who summers at the hotel and who, to Sonie, is the very embodiment of breeding and culture. Miraculously, Sonie's dream comes to pass: she becomes Miss Pride's secretary, and takes her place among the fashionable young folk of Boston society. Yet life on Beacon Hill proves to have its own sorrows, and by novel's end Sonie is dreaming of liberation from Miss Pride as fervently as she once dreamed of escape from her parents.

To read *Boston Adventure* is, among other things, to be reminded of Oscar Wilde's remark that one would have to have a heart of stone to contemplate the fate of Little Nell without laughing. Sonie is no Little Nell, to be sure, but she is almost ridiculously long-suffering, and the travails she must endure before the nearly five-hundred-page opus winds to a close are legion: her father abandons the family, her younger brother dies, her mother goes insane. Through all this, Sonie seems never to stop worrying, to stop working, to enjoy so much as an hour of her life; even once she arrives in Boston there seems to be astonishingly little light or beauty in her grim world. Nor does she really *do* much of anything; instead, she lets things happen to her. If she is to be compared to the protagonists of great novels, it is not to anyone from James or Proust but rather to such figures as Maggie Tulliver in George Eliot's *The Mill on the Floss,* Hardy's Tess, and Dickens's rags-to-riches boy heroes; for in many ways, Sonie Marburg is an English Victorian heroine in modern American dress.

She is also, in a sense, her author in disguise. Like the young Stafford, Sonie longs for a world more sophisticated than that of her parents. If Stafford's authorial ambitions seem to have been fueled, in part, by her pained awareness of her father's thwarted hopes for literary glory, so Sonie's attraction to life on Beacon Hill seems to be related to her own father's frustrated hopes for success in America as a shoemaker. If Stafford's father was an author of Zane Grey-style Western stories who spent his last forty years endlessly rewriting the same book, so Sonie's father is a perpetual rereader of *The Riders of the Purple Sage;* and if Stafford thought she had found a new family in Lucy Cooke, and later in her blue-blooded Bostonian husband, so Sonie thinks she has found a new family in the person of the blue-blooded Bostonian Lucy Pride. Read in purely biographical terms, *Boston Adventure* comes across both as a plea for pity by an author who is intent upon mystifying her childhood troubles, and as an unsettling fantasy of childhood liberation – for after her brother's death, her father's departure, and the onset of her mother's insanity, Sonie is to all intents and purposes an orphan. And, as Eileen Simpson once observed, Stafford, in her childhood, "had desperately wanted to be an orphan."

Remarkably, however, for all the autobiographical parallels, *Boston Adventure* has an extremely fabricated quality. It is, one might say, a masterpiece of false emotion. For a reader in search of something escapist, to be sure, it's a good read – an engaging, well-bred novel that is almost never rude enough to confront one with the shock of recognition. There are moments of wit, insight, and realistic dialogue, but nothing, really, that would offend or challenge a *Saturday Evening Post* subscriber. The characters, sentiments, and plot turns are all familiar – not from life, but from other books. The tone is lofty – sometimes almost absurdly so, as when Sonie (who serves double duty as protagonist and narrator) describes a dog-and-cat fight: "I saw the dreadful slaughter: the dog's eyes popping as he rent and strangled the creature, spittle mingled with blood, and I heard the cat's single wail of entreaty." When a neighbor remarks that Sonie seems pleased with her newborn brother, we are told that "immediately the words were out, a leaven commenced to resolve my wonder into the emotion the woman had assumed in me and my pity became protective." The Jean Stafford of *Boston Adventure,* in short, is an author who doesn't write "was ill" when she can write "ailed." Still, the novel does contain a handful of real-seeming episodes, most of which involve children; Stafford's insight into the sensibilities of the young, and her superb ear for their conversation, are evinced in a number of small, seemingly incidental touches:

> Betty Brunson, who rarely addressed me, was embracing a young elm tree near the door and swinging round it, her head appearing now on

one side, now on another. "Hi, Sonie Marburg, whatcha going to do this aft?"

S TAFFORD never again wrote anything as long or as popular as *Boston Adventure* (which was one of the three best-selling novels of 1944). Yet her second novel, *The Mountain Lion* (1947), marked an advance in every important way. Like its predecessor, *The Mountain Lion* is a story of childhood – specifically, of Ralph Fawcett (ten years old when the novel begins) and his sister Molly (age eight), who after a bout of scarlet fever have health problems that draw them extremely close to each other and set them apart from their schoolmates. (Like other characters in Stafford's fiction, Ralph and Molly feel superior on account of their delicate health.) They live in California with their mother and two stuck-up older sisters, all of whom revere the memory of Grandfather Bonney, a stuffed shirt who peppered his conversation with Latin epigrams and (as he continually reminded everyone) had once met Grover Cleveland; Ralph and Molly, for their part, prefer their mother's stepfather, the down-to-earth rancher Grandfather Kenyon. (As in *Boston Adventure*, then, there is an emphatic contrast between high-toned types and simple folk.) But it is not till after Grandfather Kenyon's death, early in the novel, that Ralph and Molly meet Kenyon's son Claude and begin to spend summers at the family's Colorado ranch; it is there, during their pubescence, that Ralph's health improves and he and Molly grow apart, the boy becoming attached to his uncle and learning to shoot, the girl – an aspiring author – withdrawing into her writing and developing an icy hatred for virtually everyone around her.

The novel's turning point comes when Ralph and Molly are on a train, which is, not incidentally, passing through a tunnel. Ralph, who has recently experienced a disturbing sexual attraction toward his sister Leah, takes a seat beside Molly, who despite her intelligence and curiosity retains a childlike innocence that he feels slipping away from him:

> Partly he did not wish her to read any further in his face and partly he wanted to feel her near by. He thought of her as if she were the last foothold beneath which the world fell away in a chasm: it would be so

easy to lose his footing, relax his fingerholds, and plunge downward to wedge his bones in a socket of rocks. Vile fogs baffled him and vileness was below him. Molly, alone, he thought, did not urge him to corruption.

And yet something – namely, the hormonal surge that accompanies the onset of manhood – compels him to despoil the purity that Molly represents. Aware that he is "weakening and ready to fall," Ralph whispers to his sister: "Molly, tell me all the dirty words you know." Before she can respond, the train emerges into the light of day, and the chapter concludes:

> Ralph's childhood and his sister's expired at that moment of the train's entrance into the surcharged valley. It was a paradox, for now they should be going into a tunnel with no end, now that they had heard the devil speak.

It is only a matter of time before the division between Ralph and Molly reaches its tragic apotheosis. Ralph, who has been eager to kill a mountain lion rumored to be in the vicinity of the Kenyon ranch, sees and fires at the lion one day in the underbrush – but, instead, accidentally kills Molly.

Here, as in *Boston Adventure*, the parallels to Stafford's own life appear meaningful. Molly and Ralph are clearly based on Stafford and her brother, Dick, to whom she felt very close (and who had died in an automobile accident shortly before the publication of *Boston Adventure*); the children's older sisters are based on Stafford's sisters. Like Sonie Marburg's mother, moreover, Mrs. Fawcett reflects, to a considerable degree, Stafford's view of her own mother: she is a foolish, vain, and superficial woman whose dearest wish is that her son become a "gentleman" like Grandfather Bonney and that her daughters be proper "ladies." As for the father, if in *Boston Adventure* Stafford removed Mr. Marburg from the scene after a few chapters, in *The Mountain Lion* she kills off the children's father before the novel even begins. Though the bulk of the novel is told from Ralph's point of view, it is Molly with whom the author plainly identifies, and who gradually becomes the center of interest. The girl is bright, introverted, obnoxious, and frighteningly eccentric; but the principal fact about her is that, as she approaches adulthood, she is – by virtue of her identity as an aspiring artist, a budding intellectual, and a sickly girl whose innocence refuses to die – increasingly alienated from the robust, physical, masculine environment of the ranch, and even from Ralph, who is fast growing into an altogether average young man. Plainly, Stafford's second novel can be read as a symbolic rendering of the author's own sense of isolation from her family – and, indeed, from the world – and its ending can be understood as a means of sacrificing her own life, in fiction, to save her brother's.

But of course it is not the novel's autobiographical subtext that makes it valuable; to overemphasize such matters, indeed, is to divert attention from the book's aesthetic import. And the fact is that *The Mountain Lion* is one of the most admirable short novels of its time – elegantly structured, deftly composed, and sensitively imagined. It is as taut and well constructed as a short novel by Henry James, as free of superfluities as *Boston Adventure* was swimming in them; its prose, furthermore, is as lean and temperate as that of Stafford's first novel was mannered. All of the characters are artfully drawn, but it is the portrayal of the children that qualifies the novel as a *tour de force*. For Stafford captures the world of childhood in masterly fashion, rendering details, dialogue, and thoughts for pages on end without a noticeable misstep. To recapture the way one's own mind worked at the age of eight or ten or twelve is among the most difficult of challenges for a writer, and in *The Mountain Lion* Stafford accomplishes this feat magnificently. Like Truman Capote's *Other Voices, Other Rooms* (which would appear a year later), *The Mountain Lion* is an emblematic account of the death of childhood, the end of innocence. If it has a failing, it is that the ending feels more than a bit contrived; yet there is, at the same time, a symbolic appropriateness and inevitability about it that makes it work.

THE LAST of Stafford's three published novels, *The Catherine Wheel* (1953), presents us with yet another child. Twelve-year-old Andrew Shipley is spending the summer at the New England country house of his cousin Katharine Congreve, a beautiful, charming Boston spinster in her early forties whose intimate tie with Andrew's parents is regarded as "the most winning friendship in Boston." Andrew's story – which takes place entirely during this one summer – is reminiscent in many ways of *The Mountain Lion*. Like Molly, Andrew is a sensitive, imaginative isolato. Just as Molly comes to feel rejected by her brother, so Andrew feels abandoned by his only friend in the world, Victor Smithwick, the son of his cousin's seamstress; just as Molly's brother is busy hero-worshiping his uncle, so Andrew's friend is preoccupied with his older brother, a Navy man whom he idolizes, and who is at home with a serious illness. Like Molly, too, Andrew has a pair of silly, conventional sisters and a mother who is much closer to them than to him; and just as Molly's mother leaves her at the family ranch while she circles the globe with her older daughters, so Andrew's parents leave him at Katharine's country house while they spend their summer in Europe.

Andrew is not, strictly speaking, the only protagonist of *The Catherine Wheel*. Chapter by chapter, Stafford alternately focuses on Andrew, who secretly pines for Victor and hopes that the boy's brother will either die or recover and leave, and Cousin Katharine, who has her own secret preoccupation: she's been conducting a clandestine romance with Andrew's father, whom she has loved for twenty years, and is waiting to hear whether he will divorce his wife. Neither Andrew nor Katharine is aware of the other's hidden torment; each nervously interprets the other's occasional show of anxiety as evidence that his own deepest thoughts have been perceived. Together they agonize alone, neither receiving an ounce of comfort from the other. This situation persists until the end of the summer – and of the novel – when Katharine is burned to death in a fireworks accident.

The Catherine Wheel is an unusual novel – and, in many ways, a satisfying one. The principal characters are vividly imagined, and the prose is as finely crafted as in *The Mountain Lion;* the central dramatic situation, moreover, is skillfully and often wittily managed, and Stafford's central point – namely, that we all live in individual worlds, obsessed, in spite of our best intentions, with our private dilemmas – certainly comes through clearly. Ultimately, though, the novel is less effective than Stafford must have hoped it would be. A large part of the reason is the ending. Like *The Mountain Lion, The Catherine Wheel* concludes in a burst of symbolism. Significantly, the fireworks device that kills Katharine is a Catherine wheel – a rapidly spinning wheel of colored fire, also known as a pinwheel, which is typically nailed to a tree; this, the novel's main symbol, serves much the same function as the mountain lion in Stafford's second book. We are told that when Katharine first fell in love with Andrew's father – who on that same night fell in love with his wife-to-be – there was a Catherine wheel spinning; we are reminded that the wheel is the symbol of the martyr Catherine ("They tied her to a thing like that and set it spinning, but it broke before it killed her and then they chopped off her head"); and we are informed that Katharine has ordered an image of the wheel carved into her own gravestone.

A comparison of the endings of this novel and *The Mountain Lion* is highly instructive. *The Mountain Lion* ends with the appearance of the eponymous feline and the death of Molly; *The Catherine Wheel* concludes with the appearance of the eponymous wheel and the death of Katharine. As critics have noted, both endings involve a *deus ex machina* and are thus less than completely pleasing; but there is a clear difference between them. For, despite its artificiality, the conclusion of *The Mountain Lion* manages to be quite affecting, and indeed feels somehow *right* – partly because the story is so symbolic in tone to begin with, and perhaps also in part because the conclusion represents an expert tapping into the reader's unconscious storehouse of myths and emotions relating to childhood, family and growing up. Besides, whereas it is the fire from the Catherine wheel that kills Katharine, it is not the lion but her brother who kills Molly. And the act is a direct – if hardly an inevitable – consequence of the changes that both children in *The Mountain Lion* have undergone: Molly has increasingly kept to her own company, prowling quietly around the ranch and examining the local fauna (which would explain her sudden appearance in the brush); her brother has become more of a "man," incautiously gun-happy. Hence the killing of Molly has both credibility and import. The conclusion of *The Catherine Wheel,* by contrast – for all of Stafford's skilled foreshadowing – has a facile, phony quality; Katharine's death comes off as a freak accident, and the image of the Catherine wheel has no more resonance than a naughty limerick.

By the time *The Catherine Wheel* was published, Stafford's life had changed enormously. As her marriage to Lowell disintegrated, Stafford's life fell into a grim routine of insomnia, heavy drinking, and nervous breakdowns; after Lowell left her in 1946 she broke down completely and spent most of the following year as a patient at the Payne Whitney Clinic of New York Hospital. Eileen Simpson's observation that Stafford seemed "relieved" and "comfortable" to be at Payne Whitney is not surprising; indeed, it is consistent with Stafford's lifelong preoccupation with characters, Sonie Marburg among them, who long for refuge with strangers, for a home away from home. Best-sellerdom, surely, provided no such refuge. When, some time after their estrangement, Lowell expressed the hope that she would be recognized as the best novelist of her generation, she replied that such a turn of events "would mean to me absolutely *nothing*. It could not happen and even if it could, it would not make the days here less long nor would my loss of you be made up for." The truth seems to be that without the dominating figure of Lowell in her life Stafford was lost, directionless; that his rejection of her was so destructive of her mental stability seems to have been a measure not only of her love for him but of her continued insecurity, her inadequate sense of self – which, even after the financial success of *Boston Adventure* and the artistic triumph of *The Mountain Lion*, seems not to have been altered substantially.

Stafford's second and third experiments with wedlock were more conservative than her first. Following a brief marriage, in the early fifties, to Oliver Jensen – a *Time* magazine writer who would later co-found *American Heritage* – Stafford wed the *New Yorker* writer A. J. Liebling, to whom she remained married until his death in 1963. Both of these men provided a measure of stability (and Liebling, by her own testimony, brought her considerable happiness), but Stafford's life continued, for the most part, to be an emotional roller coaster. Though she lived until 1979, passing her last fifteen years in relative seclusion on Long Island – as much of an *isolato* as Molly Fawcett or Andrew Shipley – she never completed another novel after *The Catherine Wheel*. Why? Perhaps part of the explanation is that once she had satisfied herself that she'd *made* it – in other words, that she had accomplished what her father had never done – her driving motivation to write was gone. For Stafford seems oddly to have been driven, at once, to show up her father, to vindicate him, and to duplicate his long, pathetic, unproductive decline. In fact, in a manner eerily reminiscent of her father's decades of work on his economic manifesto, Stafford spent many of her last years laboring over a novel, entitled *The Parliament of Women,* that would never be published. And, as her father had once made a habit of mailing off cranky, never-to-be-published pieces to famous magazines, so Stafford devoted the final years of her career largely to intemperate articles ridiculing the use of the honorific "Ms.," noting the ruinous effects of television on the English language, and complaining about houseguests. (One of these pieces – a 1966 profile of Lee Harvey Oswald's mother – was published the next year in expanded form as *A Mother in History.*)

More important, Stafford continued to write short stories well into the mid-sixties. Indeed, as her novels faded in the reading public's memory, she began to be known primarily for her work in that field, and, in particular, as one of the most celebrated practitioners of the controversial genre known as the *New Yorker* story. Stafford's short fiction, most of which was assembled in various volumes during the fifties and sixties and brought together in the Pulitzer Prize-winning *Collected Stories* (1969), represents one of the finest moments of the American short story. Witty, luminous, and impeccably crafted, her contributions to the genre are crowded with people named Otis and Meriwether and Fairweather, with troubled children and snobby society women, and with garden party conversations reported word for word. Extremely long sentences abound, and the vocabulary is unusually rich: a single page of the story "A Modest Proposal" contains the words *concupiscently, nares, sybarite, mufti,* and *cereus.* Yet Stafford succeeds in fashioning a lucid, well-upholstered style into which such words fit very gracefully.

To read *The Collected Stories* is to note the recurrence of certain themes, many of which recall the preoccupations of Stafford's life as well as the plots of her novels. The book abounds in protagonists who are, to some extent, Sonie Marburgs – unsatisfied with their lot and eager to be taken into someone else's world. In "The Bleeding Heart," for instance, "a Mexican girl from the West" named Rose Fabrizio longs to be adopted by a mysterious elderly man who visits the New England library where she works; but her illusions about the man are soon shattered. The most prominent of Stafford's themes, indeed, may well be the shattering of illusions – the illusions of Americans about Europe, of Westerners about the Eastern seaboard, of poor people about the rich, of naïve young people about the *beau monde*. One story after another seems to derive in some way from the young Stafford's encounter with Lucy Cooke's bohemia, with the *Kultur* of Heidelberg, or with Robert Lowell's Boston. In "Maggie Meriwether's Rich Experience," a girl from Nashville on her first trip abroad is intimidated into silence by a host of rich and titled folk at a garden party in France; in "The Echo and the Nemesis," Sue Ledbetter, an American student in Heidelberg, feels painfully inferior to the more worldly Ramona Dunn; in "The Healthiest Girl in Town," a girl named Jessie is made to feel *déclassé* by two well-to-do schoolmates who regard their delicate health as a sign of privilege. (Like Ralph and Molly Fawcett, they're *proud* of their illness.) Time and again, however, sophistication is revealed to be a mask for vulnerability, for failure, for loneliness, for a history of personal tragedy. And tragedy is certainly plentiful in these stories. Just as Stafford lost her brother immediately prior to the appearance of her first novel, so some of her characters are struck by tragedy on the threshold of their greatest joy. In the deeply haunting story "The Liberation," for instance, Polly Bay – who has been saved from a life of eternal spinsterhood in her aunt and uncle's tomblike Colorado house by a proposal of marriage from a wonderful young Harvard professor – learns just before her would-be triumphal departure that her fiancé has died.

Naturally, some of Stafford's stories are more impressive than others. Aside from those I have named, the strongest ones include "A Country Love Story," "The Interior Castle," and "An Influx of Poets." But even her weakest stories are a joy to read, if only because their prose is so lovely. The deficiencies that they do manifest are, for the most part, those which are notoriously characteristic of *New Yorker* short stories in general. For instance, like many a fiction writer associated with that illustrious magazine, Stafford places a good deal less emphasis on plot than on character. This is, to be sure, not always a weakness, but it is hard to read the *Collected Stories* in sequence without eventually becoming irritated by their mostly ambiguous, well-nigh pretentious endings; one has the feeling that the author doesn't want to push too far, doesn't want to face the difficult choices attendant upon reaching the conclusion of a story, doesn't want to risk sentimentality or conventionality or melodrama. The contrast with the emphatic sense of closure achieved in *The Mountain Lion* and *The Catherine Wheel* is striking; and the result is too often a denouement that feels dry to the point of heartlessness and pat to the point of meaninglessness. Another *New Yorker*ish problem is that the stories tend to be cluttered up with gratuitous details – inventories of clothes, furnishings, meals, and the like, with a frequent emphasis on the hoity-toity.

A failing more specific to Stafford's stories is that her sarcasm toward a character sometimes overwhelms her sympathy. This is true, for instance, of "A Polite Conversation," in which a recently married young woman is forced to endure a visit to her new home by a rich lady who lives nearby. The only apparent point of the story is to make fun of the lady, who in her fatuity, condescension, and bigotry is rather too easy a target – not to mention a *very* familiar one, whose like (in male and female form) may be found throughout Stafford's fiction. These stories, then, are not without serious flaws; to compare them to the short fiction of John Cheever – and especially to that of Eudora Welty and Peter Taylor – is to notice, on Stafford's part, a relative want of sympathy and narrowness of range. Cheever's stories are more inventive than hers, Welty's more playful and abundant, Taylor's more thoughtful; Welty's and Taylor's stories, moreover, seem markedly *realer* than Stafford's, more significant, more profoundly human. Yet the very fact that one is compelled to speak of Stafford in the company of such masters is to acknowledge that her achievement in the genre is of a very high order indeed.

WHICH, unfortunately, is more than one can say for David Roberts's biography. For despite the occasional insight, Roberts generally acts as if the biographer's chief obligation is to accumulate pointless and intimate facts about his subject: whom she slept with, what they did or didn't do in bed. To be sure, such details, handled with tact and sensitivity, can provide vital insights into a writer's character, and can even be humanizing; even the most clinical details will usually strike a sensitive reader as permissible, so long as they seem integral to a carefully exe-

cuted, full-figure portrait of the subject. But the sleaze-to-insight ratio
of this book is inexcusably high, the portrait of Stafford lacks technique
and proportion, and the portraitist himself has all the delicacy of a rhi-
noceros. Really, what can one say about a serious literary biography that
contains such a passage as this: "It is thanks to Hightower that we have
the only objective testimony, sketchy though it may be, about how Stafford lost her virginity." (Gee, thanks, Hightower.) Or this: "It is entirely possible that this half-secret romance [with one Jamie Caffery] involved no sex. If it is true that Stafford and Lowell were never lovers, as
she later claimed to Eve Auchincloss, then it is also possible that by
1948 it had been almost ten years since Stafford had made love with
anyone (the last time having been her one-night stand with Hightower
in November 1938)." Paging Leon Edel!

To be sure, in a brief passage toward the end of chapter 10, Roberts
does speculate intelligently about the reasons for the asexuality that Stafford seemed to manifest after 1940, and sensibly associates this asexuality with the minuscule role played by sex in her fiction; but there is
nothing in the biography to justify the inclusion of some of the grubbier
anecdotes that he retails in its pages. Central to this book is the assertion
that Stafford spent most of her adult life suffering from syphilis, and
that she never told anybody about it. What to say about this theory?
Yes, some of the evidence that Roberts marshals in its defense is compelling; yes, he has a point when he suggests that such a medical problem
might help to explain Stafford's mid-life antipathy toward sex and
motherhood; and, yes, if Richard Ellmann had come across such information about James Joyce he might have made use of it, too. The difference is that a Richard Ellmann would have provided a respectable and
intelligent context for such a revelation, and would have found an appropriate tone in which to treat the subject; Roberts's blunt, insensitive
approach, by contrast, reminds one of an article in a supermarket tabloid
about the Sex Secrets of the Rich and Famous. In a great literary biography, every newly introduced detail helps to sharpen a steadily developing portrait of an artist's character in action; in the present book, however, the indiscriminate tossing out of every new fact and hypothesis
only compounds the chaos. If an Ellmann, in other words, discusses a
subject's medical history in a way that makes one think, Roberts dis-

cusses it in a way that makes one want to wash one's hands.

Roberts organizes his book as if it were not a biography at all but simply a rough sketch for one. He lumps together quotations about diverse topics for no other reason than that he picked them up at the same interview; he repeats information about a pamphlet that John Stafford published late in life, and about the inclusion of Stafford's first story in a magazine called *American Prefaces.* On one page he quotes a single telegram in two different ways. As for his prose, it is alternately workmanlike and terrible. He writes, for instance, that in her later years Stafford "still carried an ambivalent torch for Robert Lowell." In a sentence about Stafford and Liebling, he manages to be both tacky and clumsy: "It is not clear how physically amorous the relationship was." Roberts claims that he was first attracted to Stafford by the beauty of her prose; but how could any writer who respected beautiful prose permit a book of first-draft quality to be published under his name?

The inclusion of some materials in this biography is downright baffling. Roberts quotes a rejection slip from the *Atlantic Monthly,* indulges in dopey chatter about his eagerness to know "what went on inside the mind and heart of this enigmatic 'coed,'" and puts unnecessary quotation marks around words like *coed.* He specializes in the self-evident: "Had Jean Stafford never become a writer, her family would have passed into oblivion unprobed." A Coloradan himself, he breaks into gratuitous anthems of praise for the state whenever he has a chance, describing the University of Colorado's summer writers' conference as "an illustrious event," referring to the state's "renowned" World Affairs Conference, mentioning (twice) that Thomas Wolfe once gave a talk at the university (and Stafford wasn't even there!), and writing that the university's 1932 faculty "included a number of scholars with national reputations and as a whole was significantly more liberal than any other body of intellectuals in Colorado." (The Denver Broncos, for example.) He devotes much of his epilogue to a series of "if onlys": "If only Stafford had married Robert Hightower instead of Robert Lowell; if only she had stopped drinking once and for all; if only she had exorcised the demons that her father, her sisters, and — at the end — her best friends came to resemble." Amen — but what's the point? If only Scott Fitzgerald hadn't met Zelda, if only Keats had been born after the discovery of antibiotics, if only Sappho had kept carbons! It simply makes no sense to speak of a literary talent as if it could be extricated from the soul in which it is embedded, isolated from the life experiences that have helped to shape it. The unwise choices of Jean Stafford's life and her finest writings are equally part of who she was.

AND WHO, in the final analysis, was she? One cannot disagree with Roberts's valedictory description of her as "perhaps her generation's outstanding investigator of abandonment, voluntary exile, and self-estrangement." To read through her fiction is to be overwhelmed by a sense of the distances between people; the typical Stafford protagonist is at a considerable remove simultaneously from those who have abandoned her, from those she has left behind, and from those with whom she aspires to associate. And Stafford, admirably enough – though her fiction draws extensively upon her personal life – keeps at a distance as well; that so emotionally fragile a woman, in fact, could transfigure the anguish of her childhood into a series of splendidly objective fictions would seem to be little short of remarkable. Indeed, if there is any value in the grimly detailed closing chapters of Roberts's book, it resides in the way that the darkness of Stafford's final years underlines the brilliance of her fiction. But the drama of this antithesis hardly justifies Roberts's emphasis upon such material. Patently, his chief purpose is to lend support to his conclusion that "Jean Stafford's career was a tragic one." It is of course fashionable nowadays for literary biographers to speak pityingly of their distinguished subjects, and to refer to those subjects' lives as "tragedies"; but no life that yielded a novel as fine as *The Mountain Lion,* and a body of short fiction that has few equals in the postwar American canon, can properly be called a tragedy.

(NOVEMBER 1988)

A Proliferation of Rabbits:
John Updike

*" – and you're so damn adolescent. There's more things in
the world than who's boffing who."*
—NELSON ANGSTROM
to his father, Harry "Rabbit" Angstrom,
in *Rabbit at Rest*

WHEN, IN 1960, a promising twenty-eight-year-old writer named
John Updike published his second novel, *Rabbit, Run,* nobody– not
even the young author himself– had any idea that it would turn out to
be the first installment of a tetralogy, or that thirty years would pass before the last volume, the newly issued *Rabbit at Rest,* finally appeared.[1]
According to a recent essay by Updike in the *New York Times Book Review, Rabbit, Run* – with its tale of a former high-school basketball star
who finds adult life less rewarding than his glory days on the court – was
contrived principally for the purpose of exemplifying what Updike calls
the "rabbit approach" to life, "spontaneous, unreflective, frightened,"
and was designed in conjunction with his third novel *The Centaur*
(1963), which depicts the "horse method of coping with life, to get
into harness and pull your load until you drop." Though Updike set
Rabbit, Run in his home state of Pennsylvania, his twenty-six-year-old
protagonist, Harry "Rabbit" Angstrom, is no self-portrait but something of an alternative self, an Updike, as it were, whose talents are physical rather than artistic, who has stayed in Pennsylvania instead of moving to New England, and who, in his mid-twenties, is not a successful

---

1. *Rabbit at Rest,* by John Updike; Knopf. The other Rabbit books are available in paperback from Fawcett.

and resolute young man who has found his vocation but a weak-willed failure who doesn't know what to do with his life.

As the novel opens, Harry is living in his hometown of Mt. Judge, a suburb of Brewer, the "fifth largest city in Pennsylvania." Both professionally and personally, things are looking down for this sometime sports hero: he's a door-to-door potato-peeler salesman with no career prospects, and Janice, his pregnant wife (and the mother of his infant son, Nelson), is an unaffectionate, dipsomaniacal mess. Oppressed by the burdens of his life and grieved by its lack of rapture, Harry runs away from home. On an impulse, he drives to West Virginia, then back; then, through his old high-school coach, he meets a prostitute named Ruth Leonard, whose affection he wins and whose flat he moves into. Jack Eccles, a young Episcopal priest from his in-laws' church (Harry's a Lutheran), urges him to go home; but though he does return when Janice gives birth to a daughter, she throws his dalliance with Ruth up at him and he walks out again. Soon afterward, when an inebriated Janice accidentally drowns the little girl in the bathtub, Harry shows up at the funeral, offhandedly forgiving ("Hey, it's O.K. . . . . You didn't mean to") and ready to give the marriage another chance; but Janice turns away coldly, and Harry goes back to Ruth, who, now pregnant and resentful over his abandonment of her, rages at him about his vacillation and undependability. "All I know is what feels right," he responds by way of explanation, to which she counters: "Who cares *what* you feel?" Harry, unable to decide whether to throw in his lot with Janice or Ruth, simply runs.

Rabbit, Run is impressive in many ways. Tense, taut, and suggestive, it is a fine example of that demanding genre, the acute, fluent study of a not very acute or fluent protagonist. What is particularly notable is that Updike, inspired by Joyce Cary's marvelous *Mister Johnson*, wrote the novel – as he would write all three of its successors – in the present tense, at the time rarely employed in American fiction. (The Rabbit books are largely responsible, of course, for its frequent use today.) Despite the congenital drawbacks of the present tense (which are manifested to a relatively minor degree in *Rabbit, Run,* but which I will elaborate upon in connection with *Rabbit at Rest*), it does lend the book a sense of movement and urgency, and captures something of Rabbit's own existential sensibility. And what a crippling sensibility it is: for while his brief tenure as a local athletic hero endowed him with inflated expectations of life, he has never learned to articulate, tame, or act constructively upon these expectations, never progressed beyond the reflexive, moment-to-moment approach that works better on the high-school basketball court than on the field of life, never recognized that what adulthood requires of him is self-discipline and intelligent decision-making, not fleetness of foot. Yet Updike wants us to *like* Harry, to sympathize with him and care passionately about his fate, and even to see a religious significance in his personal waverings. This is why Updike gives him an opportunity to debate theology with Eccles, whose views of the deity he doesn't share. While the priest believes that "God rules reality," Harry's sense of things is that living in the world entails "separation from God"; he feels that "somewhere behind all this . . . there's something that wants me to find it," a sentiment that prompts Eccles to call him a "mystic" and to explain that "Christianity isn't looking for a rainbow. . . . We're trying to *serve* God, not *be* God."

The novel's epigraph is from Pascal – "The motions of Grace, the hardness of the heart; eternal circumstances" – and Updike, like Pascal, is fascinated by the nexus between matter and spirit, between the mundane and the sublime. The epigraph to *The Centaur,* which is drawn from the theologian Karl Barth (a major influence on Updike's thinking), is relevant here: "Heaven is the creation inconceivable to man, earth the creation conceivable to him. He himself is the creature on the boundary between heaven and earth." Plainly, Harry is meant to be seen as torn between heaven and earth, drawn upward by a quasi-mystical straining after grace and downward by his worldly obligations. But Updike behaves as if these two things are mutually exclusive, as if spiritual fulfillment cannot be derived from the performance of selfless acts, as if selfishness is the surest route to spiritual intensity. (Indeed, it is only when Harry takes care of his baby daughter that *Rabbit, Run* seems to reflect an awareness that doing something for another person might actually be as soul-enhancing as doing something for oneself.) The plain truth about Harry, notwithstanding the sympathy he evokes now and then, is that most of his actions come across as symptoms not of quasi-mystical temperament but of shallowness of character. "[I]s he a good man?" Updike asks in a note to a 1977 limited edition of the novel. "The question is meant to lead to another – what is goodness?" Updike explains that when he wrote *Rabbit, Run,*

> Kerouac's *On the Road* was in the air, and a decade of dropping-out about to arrive, and the price society pays for unrestrained motion was on my mind. In the end, the act of running, of gathering a blank momentum "out of a kind of sweet panic," offers itself as containing a kernel of goodness; but perhaps a stone or a flower at rest holds the same kernel. At any rate, the title is a piece of advice, in the imperative mode, though the man giving it was sitting at a desk, in the upstairs room of a seventeenth-century house, overlooking a shady street corner in a small New England town.

At the end of the note, he says that "the Rabbit in us all remains both wild and timid, harmful and loving, hard-hearted and open to the motions of Grace."

This passage has a coy, narcissistic dodginess that is very Angstrom-ish: Updike expresses a conservative-sounding concern about "the price society pays for unrestrained motion," then subversively asserts the "goodness" of Harry's running away, then hedges by suggesting that maybe it's good only in the same way as a stone or flower (?), then tells us that "the title is a piece of advice" – that, in other words, he *likes* the idea of Harry running. More to the point, however, is the peculiarity of Updike's notion that *Rabbit, Run* constitutes a study in the nature of goodness, and his implication that it is through the most Angstromlike corners of our souls that the rest of us are most "open to the motions of Grace" – an implication that would seem to reflect a surprisingly blinkered moral perspective, or (at the very least) an idiosyncratic understanding of the meaning of the words *goodness* and *grace*. Confronted with Updike's gloss on *Rabbit, Run,* a reader may be forgiven for having his own question, namely: in a world full of more virtuous, bright, interesting, and industrious men and women, why should anyone be concerned enough about this idle, self-obsessed, tiresome, and mediocre man – whose own concern for those around him is (at best) inconstant – to read four books about him? Quite simply, Harry's chief flaw as a human being is that he has never learned to care about anyone else as much as he cares about himself; by the same token, a major shortcoming of *Rabbit, Run* is that Updike, who considers himself to be interested in the question of goodness, is at once too tolerant of Harry's solipsism and too inattentive to its repercussions in the lives of those around him. This is true, alas, not only of *Rabbit, Run* but of all the Rabbit novels.

When Harry does approach spiritual fulfillment in the company of another person, the encounter is likely to center on sex. Updike is, needless to say, notorious for his erotic passages, which have been widely praised for their combination of the clinical and the transcendent. The problem with them, however, is that they tend to jump directly from the clinical to the transcendent, largely bypassing the human. To put it a bit differently, Harry is inclined to regard a sexual partner more as an orgasm machine and a vessel of grace than as a person, deriving little or none of his joy in the liaison from a profound interest in her as an individual; Updike's perspective on these coital episodes, moreover, is not significantly removed from Harry's. A critic has suggested that "we must grant Updike his obsession" with sex; and one would hardly want to deny a novelist his obsessions. But a reader has a right, I think, to expect an author to bring some perspective to bear on those obsessions, and to manipulate them in such a way as to illuminate the human condition – especially when he makes it clear, as Updike does in the sex scenes of the Rabbit books, that those obsessions lie, for him, at the heart of the matter.

Rabbit, Run has other failings. The setup is excessively schematic: Eccles is too patently a mouthpiece for organized Christianity's slant on things, and the contrast between the dense, wan, unstable Janice and the smart, robust, sturdy Ruth is implausibly tidy. What's more, Ruth – who is not bitter and cynical about sex but generous and good-natured – strikes one as a romantic's idea of a whore. For all this, however, *Rabbit, Run* is a compelling, meticulously fashioned novel that explores serious spiritual questions and exhibits a real appreciation for the power of the unspoken, the reality of mystery. Though one may not agree entirely with Updike's metaphysics, the book renders its vision forcefully, even (at times) affectingly.

THE SAME, I'm afraid, cannot be said of the longer, slacker *Rabbit Redux* (1971). In his *Times* piece, Updike says that he wrote it partly because he owed his publishers a novel and partly because "it seemed to me that Rabbit Angstrom . . . might be the vehicle in which to package some of the American unease that was raging all around us." The word *package* strikes the right note, for *Rabbit Redux* comes across less as a novel about the way people really lived and thought during the late sixties than as an assemblage of images, arguments, and character types drawn from the newspaper headlines of that period. Set in 1969, the book finds Harry living with Janice and working as a typesetter at a Brewer printing plant. He is, plainly, a solid enough citizen; but when Janice abandons him and Nelson (who's now thirteen) and moves in with Charlie Stavros, a salesman at her father's used-car lot whom she has been seeing on the sly, Harry loses control. He takes as his concubine a rich, radical teenage runaway named Jill; she, in turn, brings into the house a violent black fugitive named Skeeter, who hates America and the white race and imagines himself to be a messiah. Both Skeeter and Jill consider Harry an ignorant bigot (which he is), and he considers them, respectively, deranged and spoiled (right on both counts); but all three, for whatever reason, are willing to talk politics together, and so much of the book consists of this unlikely threesome's implausible conversations about race, revolution, and the ruling classes. Since there is little here in the way of plot, Updike wraps the whole thing up by having Jill perish in a fire, set (apparently) by a neighbor distressed at Skeeter's presence in Harry's house.

We are doubtless supposed to view the Harry of *Rabbit Redux* as a desperate, conflicted man, torn between his responsibilities as patriot, wage earner, and family man and his long-suppressed yearning – now reawakened by Janice's departure and the advent of Jill and Skeeter – to break loose and seek the "something out there" that he feels calling to him. But it doesn't wash. Skeeter, for one thing, is a preposterous creation, coming off less as a human being than as a grotesque incarnation of late-sixties black anger at its most irrational and paranoid; he is difficult to buy on anything other than a strictly symbolic level. Nor is Harry's fascination with him credible. Of course, we're meant to recognize that Harry sees in Skeeter glimpses of the runaway "mystic" he once was, and that part of him is drawn to Skeeter even as part (the level-headed householder) is repelled. But the two parts don't fit together convincingly; Harry sounds like Archie Bunker one minute and Abbie Hoffman the next. And it's hard to believe that even Harry, irresponsible as he is, would let this sociopath stay under the same roof as his son, let alone that he would sit still for Skeeter's lessons in Marxism. Likewise, we're evidently supposed to recognize that Harry's attraction to Jill, who is young enough to be his child, is largely rooted in the loss of his baby daughter in *Rabbit, Run;* but virtually everything about Jill – who appears almost out of nowhere, the very embodiment of youth, wealth, beauty, and free love, and who readily services Harry's often kinky carnal appetite – reads like something out of an adolescent fantasy. (One might also add that it's hard to believe a middle-class American homeowner in 1969 would set fire to a house down the block from his own in order to drive an undesirable from the neighborhood.)

To be sure, the novel has a spiritual element. The conflict between Harry's support of America's Vietnam policy and his adversaries' Marxist utopianism seems designed to enact a Barthian tension between earth and heaven. But politics rules the day here; and the moral ambiguity of *Rabbit, Run* deteriorates in this book, with the movement of politics to center stage, into an offensive moral indeterminacy, a refusal to advance beyond dialectic. Equally offensive is the sex, which is more obtrusive, empty, and exploitative than in *Rabbit, Run.* Throughout the book, the characters play musical beds: aside from Harry's coital encounters with Jill and Janice's with Charlie, there's Harry's with Peggy (a friend of Janice's), Skeeter's with Jill, and Charlie's with Mim (Harry's sister); it is also hinted for a time that perhaps even Nelson and Jill are sleeping together. In addition, Harry thinks endlessly about sex, and those thoughts can be pretty bizarre. At one point, for instance, he tries to picture Charlie and Mim together, and we are vouchsafed a graphic description of both characters' genitalia as he envisions them, and an elaborate account of their imagined coupling; at another point, we are offered a detailed description of Harry's fantasy of bedding down "a hefty coarse Negress, fat but not sloppy fat, muscular and masculine, with a trace of a mustache and a chipped front tooth."

All these pairings, real and imaginary, are rendered by Updike with what can only be described as lusty enthusiasm. The idea here is plainly that sex, to Harry, is the preeminent means of establishing meaningful contact with other people, and that his fantasy, say, about intercourse with a black woman may well be seen as embodying a longing to bridge the American racial gap. Yet these sex scenes have little real human content or dramatic purport, and it is not long before they grow monotonous and redundant – and not long, either, before Updike's apparent conviction that they embody moments of transcendence comes to seem not only puerile but repugnant.

In *Rabbit Redux* Updike attempts to capture the distinct tenor of the sixties; in *Rabbit Is Rich* (1981) he seeks to do the same for the more amorphous seventies. Since, when he came to write the book, America happened to be in the grip of the 1979 gasoline crunch, Updike took as his theme the idea that the country, in the seventies, was "running out of gas." These are, in Harry's words, the "bad new days": America can't produce anymore, the Japanese have shown us up, our nation's young people are spoiled and lazy and dependent. In his *Times* piece, curiously enough, Updike all but acknowledges the artificiality of the socioeconomic motif of *Rabbit Is Rich,* noting that, despite the "running out of gas" theme, he was "feeling pretty good" when he wrote the novel and so it turned out to be "kind of an upbeat book in spite of itself." And it is upbeat, if only in comparison with its predecessors: there are no babies drowning in bathtubs, no teenage girls perishing in house fires. What's more, though not quite "rich," Harry and Janice (who have been back together for years) are decidedly well off: her father having died, the family used-car lot has passed into the hands of Janice and her mother, and is now (what else?) a lucrative Toyota franchise with Harry as its manager.

The catalytic acts in the first two Rabbit novels are, respectively, Harry's abandonment of Janice and Janice's abandonment of Harry; in *Rabbit Is Rich,* the catalytic act is a homecoming – namely, the twenty-three-year-old Nelson's return home from college (he attends Kent State, naturally) with a friend named Melanie. Harry assumes that she is Nelson's girlfriend, but soon afterward her place is taken by a pregnant young lady named Pru, whom Nelson introduces as his fiancée. Nelson announces his intention to quit school and work at the lot, and suggests that Harry make room for him by firing Charlie. Though Harry, who has become good friends with Charlie, balks at the suggestion, Janice sides with Nelson, and eventually Charlie is squeezed out. Nelson proceeds to screw up at the lot, though not disastrously, and after marrying Pru—who gives birth to a baby girl—and briefly running away from home (like father, like son), he decides to return to college, making it possible for Charlie, who has in the meantime had a pleasant affair with Melanie, to get his old job back. At the end of the book we find Harry and Janice, content as they ever have been, moving into a new house in the upscale neighborhood of Penn Park. All in all, compared to the earlier Rabbit novels, *Rabbit Is Rich* is a veritable Midsummer Night's Dream.

In no respect is this difference more pronounced than in regard to sex. Compared to the extramarital hijinks in the earlier Rabbit novels, the playing around in *Rabbit Is Rich* is relatively guilt free and out in the open; Janice's affair with Charlie is a fact of history that nobody feels uncomfortable about anymore, and sexual fidelity is so little an issue between Harry and Janice that, when they vacation in the Caribbean with two other couples, they engage readily in spouse-swapping and talk uninhibitedly about it afterward. To be sure, Harry assumes during most of the novel that he will never again sleep with anyone but Janice; when, in the Caribbean, he finds himself in bed with Thelma, the wife of his high-school teammate (and nemesis) Ronnie Harrison, and learns to his astonishment that she is very much in love with him and willing to do anything for him, Updike wants us to see their night together as revitalizing, epiphanic. If he is more successful at this here than elsewhere, it is because there is more than the usual degree of real affection involved— at least on Thelma's part (her declaration of her love for Harry is genuinely convincing, even touching)—and less than the usual degree of selfishness (the liaison, sanctioned by Janice and Ronnie, doesn't appear to be hurting anybody).

Having had one attractive young woman under his roof in *Rabbit Redux,* Harry now has two, Melanie and Pru, both of whom are at once daughter figures and objects of desire. And there is yet another daughter figure: toward the end of the book, he tracks down Ruth, his hooker girlfriend from *Rabbit, Run,* who refuses to give a clear answer when he asks whether her college-age daughter is his. If in *Rabbit Redux*, more-over, Harry's special bond with Skeeter seems to derive strength from their mutual involvement with Jill, in *Rabbit Is Rich* his sense of close-ness to Charlie is founded, in some way, upon the latter's affair with Janice a decade earlier. What's Updike's point here? It's as if he's trying to say that women serve as physical-spiritual conduits of a sort between men, as instruments of male bonding, as territories for them to fight over and as the fields of battle on which they fight. ("I'm tired of you and Nelson fighting your old wars through me," Janice complains to Harry in *Rabbit at Rest*.) Not that this earns women any recognition as human beings: if anything, Harry (who in all four books routinely re-fers to Janice as a "mutt") is more callous here than ever about women, habitually reducing them to their sex organs. "She does know some-thing," he muses darkly about Janice when he realizes she has no loyalty to Charlie. "All cunts know something." Here, as in *Rabbit Redux*, women are seen as mysterious, fickle creatures, never to be fully known or understood, whose worth is measured at least in part by their attrac-tiveness to other men. Pondering Janice's affair with Charlie, Harry re-flects: "A man fucks your wife, it puts a new value on her, within limits."

Paradoxically, the Harry of *Rabbit Is Rich* is at once more likable and more obnoxious than ever. Or maybe he just *seems* more likable, partly because Nelson is now too old for Harry's incompetence as a parent to count very strongly against him, and partly because the boy has grown up to be so egocentric, whiny, unreliable, and self-pitying that Harry now looks almost like Albert Schweitzer by comparison. Nelson is, in-deed, so unbearable that he comes across less like a character in a book than like the image that someone griping in a barroom might give you of his ingrate son. As Elliot Fremont-Smith wrote in a review of the novel, Nelson "seems more programmed by Updike's loyalty to Rabbit than by Rabbit's genes or will." Yet Updike's loyalty doesn't keep Harry from being remarkably obnoxious, too. Consider this: "It gives him pleasure, makes Rabbit feel rich, to contemplate the world's wasting, to know that the earth is mortal too." And this, at his father-in-law's fu-neral: "The great thing about the dead, they make space." Throughout *Rabbit Is Rich*, Updike fails to distance himself sufficiently from such ob-servations, fails to make it clear to us why such an odious character should merit our interest and empathy.

Yet Harry is at least consistent in his odiousness. Unlike the Harry of *Rabbit Redux,* he is someone that a reader can imagine running across in a medium-sized Pennsylvania city. His opinions line up, his voice rings true, and the shape and rhythm of his days strike one as authentic. From the opening pages, which find him lollygagging around the showroom, raking over the coals of his life and shooting the breeze with Charlie about the state of the nation and of the car business, it is clear that Updike has managed, this time, to depict a real-seeming middle-class American, and to incorporate current events into the story of his life without outraging one's sense of reality. Updike even does the impossible in this book – he makes Harry Angstrom *interesting* (and, every now and then, quite funny). The novel is longer and looser than its predecessors, but it is also richer, fuller. It is appropriate that one of its two epigraphs is a description of the "Ideal Citizen" as envisioned by Sinclair Lewis's George Babbitt, for this, more than any of the other Rabbit books, effectively captures, as Lewis sought to do in *Babbitt,* something of the life of an ordinary middle-American man at home, at work, and at play. If, in short, *Rabbit Is Rich* is a considerably better novel than *Rabbit Redux,* it is because the story is much more credible and well-constructed, the characters less given to long-winded and dubious political disputation, and Harry a more integrated and engaging presence.

As ITS TITLE may suggest, *Rabbit at Rest* lacks the energy of *Rabbit is Rich.* Set in 1989, it finds Harry semiretired from the Toyota lot; in addition to their fancy Penn Park digs, he and Janice have a house in the Poconos and a condo on the Gulf Coast of Florida, where they spend six months every year. They live a quiet life, and seem reasonably content. But their peace and prosperity are threatened when they learn that Nelson, who now runs the Toyota franchise, has been embezzling money to support a cocaine habit and to buy medicine for an employee with AIDS. Though Nelson eventually agrees to enter an addiction-treatment program and Harry acts quickly to straighten things out, the Toyota company withdraws its franchise, and its representative, in an episode all too plainly intended to symbolize the nature of late-1980s relations between the United States and Japan, makes some cutting remarks about the "rack of discipline in people of America," about Nelson's immaturity and about Harry's inept parenting. As if this weren't bad enough, Harry has serious health problems: he suffers a heart attack, after which he submits to an angioplasty but vetoes a recommended bypass. (When the doctor accuses him of toying with his life, Harry asks himself: *"what's life for but to toy with?"*)

Once he has inflicted these tribulations upon the Angstrom family, Updike proceeds to arrange things so that Harry and Pru are left alone together one evening. No reader of the previous Rabbit books should be surprised to learn that the two of them, drained and demoralized by these family crises, end up in the sack. Some time later when Janice finds out, Harry can't see why she's so upset: "Whajou put me and her in the same house at night for? Whajou think I was, dead already?" Even after following him through four novels and thirty years, one doesn't know quite what to make of this comeback. Is Harry joking nervously because he doesn't know what else to say? Or is he serious? Are we truly expected to believe that Harry has grown up so little that he *could* seriously say something like this? The episode with Pru constitutes the book's climax, but it's an ill-conceived one, which, aside from striking a reader as highly implausible, makes everything that has preceded it suddenly seem like the laboriously contrived opening sequences of a pornographic movie. Nor does it do much to enhance one's already meager sympathy for Harry, who, when asked by Pru whether we shouldn't "all be responsible for our own lives," responds: "Beats me . . . I never knew who was responsible for mine." How long, for heaven's sake, can one be expected to remain concerned about such a morally torpid being?

Nor is Harry the only torpid one here. *Rabbit at Rest* is the longest book in the series, not because Updike has more to say but because his prose is slacker, and his characters chattier, than ever. It's a surprisingly lazy book. Updike appears bored with the Angstroms, and doesn't seem well enough acquainted with the people they have become over the last decade; they sound too much alike, and say and do things that seem out of character. Would Nelson complain about "the greedy consumer society"? Would Janice, a *National Enquirer* reader, buy Harry a scholarly book about the Dutch role in the American Revolution? Even Harry seems out of focus. Early in the book we're told that "blaspheming . . . makes Harry uneasy." *Harry?* And would he actually use words like *seigneurial?* Or say "Might she ask?" instead of "You think she might ask?" Ever since *Rabbit Redux,* Harry has occasionally sounded less like the "spontaneous, unreflective, frightened" ex-jock of *Rabbit, Run* than like – well – a *New Yorker* writer; in *Rabbit at Rest* he sounds closer than ever to Updike.

Another reason for the excessive length of *Rabbit at Rest* is that it is rife with references (often quite extensive) to the sitcoms Harry watches and the news events he hears about on radio and TV. To be sure, all of the Rabbit books have contained such references: in *Rabbit, Run,* Janice watches "The Mickey Mouse Club" and Updike catalogues the pop songs, news flashes, and commercials that Harry hears on the car radio during his flight to West Virginia. But never has Updike included more such references than in the present book, and never have they seemed more arbitrary and self-indulgent. More than ever, it seems obvious that he is putting his own opinions about current events and TV programs into Harry's mouth; and it seems obvious, too, that the only reason Harry's response to a news story about Jim Bakker, say, appears on a given page is that Updike happened to have that page in the typewriter the day the Bakker story broke. (In his *Times* piece, Updike tells us that "[i]n writing, I several times had to stop to let real time catch up with my fictional time." Is this any way to write a novel?)

Updike's decision to work so many news stories into *Rabbit at Rest* may well have something to do with his newfound emphasis on history. Harry reads about the French and American revolutions, and is depressed by the thought of newfangled religious sects because "[a]t least the moldy old denominations have some history to them." It is a shame, in this connection, that the great event of the 1980s, the collapse of communism, took place too late for Updike to make major thematic use of it; the subject comes up only glancingly near the end of the book, where Harry reflects that he misses the Cold War because "[i]t gave you a reason to get up in the morning." But then, what could Updike have done with so triumphant a news story? He prefers more horrific (if less historically consequential) tidings, such as the explosions of the *Challenger* and Pan Am Flight 103, the latter of which serves here as a symbol of Harry's – and, one gathers, America's – approaching end.

The proliferation of news stories and TV plots in *Rabbit at Rest* underlines a cardinal weakness of the present tense – namely, that since life does present itself as a clutter of events, and since only with the passage of time do the trivial things fall away, the important experiences separate out entirely from the inessential, and the shape and meaning of it all become more readily discernible, the present tense is a veritable invitation to an author not to direct emphasis sufficiently. Rather than struggle against this temptation in *Rabbit at Rest* (as he has done, to varying degrees, in its predecessors), Updike succumbs to it entirely, placing the deadly serious and the picayune side by side and according them similar emphasis. At one point, for instance, Harry meditates upon Watergate, China, Gorbachev, "that evil pockmarked Noriega," and the feud between Bryant Gumbel and Willard Scott on the "Today" show. When his doctor urges him to have a bypass, Harry thinks about Kelly McGillis in *Witness*. Indubitably, the purpose of such juxtapositions is to depict the way in which every mind wanders back and forth between the important and the inconsequential. But one soon grows tired of this device, which strikes one not only as something of a tic, but as a disinclination on Updike's part to make distinctions, to tell us what really matters.

Rabbit at Rest is the saddest of the Rabbit books. But then what can one expect of a novel about a fiftyish man who, thirty years ago, was already a backward-looking, woe-begone has-been? Though Harry, after playing Uncle Sam in a Fourth of July parade, observes approvingly that America is "all in all . . . the happiest fucking country the world has ever seen," Updike acknowledges in his *Times* piece that this is "a depressed book about a depressed man, written by a depressed man." It is crowded with deaths and images of death: Janice's father has passed away; Thelma (with whom Harry has been conducting an affair for several years) is dying of lupus; in drought-ridden Florida, "even friendship has a thin, provisional quality, since people might at any minute buy another condominium and move to it, or else up and die."

More than any of its predecessors, moreover, the book seems oddly tilted against Janice and Nelson. Time and again, Harry finds himself at odds with both his wife and son, who take outrageous positions on the matter of Nelson's perfidy and find ways to blame Harry for it. Nelson won't even take responsibility for what he has done to the family business, and Janice, ignoring all evidence of his untrustworthiness, lets him remain in charge of the lot until it is too late. Emerging from therapy, Nelson spouts "AA bullshit"; Janice, for her part, speaks in jargon picked up in a so-called women's course. And both act blasé about Harry's health: when he checks into a Florida hospital, Nelson decides against canceling a flight back to Pennsylvania, and Janice announces that "there's an origami demonstration tonight at the Village I don't want to miss." It all reads like a black joke by Updike about the undevotion of wives and sons, and one cannot help feeling that there is a personal explanation for it. Nelson's belligerence toward Harry also seems designed, in part, to contrast with the compassion of a young nurse in Harry's Pennsylvania hospital who proves to be Ruth's – and maybe Harry's – daughter. Updike plainly wants us to be touched by Harry's affection for this girl, and wants us to find pathos, perhaps even tragedy, in the fact that she never knows that he may be her father, and that he never finds out whether he is. But it's not particularly moving: one can think only that (a) if Harry had really cared about the girl he would have made more of an effort before now to track her down, and (b) the girl is, in any case, better off without Harry, who would probably have ended up taking her to bed.

Though *Rabbit at Rest* may not have the same emphasis on religion as *Rabbit Run,* we are meant to understand that Harry retains his quasi-mystical strain (he declares that he's always identified with the Dalai Lama), and to admire him for – of all things! – his supposed faith in life, his eternally springing hope. As he tells Thelma, he can't believe that he won't ever fulfill his dreams (of which we've never heard before) of visiting Tibet and being a test pilot. (And yet, depressed at the "elderly sexiness" of "The Golden Girls," he reflects that "[p]eople ought to know when to give up.") Janice surprises him (and the reader) by saying that "you have to have faith. You've taught me that." Faith in what? "In us. In life." Updike would manifestly like to think that Harry has taught us that, too; but he continues to view faith as something that makes one run away rather than as something that strengthens one's resolve. (The endurance of his union with Janice strikes the reader as having less to do with Harry's faith in their marriage than with his fear and inertia.) The book is crowded with images of people as ordure, as refuse, as vermin; though he reassures a despondent Thelma that "[n]obody's trash," Harry believes otherwise: "We're all trash, really. Without God to lift us up and make us into angels we're all trash." Neither he nor Updike seems to have given consideration to the notion that perhaps it's not for us to wait for God to lift us up, that perhaps it's our duty to try to rise – by, among other things, acting selflessly and loving one another. But Harry gives no indication of knowing what it means to love someone. When Thelma worries about his health, he sees it as an example of "[t]hat strange way women have, of really caring about somebody beyond themselves." Is this meant as a joke by Updike on Harry? By Harry on himself? Or are Updike and Harry both being serious? "As you say," Harry remarks to Thelma at one point, "I still think I'm the center of the universe." And he still reduces relationships to sex, scrutinizing Thelma's grieving brood at her funeral and thinking: "When you're sexually involved with a woman, some of the focus spills down into her children, that she also spread her legs for." Thelma's widower, Ronnie, calls Harry "the coldest most selfish bastard I ever met," and complains that he never returned Thelma's love, to which Harry responds: "I *did* appreciate her. I did. She was a fantastic lay." Presumably, he thinks he's being nice, which is curious enough; but what is even more curious is that Updike seems to think there is something touching – even redeeming – about the fact that this grandfather has never advanced beyond the juvenile outlook of his thirty-years-younger self.

Harry may not have many redeeming qualities, but *Rabbit at Rest* has a few. Despite his aforementioned habit of speaking through Harry, Updike knows what average Americans think about – and knows what they *think* – and he can be splendid at capturing the way they talk about it. His prose remains smooth and readable, and he continues to display a fine eye for the telling detail. He is so observant and funny on the subject of Gulf Coast condominium life that one finds oneself wishing he had let Rabbit rest already and instead written a short novel about the people with whom Harry socializes in Florida. Finally, the relationship between Harry and his eight-year-old granddaughter, Judy, feels authentic. When he and the child are boating and the craft tips over, the thoughts that go through his head when he can't immediately locate her in the water strike one as exactly right; the episode is gripping, poignant, pathetic.

Yet there are too few such episodes here, and too much that feels bogus, inflated. One thinks especially of Harry's last-act escape from home, which seems motivated less by his circumstances than by Updike's desire for structural symmetry. And one is as troubled as ever by Updike's tendency to legitimize selfishness and dehumanize sex. Why, one wonders, have these books received such extraordinary popular and critical acclaim over the years? Perhaps it is because with the coming of the sixties – and with Updike's shift of emphasis, in *Rabbit Redux* and *Rabbit Is Rich,* from the spiritual concerns of *Rabbit, Run* to more purely sociopolitical and socioeconomic matters – it was possible for Harry Angstrom to be seen by critics not merely as a case study in the "rabbit approach" to life (such a small, *human* subject!) but as a symbol of the supposedly harried, angst-ridden middle America of the Vietnam era and afterward. One of the smaller ironies of the collapse of communism is that it should have begun just as Updike was winding up the Rabbit series, thereby underscoring just how irrelevant the story of Harry Angstrom, for all its feverish bids at timeliness, has been to the deeper truths of American life in the last thirty years. One can only wonder what would have happened to Updike's art – and to his career – had he allowed Harry, after *Rabbit, Run,* to keep on running into eternity and chosen instead to write three follow-up novels to *The Centaur.*

(OCTOBER 1990)

Donald Barthelme
and "la vie quotidienne"

WHAT WOULD the *New Yorker* have done without Donald Barthelme? And what would Donald Barthelme have done without the *New Yorker*?

These are far from idle questions, for rarely in our time have the careers of a celebrated fiction writer and a leading magazine represented so productive an example of what biologists call mutualism, with each partner serving a significant need of the other. Though it might seem incomprehensible to young readers who know him only for his slight valedictory novel, *The King* (which he completed shortly before his death in 1989), the introduction of Barthelme's barbed, idiosyncratic *jeux d'esprit* into the pages of the *New Yorker* a generation ago did the same thing for the magazine's fiction department that the introduction of guitar music into the liturgy did for the Roman Catholic Church at about the same time: namely, it helped a widely venerated institution with a reputation for stuffiness to look, in the eyes of the modish young urbanites whose patronage it sought to retain, as if it were keeping abreast of the age. To be sure, the *New Yorker* continued to publish well-made conventional fictions by the likes of John Cheever (who deplored Barthelme's work and complained that the newcomer was "taking his space" in the magazine) and Barthelme's contemporary John Updike, but readers perceived a change of direction, and it was a direction they identified with Barthelme.

Meanwhile, set in that dignified-looking *New Yorker* type, and surrounded by all that fastidious *New Yorker* prose and those solemn advertisements for Bonwit Teller and Brooks Brothers, Barthelme's clever little stories looked considerably more wild and innovative – *dangerous,* even – than they actually were. The very fact that they appeared in the

New Yorker, moreover, and not in some less prominent and less Estab-
lishment-oriented publication, encouraged readers to see them as representing a significant literary development. Certainly it seems astonishing, in retrospect, how large a reputation Barthelme acquired, and how
quickly. Place him alongside other so-called metafictionists who rose to
prominence in the sixties, such as John Barth, William Gaddis, and
Robert Coover, and Barthelme looks not only lucid but tame and un-
threatening, his language games elementary, his jabs at middle-class
American life no more serious than a stand-up comic's. Place him alongside other popular black humorists of the day, such as Joseph Heller and
Kurt Vonnegut, and Barthelme seems – well – *domesticated,* a writer
who, in his own odd way, often reads like a traditional Cheever-style
New Yorker writer after all, what with his downbeat, underplotted stories of shattered or shattering professional-class New York marriages,
and who, even when he makes use of exotic characters or settings, manages to relate them in some way to the everyday experience of the typical
New Yorker subscriber – and often, indeed, to make a joke out of their
remoteness, with that *New Yorker*ish provincialism that sees the entire
history of Western civilization as a dress rehearsal for Manhattan and all
the world as an outer borough.

    Barthelme is more likely than Heller or Vonnegut to bring up, say,
Saint Augustine or Kierkegaard, but whereas Heller and Vonnegut may
be said to be serious about being frivolous, Barthelme is frivolous about
being serious; which is to say that while he tends to form his *dramatis
personae* out of more authentic stuff than Heller or Vonnegut, he treats
them with less respect. I have compared him to a stand-up comic; but it
is perhaps more accurate to say that his work is to literary fiction what
performance art is to serious drama. The narrative arts give us people we
can believe in and care about; Barthelme gives us always and only
Barthelme. It is interesting that while few (if any) critics have credited
him with inventing memorable characters, many have praised him for
his distinctive, dead-on-target "voices." Yet we rarely fall prey to the illusion that there are human beings behind these voices: we are always
aware of Barthelme gagging it up, putting on a show.

    It is these voices that do most of the work of establishing setting and
character (to the extent that one can speak, in Barthelme's fiction, of set-

ting and character), of advancing the plot (to the extent that there is plot), of expressing ideas and conveying a vision. The voices are deployed in a variety of ways: to read through Barthelme's work is to find instances of fiction in the form of catechism, of monologue, of Socratic dialogue. Yet, as if to confirm the views of those who had always regarded his formal experimentation less as the serious manifestation of inner artistic imperatives than as a function of his desire to be seen as a body surfer on the Aquarian Age's *nouvelle vague,* Barthelme's stories grew more and more conventional in form as the seventies and eighties wore on. Witness his novels: the first, *Snow White* (1967), consists of brief segments, averaging about two hundred and fifty words each, some of which advance the bizarre narrative in relatively orthodox ways and some of which come out of left field in both form and content; here and there, between the chapters, are pages containing nothing but a single brief sentence apiece, or a fragment, or some other arrangement of words, always in large upper-case letters, its relevance sometimes clear, sometimes enigmatic (e.g., WHAT SNOW WHITE REMEMBERS: / THE HUNTSMAN / THE FOREST / THE STEAMING KNIFE"). To read *Snow White* is to be reminded one moment of Woody Allen, the next of Gertrude Stein. His second novel, *The Dead Father* (1975), is composed mostly in staccato dialogue (no quotation marks), with telegraphic bits of description provided where necessary; there is also a more expansive book-within-a-book by one of the novel's characters. The most audacious formal device in Barthelme's largely conventional third novel, *Paradise* (1986), is an intermittent series of *ex post facto* question-and-answer sessions between the protagonist and (presumably) his psychiatrist; as for *The King* (1990), its only formal curiosity is the brevity and talkiness of its chapters.

What Barthelme's novels and stories all share is a self-conscious quirkiness of incident and expression, a colloquial tone (and an implication that more formal language, which he often slips into for parodic purposes, tends under most circumstances to denote not intellectual sophistication or complexity but phoniness), and a seldom relieved irony that sometimes appears to be pointed in every possible direction. (Reading Barthelme, one always knows that something is being mocked, though one is not always sure what.) One of Barthelme's stories is entitled "Critique de la vie quotidienne," and all his fiction is indeed, in a sense, a critique of everyday life – and, especially, of everyday life in the high-tech secular culture of contemporary urban America. In *Snow White* he devotes more than a page to a detailed description of a portion of the eponymous heroine's housework, the intention of which is apparently to make housework look ridiculous and homemakers robotic. (What's more, he emphasizes the dumb-animal aspects of such work throughout the novel by consistently using the word *horsewife* in place of *housewife*.) In the story "Robert Kennedy Saved from Drowning" (which appeared, incidentally, before Kennedy's assassination), Barthelme implies that though we all share the same longings, and though our lives are all sad and ordinary in much the same way, we mortal millions live *alone*: "He hears something playing on someone else's radio. . . . The music is wretchedly sad; now he can barely hear it, now it fades into the wall. . . . He turns on his own radio. There it is, on his own radio, the same music. The sound fills the room."

WHAT CURE is there for this essential loneliness? Not fame. (An exchange from *Paradise*: "What's it feel like to be famous?" "Feels very much like not being famous.") Not getting out of the house. ("'Take me home,' Snow White said. 'Take me home instantly. If there is anything worse than being home, it is being out.'") Not "consciousness-expanding" drugs. (From *Snow White*: "Clem thrust his arm into the bag of consciousness-expanding drugs. His consciousness expanded.") Sleep, yes, but only for one night at a time. (From *Paradise*: "Q: Where is satisfaction? A: In sleep?") And love, perhaps, but not for long. Witness the story "Edward and Pia," which consists almost entirely of simple declarative sentences that describe the daily routine – and increasingly evident mutual disaffection – of a middle-aged American husband and his Swedish mistress who, after a sojourn in London, settle down on her farm. One observes in such a story some of the more lamentable hallmarks of Brat Pack minimalism of the eighties – the studied flatness, the emphasis on superficial particulars – but these traits serve a valid purpose in "Edward and Pia," whose aim is to show how even the most intensely charged relationship, in the most promising of circumstances, gets ground down by nothing more or less than the daili- ness of life. What's more, the story profits from a very un-Brat Packish waggery: "Edward worried about his drinking. Would there be enough gin? Enough ice?" Here and elsewhere, Barthelme does a genuinely witty job of pointing out how much of life consists of banal activities; he is never sharper, funnier, or more sincere than when he is capturing the state of mind of a hapless gent—a gent, it must be said, very much of Barthelme's own demographic description—who can't see any joy or love or light or certitude or peace or help for pain except in a bottle of booze.

That marriage appears in "Edward and Pia" only as an institution betrayed is far from unique in Barthelme's fiction; time and again he im- plies that to be married is, by definition, to be miserable, to be hurtful, and, yes, to betray. The story "The Rise of Capitalism" contains this *mot:* "'It is better to marry than to burn,' St. Paul says, but St. Paul is largely discredited now, for the toughness of his views does not accord with the experience of advanced industrial societies." In "The Dolt," a husband, irked by his wife's ability to answer the questions on a sample test with which he's been struggling, matter-of-factly contemplates bringing up her sordid past in order to regain the upper hand: "she had been a hooker for a period before their marriage and he could resort to this area if her triumph grew too great." And the narrator of the darkly funny "Critique de la Vie Quotidienne," slipping briefly into the second person, remarks that "[t]he world in the evening seems fraught with the absence of promise, if you are a married man." On a typical evening, "you decide to break your iron-clad rule, that rule of rules, and have eleven drinks instead of the modest nine with which you have been wont to stave off the song of twilight, when the lights are low, and the flickering shadows, etc., etc." (These lyrics from "Just a Song at Twi- light" also appear, to much the same ironic purpose, in *The Dead Fa- ther.*) Having used up all the ice, "you measure up your iceless over-the- limit drinks, using a little cold water as a make-do, and return to what is called the 'living' room, and prepare to live, for a while longer, in a truce with your circumstances." All of Barthelme's fiction is, one might say, about how one makes a truce with one's circumstances. This is not to suggest that in his stories it is always, or even often, an easy truce. "Holy hell," says the narrator of "Critique" when his infant child climbs into the marriage bed and wets it. "Is there to be no end to this *family life?*"

Don't dare to see symbolism in that child wetting the marital bed, because Barthelme repeatedly ridicules the idea of analysis – analysis of *any* variety, whether it be the kind that is entailed in psychiatric therapy or the kind engaged in by literary symbol-hunters. The first of *Snow White*'s three parts concludes with a tongue-in-cheek list of questions for the reader, among them: "Do you like the story so far?" "Does Snow White resemble the Snow White you remember?" "Have you understood, in reading to this point, that Paul is the prince-figure?" and "Has the work, for you, a metaphysical dimension?" Not only is Barthelme here lampooning the sorts of questions that follow stories in school textbooks; he is also lampooning the very idea of critical interpretation, judgment, and ranking: "Holding in mind all works of fiction since the war, in all languages, how would you rate the present work, on a scale of one to ten, so far?" When he concludes the list of questions, furthermore, by asking whether human beings should have additional shoulders ("Two sets of shoulders? Three?"), he seems to be implying that a work of fiction, however idiosyncratically constituted, possesses an organic authenticity, and that holding opinions about how a given book is put together is thus as foolish and pointless and just plain *wrong* as holding opinions about how human beings are put together. Among the stories in which he mocks the critical enterprise are "The Party" (whose narrator wonders: "Is it really important to know that this movie is fine, and that one terrible, and to talk intelligently about the difference?") and "The Glass Mountain," whose narrator scales a glass mountain for a prize that is unnamed in the opening pages, only to be disappointed at the summit: "I approached the symbol, with its layers of meaning, but when I touched it, it changed into only a beautiful princess."

Generally more diverting, and less pretentious, are Barthelme's glosses on psychoanalysis. "The Sandman" takes the form of a very funny letter from a man to his girlfriend's shrink. "I fully understand," the man writes,

> that Susan's wish to terminate with you and buy a piano instead has
> disturbed you. You have every right to be disturbed and to say that

she is not electing the proper course, that what she says conceals something else, that she is evading reality, etc., etc. Go ahead. But there is one possibility here that you might be, just might be, missing. Which is that she means it . . . The one thing you cannot consider, by the nature of your training and of the discipline itself, is that she really might want to terminate the analysis and buy a piano. That the piano might be more necessary and valuable to her than the analysis.

The message is clear: since psychiatrists are as confused, troubled, and self-absorbed as anyone else, and since there is no "happily ever after" for any of us, why not channel one's exasperation with the world into art instead of endeavoring vainly to eliminate it through psychoanalysis? "What do you do," the man writes, "with a patient who finds the world unsatisfactory? The world *is* unsatisfactory; only a fool would deny it."

PSYCHOANALYSIS, then, is absurd because it seeks to achieve an impossible deliverance from life's inevitable malaise; by the same token, literary analysis is absurd because it presupposes the idea of greatness – a concept that Barthelme, an early if unsystematic canon-basher, frequently belittles. That he agrees with the character who observes that "what an artist does, is fail" would appear to follow from his sardonic reference, in one story, to "seven high-class literary works of the first water and four of the second water and two of the third water," from his ironically solemn account, in another story, of the death of a "great waiter" (if there can be great writers, why not great waiters?), and from his inclusion, in *Snow White,* of a handful of *idées reçues* about the great Russian writers: "IT WAS NOT UNTIL THE 19TH CENTURY THAT RUSSIA PRODUCED A LITERATURE WORTHY OF BECOMING PART OF THE WORLD'S CULTURAL HERITAGE. PUSHKIN DISPLAYED VERBAL FACILITY. GOGOL WAS A REFORMER. AS A STYLIST DOSTOEVSKY HAD MANY SHORTCOMINGS. TOLSTOY. . . ." Probably because his work represents, in many ways, the antithesis of Barthelme's zany, featherweight fictions – and, of course, because *War and Peace* is widely thought of as the *ne plus ultra* of conventional novels – Tolstoy comes in for special attention from Barthelme. "At the Tolstoy Museum," a slight, unfunny jab at the idea of literary greatness, includes not only text but drawings of the imaginary museum's exhibits – among them, one of Tolstoy's coat, which, surrounded by the great man's admirers, looks to be about thirty feet high. Similarly, "The Genius" offers glimpses of the everyday life of an unnamed genius (and drunk) – a life that proves to be just as inconsequential, as full of self-doubt, and as void of meaningful accomplishment as anyone else's. ("I always say to myself, 'What is the most important thing I can be thinking about at this minute?' But then I don't think about it.")

If Barthelme derides the language of ambition in *Snow White,* wherein one of his characters complains that another plays cards "when he could be out realizing his potential" and "maximizing his possibilities," it is because nobody, however maximized his possibilities, can ever hope to ameliorate the essential misery of the human condition. And if Barthelme puts a gigantic coat in the Tolstoy museum – and, in an affected story entitled "The Balloon," imagines a monstrous balloon whose random motion, constant shape-changing, "apparent purposelessness," and lack of limitation and definition "offered the possibility . . . of mislocation of the self, in contradistinction to the grid of precise, regular pathways under our feet"—it is because both these objects represent man's longing for a godlike and transcendent Other, for some form of deliverance from *la vie quotidienne,* for (as Barthelme sees it) a father. The father image is, in fact, focal in Barthelme, virtually all of whose fiction appears to be informed by the notion that the defining circumstance of a man's life in the modern world (Barthelme doesn't concern himself overmuch with women's lives) is his boyhood sense of his father as all-knowing and all-powerful, his eventual discovery of his father's essential helplessness and mortality, and his lifelong craving for, and inability to find, a substitute for that original illusion of perfect love and authority. Which, Barthelme would have it, explains the cult of great authors, the cult of psychiatry, the power of kings and presidents, and the anomie, acedia, and anhedonia that (to his mind) typify adult life in a secular society.

The key word here is *secular,* and perhaps what makes it most difficult to dismiss Barthelme as a mere entertainer is that, unlike many serious contemporary authors, he has manifestly devoted a good deal of thought to the question of God. Just when one has decided to write him off as a nihilist, Barthelme hints at the possibility of a deity and of a moral purpose to human life. "Perhaps we should be doing something else entirely, with our lives," says one of the seven men who live and work together at menial jobs in *Snow White*. "God knows what. We do what we do without thinking. One tends the vats and washes the buildings and carries the money to the vault and never stops for a moment to consider that the whole process may be despicable. Someone standing somewhere despising us." Indeed, if at times Barthelme's work seems quite thoroughly nihilistic, at times it almost reads like a devout Christian's critique of secular life in the Computer Age. The story "Paraguay" tenders a dystopic vision of artworks being reduced to software products; in "Report," a man puts a moral sense on IBM cards. In a story called "The Leap," a character says that "[p]urity of heart is . . . to will several things, and not know which is the better, truer thing, and to worry about this, forever." No writer who has such sentences in his fiction can be described as utterly lacking in seriousness, however compelling the evidence may appear to be.

At the very least, it seems safe to say that whenever Barthelme writes about fathers he is also writing about God, and vice versa. Time and again, he links the demythification and eventual demise of the temporal father with the widespread twentieth-century loss of belief in a heavenly Father. And just as he mocks the mystique of earthly father-surrogates – psychiatrists, literary luminaries – so in several stories he takes on saints and angels. "The Temptation of Saint Anthony," for instance, recounts the saint's life in a contemporary American city, where he lives in an apartment and eats too much fried food. The saint, we are told, "was underrated quite a bit . . . mostly by people who didn't like things that were ineffable. I think that's quite understandable – that kind of thing can be extremely irritating to some people." What Barthelme is scoffing at here is not saints as such, but the idea that the glorious things they represent can have anything to do with the less-than-glorious world we live in. The fundamental problem, to his mind, is not that transcendence is a philosophically invalid concept; on the contrary, this and similar Barthelme stories evince a palpable longing for something beyond quotidian reality that imbues them with a degree of humanity, and even of

pathos, that is absent in much of his work. Rather, the problem is that
transcendence is irreconcilable with the pettiness and prurience of the
human animal: "There is a sort of hatred going around for people who
have lifted their sights above the common run. Probably it has always
been this way." For Barthelme, the bottom line is that neither man nor
his world is perfectible: there's no omniscient king or father, no happily-
ever-after paradise; short of a cure-all for life's bruises, the best one can
hope for (metaphorically speaking) is Band-Aids – which, not coinci-
dentally, occur frequently in Barthelme's fiction.

Barthelme puts colloquial language to fine ironic use in "The Temptation of Saint Anthony," the demotic narration contrasting pointedly
with the notion of sanctity. But for all their humanity, it is also in such
stories as this that Barthelme's principal failing tends to stand out most
glaringly: namely, that drawn as he is to the idea of transcendence –
whether romantic, intellectual, or spiritual – he is unable or unwilling to
transcend for long his own chronic jokiness, his position of safety, as it
were, behind his battery of cynical gags, to take the risk of representing a
compellingly imagined human soul in the grip of romantic or intellectual or spiritual passion, and, by showing the disappointment of that
passion, to afford us a richer sense of the tragicomedy of man's failure to
surmount his circumstances. One's complaint, let it be clear, is not that
Barthelme opts for surreal humor rather than for Tolstoyan gravity; it is,
rather, that his humor is thin, cautious, formulaic. One has the feeling
that he's afraid of probing too deeply, especially in matters of religion (a
subject that is notorious for making *New Yorker* editors uncomfortable).
He refuses to mourn – not for long, anyway: even if something isn't
funny, it must be put over as if it were. Thus if in one sentence he brings
up Thomism or Teilhard de Chardin, chances are that in the next sentence, like a talk-show host worried that the conversation might be getting too heavy for his entertainment-starved audience, he'll segue into
yet another goofily relevant Tin Pan Alley lyric ("You smile. And the
angels sing") or start cracking wise.

IF IN "The Temptation of Saint Anthony" Barthelme juxtaposes
the saintly ideal of self-sacrifice with the reality of human meanness and

the daily grind, in *Snow White* he sets the familiar fairy tale's romantic ideals against those same realities, re-creating the eponymous maiden as the housekeeper and lover of seven men in what might seem, on the face of it, an enticing alternative to the traditional family. (Or, as Barthelme puts it, "a mocksome travesty of approved behavior.") But Snow White doesn't appreciate what she's got, for she's too busy thinking that "someday [her] prince will come" – a sentiment of which the narrator, spoofing psychobabble, has the following to say: "By this Snow White means that she lives her own being as incomplete, pending the arrival of one who will 'complete' her. That is, she lives her own being as 'not-with' (even though she is in some sense 'with' the seven men, Bill, Kevin, Clem, Hubert, Henry, Edward, and Dan). But the 'not-with' is experienced as stronger, more real, at this particular instant in time, than the 'being-with.' The incompleteness is an ache capable of subduing all other data presented by consciousness." What bothers one, in this passage, is Barthelme's insistence on having his cake and eating it too: he wants to analyze Snow White, yet doesn't want to commit himself to his own analysis – and thus distances himself from it by means of a mock-academic persona. As for *Snow White* itself, to read it a quarter century after its first appearance in the *New Yorker* is to realize that it is very much a book of its time, and that it owed much of its original appeal to the relative freshness of a type of humor that has long since come to seem familiar, even passé, to readers who grew up on "Saturday Night Live" and David Letterman.

Barthelme's second novel, *The Dead Father,* is an intense, fantastic, often dream-like story (reminiscent of *As I Lay Dying*) about a band of men and women, among them a young man named Thomas, who are dragging to its burial place the gigantic body of someone who, though still half-alive, is referred to as the Dead Father. (He is, we are told, *"Dead, but still with us, still with us, but dead."*) He begins the journey as a powerful, godlike figure – complete with "facilities for confession" – who "controls what Thomas is thinking, what Thomas has always thought, what Thomas will ever think, with exceptions"; in the early pages he slays a host of musicians (whose names – in one of Barthelme's many lists – occupy more than a page). Over the course of the novel, however, the Dead Father declines steadily, and is deprived by Thomas, in turn, of his belt buckle, passport, and keys. The novel is, among other things, an allegory about the gradual decline of fathers from indomitability to impotence, and about the deeply paradoxical role of the son as acolyte, nemesis, and mourner. Incorporated in the book is *A Manual for Sons,* an *outré* assortment of general observations about fathers and sons ("Fathers have voices, and each voice has a *terribilità* of its own"), as well as some vividly rendered fathers' voices: "Hey son. Hey boy. Let's you and me go out and throw the ball around. Throw the ball around. You don't want to throw the ball around? How come you don't want to go out and throw the ball around? I know why you don't want to go out and throw the ball around. It's 'cause you – Let's don't discuss it. It don't bear thinkin' about." Of all Barthelme's novels, indeed, *The Dead Father* is the strongest, even though it bespeaks as much as any of them a rather adolescent and male-centered sensibility that recalls John Irving and Robert Bly.

    Paradise, Barthelme's third novel, is also his most realistic in terms of character and *mise en scène.* Simon, a fifty-three-year-old divorced architect who has failed to find meaning or happiness in either work or love, has three young, beautiful, and sexually acquiescent women move into his New York apartment. Sounds like paradise – but it doesn't last. Why not? "Your vital interests are not involved here," one of the women gripes. "You don't give a shit." It's true. Simon, we learn, "is amazed by what he doesn't care about. He's bought nothing but a couple of new shirts and a few books. He's thought of no new projects." Of course, like the title of Barthelme's collection *Great Days,* the novel's title is ironic: in such a world as this, we're meant to see, it's impossible even to *imagine* paradise. At one point the narrator thinks of the phrase "hog heaven" and tries to visualize what heaven would be like for hogs. But he can't:

> In hog heaven the hogs wait in line for more heaven. No, not right, no waiting in line, it's unheavenly, unholy. The celestial sky is quilted in kale, beloved of hogs. A male hog walks up to a female hog, says "Want to get something going?" She is repulsed by his language, says "Bro, unless you can phrase that better, you're chilly forever." No, that's not right, this is hog heaven, they fall into each other's trotters, nothing can be done wrong here, nothing wrong can be done. . . .

No less difficult to imagine than heaven is a caring God. As Simon tells his shrink: "You think about this staggering concept, the mind of God, and then you think He's sitting around worrying about this guy and this woman at the Beech-nut Travelodge? I think not." Diverting though it is, alas, *Paradise* has a loose, offhand quality that reminds one of the later novels of Joseph Heller.

What *Snow White* is to the fairy tale, *The King* is to Arthurian legend. Barthelme's last novel is set in England during the early days of World War II; the conceit is that King Arthur and his court are still in charge, listening to Ezra Pound and Lord Haw Haw on the radio, chatting about "Winston" (who thinks he's running things), and discussing the possibility that the Holy Grail is actually a yet-to-be-discovered weapon capable of unprecedented devastation. A knight talks about his book, *On the Impossibility of Paradise;* Arthur, who is journeying to his grave as surely as the Dead Father, contemplates building "a great wall around everything we hold dear, and defend[ing] that wall, to the death of course, with everything we hold dear inside it, and everything we do not hold dear outside it –." *The King* is sometimes amusing; but both Mark Twain and Monty Python have tackled this material before, and more wittily. The novel is, in fact, by far Barthelme's most unsatisfying: flimsy, tired, tedious, its plot uninspired, its characters paper-thin.

But then Barthelme was always weakest in long forms. He wrote better stories than he did novels, and better sentences than he did stories. His strength – and his real interest – was patently not in large-scale matters (character development, plot manipulation) but in the details, the fine points of style and diction. Throughout his work, he proffers bizarre coinages (*disbosom, hurlment, mortalaciousness*) that would seem to follow logically from words we use, his goal presumably being to bring to the surface the absurdity and arbitrariness of language – and, by extension, of life; likewise, his many grammatical inversions ("nothing can be done wrong here, nothing wrong can be done") invite us to consider how words work together. His reference to "literary works . . . of the second water" is one of many extrapolations from common idioms – some witty, some belabored – that are intended to call into question the assumptions underlying those idioms; and when a character declares, in *Snow White,* that "I had hoped to make a powerful statement, coupled with a moving plea. . . . I had hoped to make a significant contribution. . . . I had hoped to bring about a heightened awareness," Barthelme's goal is to make us look behind the clichés by means of which we express our ideals about life and about the expressive powers of language. He plays with double meanings, too, savoring a Swedish woman's confusion of the English words *rape* and *rapture* and finding it nicely ironic that the lewd-sounding term "interrupted screw" actually refers to something – "a screw with a discontinuous helix, as in a cannon breach" – that has less to do with sex than with war.

To READ a book like *Snow White* or *The King* is to get the impression that for Barthelme the mere act of bringing these familiar characters into the modern world and writing about them in colloquial language was a moral act; it is as if he saw his clear, forthright prose as a sort of sieve through which only a true sense of things could pass. Just as he plays games with history (in various fictions Balzac goes to a movie, Luther telephones Haydn, and two jousting knights are interrupted by a Girl Guide selling cookies), so he also juxtaposes his own down-to-earth, contemporary voice with parodically motivated voices of a more formal or archaic character, and writes, in those voices, about subjects for which they would generally be considered inappropriate. He also mimics to amusing effect the solemnity of nineteenth-century prose, incorporating in "The Dolt" a Tolstoyan narrative by the protagonist, as if to underscore the greater authenticity of Barthelme's own more homely rendering of reality. Even funnier than this story (and equally self-serving) is "The Question Party," whose opening pages are cribbed verbatim, according to Barthelme's footnote, from a story that was first published in 1850 in *Godey's Lady's Book;* as the tale progresses (and as Barthelme begins to introduce his own material), it shifts away from the artificial world of Victorian popular fiction toward the darker, more equivocal – and, to Barthelme's mind, infinitely more realistic – world of Barthelme's own fiction, in which pretenses fall away, the unspeakable is spoken, the unnatural acknowledged.

One of the more arresting sentences in Barthelme happens to be a borrowing from Kierkegaard: "What is wanted . . . is not a victory over the world but a reconciliation with the world." To a large extent, Barthelme's fiction – by turns comical and colorless, astute and asinine, fresh and deadeningly familiar – is about how hard-won that reconciliation often proves to be, and (in his view, anyway) how ungenerous the terms. For all the inherent drama of this theme, however, Barthelme's work is rarely compelling, and ultimately hollow; Barthelme never comes close to creating people whose difficulties with the world one passionately believes in and cares about. (Which is not, of course, to suggest that he tries to.) The more one reads of Barthelme, furthermore, the greater one's exasperation with what one increasingly comes to perceive as forced, facile displays of indifference and pessimism. Barthelme concludes *Snow White* as follows: "THE FAILURE OF SNOW WHITE'S ARSE / RE-VIRGINATION OF SNOW WHITE / APOTHE-OSIS OF SNOW WHITE / SNOW WHITE RISES INTO THE SKY / THE HEROES DEPART IN SEARCH OF A NEW PRINCIPLE / HEIGH-HO." Ho-hum. In similar fashion, instead of resolving the conflict established in "Views of My Father Weeping" (a weirdly gripping, quasi-Kafkaesque yarn about a young man whose father has been run over by an aristocrat's carriage), Barthelme ends the story abruptly, at the moment of greatest suspense, with the word "Etc." – as if to say that he will have no more of the conventional plot he has concocted, or (perhaps) to chide us too-conventional readers for having been foolishly drawn in by it. One can almost see him shrugging: "Who cares what happens? What does it matter?" Some might consider this a clever gambit, but it strikes this reader as yet another demonstration of a thoroughgoing timidity, a refusal on Barthelme's part to become truly involved, to dive below the surface of human emotion and see how close he can come to touching bottom. Where Barthelme differs, in the end, from a writer like Vonnegut is that while one can quite easily believe that the author of *Cat's Cradle* is every bit as simple in heart and mind as his work suggests, the occasional glimmers, in Barthelme's outwardly glib and nihilistic fictions, of a heartfelt engagement with Important Questions suggest that there were in him depths that – for whatever reason – he never dared to explore in his writing. What, one finds oneself wondering more and more, *would* he have done without the *New Yorker*?

A Genius for Publicity:
Harold Brodkey

WHAT DOES it say about contemporary American culture that two of the most celebrated novels of our time have never, in fact, seen print—namely, Truman Capote's *Answered Prayers* and Harold Brodkey's *A Party of Animals?* Think of it: for decades, while many a gifted but obscure novelist presented his work to the world only to emerge with his gifts and his obscurity intact, both Capote and Brodkey garnered an astonishing amount of media attention and critical acclaim simply by offering, in place of their respective long-awaited masterworks, the occasional newsy tidbit about how the works-in-progress were coming along and how magnificent they were going to be. Both writers demonstrated the peculiar truth that in this media-centered age, a book that actually exists between hard covers is news for only one day, while a book that remains little more than a gleam in its author's eye can stay news for years. For a time, Capote was considerably ahead of Brodkey on the publicity meter, but now that Capote is gone and Knopf is issuing a collection of Brodkey's work, entitled *Stories in an Almost Classical Mode,*[1] the file of prominent magazine pieces on Brodkey is growing apace, so that he may yet overtake Capote as the twentieth-century American writer most famous for a book he's never published.

In recent months his slender, bearded face has stared out from the pages of *New York,* which entitled its cover story (by Dinitia Smith) "The Genius," and *Vanity Fair,* in which James Wolcott concluded that "the lesson of Harold Brodkey's career is that genius can be both too much and not enough." Similar "lessons," it will be remembered, were once drawn about Capote; it is interesting that Brodkey, like the author

---

1. *Stories in an Almost Classical Mode,* by Harold Brodkey; Knopf.

of *Breakfast at Tiffany's*, thinks of himself as a genius and enjoys working the high IQ scores of his childhood into his stories and interviews.

A Party of Animals dates back almost as far as *Answered Prayers*. Capote planned his would-be magnum opus as early as 1958; Brodkey signed a contract with Random House for his book in 1964, moving in 1970 to Farrar, Straus and Giroux, and in 1979 (after Farrar, Straus had advertised the novel's impending publication in a number of its seasonal catalogues) to Knopf. As was the case with *Answered Prayers*, supposed excerpts of Brodkey's novel-in-progress have been published along the way in magazines – *Esquire*, the *New Yorker*, *Vanity Fair*, *Partisan Review*. As Capote talked about his book right up till his death in 1984 – describing its structure, pace, and atmosphere in such elaborate detail that his complete recorded comments on the subject, if brought together by some enterprising professor, might well add up to a most unusual document: the Monarch Notes to a nonexistent novel – so Brodkey has discussed at length the specifications of *A Party of Animals*.

There's one striking difference between the two writers, however: whereas Capote had already established himself as a first-rate writer when the *Answered Prayers* saga began, Brodkey had, until this year, published only one full-length work – a short-story collection entitled *First Love and Other Sorrows* (1958). To examine the stories in *First Love* – an exercise that can provide a highly instructive prolegomenon to a perusal of *Stories in an Almost Classical Mode* – is to be surprised that its author's unpublished work could be the focus of so much feverish speculation. For *First Love* is a decidedly unspectacular item – an assemblage of quiet, innocuous little fictions about midwestern boyhood, campus romance, and young marrieds. Since eight of the nine stories appeared originally in the *New Yorker*, it should not be surprising that the campus is invariably that of Harvard University, that the young marrieds are invariably fainter, more plastic versions of John Cheever's vaguely discontented New York suburbanites, and that the style is invariably spare, precise, graceful, and passionless. In most of these stories, every detail seems shamelessly tailored to the requirements of 1950s *New Yorker* fiction. As Melvin Maddocks wrote in a review of *First Love* for the *Christian Science Monitor*, "A sense of vital, untampered-with conflict is missing. These stories seem too patly, too cautiously worked out. They are Japanese-garden fiction with every pebble in place." The reviewer for the *Atlantic Monthly* agreed, noting that Brodkey "appears to be the kind of artist committed to working in the minor key which the *New Yorker* has made fashionable."

Yet not all the stories in *First Love* are equally contrived. The first three stories in the book – "The State of Grace," "First Love and Other Sorrows," and "The Quarrel" – are all told in the first person (the others are in the third person), and each of them manifestly derives from the author's own youth. They have a touch of genuine feeling and originality that the remaining stories in the book don't have; their boy protagonists are the only characters in *First Love* who come alive. Perhaps the most memorable of these three stories is "The State of Grace," whose protagonist is a thirteen-year-old resident of St. Louis; as in Brodkey's later, more blatantly autobiographical stories of boyhood, the narrator makes a point of how tall he was, how attractive, how brilliant ("I always had the highest grades – higher than anybody who had ever attended the schools I went to – and I terrified my classmates"), and how "remarkable": "I was smart and virtuous . . . and fairly attractive, maybe even very attractive. I was often funny and always interesting. I had read everything and knew everything and got unbelievable grades. Of course I was someone whose love was desired. Mother, my teachers, my sister, girls at school, other boys – they all wanted me to love them." (This – like many of Brodkey's later stories – leads one to wonder: *Was any child ever so admired?*) The story concerns the thirteen-year-old's relationship to one of these "other boys" – a "precocious and delicate" seven-year-old neighbor for whom our protagonist baby-sits and with whom he identifies, since he feels that both he and the child are unloved and unappreciated by their parents. Yet he doesn't give the boy his love because the boy, like everyone else, doesn't love *him:* "I was fierce and solitary and acrid . . . and there was no one who loved me first. I could see a hundred cravennesses in the people I knew, a thousand flaws, a million weaknesses. If I had to love first, I would love only perfection." The story ends with a rather touching paragraph, the last sentence of which is, in its modest way, probably the most emotionally unrestrained in a very restrained book:

> Really, that's all there was to this story. The boy I was, the child Edward was. That and the terrible desire to suddenly turn and run

shouting back through the corridors of time, screaming at the boy I was, searching him out, and pounding on his chest: Love him, you damn fool, love him.

Of the nine stories in *First Love,* it is the three stories of boyhood that prefigure the direction Brodkey was to follow in his later work; and of all the sentences in the book, it is perhaps the closing sentence of "The State of Grace' that comes closest to the passionate, oracular prose for which Brodkey would become famous. To read Brodkey's debut volume is to recognize that it wasn't necessarily a bad idea for him to pursue the midwestern-boyhood material that his later stories would obsess over; on the contrary, any reader who looked at *First Love* in 1958 would have had to conclude – from the strength of "The State of Grace," "First Love and Other Sorrows," and "The Quarrel," relative to the other stories – that if Brodkey wanted to produce fresh and lyrical fiction, he would stand a better chance of doing so if he abandoned the college-romance and young-suburbanite material and concentrated instead on the imaginative treatment of themes drawn from his boyhood. Yet those three stories also contain intimations of some of the cardinal failings of Brodkey's later fiction – namely, his egocentrism, his indifference to plot, and even (in that closing sentence of "The State of Grace") his addiction to sentimental, self-pitying, and overheated prose.

To be sure, the first five stories in Brodkey's new book do not exhibit these failings in profusion. Published in the *New Yorker* between 1963 and 1969, they are, like the majority of stories in *First Love,* typical *New Yorker* stories, if with a few significant differences from those fifties narratives: longer, darker, more adventurous, they represent the *New Yorker* story at a somewhat later stage in its development, the mid-to-late-sixties era of, say, Cheever's "The Swimmer." The earliest and longest of them, "The Abundant Dreamer," makes use of a present-tense narrative and a generous number of flashbacks to tell the story of Marcus Weill, a highly regarded Jewish-American film director who reacts with apparent indifference when told, on the set of his movie in

Rome, that his grandmother has just died. Gradually, the flashbacks reveal to us the intricate set of circumstances and feelings behind that reaction, and what ultimately emerges is a rather affecting evocation of the emotionally fragile boy that stands behind, and to an extent still exists within, this egocentric and seemingly self-sufficient man of consequence. Perhaps it is needless to say that there are strong similarities between Weill and Brodkey, both abundant dreamers: like Brodkey, Weill is a "genius" with a complex relationship to his Jewishness and his past; as Brodkey was raised by relatives after his mother's death, so Weill was raised after his parents' divorce by his grandmother. What's more, when Brodkey writes about Weill that "a movie is to him primarily an arrangement of recognitions, an *allée* laid out so that at every step that is being seen alters the sense of what has been seen," Brodkey appears to be offering as well, by implication, his own definition of fiction. Yet "The Abundant Dreamer" is not merely a document in self-absorption or a meditation on memory; it is an objective short story in which Brodkey does not confuse himself with Weill, does not place Weill on a pedestal, does not treat Weill's thoughts on art and Judaism and death as holy writ. Though deeply felt and abundantly human, the story steers clear of rhetorical excess; in terms of style and structure, it is as elegant as anything else Brodkey has ever published.

In nearly the same league is "Bookkeeping" (1968), the story of an evening on which Avram Olensky, a thirtyish New York Jew, finds himself caught in the crossfire between his self-destructive Dutch friend Annetje – whose parents both perished in World War II and who is experiencing the aftereffects of an LSD "experiment" – and his dinner guests, a well-to-do New England WASP and her German husband, neither of whom sympathizes with Annetje's predicament. Inevitably, the conversation turns to the Holocaust, to questions of collective guilt and individual responsibility. As in "State of Grace" and "The Abundant Dreamer," the nature of love and friendship figures importantly here; Avram must weigh compassion against gratitude, must determine the extent of his various obligations to his friends. Here, too, as in "The Abundant Dreamer" (though not quite so fully as in "The State of Grace"), the protagonist can be identified with Brodkey himself; as in both "The Abundant Dreamer" and "The State of Grace," furthermore, the protagonist's love and compassion seem to be regarded by both pro-tagonist and author as favors, as gifts to be bestowed or withheld, often for strategic reasons. As the boy in "The State of Grace" refuses to con-fer his love upon his seven-year-old charge, and as the director in "The Abundant Dreamer" decides that he doesn't have time to "fend off death" for his grandmother, so "Bookkeeping" ends with Avram con-templating not the tragedy of Annetje's life but his own virtue in being so kind to her. Is Brodkey out to make a point about human self-centeredness? It doesn't seem so. He doesn't even appear to be aware that these characters are self-centered; to his mind, this is simply the way people think about things. In the world according to Brodkey, true self-lessness doesn't exist.

By far the slightest of these five sixties stories is the short, facile "On the Waves" (1965), which depicts the unspoken rapprochement – in a Venetian gondola, of course, this being a *New Yorker* story – between a divorced ex-tennis player and his less-than-believable seven-year-old daughter (who finds Venice "insincere"). The remaining sixties stories are somewhat more impressive, though not without crucial weaknesses. "Hofstedt and Jean – and Others" (1969) is about a forty-five-year-old English professor's romance with a student less than half his age; despite certain merits, the story is rather too long and diffuse, crowded with ex-traneous and redundant details in what comes across as an amateurish attempt to capture its characters completely and definitively. The ulti-mate point seems to be that Jean's attraction, for Hofstedt, resides less in her inherent charms than in the fact that she reminds his old college buddy of the buddy's wife when she was young. Hofstedt's affair, in short, is essentially a consequence of the two men's puerile competitive-ness, which dates back to their days at Harvard (where they were, natu-rally, the top two students in their class). Though Hofstedt never tires of analyzing his own thoughts and feelings, he pays little heed to Jean's; indeed, he hardly makes an effort to know what they are. His commen-tary upon her is confined chiefly to expressions of admiration for her body, cruel ridicule of her use of slang, and a superior, dismissive atti-tude toward her deepest expressions of affection. Essentially, his take on the relationship amounts to: *I'm too good for her, of course, but being as vulnerable as the next man to human folly I find her youth and beauty irre-*

sistible. Is Brodkey's purpose here to satirize Hofstedt for this self-absorption? Decidedly not. There's no ironic distance at all between this author and his obnoxious protagonist; in fact, Brodkey seems not to realize for a moment just how obnoxious Hofstedt is. At one point in the story a friend tells Hofstedt that he "occup[ies] a private world," and this story is unquestionably set in that world. It is Hofstedt's emotions and observations, and no one else's, that we are supposed to take seriously.

Only the last of Brodkey's sixties narratives has a female protagonist. "The Shooting Range" (1969) chronicles the life of a middle-class woman named Ann Kampfel from the time of her romance, at age twenty, with a factory foreman in a small Illinois town, to her long, not particularly happy marriage to a Washington bureaucrat. Bouncing along from one period of Ann's life to the next, the story doesn't pause often to render Ann's thoughts in any depth, but instead concentrates upon capturing the shifting currents of her romantic life over the years. The picture of Ann never quite comes together: though she is a believable character, one feels as if one knows her only from a distance, like a neighbor glimpsed every so often from across the street. When Brodkey tells us that "Ann never contemplated infidelity [because] it would make Fennie [her husband] unhappy," we accept the explanation, but we don't feel as if we know Ann well enough to be certain that she would actually think this way. We don't know why she leaves the foreman (whom she loves) or why she marries the bureaucrat (whom she doesn't) or why she doesn't pursue the career for which she prepared in college. What we do know about her is not very endearing: she's grim and humorless and fatalistic, and in her whole life, as Brodkey gives it to us, there is hardly a moment of real joy or even lightheartedness; she derives no apparent pleasure from her husband, her children, or the privileges of her life in Washington. Brodkey's point, however, is not that this is an exceedingly dour woman, but that life can be an exceedingly dour affair.

He seems also to want to make a point about class. At the beginning of this extremely long story, Ann has been talked by a college boyfriend into being a Communist, a believer in "the brotherhood of man and the release of men from economic pressures that distorted them and their lives" (the year is 1934); the foreman persuades her easily enough to leave the Party, and she goes on to lead the life of a typical bureaucrat's wife. Yet it is not until the end of the story that she, now the mother of two grown daughters, complains she's "turning middle-class. . . . Why is that, Fennie?" It's a disappointing conclusion; one feels cheated to have come all this way for so feeble a fare-thee-well. It isn't even clear whether we're expected to mourn with Ann over her middle-class metamorphosis or laugh at her for not realizing that she's been middle-class all her life. Perhaps we're supposed to recognize Ann's seemingly automatic and self-defeating life choices as having been a consequence of her middle-class mentality; if so, however, the first forty-one of the story's forty-two pages must be considered extremely ineffective – for there is little justification in these pages for blaming Ann's confusing behavior on the class into which she was born. Even discounting the class-mentality theme, the story is a weak one. In its shape and tone, and of course in its attempt to present an entire unremarkable life in unadorned fashion, it much resembles Flaubert's "Un coeur simple"; but any reader who recognizes this similarity must be struck at once by everything that Flaubert has and that Brodkey lacks: not only poignancy and moral rigor, but also a humility before life, an affection for his characters, and an instinctive awareness that he is addressing an audience.

Brodkey's four substantial sixties stories, then, have their failings. To be sure, they are all highly readable, even compelling, and are blessed with poise and grace; unlike most of the stories in *First Love,* they have the texture of real life, and their characters convince. But to read through them in chronological order is to feel increasingly that they are the work of an author who is eager to render an extremely complicated vision of life, but who either has not yet brought that vision into focus or has not yet arrived at a satisfactory means of communicating it. To put it another way, Brodkey wants us to climb inside his skin – or a skin that is very much like his own – and to experience what it is like there, but he is incapable of giving us our bearings; he speaks to us in a language of the heart, but it is a language that is not quite our own, and is one for which he has failed to provide a lexicon. So it is that the protagonists of these four sizable sixties stories – Marcus Weill, Avram Olensky, Leo Hofstedt, and Ann Kampfel – are alive enough to make one believe in them and to make one angry at them, but they never grow quite familiar enough to make one understand them or care about them.

It was, of course, not these sixties stories but those of the seventies and eighties that catapulted Harold Brodkey into a position of eminence enjoyed by few writers in our time. Thirteen in number, these stories occupy more than two-thirds of *Stories in an Almost Classical Mode*. Turning the page after the end of "The Shooting Range" and beginning the first of these stories – "Innocence," originally published in the *American Review* in 1973 – one crosses a boundary into an utterly different world. Suddenly, Brodkey's prose is loose, talky, even offhand. The sense of control that is evident throughout his earlier work has disappeared. Brodkey makes little attempt to disguise the fact that he and his protagonist – here, as in most of these later stories, called Wiley Silenowicz – are essentially the same person. He makes little attempt, indeed, to pretend that what he is giving us is fiction and not autobiography. Toward the beginning of "Innocence," Brodkey unleashes what is, in view of his previous output, a remarkable manifesto:

> I distrust summaries, any kind of gliding through time, any too great a claim that one is in control of what one recounts; I think someone who claims to understand but who is obviously calm, someone who claims to write with emotion recollected in tranquillity, is a fool and a liar. To understand is to tremble. To recollect is to reenter and be riven. An acrobat after spinning through the air in a mockery of flight stands erect on his perch and mockingly takes his bow as if what he is being applauded for was easy for him and cost him nothing, although meanwhile he is covered with sweat and his smile is edged with a relief chilling to think about; he is indulging in a show-business style; he is pretending to be superhuman. I am bored with that and with where it has brought us. I admire the authority of being on one's knees in front of the event.

At the time of its original publication, a reader of "Innocence" might not have made much of this passage, but to read it where it appears in *Stories in an Almost Classical Mode* is to recognize it as a veritable declaration of independence on Brodkey's part – independence, that is, from the obligation to transfigure his obsessions into fiction, from the obligation to rein in his angst and to surmount his morbid self-obsession and to edit his rambling ruminations into something well-crafted and coherent. If in his stories of the sixties he sought an effective means of rendering his authorial vision in fictional terms, in "Innocence" he abandons that attempt, essentially renouncing, in his manifesto, the very concept of fiction. His true interest, after all, lies not in imagined lives – or, for that matter, in the real lives of other people – but in the tormented history of his own soul; with "Innocence" he announces his unwillingness to persist in pretending otherwise: his refusal to continue hiding behind some fictional characters and feigning curiosity about others, his impatience to serve up reams of vatic, well-nigh stream-of-consciousness prose in place of the taut, polished sentences he'd produced for two decades. Just as another *New Yorker* writer, J. D. Salinger, had turned from the compact, civilized prose of his *Nine Stories* to manic, effusive excursions into the eccentric world of the Glass family, so Brodkey now put his *New Yorker* stories of the fifties and sixties behind him and embarked upon a frenzied, fanatical voyage into himself.

To read "Innocence" and most of the stories that follow, then – the majority of which have been identified, at one time or another, as sections of *A Party of Animals* – is to find oneself trapped within the extraordinarily arrogant and self-obsessed soul of Harold Brodkey, a.k.a. Wiley Silenowicz, and condemned again and again to relive his agonizing childhood and youth. Brodkey's is, to be sure, a genuinely tragic personal history. He was born in 1930 in Staunton, Illinois, with the name of Aaron Roy Weintraub. His mother died when he was an infant, whereupon his father, an illiterate junk man, allowed him to be adopted by relatives named Doris and Joseph Brodkey; these new parents renamed him Harold Roy Brodkey, and raised him in a St. Louis suburb named University City. When Brodkey was nine, his adoptive father had a stroke or heart attack and became an invalid, finally passing away when the boy was fourteen; when he was thirteen, his adoptive mother came down with cancer and lingered on for years in pain and bitterness, finally dying while Brodkey was an undergraduate at Harvard. Wiley shares every bit of this personal history with Brodkey, the chief differences being that Wiley's adoptive parents are named not Doris and Joseph but Lila and S. L.

Life with Lila and S. L., as recounted in these stories, is hardly *Life with Father*. In "A Story in an Almost Classical Mode" (1973), Brodkey/Wiley describes a typical day of his youth: "I would come home from school to the shadowy house, the curtains drawn and no lights on, or perhaps one, and she [Lila] would be roaming barefooted with wisps of hair sticking out and her robe lopsided and coming open." If he said hello, she would scream: "Is that all you can say? I'm in *pain*. Don't you care? My God, my God, what kind of selfish person are you? I can't stand it." If he said, "Hello, Momma, how is your pain?" she would scream: "You fool, I don't want to think about it! It was all right for a moment! Look what you've done—you've brought it back. . . . *I don't want to be reminded of my pain all the time!*" In either case, she would end up yelling: "Do you think it's easy to die ? . . . Do something for me! Put yourself in my place! Help me! Why don't you help me?" One cannot read this sort of thing without feeling profound sympathy for Harold Brodkey and for the boy he was; if even a fraction of his anecdotes about his childhood and youth are true—and taking into account, as well, the distinct possibility that Brodkey is giving us a very one-sided view of things—then it is certainly a great credit to him that he survived and prospered. To criticize him for his continued fixation upon such memories would be not only unfair but heartless.

YET A CRITIC who is faced with the task of passing judgment on these stories—and of evaluating, as well, the legitimacy of the reputation that they have gained—cannot, alas, do anything other than criticize most of them. For the fact is that Brodkey is so fixated upon the tragic memories of his childhood and youth that he has virtually no sense of proportion about them. In one story after another, he offers up pages of gratuitous detail, straining, it seems, to squeeze every last drop of significance out of every last inane particular. Whole paragraphs are devoted to such matters as his adoptive mother's pet phrases, her opinions on a multitude of subjects, the way she dressed, the way she walked. Though these stories contain a number of affecting—and even emotionally draining—passages, the adversities and tensions and interrelationships and tastes and daily routines of the family in which Brodkey grew up are described so extensively and repeatedly that the ultimate effect of these stories is almost invariably one of numbing monotony. As a rule, not only is there no plot – there's no movement whatsoever. What power the stories do have is primarily not aesthetic but documentary in nature; the young Brodkey's diary, if he'd kept one, would doubtless be just as powerful, and in precisely the same way. Indeed, to all intents and purposes these stories do amount to a diary, the record of a man talking to himself about himself. Take "A Story in an Almost Classical Mode," for instance: it is not until the story's final sentence that Brodkey seems at all aware of or concerned about his audience, and even then his awareness comes across as little more than an afterthought. "Make what use of this you like," he says, effectively admitting that aside from sheer confession he doesn't really know *what* his intention here has been.

And confession is certainly the word for most of these stories. Brodkey is baldly, brutally, shamelessly confessional, speculating about his boyhood state of mind in the tireless, self-absorbed manner of a patient on a psychiatrist's couch: ". . . perhaps I was not a very loving person. perhaps I was self-concerned and a hypocrite. . . . perhaps I just wanted to get out with a whole skin." That such narcissistic maunderings fail to get us anywhere doesn't appear to matter to Brodkey; he seems to think that they are in themselves somehow equivalent to self-knowledge. If there is a reason for his obsessive, seemingly pointless accumulation of remembered details, it appears to be that he believes the more details he sets down, the more satisfactory a catharsis he will achieve. As for the rest of us, he seems to be suggesting, we can bloody well sit back and watch. Most writers feel that they have to earn a reader's attention; the Brodkey of these seventies and eighties pieces has the earmarks of someone who feels he has an inalienable right to that attention. If there is considerable anger on display in the last several hundred pages of *Stories in an Almost Classical Mode*, it may well be the anger of a man who is furious at the world for expecting him to earn the attention he believes he received unbidden when he was the star of the seventh grade.

So similar are most of these recent Brodkey stories that it would be an exercise in Brodkeyan monotony to describe them all in detail. This is not to suggest that there are no distinctions to be made. Two of the stories – Brodkey's Gospels, we might call them – provide most of the principal family facts, and are so long and windy that, to the reader determined to get through them, they seem positively Sahara-like. Both center on our boy hero's relationship with his adoptive mother; one is "A Story in an Almost Classical Mode" (in which Brodkey and his parents, incidentally, go by their real names) and the other is "Largely an Oral History of My Mother" (1976). These twin dissertations repeat each other almost as extensively as they do themselves. Two other stories are much shorter and markedly more tolerable. The sixteen-page "His Son, in His Arms, in Light, Aloft" (1975) makes use of a single exhilarating memory – of being lifted into the air, as a child, by his father (here christened "Charlie") – as the focal point for a meditation on their relationship; unlike most of these stories, it has at least a hint of shape and of literary purpose, and rather movingly recalls a father who had moments of "accidental glory." The nine-page "Puberty" (1975), a recollection of an experience in the Boy Scouts, is very slight, but is also the most straightforward and well written of the post-"Shooting Range" pieces. Other stories seem more peripheral, and read like forced attempts by Brodkey to develop themes from his childhood that he'd given relatively short shrift elsewhere. "Play" (1973) is a pallid twenty-one-page discourse on the games he played at age eleven; "Ceil" (1983) unconvincingly addresses the subject of the biological mother that Brodkey never knew; "The Nurse's Music" (1988) centers on his governess, "The Rain Continuum" (1976) on his sister, and "The Boys on their Bikes" (1985) on his best friend Jimmy; "S. L." (1985) rehashes the material of "His Son" at forty pages' length.

Not all of the post-sixties stories are about Brodkey's family. "Verona – a Young Woman Speaks" (1977) is an odd little monologue by a young woman about a childhood experience; the closing story, "Angel" (1985), is the collection's version of the Book of Revelations – a bizarre forty-page narrative about God and man at Harvard that begins with this sentence: "Today the Angel of Silence and of Inspiration (toward Truth) appeared to a number of us passing by on the wall in front of Harvard Hall – this was a little after three o'clock – today is October twenty-fifth, nineteen-hundred-and-fifty-one." And "Innocence" – all thirty-one pages of it – relates in exhausting physical detail how Wiley manages, during his senior year at Harvard, to give a willful, beautiful classmate her first orgasm. Since most of the story is written at an unvarying fever pitch – with numerous run-on sentences and words in italics, endless series of parallel phrases and clauses and extravagant modifiers piled up on top of each other in frantic, desperate emphasis – to quote from virtually any portion of it is to give a fair sense of the whole:

> She called out, "Wiley, Wiley!" but she called it out in a *whisper,* the whisper of someone floating across a night sky, of someone crazily ascending, someone who was going crazy who was taking on the mad purity and temper of angels, someone who was tormented unendurably by this, who was unendurably frightened, whose pleasure was enormous, half human, mad. Then she screamed in rebuke, "Wiley!" She screamed my name: *"Wiley!"* – she did it hoarsely and insanely, asking for help, but blaming me, and merely as exclamation; it was a gutter sound in part, and ugly; the ugliness destroyed nothing, or maybe it had an impetus of its own, but it whisked away another covering, a membrane of ordinariness – I don't know – and her second pair of wings began to beat; her whole body was aflutter on the bed. I was as wet as – as some fish, thonking away, sweatily. Grinding away. I said, "It's O.K., Orra. It's O.K." And poked on. In midair. She shouted, *"What is this?"* She shouted in the way a tremendously large person who can defend herself might shout at someone who was unwisely beating her up. She shouted – angrily, as an announcement of anger, it seemed – *"Oh, my God!"* Like: *Who broke this cup?* I plugged on. She raised her torso, her head, she looked me clearly in the eye, her eyes were enormous, were bulging and she said, *"Wiley, it's happening!"*

Though the story is about Orra's first orgasm, the hero of the piece is of course Wiley. Orra has been with many other men, and claims that she's "too sexual to have orgasms"; it is Wiley, with his superior wisdom and his gift for the art of copulation, who teaches her otherwise. Here as elsewhere, Brodkey habitually refers to the sex act with the word *fuck:* "I figured I had kept her from being too depressed after fucking – it's hard for a girl with any force in her and any brains to accept the whole thing of fucking, or being fucked without trying to turn it on its end, so that she does some fucking, or some fucking up; I mean, the mere power of arousing the man so he wants to fuck isn't enough: she wants him to be willing to die in order to fuck." Though with this repeated use of the blunt Anglo-Saxonism he seems to be trying to identity himself as a worldly, with-it adult, Brodkey – this man who is ever fascinated with himself at age thirteen – sounds instead very much like a thirteen-year-old boy reveling in Dirty Words. Or, rather, like a vulgar man who thinks like a boy, a man who, preoccupied with his own physical sensations and ego gratification, regards his sexual partner only as a football field upon which to demonstrate his manly prowess – orgasm as touchdown. Sex, here, has little or nothing to do with affection and everything to do with power and the aggressive assertion of self. Not even the *oeuvre* of Norman Mailer contains a more gruesome piece of self-advertisement (though, as critics have noted, "Innocence" bears a strong resemblance to Mailer's famous piece of sexual braggadocio, "The Time of Her Time," which is also about giving a formidible young lady her first orgasm).

THAT BRODKEY attributes to his orgasmic heroine "the mad purity and temper of angels" should not be too surprising, for in his hands the distinctions between such phenomena as college girls' sex lives and imagined heavenly visitations quickly evaporate. To Brodkey, nothing seems to mean anything unless it means just about everything. Even the ordinary little tussles between a boy and his sister can't be described on their own terms, but must instead be magnified beyond recognition into something cosmic and Wagnerian. "This is my first, uncertain knowledge of evil," Brodkey writes in "The Pain Continuum" of such an encounter, at age four or so. "I am about to give birth – to death. . . . Pain is less than blood. . . . Blood is the boundary of a special seriousness." And so on. Such lofty rhetoric serves only to distance the reader from the modest incident it purports to describe, to crush the event itself under the weight of its own grandiloquence. This sort of thing happens time and again in Brodkey's later stories; in the world of these fictions epiphanies abound, and, what's more, they're all pretty much alike – in kind, in degree, and in moral dimension. Orgasms, the arrivals of angels, the thrill children feel when they are hoisted in the air by their fathers: when in his later stories Brodkey attempts to describe these phenomena, they all somehow seem to come out to the same thing – a fact that doubtless goes a long way toward accounting for the stories' monotony.

To a few critics, of course, these stories are anything but monotonous. Pick up any recent magazine or newspaper profile of Brodkey and chances are that somewhere in the first couple of paragraphs you'll find quotations from one or more of the following authorities: Harold Bloom, who calls Brodkey "an American Proust"; Denis Donoghue, who pronounces A *Party of Animals* "a work of genius" and says of its author that "there is no one writing in American literature at all comparable"; and Gordon Lish, who declares that "Harold Brodkey has been creating the one necessary American narrative work of this century." According to Dinitia Smith (from whose piece in *New York* magazine most of these quotations have been taken), Brodkey himself reportedly talks obsessively about literary politics, and the curious thing is that such quotations sound less like honest critical judgments than like the remarks of a political campaign's spin doctors. One can readily figure out, in any case, why it would be in the interest of these three particular men – aside from reasons of personal friendship – to prop up the reputation of a Harold Brodkey. Bloom? Brodkey fulfills Bloom's need for a contemporary Jewish American visionary, a West Side version of Milton and Blake. Lish? The *modus operandi* of Brodkey's later stories validates Lish's own crude, ripped-from-the-gut style of shock-confessional narrative. Donoghue? Brodkey exemplifies, in extreme form, Donoghue's notion of American literature as something whose "moral and rhetorical aim" is "to separate essence from existence, and to protect essence – or call it selfhood – from the vulgarity imposed by mere conditions."

What is remarkable, though, is not that a handful of influential critics have trumpeted Harold Brodkey's name so loudly, but that literary folk have listened so respectfully. Brodkey's stories of the seventies and eighties have developed a truly towering reputation; and yet the most cursory inspection is enough to establish that they contain some of the very worst prose of our time. Brodkey writes not only like a man who is certain that his every fleeting thought and trivial act is fascinating and pregnant with meaning; he writes also like a man who is convinced that his every word, comma, and ampersand is divinely inspired. He mistakes bombast for profundity, lexical flatulence for the divine afflatus.

Some of his sentences are so wordy and abstract (not to mention pretentious) that they read like examples of bad writing in a freshman composition textbook: "It is not metaphorical or a figure of speech or a
conceit," he writes in "The Rain Continuum," "to say that as that
knowledge grew to occupy the center and the periphery of my attention,
whatever else I knew seemed unimportant, and was, in a geographical
sense, forgotten: that is, there was no room for it in my attention."
Some sentences are infected with a chatty shapelessness: "Also," Wiley
says of Lila in "Largely an Oral History of Mother," "there are certain
serious gloomy honesties in her, a pessimism, and dark insights into
people that served as a form of somewhat lazy omniscience ('No one's
really nice,' she would say), and a dark forgiveness and wonder that a
child oughtn't to know about, so she would say to me at times, 'Don't
pay attention to me. Go away now – live your own life.'" (Lazy omniscience indeed!)

Some sentences have to be read at least twice to to be understood: in
"His Son, in His Arms," for instance, Brodkey writes of his father that
"My gaze, my enjoying him, my willingness to be him, my joy at it, supported the baroque tower of his necessary but limited and maybe dishonest optimism." And quite often, as in this passage from "S. L.," he
just yammers away:

> It was a peculiarity of that moment and of my life that he was not my
> father by blood and that I was not an infant when I met him except
> that I was like an infant. I was an infant a second time, an older,
> smarter, tougher infant, and weaker and more scarred. And he was
> *like* a father. I'm trying to say that I was a peculiar example of a son,
> not an ideal example, but some of that thing of being ideal hovered
> around me, probably unwisely, as a kind of explanation of the pain of
> emotion and the poignancy of hope, and a reason for grief and for
> pleasure – the hurt urgency in the real thing, plus the charitable part,
> gave a glow of the ideal. But I was not *the son* or *his son* but only *a son
> he had*. And he was not whatever an Ideal Father actually is or would
> be – a kind of light inside a common thing – he was not it, or maybe
> he was, or maybe he was at moments, how would I *know*?

There is always the possibility, of course, that Brodkey will redeem
himself – that he will publish *A Party of Animals* and that it will be everything his champions say it is. But if the stories of boyhood that he has

collected in the present book are any indication, readers who have been led to expect a work of genius are in for a major disappointment. One particularly odd phenomenon is that even those commentators who admit their dissatisfaction with Brodkey's work have a way of turning their criticism to his advantage. When James Wolcott writes that the lesson of Brodkey's career is that "genius can be both too much and not enough," he is taking a familiar line. But the truth is in fact quite different: the lesson of Brodkey's career is that one should not be surprised when an egocentric writer who is preoccupied with his own supposed genius – and who is mesmerized by the image of himself as a suffering prodigy – produces hundreds of pages of jagged, vainglorious, even infantile prose. The Brodkey of the eighties may be bearable in small doses but is insufferable at lengths of thirty and forty pages; one can only imagine what he might be like at novel length. Then again, *Stories in an Almost Classical Mode* may be all we will ever see of *A Party of Animals*.

(DECEMBER 1988)

Postscript: As all the world knows, Brodkey's *magnum opus* finally appeared in 1991 under the title *The Runaway Soul;* my review can be found in the January 1992 issue of *The New Criterion*.

A Still, Small Voice: Penelope Fitzgerald

Among the many symptoms of the American literary scene's current infirmity is that stateside publishers have been slow to take on, and readers on these shores slow to discover, the English novelist of manners Penelope Fitzgerald. Though British critics have justly compared her to such writers as Evelyn Waugh, Kingsley Amis, Barbara Pym, and Anita Brookner – all of whom have long enjoyed sizable readerships here – and though back home she has received one Booker Prize and been nominated for three others, two of her eight novels have yet to appear in United States editions and her name is nowhere near as well-known hereabouts as that of Pym or Brookner.[1] Why is this so? The answer is not simply that Fitzgerald, now in her seventy-fifth year, is decidedly English in setting and sensibility (so, after all, are Pym and Brookner); nor is it merely a matter of her novels' temperate tone and modesty of scale. (To read through the reviews of her books is to find, time and again, such words and phrases as "slight," "delicate," "unpretentious," "economy and understatement," "an impression of sharpness and shortness," "in no sense a 'big' book"; more than one critic has compared her novels to watercolors.) Nor is it that, like Pym and Brookner, she is a writer of unsensational stories. For Fitzgerald's novels are not only unsensational: they are elliptical, elusive, episodic, at times exasperating in their deliberate slenderness of plot and lack of resolution; their most essential relationships, pivotal incidents, and intense confrontations tend to happen offstage or to be rendered very concisely.

---

1. Only four of Penelope Fitzgerald's novels are currently in print in America: *Offshore, Innocence* and *The Beginning of Spring* are in paper from Carroll & Graf; *The Gate of Angels* is newly out in cloth from Nan A. Talese/Doubleday.

Instead of action, what Fitzgerald often gives us are apparent digressions, among them conversations in which trivial matters may receive as much attention as important ones – but in which her characters, in one way or another, tellingly reveal themselves. She is less interested in storytelling, *per se,* than in the qualities that draw people together and the differences that estrange them, in the abiding and numinous mystery that the world is to human beings and that human beings are to one another, and in the disjunction between what they are and what they pretend to be (or imagine or hope themselves to be). She celebrates those who defy mean self-interest in the name of some higher cause – art, truth, love, or even a vague longing for something better – even as she is acutely aware of the hurtful ways that people can treat their nearest and dearest in the name of such causes, and of their often less praiseworthy underlying motives: a fear of losing independence, a need to control, a craving for power. She is fascinated by the dynamic of romantic love and family devotion, but never yields to anything that might be taken as a sentimental impulse; in book after book she reminds us that good and bad can coexist in one heart, and that otherwise unimpressive – and even somewhat ridiculous – people can display remarkable qualities of character. At their best, her *dramatis personae* exhibit those most English of virtues: decency, honesty, quiet fortitude, a sense of duty, an uncomplaining acceptance of one's role and responsibilities in life.

PENELOPE FITZGERALD'S first novel appeared a mere fifteen years ago, when she was nearly sixty. (It was preceded by two biographies, one of Edward Burne-Jones and the other of Fitzgerald's father, an editor of *Punch,* and her uncles, the cryptographer Dillwyn Knox and the priests Wilfred and Ronald Knox; she has since published a third biography, of the English poet Charlotte Mew.) Though now chiefly notable as the fictional debut of a writer whose artistry has since grown in leaps and bounds, *The Golden Child* is a competent whodunit, the sort of mystery that is set mostly in a single institution and whose success depends largely on the author's ability to make that setting interesting. In this case the institution is an unnamed London museum, obviously modeled on the British Museum; and the characters – many of whom might have been plucked out of an Evelyn Waugh novel – are mainly museum officials who, almost to a man, care less about art than about their own careers. During a mega-exhibition of the Golden Treasure of Garamantia, an ancient African civilization, there takes place a series of odd and troubling incidents, chief among them the murder of the distinguished resident archeologist, Sir William Simpkin. Whodunit? Why? The solution turns out to be hidden in a message composed in Garamantian pictographs and carved on a clay tablet in an exhibition display case.

If *The Golden Child* falls short of being a first-rate mystery, it is because Fitzgerald's artistic priorities clash head-on with those of the genre in which she has chosen to work. A murder mystery should be tidy and schematic; the characters may be shot through with ambiguities, and the mystery richly nuanced, but in the end there should be a firm sense of order restored, of pieces falling neatly into place. But to Fitzgerald one of the important points about life is that the pieces never fall neatly into place; she is less interested in devising jigsaw-like plots than in exploring the perplexities of the human condition. To be sure, in an apparent attempt to fit her characters neatly into their assigned roles in the mystery, Fitzgerald tries to reduce most of them to familiar comic-novel types; yet the very resistance to contrivance that makes her later novels feel so credible prevents her, in *The Golden Child,* from tailoring these characters as dexterously as a top-notch mystery writer would to the needs of her plot. Especially unsatisfactory is Waring Smith, the protagonist (and the first of Fitzgerald's many innocents). He is a surprisingly sketchy creation; his motives are never clear, so one has less sympathy for him than one might otherwise – a state of affairs that is hardly unusual in Fitzgerald (who was once told by Ronald Knox that one should write biographies about people one loves and novels about people one dislikes) but is less than desirable in a mystery. What's more, Waring is so terribly passive that it's not even he who solves the case; again, such passivity might work in a literary novel, but not in this genre.

Fitzgerald's ironies of circumstance and temperament are far sharper than her plotting. Already in this book she is a forthright critic of manners and morals. The Garamantia exhibition is plainly an allusion to the

King Tut extravaganza that helped usher in the age of the museum mega-show; and Fitzgerald captures perfectly the inanity of an era in which armies of people who wouldn't cross the street to look at a Matisse can be persuaded by relentless publicity and media hype to line up in the freezing cold for hours to view a historically inconsequential exhibition of little artistic merit. In good English fashion, moreover, she gets in a few digs at Continental art and scholarship. We learn, for example, that Waring and his wife frequently "go out . . . to see films by leading French and Italian directors about the difficulties of making a film." Fitzgerald skewers both the oppressive seriousness of Germans — a Heidelberg Garamantologist's book is entitled *Garamantischenge-heimschriftendechiffrierkunst* — and Gallic silliness: a pretentious impromptu oration by Rochegrosse-Bergson, a French scholar, includes a trendy nihilistic flourish to the effect that "[o]ur art — for every man, let us admit it, is an artist — is *to achieve absolutely nothing!*" The audience for this "arrant nonsense" consists of a pair of British journalists, of whom Fitzgerald offers a sardonic description: "exquisites for whom life could hold no further surprises, and removed by their foreign educations from crass British prejudices, [the journalists] sat in their Italian silk shirts and deerskin jackets, waiting, in a kind of energetic idleness. . . . Trained in French lycées, they were unable to resist [Rochegrosse-Bergson's] rounded sentences which now dropped a couple of tones to announce the coming peroration." These few words provide the reader with a veritable beginner's catalogue of qualities (all of them somewhat connected to Continental ways and means) that Fitzgerald holds in disesteem: pretension, foppishness, "energetic idleness," overassurance, a snobbish attitude toward middle-class bigots, a fashionably nihilistic or grotesquely scholarly approach to art. Though *The Golden Child* is far from a masterwork, then (alongside her later novels it looks decidedly primitive), it has wit and personality, and one comes away from it with a clear sense of Fitzgerald's impatience with shabby contemporary values and with the wretched prospects for Western civilization in an age of hype, self-seeking, phoniness, and philistinism, high and low.

The Golden Child is the first of several Fitzgerald novels to focus on a cultural institution and on a cast of characters who are, shall we say, not all devoted in equal measure to the good, the true, and the beautiful. In her second novel, *The Bookshop* (1978), set in 1959, a widow named Florence Green buys the Old House, a centuries-old building in her sleepy East Suffolk village, and turns it into a bookshop. Like Waring Smith, she is something of an innocent – a well-meaning, quietly plucky, but rather naïve adult with commendable moral and artistic instincts but an insufficient awareness of the degree to which other people are driven by selfishness, jealousy, and power-hunger. In place of the self-seeking museum officials in *The Golden Child*, *The Bookshop* gives us Mrs. Gamart, a society matron who, seeing her role as the local doyenne of culture threatened by Florence's shop, resurrects a plan to turn the site into an arts center and proceeds to use all her influence to have the building confiscated by the government. How does Florence react? If one expects her to be yet another mild-mannered, virtuous underdog who triumphs over the villainous powers-that-be, one will be disappointed. Nor should one expect her motives to be overly clear: as it is not entirely obvious why Waring Smith works in a museum and not, say, in some civil-service job, neither can one understand why Florence Green, of all people, has decided to go into the bookselling business. Confronted with the newly published *Lolita*, after all, she can't even decide whether to stock it – "I haven't been trained to understand the arts," she explains, "and I don't know whether a book is a masterpiece or not" – and has to turn to the well-read village recluse for an opinion. How, one wonders, did such a woman fasten upon the idea of opening a bookshop?

Here, as in *The Golden Child*, Fitzgerald contemplates with a jaundiced eye the rampant popularization of culture. An entire wall of Florence's shop is covered by paperbacks: "cheerfully coloured, brightly democratic, they crowded the shelves in well disciplined ranks. They would have a rapid turnover and she had to approve of them, yet she could remember a world where only foreigners had been content to have their books bound in paper. The Everymans, in their shabby dignity, seemed to confront them with a look of reproach." A whole cultural outlook – the sort that some might call elitist and xenophobic – is conveyed in this brief passage. Nor is this the only time that Fitzgerald weighs in on such issues. When Mrs. Gamart tells Florence that she and others in the village have long wanted to turn the Old House into an arts center, Florence at first thinks it possible to have both a bookshop and an arts center in the building and innocently decides that, in order to run the latter efficiently, "she herself would have to take some sort of course in art history and music appreciation – music was always appreciated, whereas art had a history." The aged village recluse, meanwhile, is unimpressed by Mrs. Gamart's plans: "How can the arts have a centre?"

The Bookshop was followed by the Booker Prize-winning *Offshore* (1979), which has less in common with Fitzgerald's other early efforts than with her later works, and which I shall discuss in connection with them. It was succeeded by *Human Voices* (1980), a novel about wartime London – or, to be specific, about the BBC in 1940, a place where, as in the museum of *The Golden Child*, some officials are identified not by name but by title (a device that nicely underscores the importance to Fitzgerald of roles and responsibilities). A temperate, lightly plotted book, *Human Voices* covers a few months in the lives of two programming directors, the Director of Programme Planning (DPP) and the Director of Recorded Programming (RPD), and of several young men and women who serve as assistants. Most important of these assistants is Annie Asra, a Birmingham piano tuner's sensible daughter, who falls senselessly in love with the eccentric, middle-aged RPD. Given the promising situation – inside BBC headquarters during the Blitz! – a reader may well find himself frustrated at the lack of high drama in these pages. But the frustrations he will experience are those of life itself: Fitzgerald reminds us that heroism is not necessarily glamorous and is often, indeed, a matter of quiet dedication to monotonous tasks. She reminds us, too, that heroes, like saints, can be selfish and stupid, maddeningly quirky and abundantly flawed: though the Beeb's employees "bitterly complain[ed] about the shortsightedness of their colleagues, the vanity of the newsreaders, the remoteness of the Controllers and the restrictive nature of the canteen's one teaspoon," the Corporation's loyalty to the truth (despite temptations to conceal unpleasant facts for purposes of national morale) filled them with "a certain pride which they had no way to express, either then or since." In the end, the book is a tribute to the unsung and quintessentially English heroism of imperfect people.

At Freddie's (1982) is something of a tribute as well. Like *Human Voices*, it is an account of several months in the lives of several people;

this time around, though, we're at the Temple School, a.k.a. Freddie's, an ever-destitute but widely revered London academy for child actors whose elderly founder and leader, Frieda Wentworth, a.k.a. Freddie, is a legendary figure in the theater world. Among the principal characters are two young teachers, one of whom falls in love with the other, and a pair of students, a brilliantly gifted nine-year-old named Jonathan and a vain, show-offy type (and future movie star) named Mattie. As Florence's bookshop is threatened by Mrs. Gamart, so Freddie's is endangered by a vulgar entrepreneur who wants to change it into a school for television-commercial actors; but, surprisingly, the real joker in the deck turns out to be Freddie herself, who, in her heart of hearts, proves to be devoted not to the theater but to the perpetuation, at any cost, of her own power. (Meanwhile, the school's talentless, lovestruck young teacher – whom Freddie hired only because he would accept low pay – proves to have great strength of character.) As if to emphasize that what ultimately matters is not fame or power but art, the novel concludes with a memorable glimpse of the one true artist in the place, Jonathan, who, interested not in celebrity but in the perfection of his craft, remains past dusk in the schoolyard, repeatedly practicing a leap from a wall for his role in *King John*.

JONATHAN, we are told, "was born to be one of those actors who work from the outside inwards. To them, the surface is not superficial." The surface has never been superficial to Fitzgerald either, though there are times in *The Golden Child, The Bookshop, Human Voices,* and *At Freddie's* when her meticulous portraits don't communicate quite as much as she presumably wants them to. This is far less true of her other four novels, in which Fitzgerald, though no more than ever inclined to engage in extensive mind-reading, manages with far greater success to convey, for all her concision, a phenomenally rich sense of place and character and moral tone. These later novels (though they are not all strictly "later," since I include among them the third, *Offshore*) are more ambitious and ambiguous than those already discussed; Fitzgerald's vision seems larger, subtler, more complex. She focuses less on institutional than on family relations, and even reaches beyond England for her main settings; while infatuations figure in *Human Voices* and *At Freddie's,* moreover, such later books as *Innocence* and *The Gate of Angels* examine full-fledged romances and marriages.

Fitzgerald is also more explicit, in these later novels, about her interest in matters of the spirit. The niece of two eminent priests, she takes what might be described, to an extent, as a Christian view of her creations: she notes their transgressions and names them bluntly, even bitingly; but if she scorns the sin she has compassion for the sinner. Such words as "soul" and "saint" crop up frequently in her pages, though one might miss them because of the casual, colloquial way in which they are generally introduced. (In *Innocence,* for example, she describes the perturbed young hero as rushing out of a room "like a lost soul.") Fitzgerald is preoccupied, moreover, with the nature of innocence – its assets and liabilities, moral and practical, and the myriad forms it takes, whether in small children or in supposedly sophisticated adults – and emphasizes that innocence and righteousness do not necessarily go hand in hand. Sometimes her innocents are people who lack sufficient knowledge of the world; sometimes they are very worldly folk indeed – scientists, physicians, and journalists – who possess an overweening confidence in the ability of rational investigation to determine objective truth, and about whose smug, unquestioning reverence for such things as behaviorism and the scientific method Fitzgerald can be trenchantly sardonic. Surely one reason why she shrinks from directly rendering her novels' climactic events is that she is intensely aware of the difficulty of pinning down the precise truth of a human situation.

This is not to suggest, of course, that Fitzgerald's position is that of many a contemporary academic theorist who claims that nothing is knowable. On the contrary, she patently believes in truth, and believes, too, that fundamental human truths are worth pursuing. Yet she is hesitant to delve too deeply into the human soul. So heavily, indeed, does she rely on dialogue and physical action to convey character that at times one almost gets the impression that there is, to her, something unseemly about rummaging around too much inside a protagonist's head. In any event, her emphasis is invariably not on exploring her characters' souls but on examining their conduct in the company of others. When she makes general statements, accordingly – some of which are attributed to the narrator, others to various characters – they tend to be commentaries not on psychological but on social verities: "Morality is seldom a safe guide for human conduct." "Total approval is never convincing." "Honourable men are rare, but not necessarily interesting." "Politics and business can be settled by influence, cooks and doctors can only be promoted on their skill." Manifestly, these aphoristic remarks are the work of someone who is clear-eyed but funny about human failings, someone who has firm and unromantic convictions about art, life, and civilization. Yet her best novels are characterized by a reflectiveness, a probing curiosity, an acute awareness of the contingency of the human condition that separates her dramatically from the callow certitude of many a glib, solipsistic contemporary novelist.

Such is the case, certainly, with *Offshore*. Set in a community of Thames barges on London's Battersea Reach during the early 1960s, the book focuses on thirty-two-year-old Nenna James, a former music student who lives with her daughters, Martha and Tilda, on a barge named *Grace*. Nenna bought the barge, we learn, while her engineer husband, Edward, was in Central America on a construction job; Edward, now back in London and unwilling to join them in their unorthodox new residence, has instead taken a room in a drab-sounding neighborhood that Nenna can't even bring herself to visit: "In Christ's name, who ever heard of such a place?" Fitzgerald doesn't offer a simple thumbs-up or thumbs-down verdict on all this. Nor does she tell us, in so many words, precisely why Nenna decided to move onto a barge and why she now obstinately refuses to give it up. (There are, significantly, no flashbacks to the marriage, of which we are offered the skimpiest, most objective record.) Doubtless the explanation is not a simple one, for Nenna is not a case study out of a textbook but a character who feels at every moment perversely, perplexingly, and poignantly real. By way of dialogue and gesture, however, and the occasional brief flashlight glimpse beneath Nenna's edgy, stubborn, and confused surface, Fitzgerald delicately plants in one's mind the notion that marriage has been for Nenna a string of failures and disappointments, including the frustration of her musical ambitions, and that the approach of middle age and the absence of Edward have combined to bring to a head her long-suppressed fears and resentments and to propel her into extreme, perhaps even reckless, action. In moving offshore, Nenna has moved away from the mainstream of middle-class existence, to experiment with a life on the margins that may, in her mind, provide a gratifying tie to her musical ambitions of yore and to her passing youth.

In addition to bringing Nenna and her daughters to vibrant life in very little space, Fitzgerald affords us engaging glimpses of the other lives on the Reach – those of Willis, an old man whose leaky boat finally sinks; Maurice, a sad, aimless gay man; and Richard, a married business executive with whom Nenna has a brief fling. Though the sometimes protracted episodes involving these other characters cannot be defended on strict grounds of dramatic structure, they don't feel superfluous: on the contrary, they all help to fill in the picture of life on the Reach, to illuminate the odd little corner of the world into which Nenna has chosen to withdraw. It should be noted that the Thames functions here in several ways: not only as a symbol of sexuality (especially female sexuality) and of the unremitting flow of time, but also as an image, paradoxically, both of life (it is, note well, a river of life on which the heroine and her children are kept afloat by a boat named *Grace*) and (as in *Huckleberry Finn*) of escape from life and its responsibilities. A number of events here might be interpreted symbolically: for instance, when a priest comes to ask why the girls haven't been attending school, he slips on *Grace*'s deck. But Fitzgerald isn't insistent about such symbolic implications, and the novel's details are presented so realistically that a reader might well overlook their possible figurative significance.

MUCH THE SAME might be said about *Innocence* (1986), which chronicles the romance and marriage of two bullheaded young Italians in 1955. Salvatore Rossi is a peasant boy from a rural village who has grown up to be a brilliant and successful "nerve doctor" in Florence. Excitable, antireligious, and devoted to science, he is the son of two parents with their own strong attachments: his mother (who named him for the Savior) was a devout Christian, his father an equally devout Communist. Indeed, it was a traumatic boyhood visit to his father's hero, Antonio Gramsci – who, by that time, was a hideous, broken-down old jailbird – that made Salvatore resolve never to risk his life, health, or freedom for his principles or to be emotionally dependent on anyone. His beloved is Chiara, a beautiful student at an English convent school who is the daughter of an ancient and noble Florentine family, the Ridolfi.

In the novel's opening pages, we are vouchsafed an anecdote from Ridolfi history. In the sixteenth century, the Ridolfi were midgets; a beloved daughter, kept within the walls of the family estate so that she would be protected from the knowledge of her difference from others, had a mute midget playmate who unexpectedly began to grow to normal size; whereupon the Ridolfi child, to protect her friend from the knowledge of her apparent differentness from others, had the girl's eyes put out and her legs amputated at the knees. Neither Fitzgerald nor any of her characters ever spells out a moral to this anecdote, or explains the implied thematic link between it and the story of Salvatore and Chiara; but over the course of the novel the anecdote resonates frequently, the pitch changing ever so slightly every time. Part of the point, certainly, is that innocence, far from being a guarantee of virtue, can be a wellspring of cruelty and horror; that people are capable of doing foolish and even wicked things to those they love in an attempt to improve them, to make them conform to some vision of normality or rightness; that the innate differences between people, whether of stature or sensibility, can form insuperable barriers between them; and that, in some way or another, the attributes of one's parents remain ineradicable, perhaps even disfiguring, elements of one's own identity. Family is character; family is fate.

The lovers' first encounter in *Innocence* might well be an episode from a romance novel. Introduced during an intermission at the Teatro della Pergola after a crude performance of Brahms's Third Violin Sonata, Salvatore asks Chiara politely whether she enjoyed the music; she replies: "Of course not." He falls for her immediately, and she is so taken with him that she lets him lead her out into the rain before returning to the auditorium. (Like Forster's *A Room with a View*, this novel is about a capable, experienced young man of humble origins who, amid picturesque Italian settings, introduces a sheltered, well-to-do girl to sensuality.) But nothing else here is remotely reminiscent of a romance novel. Obsessed with Chiara, Salvatore makes no effort to see her. Months pass; finally she appears at his office, only to be upbraided by him for coming. She flees; he writes her a letter, then tears it up. Perplexed by his behavior, Chiara invites Barney, a no-nonsense English schoolmate, to Italy and asks her advice. At Barney's suggestion, she arranges for herself and Salvatore to be invited to lunch by mutual acquaintances, but they both hesitate to go; the vacillations that precede their meeting are recounted in elaborate detail.

Not so, however, the ensuing affair, which begins offstage and is recounted very succinctly. Ditto the first months of Salvatore and Chiara's marriage: instead of seeing them together, we hear about their relationship in conversations between Chiara and Barney (who tells her: "You're just an innocent who hopped into bed with the first man you saw when you got out of the convent") and between Salvatore and his friends. The narrator sums up the marriage in businesslike fashion: "Chiara and Salvatore quarrelled, but not so successfully as they made love. Chiara had no gift for quarrelling at all and could scarcely understand how it was done, nor, really, had Salvatore, since his argument was with himself, and he was therefore bound to lose. . . . They loved each other to the point of pain and could hardly bear to separate each morning." The main problem with the marriage, as this quotation suggests, lies with Salvatore, who is unable to enjoy the blessing of his and Chiara's love; insecure, irrational, and suspicious, he comes to feel that he was unwise to tell Chiara everything about himself, and is sure that she doesn't need him, that she must be unhappy, that she's a dilettante when it comes to romance, and that she's secretly arranging to regain the family property that he sold in order to afford to marry her.

A friend opines that Salvatore has "a sickness and craziness about him because he has cut himself off from the place where he was born." (Note the words *cut off* – a reminder of the story of the leg amputation.) Salvatore, for his part, feels "that both Marta [his ex-mistress] and Chiara took advantage of him by attacking him with their ignorance, or call it innocence. A serious thinking adult had no defence against innocence because he was obliged to respect it, whereas the innocent scarcely knows what respect is, or seriousness either." But who's the innocent here? At one point Salvatore says that the only thing he hopes to be spared is "to know exactly what kind of man I am": what is he hoping for here, after all, except to retain a kind of innocence? One of the things that this novel is about, ultimately, is the ways in which people deprive themselves and others out of innocence – an innocence that, paradoxically, may generate guilt, and that may take the form of deficient self-knowledge or a lack of worldly experience. Chaucer's "Franklin's Tale" poses the question: "Which was the mooste fre?" Perhaps one question that *Innocence* seeks to pose is: which is the more innocent, Salvatore or Chiara? "What's to become of us?" Salvatore asks a cousin of Chiara's in the novel's closing pages. "We can't go on like this." "Yes, we can go on like this," comes the reply. "We can go on exactly like this for the rest of our lives." And that's part of the point in this novel, which concludes on a note of hope but intimates that, people being the troubled and troublemaking creatures that they are, the very notion of a happily-ever-after ending – or, for that matter, of an innocence without unsavory repercussions – is a patent absurdity.

What with its sumptuous settings, its colorful cast of aristocrats, politicians, and Vatican priests, its Latin outbursts of temper and its torrid passions (which run several degrees hotter than the passions in any previous Fitzgerald novel), *Innocence* differs significantly from its predecessors. Some reviewers seem to have thought it odd for so English a writer as Fitzgerald to set a story in Italy, but it makes a certain kind of sense: there's something in a pure English temperament that just naturally assumes a tempestuous, irrational romance of this sort should be set in hotter climes. (Think of *Romeo and Juliet.*)

FITZGERALD'S Italian novel was followed by her Russian novel. *The Beginning of Spring* (1988) is set in Moscow on the eve of revolution. It is 1913, and Frank Reid, the Russian-born English owner of a printing firm, has been abandoned by his wife, Nellie, for reasons that are apparently a mystery to him. Hiring a taciturn young woman named Lisa to take care of their three children, he asks her to cut her hair, presumably because he finds her attractive and wants her to look less tempting (shades of the Ridolfi mutilation!). More than ever in Fitzgerald, there are abundant references here to God and the soul: if Fitzgerald seems, at least in part, to have set *Innocence* in Italy so that she could write about extravagant passions, she seems to have set *The Beginning of Spring* in Russia so that she could allow certain of her characters to converse at length, and with relative unrestraint, about spiritual matters. Frank, who does "everything quickly and neatly, without making a business of it," considers himself a rational being, but isn't sure: "Perhaps, Frank thought, I have faith, even if I have no beliefs." More openly metaphysical-minded than Frank is his accountant, Selwyn Crane, a religious poet and Tolstoy disciple who is described by Frank's servant as "a good man, . . . always on his way from one place to another, searching out want and despair." "If you have a fault," Selwyn tells Frank, "it is that you don't grasp the importance of what is beyond sense or reason." Yet, as the beloved Freddie turns out to be the resident demon of *At Freddie's,* so it is the seemingly righteous Selwyn who proves to have been the reason for Nellie's disappearance: as he confesses remorsefully, they were having an affair and arranged to run off together – a plan that he did not repudiate until after Nellie had already deserted Frank.

The Beginning of Spring is set in the year before the outbreak of World War I; Fitzgerald's most recent novel, *The Gate of Angels* – which, though published in England in 1990, did not appear in America until 1992 – takes place a year earlier. (One can well understand why Fitzgerald would want to set two novels in that period, which marks the boundary between the British Empire-dominated world of the Victorians and Edwardians and the modern era.) Like *Innocence,* it follows two strong-willed young people down their separate paths to each other and through a romance marked by disagreement, misunderstanding, and estrangement; as in both *Innocence* and *The Beginning of Spring,* it is not until the very last sentence that Fitzgerald, in the most matter-of-fact way, introduces the possibility of reconciliation.

Fitzgerald gives us straightforward accounts of both these young people's lives. Fred Fairly, a former choirboy and the son of a provincial rector, has been appointed a Junior Fellow at the fictitious Saint Angelicus, the smallest college at Cambridge; known colloquially as Angels, the college is a sort of secular monastery whose charter forbids its fellows, all mathematicians and scientists, to marry. Like Salvatore, Fred is basically a good sort, a well-educated man of science with a callow reverence for rationality. "These are wonderful years in Cambridge," says

Fred; science is in its glory days, and he has decided to clear his mind "of any idea that could not be tested through physical experience." Since this includes, to his way of thinking, the idea of God, he has decided that he is no longer a Christian. Informed of this decision, his father is not surprised: "When you told me that you wanted to study Natural Sciences at university, which led, fortunately I suppose, to your present appointment, I took it for granted that you would sooner or later come to the conclusion that you had no further use for the soul." To be sure, like any good scientist, Fred is willing to keep an open mind about these things: "He had no acceptable evidence that Christianity was true, but he didn't think it impossible that at some point he might be given a satisfactory reason to believe in it."

The young lady for whom Fred falls is also something of a rationalist. A lower-class girl from the south of London, Daisy has studied to be a nurse because she wants to know how the body works. She is at once hard-nosed and sympathetic: "Hating to see anyone in want, she would part without a thought with money or possessions, but she could accept only with the caution of a half-tamed animal." Dismissed from a London hospital for violating professional bounds to help a patient, she travels to Cambridge in search of a job and is followed by a sleazy middle-aged newspaper reporter, Kelly, who seeks to take advantage of her helplessness. The two of them are bicycling to the hotel where he plans to rob her chastity when they – and Fred, who happens to be directly behind them on his Royal Sunbeam – are knocked unconscious in a road accident caused by a carter named Saul (which, if one chooses to notice it, may be taken as an allusion to Saint Paul, *né* Saul of Tarsus, the transfiguring event of whose life also took place on a road). Awakening next to Daisy in a strange bed, Fred is smitten as quickly as Salvatore is with Chiara.

Several of the signal characteristics of Fitzgerald's fiction are more pronounced in this novel than in any of its predecessors. For one thing, if her books have always tended toward brevity and directness – their chapters short, their style plain, crisp, and unadorned – the tendency is even more manifest in *The Gate of Angels*. Also, though her protagonists have often been quite calculatedly ordinary, Fred and Daisy, with their humble backgrounds and almost parodically down-to-earth names, could hardly seem less exotic – to an English reader, anyway. (They may seem especially so to readers who come to the new novel with vivid memories of the foreign settings and characters of *Innocence* and *The Beginning of Spring*.) Moreover, Fitzgerald's powers of selectivity and compression are at their zenith here. Finally, if Fitzgerald's preoccupation with spiritual matters has been increasingly evident in her last few novels, such matters figure even more prominently in *The Gate of Angels,* and her apprehension of that which lies beyond sense and reason is communicated with greater force and beauty than ever before in her oeuvre. Partly because her description of each homely particular is well-nigh allegorical in its simplicity – and partly because the place names that she chooses to include (e.g., Jesus Lane, Christ's Pieces, Bishop's Leaze) serve to remind us, in an unaggressive way, that everything around us is a part of the divine creation – the reader of *The Gate of Angels* begins to feel, before too long, as if the novel's very landscape is gently but unmistakably aglow with its own miraculousness. And what is the significance of the wind that stirs up in the first line of the novel, and then again at the very end, when, after having resolved to part forever, Fred and Daisy meet once more by what may or may not be purest chance? This is, let it be said, the rarest of novels in which an eleventh-hour coincidence, because it is in perfect figurative harmony with all that has gone before, feels not at all like an authorial contrivance but like a genuine moment of grace, a gentle brush with the hand of providence – a still, small voice in the madding crowd.

One of the things that figure importantly here is a historical anecdote. Early on, Fitzgerald tells us that Saint Angelicus "had no real existence at all, because its foundation had been confirmed by a pope, Benedict XIII, who after many years of ferocious argument had been declared not to be the Pope at all." Obstinately, Benedict refused to accept the verdict and spent the rest of his very long life holding papal audiences. Fred, we are told, is also obstinate: "Like Benedict XIII himself, he might be asked to admit defeat, but would never recognise it as legitimate, or even respectable." This story of Saint Angelicus's founding, like that of the Ridolfi ancestors at the beginning of *Innocence,* resonates throughout the book. By suggesting that the college has "no real existence," Fitzgerald is playing something of an ontological game with the reader:

for the college *doesn't* exist, of course, outside the world of the novel; but it *does* exist within the novel, Pope or no Pope. But what does it mean to say that it exists when the narrator says that it doesn't? Fitzgerald's game forces the reader to attend throughout the book to questions of reality and unreality, and, in particular, to the delicate intimations of another reality – one of spirit – with which Fitzgerald permeates her narrative. This is all very effectively done, and indeed it points to what may be this author's most distinctive achievement: namely, her ability to combine, in one novel, a convincingly detailed realistic surface with a sublime sense of the transcendent. In none of her novels has this been quite as elegantly and affectingly accomplished as in *The Gate of Angels*.

(MARCH 1992)

Passage to India:
Ruth Prawer Jhabvala

PROBABLY most Americans who recognize the name of Ruth Prawer Jhabvala know her mainly as a screenwriter, one third of the celebrated international movie-making team whose other members are the Indian producer Ismail Merchant and the American director James Ivory. In this country, at least, Jhabvala and her partners are known almost exclusively for three recent films that were based upon major modern novels: *The Europeans* (1978) and *The Bostonians* (1984) both derived from works by Henry James, and *A Room with a View* was an adaptation of one of E. M. Forster's less familiar novels. Though many reviewers carped about the casting and the slow pace (among other things) of the first two films, even the harshest critics almost invariably praised the filmmakers for their seriousness, for their wonderful attention to period detail, and for their manifest effort to be as faithful as possible not only to the word of the text but to James's tone and sensibility. The word "literate" was widely invoked – and, at a time when films often seem to be more illiterate than ever, the literateness of the Ivory-Merchant-Jhabvala productions was more than enough to inspire fervent expectations, on the part of many critics who were unhappy with the two James adaptations, that in time a truly magnificent film would be forthcoming from the team. These expectations, in most instances, seem to have been satisfied with the release of *A Room with a View.* This splendid film received better notices than either of its two immediate predecessors; it was nominated for the Academy Award for best picture and earned Jhabvala the award for best screenplay adaptation. When she appeared on the awards telecast last spring to accept her statuette, it was doubtless the first time most Americans had heard her name.

Despite her relative obscurity in this country, however, Jhabvala's writing career has been a long and distinguished one. Her motion-picture partnership with Ivory and Merchant dates back to the early six-ties; prior to the films I have mentioned, the team collaborated on a number of productions, none of which was shown widely in the United States. In addition, Jhabvala has written ten novels – the most celebrated of them being the Booker Prize-winning *Heat and Dust* – and several collections of short stories. Most of these books, if obtainable at all in this country, have hitherto been available only in British editions; but, largely as a result (one assumes) of the success of *A Room with a View,* that situation has lately begun to change. Both *Heat and Dust* and the 1973 novel *Travelers,* as well as the short-story collection *Out of India,* have recently been issued by the Fireside division of Simon and Schuster in handsome, well-distributed paperback editions. Alongside them on the bookstore shelves is Jhabvala's newly published novel, *Three Continents.* As if this were not enough compensation for years of stateside neglect, during the months of September and October the Asia Society in New York held screenings of a number of Ivory-Merchant films – six of them scripted by Jhabvala – as part of a twenty-fifth anniversary trib-ute to the team. Though she has been writing fiction and movies for more than a quarter of a century, then, it is not much of an exaggeration to say that Jhabvala is only now being introduced to a broad American public. There could hardly be a more appropriate occasion to examine some of the highlights of this most interesting – and, on these shores, largely neglected – career.[1]

Probably one important reason for America's neglect of Jhabvala's novels is that most of them – as well as the majority of her pre-Henry James screenplays – are set in the country where she has lived, whether full- or part-time, for decades: India. Though she still spends several months of the year on the subcontinent, her principal residence is cur-rently in New York. The problematical question, however, is whether Jhabvala herself – born in Germany of Polish parents, and educated in

1. *Three Continents,* by Ruth Prawer Jhabvala; William Morrow & Company. Of the other Jhabvala books discussed in this essay, *Esmond in India* is available in paperbak edition from Penguin Books U.K.; *The Householder* in paperback from Norton; *Out of India, Heat and Dust,* and *Travelers* in paperback from Fireside Books (Simon and Schuster); and *In Search of Love and Beauty* in paperback from Penguin Books U.S.A.

England – can be considered Indian. Her own answer to this question, given in an essay entitled "Myself in India" (which serves as the introduction to her recent story collection *Out of India*), is no. "I have lived in India for most of my adult life," she declares at the beginning of the essay. "My husband is Indian and so are my children. I am not, and less so every year." India, she goes on to say, is a country that one either loves or hates; it offers "a special problem of adjustment for the sort of people who come today, who tend to be liberal in outlook and have been educated to be sensitive and receptive to other cultures. But it is not always easy to be sensitive and receptive to India: there comes a point where you have to close up in order to protect yourself." Her reason for living in India, she tells us – and I quote this at length because I think it helps to explain some of the distinctive qualities of her fiction – is that

> my strongest human ties are here. If I hadn't married an Indian, I don't think I would ever have come here for I am not attracted – or used not to be attracted – to the things that usually bring people to India. I know I am the wrong type of person to live here. To stay and endure, one should have a mission and a cause, to be patient, cheerful, unselfish, strong. I am a central European with an English education and a deplorable tendency to constant self-analysis. I am irritable and have weak nerves.

She is not, in other words, the type who has come to this land of desperate poverty – a poverty of which she, in her very nice air-conditioned house, is nonetheless always vividly aware – to be of service as a doctor or social worker. "I often think," she writes, "that perhaps this is the only condition under which Europeans have any right to be here." (According to a recent article by Dinitia Smith in *New York* magazine, Jhabvala's reason for living part of the year in New York is that "by 1976, she had grown overwhelmed by the subcontinent.") If her fiction is predominantly about "modern, well-off, cultured Westernized Indians," it is because her way of adjusting to life in India is to do her best to ignore the backward and hungry multitudes (which she refers to continually as a "great animal" on whose back she rides). Yet she doesn't associate with many Westernized Indians, either, for she believes that their social lives are synthetic, their conversation empty ("Everything they say . . . is not prompted by anything they really feel strongly about but by what they think they ought to feel strongly about"), their perspective on India's poverty and backwardness thoroughly detached. They talk about India "as if it were some *other* place—as if it were a subject for debate—an abstract subject—and not a live animal actually moving under their feet." Her problem, then, is essentially one of cultural adaptation: "To live in India and be at peace, one must to a very considerable extent become Indian and adopt Indian attitudes, habits, beliefs, assume if possible an Indian personality. But how is this possible? Should one want to try to become something other than what one is?"

THIS QUESTION, in a sense, is at the center of Jhabvala's fiction. Many of the prominent characters in her novels and stories are either Indians who try to be Westerners, or Westerners who try to be Indians. Jhabvala's tone, when she writes about such people, invariably combines affection with irony—affection, because she knows that it is only human to be attracted to that which one is not, to long for that which one does not possess; irony, because she recognizes how delusory most such attractions are, how fruitless most such longings. Jhabvala is a humorist as well as a humanist: she laughs at man's moral and intellectual imperfections even as she laments his inability to transcend those imperfections. For she does perceive (it is the central perception of her fiction) that the human animal craves transcendence—transcendence of uncertainty, of mortality, of the banality of day-to-day life. Characteristically, Jhabvala sees this craving as both beautiful and foolish. Or, more precisely, she sees it as a beautiful longing that people—not knowing where they can go to find satiation—try to satisfy in foolish ways. In her novels, characters are always seeking, traveling, roaming the world in search of a *locus amenis,* making fools of themselves by reaching out for the impermanent, the inappropriate, the unnatural, the impossible.

The longing for transcendence often takes the form, in Jhabvala's work, of a passionate attachment (and *passion* is a word that she does not hesitate to use) to someone grand, exotic, forbidden, even evil—usually someone of a different race. In her novel *Esmond in India,* for instance, the sheltered young Indian woman Shakuntala is smitten with the haughty, married, extremely European Esmond; in *Heat and Dust* Olivia, the wife of a British officer, falls for the Nawab, a rich, shady local prince; and in *Three Continents* the naïve American girl Harriet adores the mendacious, mysterious Crishi. The narrator of *Heat and Dust* speaks of reaching "a higher plane of consciousness through the powers of sex."

Another form taken by the longing for transcendence is the veneration of movie stars and swamis. (Yes, movie stars and swamis.) Jhabvala recognizes that however different they may seem – the movie star an embodiment of modern Western popular culture at its trashiest, the swami a symbol of ancient Indian religion at its most sublime – they are really very closely related, in that they both represent for the common man a type of transcendence; if swamis (embodying as they do the mysteries of India) hold a special fascination for certain Westerners, so movie stars (embodying the affluence and glamour of the West) hold a special fascination for Indians. Nothing, by the way, is more characteristic of Jhabvala's unique vision and perspective than her recognition of such a bizarre cross-cultural affinity. Movie stars and swamis thus pop up frequently in her work. (One of her films – probably her most unsuccessful, in fact – was *The Guru*, a 1968 character portrait starring Michael York.) Though she pokes fun at both movie stars and swamis, however, she does not make them out to be thoroughgoing fools and rascals; in Jhabvala's fiction, even they have their moments of goodness and wisdom. This is one of the things that make Jhabvala special: she perceives that man is neither basically good nor basically evil, that neither pure materialism nor pure idealism – the struggle between which she often depicts – makes very much sense as a philosophy of life. She knows that we all have in us both good and evil, that we consist of both body and spirit; we are, in short, holy but imperfect creatures; and she writes about us with an empathy that stays well clear of bathos and a cynicism that only occasionally descends into bitterness.

Her career can be divided into two periods. Between 1955 and 1971 Jhabvala published six novels. Typical of these early books are *Esmond in India* and *The Householder*, in which Jhabvala is very much a novelist of manners in the tradition of Jane Austen, as well as a natural storyteller à *la* Chekhov. These novels also bring to mind the Indian novelist R. K. Narayan, though her characters are generally more well-to-do than his, and her novels more obviously aimed at a Western audience. Conventional in style and structure, they are strong on character development and social detail; they lie squarely in the realistic tradition of the English novel, and, among twentieth-century English novels, belong in the camp of Evelyn Waugh, Joyce Cary, and Kingsley Amis rather than with such foursquare modernists as Woolf and Conrad.

Take, for instance, her third novel, *Esmond in India* (1958), which is set in the years immediately following India's independence from Britain. The title notwithstanding, the character who is really most prominent in the novel is a young woman named Shakuntala, who has just earned her B.A. and returned home to New Delhi to live with her family. They are a wealthy clan who pride themselves on their Westernization: Shakuntala's father, Har Dayal, a Cambridge-educated government minister, spices his conversation with quotations from Keats, Wordsworth, and Matthew Arnold; her fair-skinned mother, Madhuri, remembers proudly the time a friend told her that in Europe she'd "be taken for Italian or Spanish"; her married older brother, Amrit, a businessman (and a subscriber to *Reader's Digest*), has moved up quickly because his British-owned firm is following a "policy of gradually replacing British executives by Indian ones," and he is "very suitable for this purpose, as he had attended an English university and was also very English in all other respects, except in his complexion"; Shakuntala herself is a fan of Sibelius and Liszt.

Shakuntala considers herself and her father, though, to be different from the other members of her family, especially Amrit. Her brother is a materialist, she complains, whereas she and her father are "idealists" and know that "art and culture are the only important things in life." From the outset, it is clear that Shakuntala's and Har Dayal's culture is superficial and their idealism pragmatic. The truth is that Har Dayal enjoys art and culture less than he enjoys his image of himself as a friend of art and culture.

The novel's other New Delhi family is strikingly different. Its patriarch, Ram Nath – once Har Dayal's friend and mentor and a respected leader of the struggle for Indian independence – has lately gone down in the world as steadily as Har Daval has gone up. So traditionally Indian is Ram Nath's clan, moreover, that his niece Golub, to the disgust of her despicable English husband, Esmond, cannot even make conversation with his European friends. When this family enters Shakuntala's life it is because Ram Nath wants her to marry his son, Narayan – a brilliant young doctor who has rejected a lucrative practice to care for the rural poor. Unbeknownst to everyone, however, Shakuntala has fallen in love with the superficial Esmond, who represents to her everything Western, and who doesn't care for her in the slightest. Esmond or no Esmond, though, one never has any question about the outcome of Ram Nath's proposal. One knows that Har Dayal, for all his supposed devotion to Ram Nath, will manage to argue slickly against the marriage. And one knows that the idealistic Shakuntala will decide that "my ideals are different than [Narayan's]. . . . I love Art and Beauty and Poetry, how can I give these things up as I shall have to if I go and live with Narayan in a village to do good to the poor?"

It should be said that some of the characters in *Esmond* are less credible than others, their motivations more dubious and their fatuities too strongly exaggerated. It is hard to believe, for instance, that the pathetically meek Golub could ever have worked up the nerve to marry Esmond against her family's wishes – especially since she cannot now summon up the same nerve to leave him, though she and her whole family realize that the marriage is a lost cause. Equally difficult to swallow is that a rich, sheltered young Indian woman of the 1950s would have opened her chaste treasure, especially to a married man, as readily as Shakuntala opens hers to Esmond. In any event, one sometimes wishes, while reading *Esmond,* that Jhabvala would let up a bit on the irony, particularly when she is writing about Shakuntala. Quite often the girl is just too foolish to be believed. When her mother asks her, on one occasion, what she is doing, Shakuntala replies, with a child's solemnity, "I am thinking quite hard"; at the end of the novel, when she has a marketplace rendezvous with Esmond, she is absurdly deluded and happy, and Jhabvala, who wants to indicate that life is nowhere near as wonderful as Shakuntala thinks, makes her point with less subtlety than might have been desirable: "She knew now that life was more wonderful, a hundred times more wonderful, than even she had suspected. It was not the moment, nor was she the person, to hide such a sentiment, so she told him, 'Life is wonderful – wonderful!' letting her hand slide from his arm down to his hand which she firmly and fearlessly held as they made their way through the crowd." Though Jhabvala's affectionate attention, then, to the little details of human relations, attitudes, and customs is very charming, she is at times so ironic in this novel that she comes off as downright misanthropic.

The Householder (1960) might be read as something of a companion piece to *Esmond in India*. Instead of concerning herself with a rich young lady who has returned to her father's house after being graduated from college, Jhabvala gives us a middle-class boy named Prem who, as the novel opens, has recently earned a second-class B.A., has undergone an arranged marriage with a girl named Indu, has taken up residence with her in a seedy little flat in Delhi, and has entered upon a low-paying teaching job at a seedy little private college. He is, then, a brand new "householder" – which is, according to the ancient writings, the third (after child and student) of the four stages of a man's life. The novel is concerned with describing his period of adjustment to this role. For this timid, unambitious, and only moderately intelligent young man is not quite ready for the responsibilities of manhood. Though Indu is with child, he does not find her attractive, and considers her pregnancy a "terrible embarrassment," for "[n]ow everybody would know what he did with her at night in the dark." He tries to behave in a manner befitting a proper Indian husband, but is not very good at it; Indu blithely ignores his orders. At the college, too, his attempts at discipline are ineffectual. Though he spends much of the book, moreover, trying to work up the nerve to ask Mr. Khanna for a raise in salary and his landlord for a lower rent, one knows from the start that when he finally manages to choke out these requests, they will be brushed aside breezily: one knows this as surely as one knows that Shakuntala will never marry Narayan. (One reads Jhabvala novels like *Esmond in India* and *The Householder* not to discover what will happen – one knows pretty much what will happen – but to delight in, among other things, the perceptiveness with which Jhabvala depicts self-important, self-deceiving people like Har Dayal and Mr. Khanna in the act of justifying their ignoble actions.) But one also knows that eventually – and very gradually – things will improve for Prem. Perhaps he will not come to enjoy his new life, but he will grow used to it; it will come to seem less of a burden, and at times even pleasurable.

About Prem: although he is a believable and pitiable character, he is not an extremely likable one. Like Shakuntala, he seems abnormally puerile for a college graduate, buying candy on the way home and eating it quickly so he will not have to share it with Indu. As in the case of Shakuntala, the irony Jhabvala brings to his characterization is sometimes excessive; on occasion he is so passive and ineffectual that one feels as if one is being invited not to sympathize with him but to feel superior to him. This is true not only of Prem, to be sure, but of many of the characters in the book, whose banality is of grotesque dimensions. Prem's fellow teachers, for example, speak almost entirely in clichés. Since they are minor characters, however, this is not a crucial failing, and the results are admittedly very funny; the inane pretentiousness displayed at Mr. Khanna's tea party, for example, is reminiscent of Dickens:

"As I was saying," said Mr. Khanna; he took up his position in the centre again and replaced his thumb in his armpit. "It is very pleasant to have the ladies with us. Very agreeable." The ladies all stared straight in front of them, without any change of expression. Only Mrs. Khanna said, "I think the tea-water is nearly boiling."

Mr. Chaddha said, "The society of ladies is said to have a very softening effect." He was wearing a cream-coloured silk suit which seemed to have been washed quite a number of times, and he sat with his arms and his little bird legs crossed in an attitude of ease suitable to a tea-party.

"It is not for nothing," suggested Mr. Khanna, "that they are known as the gentle sex." Led by Mr. Chaddha, the gentlemen politely laughed. "It is good sometimes to break off in the midst of toil," Mr. Khanna continued, "and enjoy an hour's leisure and ease in their charming company."

"As our heroes of old," said Mr. Chaddha, "withdrew for respite from their battles to have their wounds dressed and their brows soothed by the hands of their consorts." He seemed pleased by this remark; he cleared his throat and crossed his legs the other way. The other teachers looked at the Principal, and when they saw him smile in appreciation, they too smiled in appreciation.

Outlandish as they are, furthermore, the teachers are a lot easier to take than Hans Loewe, a German boy who befriends Prem. Hans has come to India from "materialistic" Europe because he thinks this is "the country where people renounce the flesh and think only of the Spirit!" Nothing, apparently, can make him see things any differently. (He is as obtuse about the real nature of India as Shakuntala is about Esmond's lack of affection toward her.) He says to Prem,

> "Only think – in this country where everything is beautiful, the sunset and the fruit and the women, here you call it all Illusion! How do you say – Maya?"
> Prem said, "Yes, Maya," though he was not quite sure.

"How I love your India!" Hans tells Prem, but *his* India is not at all the same as Prem's; when Prem begins to speak of India's independence and its economic progress, Hans seems not even to hear him: "Everything is so spiritual – we can wash off our dirty materialism when we come here to your India!" At first these speeches are somewhat amusing, and this Westerner's admiration of India's supposed spiritual *richesse* is certainly deliciously ironic in light of post-revolutionary India's desperate longing for a Western-style material affluence. But though Hans appears several times in the book, Jhabvala never develops him any further than this; he remains incredibly obtuse and deaf to Prem's practical-minded conversation. To Hans, indeed, Prem is little more than a symbol of India. Of course, Jhabvala finds Hans ridiculous for taking this simplistic, condescending attitude. But Hans is such a blatant, uncomplicated stereotype of the European in India that it could be argued that Jhabvala herself, in creating such a character, is as guilty of gross simplification and condescension as he is.

The most peculiar episode of *The Householder* is one in which Prem spends part of an evening with a swami and his followers. Nobody says anything profound during this encounter, but the mere fact that the swami and his followers speak – even in the vaguest terms – of God and of the heart's longings and of "what is valuable in the world and what is not" makes the experience overwhelming for Prem; the "unaccustomed purity" of the meeting goes to his head, and causes him to laugh and feel drunk and experience, like Shakuntala at the marketplace, a brief sense of transcendence:

> He thought yes, this is how one must live – with love and laughter and song and thoughts of God. All his former worries about his rent, his rise in salary, his lack of authority as teacher and husband, were nothing but a thin scum floating on top of a deep well of happiness and satisfaction. Nothing, he thought, would ever trouble him again. From now on he would live in contemplation only of spiritual things. Indu would be like a sister to him – he would love her as a sister and both would sit at the feet of the swami and think of God and indulge in happy, innocent play.

But of course the pressing circumstances of daily life make Prem's determination to live such an existence fade quickly away. Though this episode is well done, Prem seems in it to be rather out of character; one feels as if he has been led to the swami less by the longings of his soul than by Jhabvala's desire to work a swami into the novel, and to have somebody speak of transcendent things.

The strength of *The Householder* – and a great strength it is – is that Jhabvala manages to make an unremarkable phase of an unremarkable life very touching and compelling. Like many contemporary English novelists – the late Barbara Pym comes to mind – she seems deliberately, in these early novels, to cultivate a certain smallness; in size, style, setting, scope, intentions, ideas, and range of feeling, *The Householder* is a modest book. Jhabvala concerns herself with a protagonist who we know from the start will not change dramatically, will not do anything admirable, will never amount to much. Jhabvala's restraint is remarkable, as is her understanding of character. She captures with great skill Prem's feelings of fear, uncertainty, deprivation, and hopelessness. (In fact, she makes the life of these middle-class Indians seem so barren and banal – which I don't doubt for a moment it is – that one can only be grateful she doesn't take on the life of the abject poor.) She has extra-literary goals, of course: here – as throughout her fiction – she is out to destroy the sentimental views that Western readers may have of India. Furthermore, her attention to homely details seems to be designed, in part anyway, to ridicule the grandiose pretensions of characters like Mr. Khanna. Whatever the case may be, *The Householder* is wonderfully attentive to the details of Indian life – the jarring of pickle, the making of poori and chapati, the conversations about the desirability of government jobs, the entreaties of beggars ("You are my mother and my father"). As for the novel's prose, it is even more lucid and luminous than that of *Esmond in India*. Compared to that novel, *The Householder* is shorter, simpler, more focused, more austere in its manner, and more concerned with conveying a sense of everyday Indian life; in the latter regard, in fact, it is, despite its drawbacks, a veritable *tour de force*.

ASIDE FROM the swami, the one thing in Prem's life that seems to transcend everyday reality is the cinema. Jhabvala's novels poke merciless fun at the film world – at the shoddiness of most of its products, at the large role it plays in most Indians' lives (and imaginations), and at the preoccupation of many Indians with the romances and scandals described in movie magazines. (In *The Householder* a paper-man passes by Prem's mother's train, shouting, *"Film-Fun, Film-Fare, Film-Frolic!"*) It seems ironic, then, that Jhabvala has herself made such a large contribution to Indian film. The first motion picture on which she collaborated with Merchant and Ivory was a charming black-and-white adaptation of *The Householder* (1963), starring Shashi Kapoor as Prem. Though the film has the same story, and much the same grim, claustrophobic atmosphere, as the book, there are a few notable differences: several episodes are shuffled around; Prem is not quite as spineless as in the book, and is rather more talkative; and Hans from Germany – who probably should have been an American in the first place – is transformed into Ernest from Philadelphia.

The film of *The Householder* was succeeded by two good films about India, the West, and the decline of culture. *Shakespeare Wallah* (1965) concerns a small traveling company of English Shakespearean actors who have spent years in India but who, thanks to the growing popularity of movies, have had increasing trouble finding employment, and are thus beginning to feel as if there's nothing left for them in India. "We should've gone home in '47 when they all went," complains the company's lead actor, Mr. Buckingham. But his wife (and leading lady) observes that "We always used to think *this* was our home." Indeed, the Buckinghams' teenage daughter, Lizzie, has never even been to England. Nor, in spite of her family's wishes, does she want to go there to be educated – especially after she meets, falls in love with, and begins an affair with a rich, handsome young man named Sanju (Shashi Kapoor). The affair is doomed from the start, of course. For one thing, Sanju's values and way of life contrast sharply with those of the Buckingham family; for another, Sanju already has a woman in his life, the glamorous film star Manjula, who is as wily and superficial as Lizzie is sincere and sensitive. *Shakespeare Wallah* may be the best of Jhabvala's early films: it is a gentle comedy with the audacity (and the good sense) to imply that certain products of a foreign culture – that is, Shakespeare's plays – might be better for Indians than certain products (i.e., tacky films) of their own culture.

After *Shakespeare Wallah* came *Bombay Talkie* (1970), yet another Jhabvala movie whose primary concern is to deplore the influence of movies. The heroine is Lucia Lane (Jennifer Kendal), a restless, superficial, several-times-married hack writer from England who has come to India hoping to change her luck. On a Bombay soundstage – where a musical number featuring a giant typewriter is being filmed – she meets two men who are attracted to her. One of them is a good-hearted bachelor screenwriter named Harry; the other is the dashing movie actor Vikram (Shashi Kapoor again), who is as superficial as she is. Though Vikram is married, Lucia has an affair with him; so insensitive is she that even when his meek little Indian wife walks in on the two of them in the couple's bedroom, it doesn't occur to Lucia to feel guilty or uncomfortable. Vikram is one of many men in Jhabvala's work (Esmond is another) who blithely cheat on their Indian wives with Western women; to these husbands, their wives represent tradition and permanence, whereas Western women – who need not be taken seriously anyway, because they are prostitutes by nature – represent adventure, sophistication, modernity. Of course, no Jhabvala story about restless Westerners in India would be complete without a swami, and so Lucia spends some time in an ashram, trying (without much success) to adapt herself – and her very healthy sex drive – to a disciple's ascetic life. *Bombay Talkie* is a good movie; if it is less satisfying than *Shakespeare Wallah*, it's because the principal characters are less sympathetic, the theme more familiar (with only a few changes, the story might have been set in Rome or London), and certain developments (notably, the stabbing at the end) downright corny.

B EGINNING WITH *Travelers* (1973), Jhabvala's novels represent quite a different sort of accomplishment from their predecessors. If the early novels tend to depict India from Indian points of view, in these later novels the subcontinent is more usually seen through the eyes of Westerners. In these books the country seems more exotic, somewhat less a geographical entity, a way of life, and somewhat more a state of mind; her view of the country, that is to say, is less down-to-earth, more cosmic – more symbolic. Whereas in the early novels the story is paramount, and narrative coherence a priority, the later novels are more fragmented; Jhabvala is less interested, in these books, in telling a story than in painting a single broad canvas; she seeks to give us India, it seems, not by offering us a series of discrete connected images but by depicting one image, as it were, from a multiplicity of angles. These later Jhabvala novels are more sensual, experimental, modern; though the later Jhabvala, like her earlier incarnation, has affinities to Waugh and Cary, say, she is closer than the early Jhabvala to the camp of Virginia Woolf, Conrad, Lawrence, and Joyce.

Travelers reads like a sort of trial run for the new Jhabvala. In it she moves back and forth between the points of view of four characters whose paths cross in India. Raymond, a pleasant young Englishman, is a Cambridge graduate who lives in New Delhi and is in love with Gopi, a college student; Asha is a rich middle-aged woman who also becomes smitten with Gopi, and Lee is a young Englishwoman who has come to India "to lose herself in order . . . to find herself," and who spends time in an ashram as a swami's disciple and lover. The stories of these characters' lives, as they develop over a period of several months, are told in brief chapters, many of them no longer than a page or two, some of them in epistolary form; they carry flat, descriptive titles such as "Raymond and Gopi Meet Lee," "Lee Writes to Asha," and "Raymond Arrives in the Ashram."

There is much talk about India and what it means, and in this connection many characters and settings take on symbolic dimensions. Raymond grows very fond of Indian music because it has become for him "a distillation of everything he loved in Gopi and everything he loved in India. These two were now inextricable." Lee notes that her friend Margaret looks down on Miss Charlotte, an elderly English missionary, because

> she can't sympathize with her *attitude,* which she says is old-fashioned and patronizing. She says people just don't come any more to India to do good, those days are over. What they come for now is—well, to do good to themselves, to learn, to *take* from India. That's what Margaret's here for. Above all she wants to be pure—to have a pure heart untainted by modern materialism. Margaret hates modern materialism. Of course, so do I; that's why we're both here.

It is this hatred of "modern materialism" that leads Lee to the swami, who plans to develop his following into the Universal Society for Spiritual Regeneration in the Modern World, "a worldwide religion uniting men of all creeds and all colors into one family and so bringing peace and harmony into the world." It is Lee's naïve faith in the swami that provides Jhabvala with her biggest opportunities, in this novel, for irony. "[H]e's so *phenomenal,*" Lee exults, "I mean it's so fantastic the way his mind is always alert. . . . [H]e has this power of knowing people before he's actually physically met them." Contrasted with the swami and his thriving ashram are Miss Charlotte and her mission—an institution that has actually done a great deal of good, but which is closed by the Indian government because "philanthropy is a form of charity that the government of India, indeed I may say the people of India, can no longer allow themselves to accept."

The travelers of this novel are in search not only of a number of great abstractions—truth, enlightenment, spiritual regeneration—but of one thing that is very concrete: family. If he is so easily taken in by the swami, it is because he has made it possible, at his ashram, for her to be part of something that resembles a family; likewise, Gopi becomes attached to an old swami-like woman named Banubai of whom he says, "She is my mother. She is everyone's mother." Appropriately, the novel ends with two of its protagonists making traveling plans: Raymond arranges to return to his only real family, his mother in England; Lee – who has left the ashram – decides to return to it, because it is the only real home she has.

Travelers is an odd book. The writing is crisp and vivid throughout, and some of the episodes are wittily done. At a high-toned dinner, for instance, the English host and an Indian minister get into a friendly argument over whether there is a "special relationship" between England and India; it's an absurd argument, because the Indian – who denies the existence of such a relationship – sounds as English as the Englishman. But after the smoothness, concision, and focus of *Esmond in India* and (even more so) *The Householder, Travelers* seems choppy, sprawling, meandering. Yes, the directionlessness of its characters and plot is part of the point; this is a book about four confused people meandering through life – and, to an extent, across the landscape of India – in search of something. Such a book can certainly work, but more than anything else it needs particularly appealing and sympathetic characters in order to do so; and the fact is that the characters in *Travelers* simply are not all that engaging. Even at the end of the book, one does not feel as if one knows them very well or cares strongly about any of them. Interestingly, the words of praise quoted on the back cover of the Fireside paperback edition point directly to the book's cardinal weakness. The quotation from the *New York Times Book Review* describes *Travelers* as a "distinguished psychological survey"; Ved Mehta observes that the "central character in *Travelers* . . . is India, which for [Jhabvala] is not so much a country as an experience, after which no one is ever the same." Both Mehta and the *Times* critic are correct. But to refer to the novel as a "psychological survey" is to suggest – with justification, I think – that Jhabvala's characters seem more like case studies of personality types than they do like distinctive individuals; and to say that India is the novel's central character is plainly to admit that the human characters in the book are overwhelmed by the setting.

JHABVALA'S most celebrated work of fiction, *Heat and Dust* (1975), has several affinities with *Travelers,* the most important being that it, too, is concerned with Anglo-Indian relations and cross-cultural romances; as with the earlier novel, moreover, it might be said of *Heat and Dust* that one of its central characters is India itself. Here, too, Jhabvala presents us with more than one protagonist – with a pair of them, in fact – but, unlike the foursome in *Travelers,* they never meet each other. They are, as it happens, two women who are divided from each other by time, but who belong to the same family and have a great deal in common. One of them, Olivia – whose story is set in 1923, in the Indian town of Satipur and its environs – is the bored young wife of Douglas Rivers, a British officer; she loves him, yet gradually finds herself becoming fascinated by the Nawab, a charming but dissolute (and married) prince whose palace is in the nearby town of Khatm and whose income appears to derive largely from the petty crimes of various sordid hirelings. The attraction is mutual, and in the end Olivia runs off with the Nawab, lives out her days in his house in the remote town of X, and is never seen again. The other protagonist is a young lady – Douglas's granddaughter by his second wife – who, fifty years later, having read through a trove of Olivia's old letters, journeys to India in an attempt to understand this woman whose story is now a skeleton in the family closet. The novel alternates between a straightforward recounting of Olivia's story – as revealed, we are to understand, by the letters – and the granddaughter's successive entries in the journal she keeps of her several months' visit to Satipur, during which time she has her own affair with an Indian.

As is to be expected in a Jhabvala novel, however, the narrator's reasons for coming to India are not entirely related to Olivia. She explains that "many of us are tired of the materialism of the West, and even if we have no particular attraction towards the spiritual message of the East, we come here in the hope of finding a simpler and more natural way of life." Inder Lal, her lover, considers this attitude a mockery; he is as acutely and painfully aware of his material poverty, as compared with the lot of the typical European, as she is aware of what she considers her spiritual poverty, *vis-à-vis* the average Indian: "He says, why should people who have everything – motor cars, refrigerators – come here to such a place where there is nothing?"

Esmond in India and *The Householder* have strong story lines that develop clearly and fluently, and characters that blossom rapidly into life; *Heat and Dust* is a more elliptical work, its characters more enigmatic, their motives less readily apprehended. Its feel – the tone peculiarly dry, the episodes often crabbed and unyielding, the chronological leaps disorienting, even jerky – is similar to that of *Travelers,* but it is far more surefooted, almost as if *Travelers* were the rough draft and *Heat and Dust* the finished work; there is a symbolic force to the latter book that *Travelers* doesn't quite achieve. If in *Travelers* the landscape of India seems to dwarf the characters, in *Heat and Dust* the characters partake of the country's vastness; the simple, mysterious stories of Olivia and the narrator have an archetypal, a legendary, quality that the muddled, prosaic case histories in *Travelers* don't.

The stories of Olivia and the narrator are at once similar and different; in this they reflect the similarities and differences between the British India of Olivia's day and the independent India that the narrator visits – connections which Jhabvala draws with a fine subtlety and elegance. Of course it is the differences – especially those between the nature of Anglo-Indian relations in 1923 and in the 1970s – that are most dramatically apparent. The house in which Olivia and Douglas lived now contains Indian government offices; there is a chumminess now between Englishmen and Indians that would have been rare in Olivia's time. But in all essential things, the India that the narrator becomes familiar with is the same India that Olivia knew. The heat and dust, for instance, persist. India is the same intolerably hot and dry land that it was half a century ago – or, for that matter, half a millennium ago. India is still a land that "always changes people." Though, in comparison to Jhabvala's other novels, it seems to have received somewhat more than its share of critical attention and praise, *Heat and Dust* most assuredly represents a high point of Jhabvala's art.

In the same year that this most substantial novel (which became a film in 1982) was published, there appeared a surprisingly slight Merchant-Ivory-Jhabvala movie entitled *The Autobiography of a Princess.* It is of interest, though, for its thematic similarity to *Heat and Dust.* Far from the sweeping spectacle that the title might lead one to expect, this film takes place in a modest house where, one afternoon, a middle-aged Indian princess (Madhur Jaffrey) has an elderly English bachelor

(James Mason) to tea. This is, one gathers, an annual ritual; her guest—who was once right-hand man to her late father, a maharajah—has come to celebrate with her the birthday of her father by watching home movies and sharing memories. During most of the film, the princess talks incessantly of Papa, whom she remembers as a great and cultured man, but who—one gradually realizes—was actually very much like the Nawab in *Heat and Dust:* a tyrant, a criminal, and an adulterer, who romanced a film star and lost his throne as the result of a scandalous affair with a lower-class Englishwoman. It is not till the last minutes of the film that the guest speaks at length of his relationship with the maharajah, which sounds exactly like that between the Nawab and his homosexual English friend Harry (who, in turn, rather reminds one, with his endless letters home to mother and his quiet worship of his Adored One, of Raymond in *Travelers*). So ends the film.

It is a baffling piece of work: barely an hour long, set in one room in "real time," it has no plot, no action, no dramatic conflict, and consists mostly of one rambling, interminable speech. As for the home-movie-within-a-movie, it is a bizarre compilation containing, among other things, a "60 Minutes"-style interview with disenfranchised Indian nobles, grainy scenes of elephants on parade, and truly repulsive footage showing the beheading of goats. Its only apparent points are that daughters often have highly selective memories of their fathers, and that for many high-born Indians who now live in reduced circumstances, British India is a glorious memory and independent India a nightmare. At best, the film is an *outré* footnote to *Heat and Dust*—a drastically less effective variation, that is, on the family memories of British India.

THE NOVEL that directly preceded Jhabvala's new novel is of interest for several reasons. For one thing, it is the first of her novels written during her residency in New York. For another, it has many similarities to *Three Continents*. Interestingly, *In Search of Love and Beauty* (1983) is set mostly in America—in Manhattan, to be specific—and takes place over several decades of the mid–twentieth century. At its center are three generations of a well-heeled West Side family: Louise (whose husband Bruno dies young), her businesswoman daughter Marianne (who calls herself Marietta), and the grandchildren, the world-traveling real-estate entrepreneur Mark and the otiose, idealistic homebody Natasha. The family is surprisingly close-knit – more like an Indian family, one cannot help thinking, than a typical New York family; Marietta's fulfillment, we are told, lies in Mark, and for the utterly friendless Natasha, her grandmother, mother, and brother are "her home, her life, everything she knew and cherished." Yet family attachments are not enough to sustain and satisfy them. All four – aside from Natasha, who never even has a boyfriend – share a history of unorthodox, intense, and impermanent romantic entanglements, as well as a vague but persistent dedication to spiritual realization. They also share a fascination with a man named Leo Kellerman, whom Louise first meets in the 1930s, recognizes as "a yet undefined genius," and remains enthralled by for the next several decades. Leo is a swami in everything but name: he gives lectures and workshops, has a group of followers, and seeks to establish an Academy of Potential Development – a goal that Louise's family, of which he becomes something of an associate member, helps him to achieve.

Here, as in *Heat and Dust,* Jhabvala eschews a straightforward chronological structure. Instead, she leaps back and forth through the history of Louise's family, favoring us now with an episode set in the 1970s, now with one set in the 1940s. This practice of skipping around in time has a striking effect: it makes the family's life seem like a *fait accompli* rather than like something that mysteriously unfolds from moment to moment and can be changed by the characters' actions. This, in turn, makes the characters' incessant spiritual searching seem particularly pathetic and useless: we already know, after all, that they will never find transcendence. (Alas, Jhabvala doesn't get Americans quite right. She has them speak of "laundrettes" instead of "Laundromats," of "blocks" instead of apartment houses; she has them drink too much tea and use British colloquialisms.)

This being a Jhabvala novel, there must be at least one Indian in the cast. That quota is filled in part by Ahmed, a musician whose recital at a converted New York porno theater Marietta attends. She is attracted not so much to Ahmed, she insists, as to "his sarod [a sort of Indian lute], his music; and not even that but the world it opened – the world beyond worlds – the promise of peace and fulfillment that was like a hand laid on her restless heart." Marietta hires Ahmed to give her sarod lessons, and she thereafter invites him (as Raymond does Gopi in *Travelers*) to move in with her. He does so, only to return eventually to India, which Marietta thereafter visits yearly, often passing through ashrams in the course of her travels; on one of her trips she forms an intense friendship with a woman musician named Sujata who represents her "most meaningful encounter there, or her deepest immersion and enchantment." (Like Asha, by the way, Sujata is in love with a boy who is young enough to be her son; she asks Marietta "if it was so wrong to have these feelings, then why were they sent?") Mark, for his part, devotes his life to a series of homosexual affairs. In a conflict over a mutual lover named Kent, an older man stops just short of stabbing Mark with a carving knife; Mark handles the crisis well, but the object of their affections breaks down in tears. Jhabvala explains:

> He was still very young, only at the beginning of his career, and knew nothing of what could sometimes happen among people with very strong feelings.
>
> About these feelings: Leo had once likened them to the voices of the great *castrati*, in which a man's vigour was made to give body to a woman's nervous delicacy. Unhuman voices, Leo called them; unnatural hybrids. "All the same," Mark had replied, "no one ever said they weren't beautiful."

This is what *In Search of Love and Beauty* is about: the way that unnatural, strong, and beautiful longings can lead people into foolish acts and harmless liaisons. For the truth about Louise, Marietta, and Mark seems to be that, though they cherish the family bond, each of them still hopes for some more transcendent form of human connection than that which they have. Leo, Ahmed, Kent are all ways of trying to build a new kind of family, a more nearly perfect union of souls. But one never really understands why one generation after another of this family should be so restless, so dedicated to the intercontinental search for "inner fulfillment," so devoted to the Leo Kellermans and Ahmeds of the world. Indeed, though one wants very much to believe in these extremely interesting people, one doesn't.

JHABVALA'S new novel, *Three Continents,* is in many respects similar to *In Search of Love and Beauty.* For one thing, the new novel – which in style and structure is Jhabvala's most conventional in over a decade – centers upon three generations of an affluent American family. The narrator is a young woman named Harriet Wishwell, who begins with a capsule family history: she and her twin brother, Michael, are the product of a broken marriage between a spoiled father, Danton, who has spent his life drawing on a trust fund, and a mother, Lindsay, who lives on the family ranch with a woman named Jean; since neither parent has very strong parental instincts, both Harriet and her brother were brought up largely by their paternal grandparents, a diplomat and his wife, in a number of Asian capitals. This upbringing bred in the children a "restlessness, or dissatisfaction with what was supposed to be our heritage – that is, with America." Neither lasted in college more than a year; both always "wanted something other – better – than we had. Of course people would say that what we had was pretty good, and from a materialistic point of view that would be true."

But, needless to say, theirs is an idealistic rather than a materialistic point of view. And it is not until their twentieth year – when Michael shows up at Lindsay's ranch house, fresh from yet another restless swing through Asia, with a swami and several disciples in tow – that things start looking up for them, idealistically speaking. The Rawul (for so the swami calls himself) is "as idealistic as Michael," the founder of something he calls the Fourth World movement. He has, as Harriet puts it, "this simple but forceful idea of constituting himself the savior of world civilization." In the new world – the Fourth World – "all that was best in the other three would come to fruition." Sharing this goal with him are the Rani, his consort, and Crishi, whom Harriet takes to be their adopted son. Michael himself declares, "This is it, Harriet. Om, the real thing." It is, in other words, what the two of them have been seeking all their lives. Harriet explains:

> While our parents were having marital squabbles and adulterous love affairs and our grandparents were giving diplomatic cocktail parties, [Michael] and I were struggling with the concepts of Maya and Nirvana, and how to transcend our own egos. Anything smaller than that, anything on a lower plane, disgusted us. I was used to following

Michael's lead, so when he said that the Rawul and Rani and Crishi operated on the highest level possible, I didn't contradict him, although it seemed to me at that time that they were very worldly people.

This impression would seem to be confirmed by the reaction of Manton's girlfriend, Barbara, the daughter of a famous movie actress: the atmosphere around the Rawul, she says, reminds her of the atmosphere around her mother. (Like previous swamis in Jhabvala's work, in short, the Rawul seems to be to idealism what movie stars are to materialism.)

Before long, however, Harriet has become not only the Rawul's disciple but Crishi's wife. It is plain to the reader – though not at all to Harriet – that Crishi's main reason for marrying her is his desire to control the ranch, which the twins will inherit on their twenty-first birthday, and which Michael wants to donate to the movement. And little by little the Rawul's people do take control of the ranch. The gradually increasing sense of domination, as communicated by Jhabvala between the lines of Harriet's placid narrative, is chillingly reminiscent of *Animal Farm;* these sections of the book represent an impressive accomplishment in *mise-en-scène*. But the characterizations give one pause. For why in heaven's name does almost nobody at the ranch notice how chilling these developments are? What is it about Harriet, Michael, and Lindsay that causes them to succumb so readily to the Rawul's empty rhetoric? Why is the only voice of common-sense reality that of Jean, who pleads with Harriet: "How could you allow these people – these strangers – to take over your house? Our house? It's like a nightmare." How is it that Harriet is able to recognize momentarily the truth of Jean's remark, only to drift back into mindless passivity? In short, why has Jhabvala chosen to create a family all of whose members are capable of being swallowed up by a cult in record time? Surely we are meant to understand that the Wishwells have been deprived of a strong sense of family and, like the clan at the center of *In Search of Love and Beauty,* yearn for a feeling of spiritual transcendence and for something larger than themselves to belong to; in a way, obviously, we are meant to see them as representative of the contemporary decay of the Western family and of family values. But the Wishwells are so grotesque a family that it is impossible to see them as representative of anything in the real world. Though it would be difficult enough to believe in any of them in isolation, to expect a reader to accept them all as members of a single family seems rather too much to ask.

And of all of them, the hardest to believe in is Harriet. She reminds one less of any real individual than of Alice Mellings, the obtuse protagonist of Doris Lessing's *The Good Terrorist,* who, desperate for a family of her own, falls for a third-rate terrorist group even more readily than Harriet falls for Crishi and the Rawul's cult. In Harriet, Jhabvala has created a textbook example of an unreliable narrator. Things are quite clearly not the way Harriet would have us think they are – or, indeed, the way she herself perceives them to be. Take her marriage, for instance. When the Rawul and his cohorts relocate to London, Harriet and Michael go with them; there Harriet meets Rupert, an art gallery owner who turns out to be the Rani's husband. Though Harriet doesn't realize it at all, the circumstances strongly suggest that the Rani married Rupert for his money, his government connections (which she used to straighten out her visa problems), and his family's seventeenth-century house (which the Rani liquidated soon after the marriage). Just as the Rani has used Rupert, so it is clear that Crishi, in marrying Harriet, is out to use her; indeed, as the party moves (in the book's second section) from America to London, and then (in section three) from London to India, everyone seems to await her twenty-first birthday as if it were the coming of the Messiah.

What's more, Harriet never faces squarely the facts about the Rawul's cash flow: like the Nawab's wealth in *Heat and Dust,* the movement's money appears to derive largely from crime. And Harriet knows this. She sees Crishi and Michael beat people up; she sees the Rawul's followers being trained in the use of weapons; she hears stories about Crishi's criminal past; and she speaks in passing of the arrest of some of the Rawul's followers "at certain borders," with each arrest representing "a considerable financial setback with the impounding of whatever it was that was being carried from one place to another." But she only mentions these things *en passant.* What *is* it that is being carried from one place to another? If Harriet knows, it's apparently not important enough to her to deserve mention. She seems incapable of adding it all up – the violence, the guns, the smuggling – and seeing the Rawul's movement for the sleazy enterprise that it really is. Why doesn't it occur to her to address the movement's blatant criminality as a moral issue? Why can't she see the utter divergence between the brutal reality of the movement and her image of it as a force for peace and love and brotherhood? The answer is, simply, that though her mother refers to her and Michael as the family "intellectuals," actual ratiocination is alien to her; it is not in her nature to *think* about her experiences. Although she considers herself a devotee of the movement, her understanding of it never progresses beyond the public-relations level; she fails to notice that the "ideas" in the Rawul's "program" are nothing but fuzzy platitudes.

To write a long novel – and this is one of Jhabvala's longest – in the voice of such a character seems an inordinately challenging task, and that Jhabvala does it as well as she does is a tribute to her gifts. This is a very smoothly written book – stately, lucid, and balanced. But the character of Harriet weakens it enormously. Like Shakuntala, Harriet is a heroine created expressly to be looked down upon; her unmitigated stupidity, and Jhabvala's incessant irony, eventually become too much to take. What's more, for all her sarcasm about people who are drawn to swamis, *Three Continents* seems to me to demonstrate – as if any more demonstration were necessary – that Jhabvala herself is in the grip of an inordinate fascination with them. To read the first few pages of this novel, with its multigenerational swami madness, is to get the mistaken impression that it is set somewhere around 1970, at the height of many Americans' love affair with gurus, mystics, and Ravi Shankar. So narrowly limited is Jhabvala here by her longtime theme of Indians who try to be Westerners and Westerners who try to be Indians that *Three Continents* comes off as stale and anachronistic, a recycling of dated and familiar motifs. It is encouraging, to be sure, that here, as in her preceding novel, Jhabvala's principal characters are Americans; both novels suggest that she is determined to bring new settings and concerns into her work, to move beyond her usual material. But just as her American protagonists, in these most recent novels, are pulled, as if by some force beyond themselves, to India, so for Jhabvala herself India remains unwaveringly the final destination, the figure in the carpet. In a very real sense, India has made Jhabvala; let us hope now that her preoccupation with the subcontinent is not her undoing as well.

(DECEMBER 1987)

Under the Aspect of Eternity: Flannery O'Connor

I$_T$ $_{IS}$ $_A$ $_{MEASURE}$ of her greatness, perhaps, that although she would be only sixty-four years old if she were still among us, Flannery O'Connor – who passed away a quarter century ago in her native Georgia, at the age of thirty-nine – seems already to belong to the ages. Typically, an author's literary reputation declines precipitously once he is no longer around to keep it going, but O'Connor's reputation has grown steadily in the years since her death; her two extremely impressive (if ultimately unsuccessful) novels, *Wise Blood* (1952) and *The Violent Bear It Away* (1960), have continued to earn the respect and interest of intelligent readers, and – far more important – a number of her three dozen or so short stories, the majority of which appeared originally in either *A Good Man Is Hard to Find* (1955) or *Everything That Rises Must Converge* (1965), have deservedly attained the status of classics in the genre. Indeed, though her position as a novelist is highly arguable, it seems eminently fair to say that the career of Flannery O'Connor, like the careers of Hawthorne, Poe, Stephen Crane, and Henry James before her, constitutes a major chapter in the history of the American short story. How appropriate, then, that the publishers of the splendid Library of America series, whose list of collected works already includes all or part of the oeuvres of the aforementioned nineteenth-century masters, have seen fit to add the name of Flannery O'Connor to that distinguished roster – a selection that makes her, whether by design or happenstance, the first author born in the twentieth century to appear in the Library of America series.[1]

---

1. *Collected Works*, by Flannery O'Connor; edited by Sally Fitzgerald; Library of America. Includes *Wise Blood, A Good Man is Hard to Find, The Violent Bear It Away, Everything that Rises Must Converge, Essays and Letters.*

Yet O'Connor is a twentieth-century writer with a difference. In an age when serious authors were all but expected to experiment with form and style, to disavow or rewrite the conventional Judeo-Christian moral code, or at least to exhibit a few unmistakable signs of alienation and nihilism, O'Connor did none of the above. She was a literary rebel, but not in any of the approved ways. She rebelled, rather, by attaching herself fervently to a distinct set of traditional – and, in the corridors of American literary power, decidedly bewildering – ideas about the human condition. Those ideas, as she explains in a handful of cogent essays that have been reprinted in the Library of America volume, derive largely from her devout Roman Catholicism. "[W]hen I look at stories I have written," she observes in "The Fiction Writer and His Country," "I find that they are, for the most part, about people who are poor, who are afflicted in both mind and body, who have little – or at best a distorted – sense of spiritual purpose, and whose actions do not apparently give the reader a great assurance of the joy of life." These characters, she adds, are often described as "grotesque," and the stories themselves are criticized by some for their violence.

Why does O'Connor write about such unfortunate, spiritually deprived people? Largely, she explains, because she wants to write about spiritual redemption. "[F]or me the meaning of life is centered in our Redemption by Christ and . . . what I see in the world I see in relation to that." Since the South is "Christ-haunted," poor Southerners make the best subjects, because "[w]hen the poor hold sacred history in common, they have concrete ties to the universal and holy which allow the meaning of their every action to be heightened and seen under the aspect of eternity." As for the supposed grotesqueness of her vision, she argues that "writers who see by the light of their Christian faith will have, in these times, the sharpest eyes for the grotesque, for the perverse, and for the unacceptable." For "[t]he novelist with Christian concerns will find in modern life distortions which are repugnant to him, and his problem will be to make these appear as distortions to an audience which is used to seeing them as natural; and he may well be forced to take ever more violent means to get his vision across to this hostile audience." Her fiction is violent, in other words, because when your audience does not hold the same beliefs that you do, "then you have to make your vision apparent by shock – to the hard of hearing you shout, and for the almost blind you draw large and startling figures."

So it is that both of O'Connor's novels are about wildly unbalanced young fellows who, in the course of resisting their true spiritual vocation – that of prophet – go so far as to commit murder. *Wise Blood* presents us with twenty-two-year-old Hazel Motes, whose grandfather was a small-town Tennessee circuit preacher and who at the age of twelve knew that he, too, was going to be one. Yet Hazel, resisting the truth of Christ's sacrifice ("I don't need Jesus. . . . What do I need with Jesus?"), goes to the city of Taulkinham to preach "a new church – the church of truth without Jesus Christ Crucified." When his idea is stolen by a cynical local operator, Hazel furiously kills the operator's hired prophet and then blinds himself. Similarly, *The Violent Bear It Away* sets before us the case of fourteen-year-old Francis Marion Tarwater, whose uncle, a fanatical backwoods prophet, raised him to be a prophet as well. After the old man's death, the boy finds his way to the house of his other uncle, a young widower and urban schoolteacher named Rayber who was similarly raised but who (despite the constant pull of his childhood beliefs) has struggled to believe only in reason. Rayber, who seeks to break Tarwater of his faith, knows that the boy has been enjoined by the old prophet to baptize Rayber's small retarded son, and assumes this is why the boy has come; yet Tarwater, like him, is engaged in a struggle against the old man's teachings, a struggle that concludes with Tarwater drowning the retarded boy and (at the last minute) also baptizing him, and that leads finally to his acceptance of his prophetic vocation.

There are several reasons why these novels are less effective than O'Connor's stories. In many ways, O'Connor's talents were more suited to short-form than to long-form fiction; both her novels feel episodic and repetitive, deficient in the shape, tautness, and resonance of her stories. But there can be little doubt that many readers' lingering discomfort with the novels relates directly to the fact that their protagonists are prophets – or, more precisely, prophets-in-the-making – and that it is in the matter of prophecy, perhaps, that O'Connor's convictions are most drastically at odds with those of the average modern secular reader. To such a reader, Hazel and Tarwater are about as far from sympathetic characters as one could get: they're mad, they're monotonous, they're murderous. To O'Connor, however, these characters' passion – murderous though it may be – is, in the deepest sense, not mad but holy; these young men are not out of touch with reality but have gazed upon (or at least glimpsed) a profounder reality than the rest of us know, a reality with which we, not they, are out of touch. If the sight of it has driven them to insane acts, it is not because they are themselves insane but because of the impediments to the attainment of grace that have been thrown in their paths by modern civilization.

What, one may ask, would draw a Catholic novelist to treat so Protestant a theme as Bible-thumping Southern fundamentalism? O'Connor answers this question in an essay entitled "The Catholic Novelist in the South." Such a novelist, she explains,

> is forced to follow the spirit into strange places and to recognize it in many forms not totally congenial to him. His interests and sympathies may very well go, as I find my own do, directly to those aspects of Southern life where the religious feeling is most intense and where its outward forms are farthest from the Catholic and most revealing of a need that only the Church can fill. The Catholic novelist in the South will see many distorted images of Christ, but he will certainly feel that a distorted image of Christ is better than no image at all. I think he will feel a good deal more kinship with backwoods prophets and shouting fundamentalists than he will with those politer elements for whom the supernatural is an embarrassment and for whom religion has become a department of sociology or culture or personality development.

Many of us, I think, would have trouble agreeing that "a distorted image of Christ is better than no image at all." There are distortions, after all, and there are distortions; and a Christ turned into a murderer or a rapist, say, is no Christ. What O'Connor is effectively saying, in this unusual apologia, is that Hazel Motes and Francis Marion Tarwater may be murderers, but at least they have passion. If the rest of us don't find ourselves tempted, as they are, to commit acts of violence, it's not because we're better than they but probably because, on the profoundest level, we're dead to the world. For this reader, anyway, such an argument falls a good distance short of convincing; surely, if the world and characters of *Wise Blood* and *The Violent Bear It Away* are meant to correspond in any manner whatsoever to the real world and to actual human beings, the conclusion cannot be avoided that both Haze and Tarwater are insane, and that Tarwater's acceptance of the role of prophet is hardly a consummation devoutly to be wished. One may, to be sure, line up behind such critics as Dorothy Tuck McFarland, who considers O'Connor's second novel "an objective correlative, as it were, of man's experience before the Infinite." Yet in the final analysis, both novels demand that one throw psychological complexity overboard – and despite the abundance of beautifully written passages and dramatically powerful episodes, neither novel manages to persuade the typical modern reader to do so. To such a reader, these novels must remain, in the end, case studies not in religious passion but in abnormal psychology – indeed, in psychology that is much too abnormal to seem particularly relevant to one's own experience of life.

No such difficulty, to say the least, attends the reading of O'Connor's short stories. Few of these stories, for one thing, directly concern preachers and prophets; none involves itself overmuch with the relation between madness and godhead. They are in fact more catholic than Catholic, accessible in every way to all readers of good will; more than that, they are magnificently affecting stories, capable of exerting an astonishingly powerful effect upon the reader's sensibilities (about which more later). Yet, like many great writers, O'Connor possesses a voice and a vision to which even a highly sensitive and intelligent reader may not immediately respond, and which may actually, for many reasons, put him off at first blush. Certainly a contemporary reader who comes to O'Connor with the standard notion of post-World War II American fiction – a notion, that is, that has been formed by a steady diet of Mailer, Updike, Roth, Kerouac, and the like – may face a certain amount of difficulty in becoming accustomed to her distinctive way of seeing the world.

For though they may (for the most part) maintain a respectable distance from the fanatical prophets of the world, O'Connor's stories are possessed of an intense religious feeling, a feeling that has continued to spawn, as it did during O'Connor's lifetime, a considerable degree of controversy, and to disturb some readers more than it should. There is no question but that, to many a contemporary reader, the mere presence in O'Connor's stories of words like *grace* and *redemption* and of images of Christ, Satan, and the Holy Ghost makes her seem as remote a figure as Hawthorne himself; without question, her grim preoccupation with mystery and evil, coupled with her thoroughly traditional approach to style and form and character, recalls the author of *The Scarlet Letter* far more than it does any contemporary writer of note. It has always been one of the chief arguments of O'Connor's detractors that her religious convictions were so extreme and unyielding, and that they so deeply infuse the bulk of her short fiction, that their very presence serves to weaken appreciably (for readers who do not share her theology) that fiction's value as literature, and renders O'Connor a less than universal writer.

Where, one wants to ask, does this leave Dante? And yet such complaints do point up a valid concern. For even the most respectful newcomer to O'Connor's stories may well find himself confused and troubled – and, in some instances, positively angered – by many of the ideas, assumptions, and images that he discovers (or thinks he does) in these stories. Even a long-standing admirer of O'Connor, for that matter, may, on returning to her short stories after a long separation, find himself in need of a period of readjustment to these aspects of O'Connor's fiction – most of which are related, in some way, to O'Connor's religious faith and to her sense of its proper place in her writing.

The stories take place, for instance, in a world of illness and retardation, of missing and mutilated limbs, of senile old men and suicidal children. It is a world where violence abounds: a vacationing family is slaughtered by an escaped criminal; a boy taken to a river baptism returns later and drowns himself; a farm worker is flattened by a tractor; a woman is gored to death by a bull; an old man, attacked by his small granddaughter, kills her by smashing her head against a rock; a young man mistakenly shoots his mother to death; a ten-year-old boy, eager to join his mother in heaven, hangs himself. There are few warm and selfless characters here, few loving and mutually rewarding relationships; in one story after another, a family is done in by the narcissism of one of its members, and time and again (as in many a nineteenth-century

American work of fiction) city meets countryside with harrowing results.

Nowhere, moreover, does O'Connor offer a fair representation of a morally upstanding and emotionally healthy rationalist. Invariably, the self-declared rationalists in her stories and novels are selfish and unreflecting; often they are not really rationalists at all, but are running away from the faith in which they were raised. What's more, O'Connor consistently implies a connection between atheism and amorality, failing to acknowledge that people can be virtuous simply for the sake of being virtuous, and not because their eternal souls are on the line. (At the same time, of course, she realizes that people who profess Christian faith can be amoral, too.) Her incisive, elegant letters – a generous compilation of which was published in 1979 as *The Habit of Being,* and a selection of which occupies several hundred pages of the Library of America volume – at times demonstrate her contempt for her friends' value systems, even as she maintains her affection for the friends themselves; in her stories there often appears to be a similar contempt – or, one might say, condescension – in operation. "You have to be able to dominate the existence that you characterize," she insists in a letter to one of her most frequent correspondents, a woman identified only as "A." "That is why I write about people who are more or less primitive."

Indeed, nowhere in her fiction is there a character as astute, as ethical, or as serious as O'Connor herself: On the contrary, the stories are crawling with arrogant, unreflecting mothers and their captious, pseudo-intellectual grown children, with inattentive rationalist fathers and their pathetic sons, with lazy white-trash hired men and their cliché-spouting wives. Those characters who think themselves smart and sophisticated generally learn otherwise by the end of the story. One such character is Rayber, the desperately secular schoolteacher in *The Violent Bear It Away,* who erroneously thinks he knows "exactly what [goes] on inside" the boy Tarwater's mind. Another is Hulga, an atheistic, virginal Ph.D of thirty-two who, in "Good Country People," leads a seemingly naïve teenage Bible salesman to a barn loft with the intention of seducing him. But Hulga turns out to be the naïf: the salesman makes off with her artificial leg, remarking indignantly that "I may sell Bibles but I know which end is up and I wasn't born yesterday and I know where

I'm going." (Clearly, not only the hired hands' wives spout clichés in these stories.) As obtuse as Hulga – though no Ph.D., she – is Mrs. Shortley, the wife of a hired hand in "The Displaced Person," whose sense of innate superiority to the black and Polish refugee farm workers around her prevents her from recognizing what the reader knows early on: that she and her husband are going to be sent packing by his employer. ("You reckon he can drive a tractor when he don't know English?" she asks about the Pole who is destined to supplant her husband; such numbing ignorance is far from rare in the world of these stories.)

The conventional dramatic reason for creating such characters is evident: the writer wishes the reader to regard them as insufferably smug, to look down upon them, and to look forward to their comeuppance. This device is not in itself objectionable. But to some readers – particularly those who are relative newcomers to the art of Flannery O'Connor – it may seem insufferably smug of her to manufacture all these insufferably smug people for them to look down upon. Yes, one can sympathize with such characters even as one is deploring their monstrous vanity. But one may long as well to share a character's surprise once in a while, to share his hurt and not experience it from a distance. At times, a newcomer to O'Connor's fiction may even have the impression that mixed in with her sympathy for her characters is a vindictive, almost sadistic feeling of it-serves-you-right. In one story after another, O'Connor's domination of her characters' existence may well make her seem as if she has forgotten her own humanity and is attempting to play God – and what could be more insufferably smug than that?

There is, in short, little compassion here – an emotion about which O'Connor herself, as it happens, has something to say. "It's considered an absolute necessity these days for writers to have compassion," she remarks in an essay entitled "The Grotesque in Southern Fiction." "Usually I think what is meant by it is that the writer excuses all human weakness because human weakness is human. The kind of hazy compassion demanded of the writer now makes it difficult for him to be antianything. Certainly when the grotesque is used in a legitimate way, the intellectual and moral judgments implicit in it will have the ascendancy over feeling."

Such is the case in O'Connor's fiction: here, feeling always takes a backseat to intellectual and moral judgment. It must be said, however, that a casual reader's discomfort with the severity of the tone O'Connor typically assumes toward her characters has less to do with any real deficiencies in her fiction than with the nature of the modern temper and the norms of contemporary fiction. An attentive reader, indeed, does not take long to begin to adjust to O'Connor's vision, and to see beyond her seeming lack of concern for her characters, and the apparent smugness with which she contemplates their fates, to the essential truth of the matter. That truth, to put it plainly, is that O'Connor violates the unwritten rule of twentieth-century relativism, which dictates that having a religion of some sort is perfectly fine, but that actually believing in its teachings and acting upon such belief is in bad taste, is backward and undemocratic, is (for that matter) to betray the secular gods of self-discovery and self-fulfillment to which many of O'Connor's contemporaries – and our own – have solemnly dedicated their lives. One of the central concerns of O'Connor's fiction is to underline the inanity of this modern craving for self-fulfillment. She does so quite humorously in *Wise Blood*, when Sabbath Lily Hawks, the randy daughter of the evangelist Asa Hawks, tells Haze of her letter – about sex, sin, and the kingdom of heaven – to a Dear Abby-type newspaper columnist, and quotes the columnist's response: "Dear Sabbath, Light necking is acceptable, but I think your problem is one of adjustment to the modern world. Perhaps you ought to re-examine your religious values to see if they meet your needs in Life. A religious experience can be a beautiful addition to living if you put it in the proper prespective [*sic*] and do not let it warp you. Read some books on Ethical Culture." Likewise, O'Connor memorably pokes fun at the jargon of secular self-obsession in *The Violent Bear It Away*, when Rayber explains to Tarwater that the boy's late (and unwed) mother was not a "whore," as their recently deceased uncle maintained, but that "[s]he was just a good healthy girl, just beginning to find herself when she was struck down."

O'Connor's barbs can sting. Yet her point is manifestly not to hold these characters up to ridicule, but rather to offer each of them as an example of a flawed and troubled human soul on its way to an epiphany. If they often appear to be teeming with ignoble thoughts and emotions, it is because some of the things that cross an average human mind in the

course of a day *can* be chillingly ugly, and O'Connor considers it a crucial part of her obligation as a writer to drag every unworthy thought
and emotion relentlessly out into the light of day and to call it by its
proper name. Part of the writer's responsibility, she tells "A.," is "the accurate naming of the things of God.") She wants to get at the core of
things, to confront her reader with the nastiest truths about human nature, and she is not afraid to do so in a blunt, disturbing, and brutally
straightforward manner. There is a kind of compassion in these stories,
but it is a hard compassion, the compassion not of a sentimental aunt
but of a tough old priest whose belief is strong, whose priorities are in
order, and who is able to stare unflinchingly into the impure hearts of
men and love them in spite of their impurity.

GRATIFYINGLY, the epiphanies into which O'Connor leads these
characters are possessed of a dramatic force that does not depend in the
slightest on one's belief system, even though in some cases the epiphanies draw heavily upon Christian rhetoric and imagery. The epiphanies
of some of O'Connor's stories, to be sure, are relatively free of such
overt religious touches. At the end of "Everything That Rises Must
Converge," for instance, a snappish, supercilious young man watches
his good-hearted mother suffer a stroke, and while running for help he
begins to realize what he has done and what he is losing: "The tide of
darkness," O'Connor writes, "seemed to sweep him back to her, post-
poning from moment to moment his entry into the world of guilt and
sorrow." End of story. In other epiphanies, however, the Christian elements are considerably more pronounced. "The Enduring Chill" presents us with another insufferable young man, a would-be intellectual
named Asbury who has returned south to his mother's dairy farm after a
failed attempt to become a writer in New York; weak and febrile, he
thinks he is dying, and since he "ha[s] never been a sniveler after the ineffable," he seeks to create out of his own intelligence some "last significant culminating experience." But the experience doesn't come – and
neither does death, for he proves to have nothing more dangerous than
a bovine fever which he caught by drinking unpasteurized milk as a
childish act of defiance against his mother. At this news he feels numb.
"The old life in him was exhausted," O'Connor writes.

He awaited the coming of the new. It was then that he felt the beginning of a chill, a chill so peculiar, so light, that it was like a warm ripple across a deeper sea of cold. His breath came short. The fierce bird which through the years of his childhood and the days of his illness had been poised over his head, waiting mysteriously, appeared all at once to be in motion. Asbury blanched and the last film of illusion was torn as if by a whirlwind from his eyes. He saw that for the rest of his days, frail, racked, but enduring, he would live in the face of a purifying terror. A feeble cry, a last impossible protest escaped him. But the Holy Ghost, emblazoned in ice instead of fire, continued, implacably, to descend.

One need not believe in the Holy Ghost – indeed, many who do so believe might be hard put to recognize the third member of the Trinity in this nightmarish image – in order to be moved by the exquisitely evoked spectacle of this young man forced, for the first time in his life, to confront the truth about himself and to live with it. This story, like O'Connor's other stories, asks nothing of one in the way of allegiance to any specific denomination or doctrine: it requires only that one recognize the objective existence of good and evil, the importance of human beings' responsibilities to one another, the significance of mystery, and the lamentability of our century's preoccupation with scientific knowledge at the expense of all other forms of truth. To put it a bit differently, the author of "A Temple of the Holy Ghost" does not expect us to believe, with her, that people are indeed temples of the Holy Ghost; she asks only that we believe that people are temples of some sort, that we recognize their hearts and minds as fields on which the forces of right and wrong do battle, and that we see that battle as an event of utmost significance.

WHAT A REMARKABLE writer Flannery O'Connor is! Not only do her stories survive comparison with the best works of her generation; to read her stories alongside those of almost any of her contemporaries is to see, in those other writers, a frivolousness and superficiality of which one was hardly aware beforehand. O'Connor makes one realize how extensively the characters in those other writers' work – and one's response to them – are shaped not by real life but by other fictions. She makes words like *traditional* and *avant-garde* seem less meaningful, for whereas her prose is invariably pellucid, controlled, and unadventurous, her stories provide one with a shock of recognition that makes most fiction – avant-garde or otherwise – seem pallid, lifeless, and derivative. Acts of murder, arson, mutilation, and such – the sort of events, that is, that leave one cold when communicated in the artless, hyperbolic prose of, say, a William Burroughs – are truly overwhelming when related in the civil, serene prose of O'Connor. One responds to O'Connor's stories, indeed, as one does to an intensely charged encounter with an outlandish stranger – and yet what one finds oneself to be looking at is not a stranger but one's own reflection. Hers is, in short, an avant-garde not of style but of vision; her stories examine human life with a degree of seriousness that few postwar American writers can even approach, and much of the anger and anxiety that a reader is liable to feel on first exposure to her writing derives precisely from a fear of that seriousness, an unwillingness to match the exhausting intensity with which she carries out her inquiry into the human condition. Her stories are, in the most urgent sense, works of moral compulsion: they compel one to look critically into one's heart, to question one's most long-settled assumptions about oneself. They are not easy to pass the time with – O'Connor rightly distinguishes between herself and the type of modern writer who seeks to "lift up" a reader's heart "without cost to himself or to her" – and they are impossible to forget.

(JANUARY 1989)

This book was designed by Tree Swenson.

It is set in Galliard type by Typeworks

and manufactured by Edwards Brothers on acid-free paper.